THE ROYAL AIR FORCE IN AMERICAN SKIES

THE ROYAL AIR FORCE IN AMERICAN SKIES

The Seven British Flight Schools in
the United States during World War II

Tom Killebrew

Denton, Texas

10 9 8 7 6 5 4 3 2 1

Permissions:

University of North Texas Press
1155 Union Circle #311336
Denton, TX 76203-5017

The paper used in this book meets the minimum requirements of the American National Standard for Permanence of Paper for Printed Library Materials, z39.48.1984. Binding materials have been chosen for durability.

Library of Congress Cataloging-in-Publication Data

Killebrew, Tom, author.

The Royal Air Force in American skies : the seven British flight schools in the United States during World War II / Tom Killebrew.—Edition: First.

pages cm

Includes bibliographical references and index.

ISBN 978-1-57441-615-2 (cloth : alk. paper) -- ISBN 978-1-57441-624-4 (ebook)

1. Aeronautics, Military—Study and teaching—Great Britain. 2. Aeronautics, Military—Study and teaching—United States. 3. Air pilots, Military—Training of—Great Britain—History--20th century. 4. Air pilots, Military—Training of—United States—History--20th century. 5. Flight schools—Great Britain—History--20th century. 6. World War, 1939-1945--Aerial operations, British. 7. Great Britain. Royal Air Force—Foreign service—United States. 8. Great Britain. Royal Air Force—History—World War, 1939-1945. I. Title.

UG639.G7K55 2015

940.54'49410973--dc23

2015025346

The electronic edition of this book was made possible by the support of the Vick Family Foundation.

To all those who participated in the British
Flying Training Schools, and especially to the
Royal Air Force students who eternally remain.
and
Dr. Gilbert S. Guinn 1929–2014

Let us go whither the omens of the gods
and the iniquity of our enemies call us.
The die is cast.

Julius Caesar

TABLE OF CONTENTS

List of Figures

Acknowledgments

Dr. Gilbert S. Guinn, history professor emeritus at Lander University, Greenwood, South Carolina, became interested in World War II British aircrew training in the United States while studying under a Fulbright scholarship in England in the early 1980s. Dr. Guinn conducted interviews and began researching the several different programs that included British students inducted directly into the U.S. Army flight training program (Arnold Scheme), the U.S. Navy flight training program (Towers Scheme), the Pan American Airways navigation school in Coral Gables, Florida, and the British Flying Training Schools. Dr. Guinn continued to amass considerable information on British aircrew training in the United States during his tenure at Lander University with a view toward writing the definitive history of these unique and little-known programs. His efforts resulted in his book, *The Arnold Scheme: British Pilots, the American South and the Allies' Daring Plan*, published in 2007 and his co-authorship of *British Naval Aviation in World War II: the US Navy and Anglo-American Relations*, published in 2012. Only Dr. Guinn's desire to write the history of the British Flying Training Schools remained unfulfilled.

After the publication of my book *The Royal Air Force in Texas: Training British Pilots in Terrell during World War II*, Dr. Guinn offered his research material and student interviews, which when combined with my own research resulted in this book. I owe a deep debt of gratitude to Dr. Guinn, not only for his material, but for his guidance, comments, and unfailing support during this project.

Special thanks are due to the former students and staff of the British Flying Training Schools who gave unselfishly of their time to aid this project. Due to the passage of time, these interviews could not be duplicated today. Also deserving of thanks are the legions of librarians and archivists from national archives, university repositories, and municipal libraries who never fail to go above and beyond.

And a very special thanks to my wife Ann, whose encouragement and support is so very much appreciated.

PREFACE

This book tells for the first time the story of a fascinating and little-known aspect of World War II flight training history. In early June 1941 young British flight students entered a neutral United States in civilian clothes destined for specially constructed flight schools. These schools, owned by American operators and staffed by American civilian instructors and maintenance workers, used U.S. Army Air Corps training aircraft supplied under lend-lease, were supervised by British Royal Air Force officers, and used the standard RAF flight training syllabus. Unlike any other military flight training program of the time, all aspects of flight training from the first flight through advanced training and graduation occurred at these schools.

There would ultimately be seven British Flying Training Schools in the United States. The lasting contribution made by these schools was not only in the number of pilots trained for the Royal Air Force, but in the close ties that developed between the young Englishmen who journeyed so far from home and the Americans who befriended them. These friendships endured after the students' flight training ended, continued throughout the war, and existed long after the end of the war.

On the international level, the British Flying Training Schools program was part of one of the greatest cooperative ventures ever undertaken between nations. Aircrew training, along with other cooperative ventures such as lend-lease, cemented the alliance between Great Britain and the United States that transcended national interest and continued after the war, throughout the cold war, and exists to this day.

THE ROYAL AIR FORCE
IN AMERICAN SKIES

INTRODUCTION

Early training of British pilots during World War I often consisted of little more than fifteen to twenty hours of instruction in underpowered temperamental aircraft such as the French Maurice Farman Longhorn or Shorthorn, machines which had been withdrawn from front line service. American Elliot Springs described the Shorthorn as "an awful looking bus . . . They say you test the rigging by putting a bird between the two wings. If the bird gets out there's a wire gone somewhere."[1]

On early dual instruction flights the student sat behind the instructor in order to observe the operation of the controls and occasionally reached around the instructor and briefly took the controls. Later training machines were equipped with dual controls. The student's first solo flight often came after as little as thirty minutes to an hour of dual instruction. Two hours of flight sufficed for a civilian pilot's license issued by the Royal Aero Club and possible acceptance by the Royal Flying Corps. If selected by the RFC, the new pilot reported to the Central Flying School at Upavon for the "long course," which consisted of ten hours of instruction.[2] The most important trainer of the war, the Avro 504, had also been withdrawn from front line service, but unlike the Farmans, the Avro proved to be an excellent trainer. A few 504s were still in service on the eve of the World War II.

As flight training matured, Major R. R. Smith-Barry developed the Gosport System (named after the English town of Gosport). This system incorporated knowledge of the fundamental principles of flight, a thorough mastery of every phase of flight including extreme low level aerobatics (which many found to be nothing short of reckless), as well as a crude method of in-flight communication between the instructor and the student which would still be in use during World War II.

British officials also realized that flight training in Britain during wartime had serious disadvantages due to limited land area, congested aerodromes, and often inclement weather. In 1917 Canada became the home for much of the British flight training. When the harsh Canadian winter arrived, some of the training moved south to the state of Texas in the United States. These lessons would be reapplied twenty-four years later.

The 1920s and 1930s were lean years for the Royal Air Force with severely reduced budgets, a civilian population opposed to armament expenditures following the carnage and utter waste of trench warfare during World War I, and successive British governments committed to limited military funding and a policy of appeasement toward Germany. Only an out of office Winston Churchill, along with a few supporters and public men, warned of the growing threat of Adolf Hitler's Nazi Germany and repeatedly called for rearmament and strengthening the Royal Air Force. These proposals met with widespread hostility and derision across the nation, both in the press and in Parliament.

Prior to 1935, Royal Air Force flying schools produced about 300 pilots a year who, according to the official history of flying training, had "the bare ability to fly an aeroplane." Pilot training lasted a year and most operational training took place in the active squadrons. Little attention was paid to navigation, all-weather flying, or night flying (even though the RAF had pioneered the concept of night flying in World War I).[3]

In response to concerns following the confirmation of massive German rearmament, the British government reluctantly agreed to Royal Air Force expansion. During the late 1930s, eight RAF expansion schemes were formulated, but only one of these plans (Expansion Scheme F) was fully implemented. British rearmament proceeded in disorganized fits and starts. The various RAF expansion plans were developed, debated, approved, modified, partially implemented, and usually replaced by new schemes before the old schemes were fully implemented. As the often disorganized RAF expansion began to gain momentum, Training Command had to vie with other commands for limited supplies of personnel and facilities. The entire and complex apparatus of recruitment, training, housing, logistics, and support had to be expanded or created. Land, a scarce commodity in Britain, had to be appropriated for new aerodromes and facilities, often against adamant local opposition. Acquisition of the necessary bombing and gunnery ranges proved to be particularly difficult due to well-organized resistance from wildlife groups.

As part of an early expansion scheme, Air Commodore Arthur Tedder, director of Flying Training in the Air Ministry, proposed a new system designed to increase pilot production. Flight students were first sent to a Civil Contract Elementary Flying Training School for eight weeks of instruction, which included fifty hours in the de Havilland Tiger Moth elementary trainer. Graduates of these short courses then reported to the RAF Depot at Uxbridge where the RAF pilots were divided into courses and posted to one of several flying training schools for nine months of further instruction. The first four and a half months were spent in both single-engine and twin-engine aircraft and the final four and a half months were devoted to improving navigation and instrument flying and introducing gunnery and bombardment training. The Tedder plan kept the flying training sequence within twelve months, cost less than earlier plans, and by shifting elementary flying to civilian contract schools, the RAF conserved experienced service personnel. But the plan was not fully implemented.

Tedder proposed another training scheme, but this plan also did not work as planned. There were shortages of instructors and training aircraft and an official course syllabus had not been developed for every stage of training. Night flying was restricted to six hours of mostly take offs and landings known as "circuits and bumps" and one short cross-country flight of some twenty miles. Although pilots destined for Coastal

Command or the Fleet Air Arm were well trained in navigation, the RAF official history asserted that navigation training for RAF pilots, "remained very much where it had been since 1918."[4]

A later RAF expansion plan (Expansion Scheme L) required the creation of eight new flying training schools. Officials, however, decided that Britain had sufficient personnel to staff only four new schools. But this plan was not fully implemented.[5]

In spite of RAF expansion and proposals by Air Commodore Tedder, Training Command remained understaffed and underfunded. This situation continued until the start of World War II and would lead to an acute shortage of pilots, especially after early operational losses during the Battle of France and the Battle of Britain.

When Air Chief Marshal Sir Edgar Ludlow-Hewitt became commander-in-chief of Bomber Command in 1937, he immediately pointed out deficiencies in the service in terms of equipment, personnel, organization, tactics, and training. Although a farsighted and intelligent officer who clearly recognized defects (those qualities would make him unpopular and lead to his dismissal), Ludlow-Hewitt erred when he stated that the next war could not be fought with "mass-produced pilots and crews."[6]

In fairness, Ludlow-Hewitt was correctly concerned with the need to adequately train bomber crews for the new aircraft then coming into service. But the next war would be fought precisely by mass-produced pilots and aircrews.

CHAPTER 1

OVERSEAS TRAINING

Even before the beginning of World War II, British Air Ministry officials, drawing on the flight training experiences of World War I, recognized the need to move some aircrew training out of Great Britain in the event of war. Drawbacks to flight training in Britain during wartime included the limited size of the country, an urgent need for airfield and support facilities for operational squadrons, the often abysmal weather, and the very real possibility of enemy attack.[1]

In spite of the advantages of moving some flight training to Commonwealth countries, officials also recognized several drawbacks to any overseas training plan. The distances involved were in many cases daunting, literally involving potential locations on the other side of the world. Another concern involved dealing with other governments.

Initial discussions with Commonwealth governments before the war concerning aircrew training produced mixed results. Australia, New Zealand, Kenya, and Southern Rhodesia responded quickly and favorably. Other Commonwealth nations were agreeable. Even with the favorable responses, the extreme distances flight students would have to travel to and from training sites and the associated supply and support problems would be sizable. The political climate in South Africa, not always friendly to Great Britain, precluded negotiations with that country. Even in the best of political climes, the sheer distance between South Africa and Great Britain, along with primitive conditions and limited facilities in much of the country presented considerable disadvantages to training at the bottom of Africa.

British Air Ministry officials, prompted by the recommendations of Group Captain Robert Leckie, DSO, DSC, DFC, serving on the staff of Air Commodore Arthur W. Tedder, RAF Director of Training, realized the advantages of training facilities located in Canada. The vast and largely undeveloped expanse of Canada offered unlimited training areas, a location close to Britain, as well as a strategic position along the crucial ferry route between the United States and Great Britain. The highly industrialized United States would be an invaluable source of raw materials, fuel, and armaments such as aircraft and engines in the event of war.

The weather presented an obvious drawback to air training in Canada. Canadian winters are noted for harsh brutality. During World War I much of the embryonic Canadian flight training program had been moved to Texas during the winter of 1917–18 in order to continue training. In spite of the obvious weather limitations, which officials believed could be diminished to an acceptable level by modern equipment, the British considered that Canada offered the key to any future overseas flight training program. The Canadian prime minister, however, proved to be particularly uncooperative.

W. L. Mackenzie King, a lifelong bachelor and career politician who used fortune tellers and the occult to make many of his political decisions, had served as prime minister twice before and would be the longest serving Canadian prime minister. King stubbornly refused to consider RAF flight training on Canadian soil. In 1936 King responded to the first British training overtures: "It would be inadvisable to have Canadian territory used by the British Government for training school purposes for British airmen."[2]

Further talks over the next several years revealed considerable differences, as well as confusion between the Canadian and British positions. Each side came away from the talks with different impressions. One area held no ambiguity, however. King insisted that any training program on Canadian soil would have to be controlled by Canada. The British were welcome to come and train in Royal Canadian Air Force flight schools under Canadian authority. King took this unrealistic position out of a sense of nationalistic pride even though Royal Canadian Air Force resources were limited to training about fifty pilots per year. The Royal Canadian Air Force had only been created in 1924 with a largely civilian role.[3] During World War I Canadian aircrew served in Britain's Royal Flying Corps and the Royal Naval Air Service. The RCAF did not assume a totally military role until the mid-1930s.

King also insisted on autonomous Royal Canadian Air Force units serving alongside British air units. British officials wanted to utilize Canadian recruits in Royal Air Force units as needed. Other areas were in dispute and negotiations produced no results until war broke out in the autumn of 1939.

Canada declared war on Germany one week after the 3 September 1939 British declaration. Following a personal appeal from British Prime Minister Neville Chamberlain, King agreed in principle to the training of British and Commonwealth aircrew including pilots, air observers (navigators), and wireless operators in Canada, but did not moderate his insistence on Canadian control. The British, now faced with a war they were ill prepared to fight, had little choice but to agree.

King and other Canadian officials were staggered to learn that the Canadian phase of the British overseas training plan, known as the Empire Air Training Scheme, called for training 50,000 aircrew annually. King proceeded cautiously out of fear that this level of commitment would consume the entire Canadian war effort. King and the Canadian finance minister J. L. Ralston felt that implementation of the plan would have a disastrous effect on the Canadian economy. The Canadians also felt that the initial British proposal assigned too much of the cost to Canada and not enough to Great Britain.

The Empire Air Training Scheme contemplated a European war. British students would be sent to Canada to complete all phases of flight training. Students from other Commonwealth nations, primarily Australia and New Zealand, would be trained in their respective countries through the first or elementary level of flight training, then go to Canada to complete the advanced stage of training. All graduates of the Canadian schools would then travel to Britain and receive further training in an Operational Training Unit before assignment to an operational squadron. Any discussion of the allocation of resources and shared costs had to include representatives from Australia and New Zealand. These joint negotiations were lengthy and complex.

After two and a half months of talks, the negotiations almost broke down over King's insistence on autonomous RCAF units in the field. The British negotiator, Lord Riverdale, was described as being "at his wits' end" and telegraphed Dominion Secretary Anthony Eden that the entire plan was "imperiled."[4] The British agreed to King's demands.

The negotiators from the four countries finally agreed on a scaled-back plan that would train 29,000 aircrew annually in Canada. This program included approximately 11,050 pilots, 6,630 air observers, and 11,320 wireless operators. The negotiators also agreed on an allocation of costs based largely on each country's relative population. In return, Great Britain would buy Canadian wheat to help offset the cost of the aircrew training program. The parties signed the final agreement on 17 December 1939, Prime Minister King's sixty-fifth birthday.

One minor example of the magnitude of the Canadian training program is revealing. The final scaled-down plan would require 720 North American AT-6 Harvard advanced trainers. When the parties signed the agreement, Canada possessed only fourteen Harvards, with fifteen more on order.

The resulting Canadian commitment to aircrew training quickly became a herculean undertaking. In only a few short months, fields of virgin forest were cleared, drained, and leveled, and rudimentary airfields appeared in record time all across Canada. Many of these airfields were occupied and operational before all utilities and other support facilities were complete. Students, instructors, and other school staff lived in primitive conditions alongside construction crews as training commenced. This immense undertaking would ultimately result in more than one hundred Canadian training schools. Besides the training schools for pilots, observers, and wireless operators, the training establishment came to include schools for air gunners and bomb aimers, as well as Initial Training Schools (pre-flight ground instruction, equivalent to British Initial Training Wings), general reconnaissance schools, operational training units, flying instructors' schools, a school for naval gunners, and another school for flight engineers. At its height, the various Canadian air training schools graduated 3,000 aircrew each month.

The prewar RCAF strength of 4,000 men rapidly increased to 33,000 men and women. Since the aircrew training program made extensive use of existing Canadian flying clubs and their civilian instructors, mechanics, and administrative staffs, 6,000 civilian personnel augmented the increased military strength.[5]

Some sources have suggested that King objected to the term "Empire" in the plan's name and the British agreed to rename the crucial Canadian phase of the plan the Commonwealth Air Training Plan.[6] In other Commonwealth nations the original Empire Air Training Scheme name remained in use. Under either name, British pilots and aircrew were trained in a number of Commonwealth countries including Canada, Australia, New Zealand, Kenya, Southern Rhodesia, South Africa, India, and even Hong Kong before the Japanese occupation. The first school in the new plan, located in Kenya, was ready for operation at the outbreak of the war. The first courses in the new schools in Canada, Australia, and New Zealand began training in April 1940.[7]

The inauguration of the immense Canadian training program resulted in a severe shortage of personnel even with the inclusion of existing civilian flying school staffs. South of the border many young men in the United States were eager to join in the newly declared war. Some of these men had a genuine desire to aid Great Britain against a Nazi foe that many considered to be the personification of evil. But for most of these young men the overriding reason for joining was the sheer joy of flying and the opportunity to fly military aircraft. These young men had been captivated by the romance of aviation typified by the barnstormers and flying circuses, which crisscrossed the United States in the 1920s and 1930s thrilling crowds at county fairs and by events such as the national air races. But America, still in the grip of the Depression, offered little in the way of gainful employment in the field of aviation and the limited U.S. Army and Navy flight training programs required at least two years of college, which most of these young men did not have.

The Canadian war effort offered opportunities for Americans who wanted to serve. Besides the need for pilots and aircrew in operational squadrons, the Canadians had an urgent need for flight instructors, ferry pilots, and pilots to fly routine training flights for bomb aimers, air gunners, wireless operators, and navigators. The Canadians also needed ground school instructors, mechanics, ground crew, and other trades. The shortage of pilots presented the most pressing need. As with every other phase of this enormous undertaking, enlisting Americans posed a problem. American neutrality laws made it illegal to openly recruit personnel in the United States for foreign service.

Billy Bishop, World War I Canadian flying ace, recipient of the Victoria Cross, and national hero, had been promoted to Honorary Air Marshal of the Royal Canadian Air Force and placed in charge of recruitment. Concerned with the pressing need for men, Bishop called his old friend Clayton Knight, a noted aviation artist and publicist. Knight had flown with the RFC and RAF in World War I. Worried about the slow development of the Royal Canadian Air Force, Bishop wanted Knight to recruit and screen experienced American pilots for service as flight instructors in Canada.

Bishop also enlisted Homer Smith to aid Knight in his recruitment efforts. Smith, a wealthy Canadian resident of New York City and Palm Beach, Florida, had been a Royal Naval Air Service pilot in World War I. Knight and Smith formed an organization, known as the Clayton Knight Committee, to recruit Americans for service in the RCAF. Ostensibly a private venture, the Clayton Knight Committee in fact operated secretly as an arm of the Canadian Air Ministry.

Knight and Smith set up headquarters in the Waldorf Astoria Hotel in New York City. They traveled around the country and used their contacts in the aviation community. Word quickly spread that the Clayton Knight Committee was recruiting American pilots for Canadian service.

Following the implementation of the newly negotiated Commonwealth Air Training Plan, Clayton Knight and Homer Smith attended a meeting of the Air Council in Ottawa. The meeting included a delegation from the British government, administrators of the Canadian air training plan, RCAF officers, and representatives of Canadian pilots and commercial airlines. The meeting focused on the immediate need for pilots to staff the numerous flight schools contemplated by the new plan. Members of the Air Council were shocked when the Canadian aviation representatives stated that they could recruit only a limited number of pilots. Knight and Smith then reported that their brief survey of American cities and airports had produced the names of 300 potential pilots willing to serve in Canada. Even though Mackenzie King and other Canadian officials had reservations about Americans in Canadian service, the Air Council approved the recruitment of American pilots.

Ever mindful of the questionable legality of their efforts and sensitive to American feelings, Knight and Smith met personally with Major General Henry H. Arnold, chief of the U.S. Army Air Corps, and Vice Admiral

John H. Towers, Chief of the U.S. Navy Bureau of Aeronautics. Once the American officers understood that the Clayton Knight Committee's efforts would not conflict with the recruitment of U.S. Army or Navy airmen or involve the release of existing service personnel, they did not object to the proposed plan. After those first favorable meetings, New York City Mayor Fiorello LaGuardia, an Army Air Service officer in World War I, arranged for Knight and Smith to speak with a U.S. State Department representative. This meeting, however, did not go well. The State Department official simply reiterated that it was illegal to recruit American citizens for foreign military service.

American neutrality laws defined "hiring or retaining another person to enlist or enter himself in the service of a belligerent" as an illegal act.[8] Knight contended that he did not recruit, but only provided "a center to advise volunteers and to facilitate their training and journey to Canada and England."[9] This barely plausible explanation actually survived an FBI investigation into Knight and Smith's activities, which found no illegality.

The matter of citizenship also presented a problem. The Citizenship Act of 1907 provided that any American citizen who took an oath of allegiance to a foreign state automatically forfeited their American citizenship. This provision had caused significant legal problems for American volunteers serving with foreign military services during World War I. Twenty-five years later, with the concurrence of both Canadian and British authorities, American volunteers destined for the RCAF or RAF were allowed to swear only to obey the orders of their commanding officers, without swearing allegiance to the king.

In spite of the State Department's reservations, which quickly developed into open hostility, the Clayton Knight Committee opened additional offices in Spokane, San Francisco, Los Angeles, Dallas, Kansas City, Cleveland, Atlanta, Memphis, and San Antonio. Even though the group could not openly advertise, their presence and purpose became well known through word of mouth and airport notices. Several newspaper articles even reported on the committee's activities. Physicians approved by the Civil Aeronautics Authority were engaged to examine and certify the physical condition of applicants, while local CAA-authorized flight inspectors tested each applicant's flying ability. Approved applicants were sent to the Waldorf Astoria Hotel in New York where Knight and Smith met each applicant, reviewed their documentation, and then provided funds and reservations for their train trip to Ottawa.

The group's increasing notoriety resulted in complaints from isolationists and anti-British groups to the U.S. State Department and the Justice Department, as well as inquiries from Congress. Oregon Representative Walter M. Pierce received a letter from Mr. and Mrs. F. A. Everett advising him that their son had been recruited for Canadian military service. Pierce asked Secretary of State Cordell Hull to investigate the matter. In late 1940 the U.S. State Department sent a sharply worded note to Ottawa concerning the Clayton Knight Committee's recruitment of Americans for Canadian service.

Mackenzie King and other Canadian officials had always harbored reservations about possible negative American reaction to the Clayton Knight Committee's activities. Following the State Department note, Canadian authorities considered abandoning the program altogether, but personnel, especially trained men such as pilots, were desperately needed. A new procedure introduced the civilian Dominion Aeronautical Association as a buffer between the Clayton Knight Committee and the RCAF. This new organization, which listed Homer Smith as director and Clayton Knight as one of the associate directors, maintained offices in Ottawa's elegant Chateau Laurier Hotel. Candidates recruited by the Clayton Knight Committee first applied to the Dominion Aeronautical Association only to be told that no positions were available, but the applicant might check with the Royal Canadian Air Force, which just happened to have an office next door.

But American attitudes, both official and private, were changing in favor of growing support for England. This support grew after the German occupation of Norway, the fall of France, the Battle of Britain, and the initiation of German air attacks on London and other British cities that resulted in civilian casualties and considerable damage (vividly reported by American news outlets). By late 1940 it became obvious that President Roosevelt not only supported, but in fact encouraged, programs such as the Clayton Knight Committee and exerted considerable political pressure for their acceptance. Secretary of State Cordell Hull replied to Congressman Pierce's letter, "The Department of State are not anxious to impede all legal activities of the Clayton Knight Committee in securing recruits for the RCAF." Thereafter, the State Department answered inquiries or complaints especially those by isolationists or anti-British groups with "a good meaningless bureaucratic answer"[10] (although friction continued between the State Department and the Clayton Knight Committee).

The Clayton Knight Committee staff at the Waldorf Astoria had increased dramatically as had the number of personnel assigned to the various hotels located across the United States. Recruitment efforts, however, still relied exclusively on airport notices and word of mouth.

After vetting in the United States and travel to Canada, American pilots recruited by the Clayton Knight Committee were interviewed by RCAF officials, given another flight physical, received their kit, and underwent RCAF commissioning ceremonies. The newly commissioned pilots were then posted to RCAF stations and received additional instruction from experienced Canadian pilots in RCAF administrative and training procedures. From there they were assigned to RCAF flight schools located across the vast reaches of Canada.

As increasing numbers of American pilots began to serve in Canada, the British Air Ministry asked the Clayton Knight Committee to expand its efforts by recruiting applicants for service in the Royal Air Force. Besides recruiting qualified pilots for RAF operational squadrons, older pilots were recruited to ferry aircraft from Canada to Britain and both men and women pilots were recruited for service in the Air Transport Auxiliary to ferry aircraft within Britain.

In time a new organization, the Canadian Aviation Bureau, replaced the Clayton Knight Committee, but Clayton Knight and Homer Smith remained directors. Canadian authorities could reply to any criticism, with at least some superficial truth, that the Clayton Knight Committee no longer existed.

At least 900 trained pilots and 1,200 aircrew trainees entered the RCAF through the pipelines of the Clayton Knight Committee and the Canadian Aviation Bureau. Many other Americans received information from the committee and then journeyed to Canada at their own expense. By the end of 1941, 6,129 Americans were serving in the RCAF and at least another 244 were in the RAF. After the Japanese attack on Pearl Harbor and the American entry into the war, most of these men returned to the United States with the blessings of the RCAF and RAF and entered the American armed forces. As the Americans departed, Canadian Air Minister C. G. Power reflected, "It is, with sincere regret, but pride in the part that they played, that we part with the Americans who fitted into our organization and formed such a formidable team with our own Canadian airmen."[11]

The request by the British Air Ministry for the Clayton Knight Committee to also recruit for the RAF added an additional burden to the recruitment of American pilots. At the onset of the Canadian training program, American pilot applicants needed a minimum of 150 hours of flying time (preferably 250 to 300 hours), 20/40 correctable vision, and a high school diploma to be accepted. Clayton Knight realized that a number of American pilots who applied for positions either in operational roles with the RCAF or RAF or in training roles had flying experience. Many held a private pilots license, but did not have sufficient flight time to be accepted. These pilots had an average of around 80 to 100 hours of flying time and obviously represented potential to a service in desperate need of pilots. The Clayton Knight Committee came up with a novel and little-known program to utilize this potential source of pilots.

With the approval of Canadian and British authorities, Air Commodore George Pirie, MC, DFC, the British air attache in Washington D.C., entered into agreements with three American civilian flight schools to provide additional training to those applicants who had flying experience, but did not meet the initial requirements for service in either the RCAF or RAF. The operators were Major William Long of Dallas, Texas, Major C. C. Moseley of Los Angeles, California, and Captain Maxwell Balfour of Spartan School of Aeronautics in Tulsa, Oklahoma. These schools all held the highest accreditation from the United States Civil Aeronautics Authority for commercial flight schools. Students selected for the program would be brought up to a "specified standard," which included fifteen hours of night flying "with the confidence to take off and climb on instruments to 2,000 feet" and thirty hours of instrument flying including triangular cross-country flights consisting of legs of at least forty miles on instruments and "normal standards of navigation."[12]

The actual hours necessary for each student would depend on the experience of the individual. Everyone agreed that the program, or more correctly the experiment, might come to nothing because "in some instances the expenditure for a considerable number of flying hours might be worthless, in that the pupil might be found unsatisfactory."[13]

Records of the Clayton Knight Committee were reviewed and around fifty candidates were selected for this new program, now known as Refresher training. Each school needed to have at least one advanced trainer with retractable landing gear, controllable pitch propeller, and flaps, as well as aircraft equipped for instrument flying, aerobatics, and night flying, a Link trainer for simulated instrument training (the forerunner of the modern flight simulator), and suitable ground school facilities. The British briefly considered twin-engine training for Refresher students, but none of the schools had the necessary equipment or qualified instructors and the limited number of students did not justify the purchase of twin-engine aircraft by either the school operators or the British government.

The contractors received $30 per hour for flight instruction (Spartan charged $45 per hour for aircraft with more than 400 horsepower) and also $1.66 per student per day for housing and meals. Refresher students were paid $2.50 per day during training. In one of the first (and inaccurate) public accounts that mentioned Refresher training, a March 10, 1941, *Dallas Morning News* article on Major Long's Dallas Aviation School reported "present enrollment is 236 including a group of eighteen American citizens being paid by the British government. They are being given training that will qualify them for ferrying planes across the Atlantic in the service of the Canadian Civil Ferrying Pilots, Inc."

By early 1941 the results of the new program were disappointing. Pirie complained that his numerous duties in Washington kept him from supervising or even visiting the three schools, "none of which is less than 1,000 miles away, and one nearly 3,000." In December 1940, Squadron Leader Stuart Mills, DFC, arrived at the British Embassy in Washington as the assistant air attache and his responsibilities included a review of the new Refresher training.

Mills had considerable combat experience in Norway, France, and the Battle of Britain. In Norway with 263 Squadron, Mills shot down a Heinkel 111 bomber, damaged several others, and received the Distinguished Flying Cross. During the Battle of Britain, Mills had been wounded while commanding 87 Squadron equipped with an early night fighter version of the Hurricane.

After his arrival in Washington, Mills spent his first week at the embassy, "reading up the files on the subject and recovering from his first bewilderment at the complexities, legal and otherwise, resulting from the necessity of observing the various neutrality laws of the country."[14] His studies were interrupted by a meeting with General Arnold and then by a summons to the White House. In a private meeting, Mills gave President and Mrs. Roosevelt a firsthand account of the fighting in Europe.

Mills then set out to visit the three Refresher schools to assess the progress and his report is revealing. The quality of the training given by the schools varied considerably and Mills immediately recognized the requirement for a uniform training syllabus.

Mills first visited the Spartan School of Aeronautics managed by Captain Maxwell Balfour. Spartan had sixteen Refresher students and four had just graduated. The four recent graduates had been at the school for three months, which Mills considered "too long." Although Mills found the navigation training to be "incorrect" he did not elaborate further. Otherwise, Spartan made a favorable impression and Mills reported, "An excellent school and a thorough training is given to the pupils." Air Commodore Pirie appended an additional comment to the report: "As expected this school is doing well. Capt. Balfour is very pro-British, keen, enthusiastic, reliable and sound; and is going to make a success of our venture. The training seems very thorough."[15]

Mills next visited Dallas Aviation School, owned and operated by Major William Long. This school did not impress Mills. Long's school enrolled seventeen Refresher students and ten had already graduated. Air Commodore Pirie had previously expressed doubts about the quality of instruction in the Dallas school. "I have a suspicion that the training is not as through and certainly not as efficient as at Tulsa."[16] Mills found the general level of instruction "below average" with very little instrument or night flying and minimal ground school instruction. Mills' final comments did note that his suggestions were already being acted upon by the time he left. "Not at all satisfactory and a great deal of pressure must be brought to bear on Major Long to put the course on a proper basis. A start has been made on this."[17]

Mills reserved his harshest criticism for the third school, Polaris Flight Academy, owned by Major C. C. Moseley. Even though Pirie had noted, "Moseley is regarded by the Army as the star civilian flying training expert in this country" he also expressed "a certain amount of anxiety and we are not by any means satisfied with the quality of the training there."[18]

At the time of Mills visit, Polaris Flight Academy had nineteen Refresher students; six of these were almost ready to graduate and five students had graduated the previous month. Mills found that many of the school aircraft were out of service undergoing overhaul. In addition to the limited flying activity, the school was poorly organized with insufficient ground school facilities and had bottlenecks created by a lack of aircraft or instructors, which hampered the training. The school needed additional flight instructors, as well as ground school instructors, and the instructors showed favoritism toward the school's existing students. Mills concluded his report: "The school has not made any great effort to give good training and needs constant supervision." Air Attache Pirie appended his own remarks to the report. "Unsatisfactory, and close supervision needed. This will be done."[19]

During his visits to the three schools, Mills was especially interested in the quality of the American students selected for training since this was a radically different concept from any other military flight training program. Although for the most part favorably impressed, Mills noted the effect the individual schools had on students. At Spartan School of Aeronautics Mills found the students, "generally good and likely to make good officers." At Dallas he again found "a good type of student" but noted, "the present course is unlikely to make them efficient officers." At Major Moseley's school, Mills again found the students "good" but, "likely to make [only] average officers."[20]

Despite the school and course deficiencies, and the well founded criticisms by the air attache in Washington, the American students apparently went on to do surprisingly well. An undated memorandum from the Air Ministry in London from around March 1941 contains a status update on the early graduates from Refresher training. "Up till now sixteen pupils trained under the scheme have arrived in this country. The reports so far received from Operational Training Units on these personnel have been excellent. Some have already gone solo on Hurricanes."[21]

One of the most interesting aspects of Mills' report is found in comments on the interaction between the Clayton Knight Committee and the individual schools, comments which were universally negative. The diplomatic Captain Balfour simply requested that the Clayton Knight Committee not make unannounced visits to the school. Major Moseley complained that members of the committee had interfered to the point of giving check rides to students and implied other evaluations and even transfers had been made without his knowledge or permission. The most virulent comments came from the Dallas school. After his visit with Major Long, Mills noted, "It is suggested that supervision by the Clayton Knight Committee, ie Miss Bennett had all but destroyed the goodwill of the owner of the school which is so vitally important."[22]

This is the only reference in the sketchy official records of discord between the civilian school operators and the Clayton Knight Committee. At this late date, other details, especially the intriguing role of the enigmatic Miss Bennett, are not known.

Another school, Aeronautical Training Centre, located in Bakersfield, California, operated by Joe Plosser and Charles Prince, joined the Refresher program in June 1941. After the Japanese attack on Pearl Harbor the War Department compelled the Refresher students to move to a new field in Seeley, California, in the Imperial Valley due to Army Air Forces expansion.

After passage of the Lend Lease Act, army training aircraft such as Stearman primary trainers, Vultee BT-13 basic trainers, and North American AT-6 advanced trainers were added to the Refresher schools. British supervision also increased. The RAF assigned Squadron Leader George Greaves, AFC, to oversee the Refresher schools.

The limited and virtually unknown Refresher training lasted until August 1942, nine months after the United States entered the war. During this time the program made considerable progress. The British added a regular RAF officer at each Refresher school and developed a training syllabus, but this effort remained somewhat limited due to the different experience levels of the individual students. The British were able to define the flying and ground school standards for graduates, then left the actual training regimen for each student up to the schools. By the first week in September 1942 when the last Refresher students graduated and left for Canada, approximately 598 Americans had completed this unique program.

American Refresher students entered the war during one of the most critical phases. Great Britain literally stood alone against the aerial might of Germany. This resulted in some of the most intense air battles of the war and British casualties were correspondingly high. The exact number of American casualties among Refresher graduates is unknown, but officials of Spartan School of Aeronautics tried to keep track of their graduates and these notes are revealing. Captain Balfour reported that at least twenty graduates of Refresher training from Spartan had been killed in action, three others had been wounded, and six were missing in action. Another had been captured after being shot down over France in an unequal battle with five German fighters. The captured pilot, Pilot Officer LeRoy Skinner from Webb City, Missouri, had originally been listed as killed in action. Skinner flew with one of the RAF Eagle Squadrons and had several aerial victories to his credit. These losses from only one school are extremely high considering the limited number of Refresher students and accurately reflect the intensity of the aerial fighting at this stage of the war.

Several exceptional American pilots received Refresher training including Gilbert Halsey, Seldon Edner, and Lance Wade. After serving in the Eagle Squadrons, both Halsey and Edner transferred to the U.S. Army Air Forces. Promoted to major, Halsey commanded the 335th Fighter Squadron of the famed Fourth Fighter Group and Edner rose to the rank of lieutenant colonel.[23]

At least three graduates of Refresher training from Spartan Aeronautics received the British Distinguished Flying Cross and one Spartan graduate, Wing Commander Lance Wade, DSO, DFC and two Bars, received the Distinguished Service Order, second only to the Victoria Cross in British service. Wade is considered to be the outstanding example of the success of Refresher training.

L. C. Wade (he had only initials until enlistment required a formal name, which he created) grew up in dirt-poor circumstances in the piney woods of East Texas and from an early age dreamed of becoming a pilot. As a teenager working odd jobs, which included a short stint with the Civilian Conservation Corps, Wade saved enough money to earn a private pilots license. With fifty-four hours of flying time, and no college credits, Wade was rejected by the Army Air Corps for flight training.

The Clayton Knight Committee, however, accepted Wade and sent him to Spartan School of Aeronautics in Tulsa for further training. After he graduated from Spartan in April 1941 the RAF accepted Wade, then sent him to No. 52 Operational Training Unit followed by a posting to the Middle East. Wade flew a Hurricane from the aircraft carrier HMS *Ark Royal* to reinforce the defenses of the beleaguered island of Malta. Wade later transferred to Egypt where he joined 33 Squadron as a pilot officer. The squadron moved to Libya in support of ground operations against the German *Afrika Korps* commanded by General Erwin Rommel. There Wade participated in aerial combat against both German and Italian squadrons. On one occasion Wade made a forced landing in the inhospitable Libyan desert after being hit by ground fire and debris from exploding aircraft during a strafing run on a German airfield and then managed to walk back to his unit.

Wade's score of personal victories mounted steadily and when his first combat tour ended Wade had fifteen confirmed kills and had been awarded the Distinguished Flying Cross. After his first combat tour Wade returned to the United States for a well-earned rest and a hero's welcome, which included a visit to Spartan in Tulsa where he had received his Refresher training.

Wade returned to North Africa to command 145 Squadron equipped with Spitfires. The squadron moved to support the invasion of Italy and Wade's score of personal victories continued to rise. Following his second tour in which he earned a bar to his DFC, Wade received a promotion to wing commander.

Following his promotion, Wade joined the staff of Air Vice Marshal Harry Broadhurst, air commander for the Mediterranean Theater, but died in a flying accident in Foggia, Italy, in January 1944. At the time of his death Wade was one of Britain's top scoring and most decorated fighter pilots (he received the Distinguished Service Order posthumously) with twenty-three aerial victories.

Such was his loyalty to the Royal Air Force that when Americans serving in the RAF were offered the opportunity to transfer to the American services after the United States entered the war, Wade decided to stay in the RAF. Even though the Army Air Forces offered him higher rank and more pay, Wade is reported to have told the AAF, "Thanks, that's mighty fine, but I'd rather keep stringing along with the guys I have been with so long now."[24]

Today, Lance Wade, a product of Refresher training and one of the most successful and highly decorated Allied fighter pilots of World War II, is virtually unknown.

Refresher training is also virtually unknown and is only a minor footnote to the global story of World War II flight training. But Refresher training introduced the Royal Air Force to the possibilities, as well as the problems, in dealing with civilian flight schools in the United States. The school operators also received a working introduction to British flight training standards and instruction methods. This knowledge would prove invaluable to both the British, who had no experience with American civilian flight schools, and these school operators who would all be involved in the greatly expanded and more significant British Flying Training Schools.

CHAPTER 2

THE AMERICAN OFFER

Even after implementation of the Empire Air Training Scheme and finalization of the Canadian training agreement, British officials still had many concerns. As impressive as the final Canadian phase of the overseas training plan appeared on paper, British officials worried that the magnitude of the program might prove beyond the capabilities of the Canadians or that such an immense undertaking might run into difficulties that could result in unacceptable delays. Officials sought alternative training plans not only as an additional source of pilots and aircrew, but also as a safeguard against the possible failure or lengthy delay of the Canadian plan. Even though other Commonwealth governments were agreeable, even desirous, of expanding their training plans (and later expansion would occur), the distances involved and in some cases the extremes of nature and geography limited these considerations. As a result, the British looked to the United States for possible assistance.

Conversations in the spring of 1940 between Lord Halifax, then British Secretary of State for Foreign Affairs, and Joseph Kennedy, the United States ambassador to Britain, concerning the possible training of Royal Air Force pilots in the United States were encouraging. Later conversations, however, between Lord Lothia, the British ambassador to the United

States, and Under-Secretary of State Sumner Wells were not so positive. Several factors concerned Wells, including American neutrality, the strong isolationist feelings in the country, and the possible negative effect on President Franklin Roosevelt's reelection campaign for an unprecedented third term. The United States also had many citizens of German and Italian descent possibly sympathetic to the Axis cause, as well as a large population of Irish-Americans who harbored no love for Great Britain. In June 1940, after conferring with President Roosevelt, Wells denied the British request.[1]

There also existed considerable doubt that the necessary military facilities and equipment could be made available to Britain due to the extensive United States rearmament program. In particular, there existed a shortage of advanced training aircraft. While several types of civilian light aircraft could theoretically be used for the initial phase of flight training, known as primary ("elementary" in British training), advanced trainers, which offered the performance and sophisticated systems of operational aircraft, were in short supply.[2] A British memorandum noted, "Elementary trainers should present little difficulty and could probably be obtained from U.S.A. sources or elsewhere. Intermediate and advanced trainers were not available from our own suppliers."[3]

Despite the official rejection of the British request for training facilities, conversations at various levels and on both sides of the Atlantic continued. Colonel Martin Scanlon, the American air attache to Britain, arranged a meeting on 28 August 1940, in London between visiting Army Air Corps Colonel Carl Spaatz (on a fact-finding mission to evaluate British training methods) and Acting Air Marshal A. G. R. Garrod, the new British Air Member for Training. As an example of the fluid nature of the discussions at this time, Colonel Scanlon had previously suggested that the Army Air Corps might be willing to turn over several existing army training bases intact to the British. In their meeting, however, Colonel Spaatz stated that the army could not spare the training facilities or equipment for British training. "Such a proposal would not be feasible even if the U.S.

Army Air Corps could spare the schools. The American public would be bound to hear and would raise the strongest opposition."[4]

Spaatz suggested that the British might establish training schools in the United States utilizing existing civilian aerodromes and specifically recommended the favorable conditions in Oklahoma and Texas. Colonel Scanlon reminded Air Marshal Garrod that some Canadian flight training had been temporarily relocated to Texas in the winter of 1917–18 during World War I. Specific details were vague and Spaatz went on to say that the British would probably have to let contracts to build the facilities, as well as furnish the training aircraft, instructors, and maintenance crews from Great Britain for these schools. This idea fell far short of the "ready-made" facilities the British were seeking. Although Garrod realized that the plan allowed the British to "gain a footing in the U.S.A." he noted, "The proposal in fact amounts merely to forming in the U.S.A. schools which we should otherwise form within the British Empire."[5]

On the same day in New York City, U.S. Treasury Secretary Henry Morgenthau met with Captain Harold H. Balfour, British Under-Secretary of State, and also discussed the possibility of British flight training in the United States. Morgenthau had been entrusted by President Roosevelt with coordinating American aid to Britain. This discussion raised the prospect of utilizing existing American civilian flight schools for British training. Unfortunately any training plan of this nature would involve the expenditure of considerable British capital funds, but Balfour reported, "The scheme will provide a further opportunity of training pilots in essential subjects without the restrictions which exist at present in the United Kingdom."[6] Captain Balfour's impression of his meeting with Morgenthau was considerably more positive than Air Marshal Garrod's meeting with Colonel Spaatz in London.

Both Morgenthau and Spaatz stated that for such a plan to be politically acceptable, and to avoid the necessity for congressional approval, British students would have to enter the United States in civilian clothes through Canada and training could not include live gunnery or bombing practice. Even though these discussions were encouraging, the shortage of advanced training aircraft remained a major obstacle. Morgenthau hinted that President Roosevelt might consider diverting the necessary aircraft from American production schedules, but made no commitment.

After his meeting with Morgenthau, Captain Balfour arranged a meeting with President Roosevelt. Also in the meeting were Harry Hopkins and Air Commodore George C. Pirie, MC, DFC, the British air attache. They found the president receptive to the idea of training British pilots in American civilian schools. Balfour cabled the Air Ministry, "The President of the United States is well disposed toward such a scheme and would take a personal interest in it" and concluded, "I attach the highest importance to this scheme."[7]

Captain Balfour's warm reception in the White House probably stemmed from a report the president received earlier that day from Colonel William Donovan. Roosevelt had sent Donovan, a New York City attorney, World War I veteran, and recipient of the Congressional Medal of Honor, to Britain as the president's personal envoy to evaluate conflicting assessments as to whether Britain could withstand a German invasion. Donovan traveled quietly throughout Britain and then conferred privately with several high-ranking British officials including Air Chief Marshal Sir Cyril Newall, Chief of Air Staff. Back in Washington, Donovan told President Roosevelt that Britain did indeed have the will to resist invasion, but desperately needed American aircraft, equipment, and training facilities.

After his meeting with the president, Captain Balfour sought more specific information about American civilian flight training. In a meeting arranged by Homer Smith of the Clayton Knight Committee, Balfour met with three flight school operators in the St. Regis Hotel in New York. Accompanied by Homer Smith, Air Vice Marshal L. D. D. McKean, Air Officer Commanding the United Kingdom Air Liaison Mission in Canada, Air Commodore Pirie, and W. W. Wakefield, representing the British Purchasing Commission, Balfour met with Major Long from Texas,

Major Moseley from California, and Captain Maxwell Balfour of Spartan School of Aeronautics in Oklahoma (the operators who would later undertake Refresher training). At this meeting, Balfour received specific information from the flight school operators and learned firsthand many of the concerns, as well as the potential problems involved in such a new and complicated venture.

Following these discussions, and irrespective of the fact that these meetings had produced no results, the British Air Ministry drew up plans to establish eight civilian flight schools in the United States. These plans, "on a civilian basis politically acceptable in the United States and such as not to require approval of Congress" anticipated an output of 300 pilots a month from an eighteen-week course. Using the British training ratio of two students per training aircraft, which allowed one-third of the trainers to be idle in order to provide for "immediate reserve, routine maintenance and repair," the plan would require 320 elementary trainers and 650 intermediate and advanced trainers for a total of 970 aircraft (subsequently scaled back to 720 aircraft).[8]

This detailed proposal included a specific flight training syllabus and projected that courses could begin training by December 1940 and would graduate the first pilots by April 1941. Developed two months before the American presidential election, this unrealistic plan ignored the realities of both the American political scene and the availability of training aircraft. The proposal never progressed beyond the preliminary planning stage, but it does indicate the importance that British officials placed on the potential for training pilots in the United States.

Realistic plans to train British pilots in the United States gained momentum after the November 1940 reelection of President Roosevelt. The president actively sought to assist Great Britain short of war and four days before the election stated, "Our policy is to give all possible material aid to the nations which still resist aggression."[9] From this desire to aid Great Britain, emerged the concept of lend-lease.

In 1939, at the urging of President Roosevelt, Congress had passed an amendment to the Neutrality Act that allowed the sale of supplies and armaments to belligerent nations as long as those nations purchased the supplies in cash and then transported the supplies in their own ships. This new policy became known as "cash and carry." British purchases of aircraft, engines, and other equipment, along with direct British investment in certain American defense companies, combined with President Roosevelt's extensive rearmament program, allowed American manufacturers, which had struggled just to survive during the Depression, to build new plants and purchase vital machine tools which would later prove invaluable to the Allied success in World War II.

By the end of 1940 the "cash and carry" system of purchasing war materiel had seriously depleted British treasury reserves and doubts existed as to the British ability to continue the war. Churchill conveyed the economic realities to President Roosevelt in brutally frank terms in his 8 December 1940 letter on the status of the war: "as you know, the orders already placed or under negotiation . . . many times exceed the total exchange resources remaining at the disposal of Great Britain. The moment approaches when we shall no longer be able to pay cash for shipping and other supplies."[10]

President Roosevelt proposed a new system, known as lend-lease, in which war materiel would be purchased from private manufacturers and "loaned" to the British under a central allocation system managed by the United States government. After passage by Congress, Roosevelt signed the Lend-Lease Act (U.S. House of Representatives Resolution H.R. 1776), on 11 March 1941. Churchill described the legislation as, "The most unsordid act in the history of any nation."[11] The Lend-Lease Act offered vital relief to the British economy, which allowed Britain to remain in the war, gave a much needed boost to American manufacturers, and also paved the way for training British pilots and aircrew in the United States.

At this time the U.S. Army Air Corps had its own problems. The American air service had suffered during the Depression from a particularly miserly Congress in much the same way as the Royal Air Force had suffered in Britain. With war clouds rising on the European horizon and a deteriorating diplomatic situation in the Far East following the Japanese occupation of Manchuria and subsequent invasion of China, President Roosevelt called for a massive rearmament program. In a 12 January 1939 address to Congress Roosevelt asked for increased expenditures for aircraft procurement and a drastic expansion of the Army Air Corps and Naval Air Service.

The previous year the army had graduated about 300 pilots from its only training facility at Randolph Field in San Antonio, Texas (which had an annual capacity of no more than 500). The proposed expansion program far surpassed the capabilities of the Army Air Corps training command. Maj. Gen. Henry H. Arnold, Army Assistant Chief of Staff and Chief of the Air Corps, knew that even with adequate funding, the time required to construct new training facilities, train personnel, and order new aircraft on a scale envisioned by the president would be prolonged.[12] Against considerable internal resistance, Arnold decided to enlist civilian flight schools in the expanded army flight training effort.[13]

In May 1939 ten civilian flight school operators met with General Arnold and members of the Army Air Corps training staff in the old Munitions Building in Washington. These men held the highest commercial flight training school certification from the Civil Aeronautics Authority. Eight of these contractors, Allan Hancock, E. S. Sias, Oliver L. Parks, T. Claude Ryan, Major William F. Long, Major C. C. Moseley, Captain Maxwell W. Balfour, and Harold S. Darr, would form the initial army contract civilian flight training program.[14]

These original contractors provided primary training, the first of the three phases of army flight training, in a twelve-week course consisting of 65 hours of flying and 225 hours of ground school.[15] Graduates of the civilian primary schools were then posted to a regular Army Air Corps basic flight school, and afterwards went on to an army advanced flight school. Someone asked Arnold about funds for the new program.

Arnold replied, "you can borrow the money, can't you, until I can get congressional appropriations?"[16] With nothing more than Arnold's promise to try and pay them, the operators agreed to the new plan. Congress passed the initial funding bill for the new contract civilian flight training program by two votes.

By mid-1940, the Army Air Corps increased its pilot production goal to seven thousand pilots annually and later to the astronomical figure of twelve thousand pilots annually (and later to much higher outputs). In order to train that many pilots the Army Air Corps had to double the number of civil contract primary schools and then almost immediately it became necessary to add still more schools. General Arnold asked the original operators to double the size of their existing schools, and then add more capacity. This level of expansion entailed the construction of new schools and additional contractors were brought into the program.

By the end of 1940 the army expansion plans were well underway, but even with the use of civilian contractors and an expanding aircraft production base, these plans were still a long way from achieving the army's goals. Against the harsh realities of American expansion, President Roosevelt wanted to give all possible assistance to Great Britain, now alone after the fall of France, alone in a struggle for national survival. Roosevelt pressured Arnold to give assistance to Britain in the form of the latest aircraft such as the long-range Boeing B-17 heavy bomber and fighter aircraft such as the Curtiss P-40, but also in the allocation of training facilities.

General Arnold, as well as other high-ranking army officers, greatly admired the British and sincerely wanted to help, but the practical dilemma always came down to a question of the proper allocation of scarce resources. These resources included aircraft, engines, equipment, and facilities, which were needed for the American rearmament program and might be desperately needed for the defense of the United States. After conferring with army planners, various army departments, and finally Army Chief of Staff General George C. Marshall, Arnold held various lengthy, often acrimonious, discussions with representatives of the administration.

From these arduous discussions, the various parties finally agreed on an allocation ratio of American aircraft for Britain.[17] Arnold also agreed to make available one-third of the army's increasing flight training capacity to train British pilots. The army estimated that this plan would provide a minimum of 3,000 pilots per year for Britain. Since the Army Air Corps was already engaged in an ambitious expansion program, this offer allowed even greater expansion. Arnold felt that the excess capacity (paid for by lend-lease funds which did not require new congressional appropriations) could be temporarily used by the British and would then be available later for American needs.

The British air attache in Washington transmitted the American proposal to Air Ministry officials. General Arnold then traveled to Britain in April 1941 to meet with British officials and senior RAF officers to discuss aid requirements and get a firsthand view of British operations. Arnold planned a low-keyed trip, but the British gave him VIP treatment. While in England, Arnold met with British air officials and members of the Air Council such as Sir Arthur Street, Permanent Under-Secretary of State, Air Chief Marshal Sir Charles Portal, Chief of Air Staff, and Air Marshal Sir John Babington, Air Member for Personnel. Arnold also discussed the proposed training schemes with Captain Harold Balfour and Air Marshal A. G. R. Garrod. These two men had participated in the initial training discussions and would be closely associated with British flight training in the United States throughout the war.

The one-third capacity of the Army Air Corps pilot training program offered by Arnold equaled the equivalent of seven and a half Royal Air Force elementary and service flying schools. The army would provide, "free of charge the aircraft, the aerodromes, the accommodation and the instructors" for the basic and advanced training, but the British would have to pay for the primary training since these schools were civilian owned. Aside from the civilian primary schools the only cost to the

British would be pay, feeding, and transportation of the students, along with fuel and oil used by the basic and advanced aircraft (fuel and oil would later be included under lend-lease). In a memorandum to the Air Ministry, Garrod summarized the American offer and concluded, "This happens to suit our book extremely well because it gives us ready made facilities at a time when the creation of such facilities would be a heavy drain on our resources."[18]

Arnold also offered to provide American pilots to ferry British aircraft purchased in the United States across the Atlantic to Britain, but told Garrod that the army had no capacity in its navigation schools (British "air observers"). As new army navigation schools were being built, Army Air Corps student navigators were attending the Pan American Airways navigation school located on the University of Miami campus in Coral Gables, Florida. Arnold suggested that British students could take open positions in the Pan American Airways school as army students departed, with a view toward taking over the school completely within four to five months. The British would also pay for instruction in this school due to its civilian ownership, but "it would be complete with aircraft, accommodation, instructors, aerodrome and equipment."[19]

Arnold's "low keyed" trip expanded to include meetings with Field Marshal Sir John Dill, Chief of the Imperial General Staff, Lord Beaverbrook, British Minister of Aircraft Production, Sir Dudley Pound, First Sea Lord, and several cabinet members. Arnold toured aircraft factories, operational units including the Eagle Squadron, an RAF fighter squadron made up of American pilots, and air defense command centers.

After several days of endless meetings and conferences, Arnold had dinner with Prime Minister Churchill, his wife, and a small party of dignitaries on two successive evenings. Both nights Churchill and Arnold stayed up long after dinner until the early morning hours discussing the war situation. Toward the end of Arnold's trip the British arranged an audience with King George VI.[20]

Aside from the purely official aspects of his visit, Arnold made a favorable impression on the British and established a rapport with high-ranking RAF officers and Air Council officials, which would pay considerable future dividends. When Arnold left Great Britain, Captain Balfour wrote to him: "May I conclude by saying how, personally, it has given me such pleasure to have had the privilege of meeting you, and I hope that your visit over here is going to be the first of many such. You were the bringer of good tidings, but quite apart from the great help which you are giving and are going to give in the future, I feel that it has been a real pleasure to have met you."[21]

Several plans emerged to train British aircrew in the United States. The plan that incorporated British students directly into the Army Air Corps flight training program became known as the Arnold Scheme. A similar program trained British students destined for Coastal Command (flying boat pilots and navigators) or the Royal Navy's Fleet Air Arm (fighter, dive bomber, and torpedo plane pilots) in the United States Navy flight training program. This plan became known as the Towers Scheme, named after Vice Admiral John H. Towers, Chief of the Bureau of Aeronautics.[22] The British also assumed the entire capacity of the Pan American Airways navigation school.[23]

Royal Air Force and Air Ministry officials were genuinely grateful and a little overwhelmed by the generosity of the American offer. They also had concerns about the American training proposal.

These training plans involved not only the obvious process of learning to fly, along with the immense logistical problems of transportation, scheduling, housing, feeding, and processing large numbers of men, but on a more subtle level they involved the sensitive collective egos of two great nations. Air officials on both sides of the Atlantic naturally considered their respective training methods to be superior to those found in any other nation. The Royal Air Force handbook included the comment, "Indeed, it is acknowledged that training in the British service reaches a higher degree of efficiency than in any other air service in the world."[24] British officials faced the conflicting emotions of gratitude for the generous offer of American help at a critical period when thousands of young men selected for aircrew training were waiting postings to overcrowded training centers, while at the same time they had concerns about the quality of American training methods.

These collective emotions were by no means simple or easily defined and existed in both the British and American air services. Many Army Air Corps officers openly admired the British stand against Hitler, while others harbored a certain, but ill defined, resentment against Great Britain. British officers exhibited the same range of emotions when considering their American cousins. Air Commodore Pirie summed up this attitude in a 7 April 1941 letter to the Air Ministry. "The standard of training in this country is not as good as ours by a long way . . . the American thinks that everything in America is superior to everything in any other country and one has to play up to this vanity—or is it inferiority complex?"[25]

In spite of individual prejudices to the contrary, flight training was not drastically different in the United States and Great Britain, but each had been influenced by disparate circumstances. After the beginning of the war, Britain faced with national survival had lowered RAF flight training standards to 130 hours. Pilots in some Commonwealth countries in the Empire Air Training Scheme had graduated with as few as 100 hours of flight time.

The United States Army Air Corps had developed a peacetime training regimen influenced by the financial constraints of the Depression. The army flight training program also stressed safety. American officers believed that students should master basic flying skills in the first or primary phase of training and the more advanced aspects of flight training such as instrument flying and night flying should be incorporated later in the program. Faced with a severe shortage of funds, the American system also demanded the utmost utilization of scarce aircraft and equipment. The British believed in smaller flight classes and a lower ratio of students to training aircraft, which the Americans considered wasteful. This difference between the two services would be a bone of contention throughout British training in the United States.

The American system consisted of three levels of training: primary, basic, and advanced. Each stage utilized a different and progressively more sophisticated training aircraft. The advanced trainers used in the final stage of flight training employed complex systems found in operational aircraft such as retractable landing gear, flaps, controllable pitch propellers, radios, lights, and full instrumentation. Each level of flight training occurred at a training base dedicated to that level of training. After completing the first or primary stage of training, students traveled to another base for basic training, and then after graduation from basic, moved to another base for advanced training. This added to the overall time required to fully train a service pilot.

On the eve of the American entry into World War II, the Army Air Corps flight training program consisted of approximately 240 hours in a thirty-six-week course. The British considered this peacetime syllabus to be too long. In the British system, students had completed eight weeks of ground instruction in an Initial Training Wing, both phases of flight training (six weeks of elementary and ten weeks of advanced), graduated from an Operational Training Unit, and were reporting to operational squadrons after thirty weeks. In addition, students completing the American courses would have had no training in live gunnery or bombing practice due to American neutrality laws. British officials also worried that student skills might deteriorate due to the lengthy travel time back to Britain after graduation from the American schools, which were mostly located in the southern United States.

Royal Air Force and Air Ministry officials hoped to influence American thinking to either adopt British flight training methods and the RAF syllabus, or to shorten the American syllabus to reflect British practice. During his trip to Great Britain, General Arnold had expressed a willingness to consider changes based on British wartime experience. British officials wisely decided not to press this point too forcefully.

"We are taking the line that their very generous offer will provide us with a training organization which is fully efficient and, except in minor details where we have the advantage of war experience, turning out first-class pilots."[26]

These differences, both real in terms of distance, facilities, and logistics, as well as disparity and concerns stemming from national egos, would probably have killed any proposed program had it not been for the overriding demand for trained aircrew. As the war progressed, these problems, differences, and concerns were solved or overcome, or simply diminished with time.

The British had always wanted a flight training program under British supervision and, if possible, tailored to the RAF syllabus. As an example of the uncertainty and wide range of discussions at this time, British officials faced with moving nine service flying schools (advanced flight schools) intact out of Britain seriously considered the possibility of moving these schools to the United States and specifically considered Texas and Oklahoma as possible locations. With Canadian efforts at full capacity, several informal discussions were held between Air Marshal Garrod and high-level United States administration officials such as Harry Hopkins and Averell Harriman. These conversations, usually over dinner, were so encouraging and the Americans' attitude so positive that Garrod remarked, "Personally, I believe the USA is ready for us to ask for everything that we require."[27]

In fact nothing came of these informal conversations. Looking back at this late date and considering the political realities, it is hard to visualize complete Royal Air Force service schools relocated intact to a neutral United States, even allowing for a pro-British Roosevelt administration. Just before the passage of the Lend-Lease Act, however, another program emerged from the various discussions, and this program would prove highly successful.

In addition to the various official British positions concerning aircrew training, Air Commodore Pirie had also made certain unofficial desires clear to his American counterparts. Therefore, it did not come as a complete surprise when Pirie received a phone call on 5 March from General Arnold.[28] When Pirie arrived in Arnold's office twenty minutes later, he found fifteen others present. "I think you know all these people," Arnold said with a wave of his hand, and then continued without waiting for an answer. "You've been worrying me for about a year and a half. Now let's talk turkey. As soon as the Lend-Lease Bill is through we are going to offer you up to 260 Stearmans and Fairchilds and up to 285 Harvards or Yales on loan for training purposes. I understand these aircraft are to be used in this country; and here are six of our best civilian school operators who are prepared to cooperate with you on this scheme."[29]

The six civilian contractors hastily summoned to Washington were John Paul Riddle, Major C. C. Moseley, Harold S. Darr, Major William Long, Captain Maxwell Balfour, and T. Claude Ryan. All of these men held contracts for training army pilots and Moseley, Long, and Balfour were already working with the British on Refresher training. This small program had produced good results despite a shaky start and interference from the Clayton Knight Committee. Pirie cabled the Air Ministry in London with the encouraging news of his meeting with Arnold and the civilian contractors.

This new program, known initially as British Civil Flying Training Schools and later shortened to British Flying Training Schools, would be all-new civilian operated schools dedicated to RAF flight training and supervised by Royal Air Force officers. The schools would provide students with flight training from primary through advanced at the same location. This innovation, unique among the various training schemes, offered faster training and greater efficiency. The civilian flight schools provided the facilities, including civilian instructors, maintenance personnel, and administrative staff. The Army Air Corps would provide the necessary aircraft and possibly other items under lend-lease. The exact contribution from the new lend-lease legislation and myriad other details, as well as certain legal aspects of the new program, were somewhat vague.

The Air Council, which consisted of prominent Air Ministry officials, met in London as soon as Air Commodore Pirie cabled news of the new program. Even though details of the new plan were sketchy, those summoned to the meeting moved quickly to implement a wide range of considerations inherent in the offer.

British officials considered training in an Initial Training Wing, which taught basic ground school subjects before flight training, to be essential for students destined for the United States in order to "weed out unsuitable pupils." Officials estimated a failure rate of 20 percent for British students even though U.S. Army Air Corps student failure rates were known to be considerably higher. British ITW capacities and schedules had to be reviewed and possibly revised. Even mundane matters such as provision for subsistence while en route to the new schools had to be considered. Since the new schools would provide all phases of flight training, officials sometimes referred to the new program as "Ab Initio Flying Training in the U.S.A." and later as the All-Through Scheme.

Air Council officials, concerned about the possible negative effect of the lengthy travel time to and from the new schools in the United States, took the RAF flight training time of 130 hours and added an additional 20 hours for a total of 150 hours. The Royal Air Force flight training course contained two segments: fifty hours of elementary and eighty hours of advanced training. Officials included the additional 20 hours in the elementary phase of training ("primary" in the American schools) and noted, "the 70 hours in 225 horsepower Primary Types should give them a much better foundation than the 50 hours which we give them on Moths or Magisters."[30]

Even with the additional flight time, the course duration was lengthened over that normally considered necessary for a 150-hour course. Officials decided on a twenty-week course and explained that the longer time would "allow for the fact that United Kingdom pilots might take time to settle down in a new country and that the instructional staff would not be experienced in our training requirements."[31] Officials also recommended one week of leave during training, but left the scheduling up to Air Commodore Pirie noting, "we have definite evidence in this country that a spell of more than 10–12 weeks on end leads to staleness, and that a few days leave is essential if students are to retain their freshness."[32]

There existed considerable uncertainty about the actual syllabus to be used in the new schools, as well as other details. Air Ministry officials felt that the American civilian flight school operators would impose their own training methods and syllabus, but went ahead and prepared a pamphlet with a suggested syllabus. "We have no intention of asking these schools to accept our methods, but it seemed desirable that they should be aware of our methods and sequence of flying instruction, and these are given in summarized form in the pamphlet."[33]

From previous conversations with American officials the members knew that students would have to enter the United States in civilian clothes and that no live gunnery or aerial bombing practice would be possible. They had some concern over the perceived lack of military discipline for students training in civilian schools in a foreign country, but that could not be helped. The British would insist on instrument training and night flying in the first or primary phase of flight training, which differed from the American system and might necessitate modifications to the primary training aircraft.

With the increasing emphasis on the bomber offensive in Europe, British officials hoped that some training in multi-engine aircraft might be possible, but realized that due to a shortage of suitable equipment, all training would probably be in single-engine aircraft. That was another area that could not be changed.

It would also be necessary to consult with the Treasury and estimate costs and how much could be expected from the new American "Lease and Lend" legislation. Air Ministry officials decided that Royal Air Force supervisory personnel would be one chief flying instructor for each pair of schools and a chief ground instructor at each school (experience would quickly show this staffing level to be woefully inadequate). Officials also expressed the feeling that American volunteers would make up the complete enrollment of one or possibly two of the six schools. Although some American volunteers did train at British Flying Training Schools, their numbers were insignificant. As a final thought, the officials asked the air attache "to convey our thanks to the U.S.A. Administration."[34]

General Arnold slightly dampened the initial British enthusiasm in response to a question. The British Supply Board in Washington had placed a preliminary lend-lease request for 200 North American AT-6 Harvard advanced trainers to be used in England. The air attache hoped that the new American offer was in addition to those Harvards. Arnold quickly clarified the situation; the British could have the Harvards currently on order or the 285 Harvards offered for the new British Civil Flying Training Schools, but not both.

The British opted for the new program, but were not overly disappointed since the American offer was still extremely generous in view of the limited supply of advanced trainers. In a letter to the Air Ministry, Pirie noted the advantages of utilizing the aircraft in the new program. "By retaining Harvards in U.S. we save extremely valuable shipping space, better weather, and no interruption [from] enemy action." But the old concerns about the quality of American training remained just beneath the surface. Pirie noted the familiar British view of the disadvantages of any flight training program in the United States: "We cannot exercise the same rigid control as we can in England over the operators . . . the actual instruction is probably less efficient than in England."[35]

The civilian flight school operators proposed a cost of $25 per hour for primary flight training and $35 per hour for advanced training, which the British considered excessive. Pirie knew this was more than the Army Air Corps paid the same contractors for flight training and brought the matter up with General Arnold. Pirie commented on the civilian contractors and the proposed cost in a letter to the Air Ministry. "I have known them all pretty well for 2–3 years and they are all fine fellows and will do a grand job. But I have no qualms about beating them down to the last penny!"[36]

The contractors did not intentionally intend to gouge the British, whom they all respected, but they had survived the Depression by being tight-fisted businessmen in a highly risky business. They were now faced with the prospect of constructing new and expensive facilities for an entirely different national government. No one knew how much help might be provided from lend-lease funds other than aircraft and possibly fuel.

Costs for the new program were negotiated down to $21.60 per hour for primary flight training, $32.70 per hour for advanced training, and $5.00 per hour for the Link trainer. The British still considered the cost to be high, but agreed to the plan.[37] In one colorful story concerning the negotiations, Major Long reportedly told Captain Harold Balfour, British Under-Secretary of State for Air, not to worry about the expense; he would take prized British Hereford bulls for breeding stock on his West Texas ranch as partial payment, since "they're going to be bombed to hell anyway." According to the story, the British agreed to the proposal, but the plan fell through due to wartime restrictions on transporting cattle.[38]

The British Treasury, unfortunately, did not share the enthusiasm of the air attache in Washington or the Air Ministry in London for the new British Civil Flying Training Schools. Air Commodore Pirie came away from his first meeting with Sir Frederick Phillips, the Treasury representative to the British Supply Council in North America, "feeling very discouraged." But others in the meeting encouraged Pirie to look on the bright side, "both Self and Pinsent (our Financial Counsellor) said we had got on very well, in that Phillips had not said it would be impossible to find the money!"[39]

One of the major obstacles to effective planning was the uncertainty concerning the actual items to be covered under lend-lease. After several discussions with U.S. officials, Pirie reported, "Generally speaking, it seemed that aircraft, hangars, hangar equipment, replacements of aircraft, petrol, oil, repair (but not maintenance or servicing) of aircraft, ground equipment, any facility for servicing (but not the actual cost of servicing) and the necessary flying equipment could be met out of Lend-Lease funds."[40] But that was by no means certain.

If that were not enough, the U.S. State Department objected to the use of RAF "publications, log books, etc." in the United States as a violation of the neutrality laws. This bureaucratic triviality came after the plan to train British pilots in the United States had been approved at the highest governmental levels. Pirie reported, "but we may get round it in some way."

In the end, and under pressure from the Air Ministry, the Treasury agreed to the proposal based on costs that "appeared likely" to be one and one-half million to five million dollars in capital expense and three and one-half million to five million dollars in annual operating costs, although, according to Pirie, Sir Frederick Phillips "thought it rather sad to throw good dollars away on flying training."[41] Apparently the State Department did not press its objection to the use of RAF publications in the United States.

RAF officials optimistically projected that British students could begin training in the new schools by the middle of May 1941.

CHAPTER 3

ROYAL AIR FORCE DELEGATION

Air Ministry officials realized that the sheer magnitude of the proposed training schemes in the United States would require considerable coordination and liaison between British and American military commands, as well as a close working relationship with the individual civilian school operators. Besides the obvious need for training supervision, accounting personnel would need to be involved due to the financial aspects of the new training programs and the complexities associated with payments to the civilian schools. Detailed records would be necessary to account for Crown funds as opposed to lend-lease expenditures. Many decisions would require approval by the British Treasury. Consideration had to be given to the maintenance of personnel records and the issuance of the necessary movement orders for the British students training in the United States, as well as the RAF officers assigned to the various schools.

The work load required by these tasks far surpassed the capacity of the limited staff of the air attache at the British Embassy and the tasks were not compatible with the British Purchasing Commission or British Council. These organizations were departments of the Ministry of Aircraft Production (later the Ministry of Supply) under the direction of Lord Beaverbrook. The relationship between the Air Ministry and the

Ministry of Aircraft Production had not always been the most harmonious. Obviously a new organization would be required.

At the time of General Arnold's April 1941 trip to Britain, the most pressing need concerned liaison with the new training schemes. The person heading this difficult task would have to be well versed not only in the field of military flight training, but would also need to be a skilled diplomat capable of dealing effectively with British and American requirements, as well as national sensitivities.

During General Arnold's visit, Air Ministry officials appointed Group Captain D. V. Carnegie to coordinate the new training programs in the United States. Carnegie, who had only arrived at the Air Ministry a fortnight earlier as Deputy Director of Flying Training, had previously commanded a fighter Operational Training Unit and had been station commander at RAF Wittering and RAF Grangemouth. An outgoing and personable Scotsman, Carnegie had traveled extensively in the United States before the war where he developed many friends in civilian and military flying circles, including Admiral John Towers, director of the U.S. Navy Bureau of Aeronautics. Carnegie had even lived for a while in Montana.[1]

Air Commodore R. A. Cochrane, CBE, AFC, temporary Director of Training at the Air Ministry, wrote a letter to Air Commodore Pirie introducing Carnegie. "He has had a very wide experience of all forms of flying and has just come from commanding a fighter O.T.U. He knows America well and has many friends in the U.S. Army Corps. He thoroughly appreciates the very generous nature of the offer which we are accepting and will provide just that quiet advice based upon war experience which should enable us to obtain the best results from the training organization."[2]

Carnegie received a hasty verbal briefing from Air Ministry officials that outlined the proposed training plans in the United States. The briefing also included British concerns about American training methods, the possibility of incorporating RAF experience into the American flight training syllabus, and the desire to reduce the training time in the American military schemes if possible. Evaluating the feasibility of these goals and then achieving them were left largely to Carnegie, who returned to his quarters and packed in order to catch the next commercial airline flight to neutral Portugal. In Portugal the passengers would take a Pan American Airways Clipper flying boat to the United States. This would also be the flight home taken by General Arnold and his staff.

Passengers, including General Arnold, his staff, and Group Captain Carnegie, boarded a KLM Royal Dutch Airlines Douglas DC-3 in Bristol. After takeoff the aircraft flew southwest far out across the Bay of Biscay, skirting occupied France and German Luftwaffe air patrols, before landing in Portugal. The next day the twenty-seven passengers and crew of twelve boarded a Pan American Airways flying boat destined for the western edge of Africa. After flying over Dakar, the flight landed in Bolama, near Bissau in Portuguese Guinea and spent the remainder of the day. The next day the Clipper crossed the South Atlantic at 12,000 feet and landed at Belem at the mouth of the Para River in Brazil "after a very comfortable trip." The Clipper now turned north toward Trinidad and then on to Bermuda before heading northwest for its final destination, New York City. After landing, Carnegie joined General Arnold and his staff in Arnold's personal DC-3, for the last leg of the trip from New York to Washington, arriving "in time for lunch." The entire 9,000-mile trip took the forty-two-ton Clipper carrying 3,980 gallons of fuel slightly less than sixty-one flying hours at an average speed of 150 miles per hour.

The trip gave Carnegie an excellent opportunity to get to know the American officers and also to learn firsthand the extent of the mission entrusted to him from the American point of view. From lengthy conversations with General Arnold and his staff, Carnegie became convinced of Arnold's "keen desire to do all he could for us."[3] From these informal conversations he also gained valuable insight into the problems associated with this entirely new undertaking. Carnegie would not have a predecessor's experience for guidance. Not only was he starting from scratch, but time was critical.

The logistics associated with screening, housing, feeding, and transporting students bound for the new American training programs were enormous and time consuming. Even at this early date, plans were already being set in motion to transport the first British students for the Arnold Scheme and the initial drafts for the first four British Civil Flying Training Schools from dispersal centers in England, across the Atlantic Ocean to Canada, and then on to the United States. Additional drafts would follow. These drafts would provide each of the six British Civil Flying Training Schools with the first course of fifty students. Intakes would continue every five weeks until each school had a full complement of four courses for a total of 200 students. In case the new schools were not ready in time, the operators had promised to accommodate the British students in their nearby army contract schools.

The same Pan American Airways flight carried a Mr. Frankel, a service representative with the Aeroplane Division of Curtiss-Wright Corporation, returning from England after coordinating the introduction of Curtiss P-40 Tomahawk fighters purchased by Britain. Frankel complained that British bureaucracy had completely frustrated his efforts and "he found it quite impossible to get anything done in the U.K." According to Frankel, some thirty-odd departments within the Air Ministry and the RAF issued conflicting orders concerning the aircraft, but no one seemed to be in charge. The Air Ministry had even demanded that the aircraft be fitted with deicing equipment in spite of the fact that the Army Air Corps had operated P-40s in Alaska for several years without deicing equipment and without problems.

The British had developed several different operating procedures for the P-40 which not only conflicted with each other, but totally disregarded the Curtiss manual, resulting in operational problems that Frankel said he had not encountered "servicing Tomahawks from Alaska to Panama."

Frankel also knew of eighteen tons of spare parts that had arrived in England, but nobody in the Air Ministry could tell him where they were.[4]

This story obviously has nothing to do with training, but it does illustrate the often strained relationship at this time between the Americans and the British on an operational level. Many American officers felt that the British were not effectively utilizing aircraft and equipment, which had been diverted from much-needed American supplies.

American officers also resented the high-level political decision to divert twenty Boeing B-17C four-engine heavy bombers from scarce American production and make them available to Britain. American officers had warned British officials that the B-17C was little more than a service test model and was not combat ready. As the Pan American Airways Clipper containing General Arnold, his staff, and Group Captain Carnegie crossed the South Atlantic, the first B-17Cs had just arrived in England. The British were preparing to press these first bombers into combat, flying in daylight, without fighter escort, in small formations at extreme altitudes (which presented unique problems in unpressurized aircraft), against heavily defended targets. After numerous training problems and several accidents, the operational results would be disappointing and costly. Later British criticism of the B-17, in which the Americans had invested so much of their limited resources during the last half of the 1930s, further infuriated American officers. Stories would soon circulate that new B-17s sent to England remained crated on docks or languished out of service in modification centers for long periods of time. The British, acutely sensitive to American feelings, sought to dispel the negative rumors, but with little success.

Most (but certainly not all) of this friction between the Americans and the British would diminish with time due to the overriding priority of defeating a common foe. But it does illustrate the often delicate national sensitivities Carnegie had to contend with as he assumed his new duties in the United States.

In Washington, Carnegie first reported to Air Commodore Pirie and then to recently promoted Air Marshal Arthur Harris who arrived to head the British Air Commission. No one knew exactly where to put Carnegie due to the tenuous early organization and a scarcity of office space in Washington. Carnegie initially felt that he might be more useful attached to the staff of the commanding general of the South Eastern Army Air Corps Flying Training Center located at Maxwell Field in Alabama since all of the Arnold Scheme schools and two of the British Civil Flying Training Schools would be located in the southeastern United States.

Legal questions, however, concerning implementation of lend-lease confronted Carnegie upon his arrival. Air Commodore Pirie noted the status in a report to the Air Ministry. "Carnegie's arrival on May 1 unfortunately coincided with severe set back in training scheme owing new interpretation of Lend Lease bill" and then concluded, "meanwhile no action as regards acquisition of sites or building has been possible."[5] Since these questions, which Carnegie described as "disheartening," occupied most of his time immediately after his arrival in Washington, the War Department gave Carnegie an unused desk in the training section.

Even though President Roosevelt had given General Arnold complete authority to set up the Arnold Scheme and the British Civil Flying Training Schools, these plans were hindered by a series of legal and procedural questions. None of the myriad questions and rulings by attorneys from the U.S. Army, Treasury Department, State Department, and other agencies specifically set up to deal with aid to Britain and lend-lease, endangered the programs, but were nonetheless frustrating and time consuming.

As one example, a letter dated April 29, 1941 (two weeks before the British schools were originally scheduled to open) from Robert A. Lovett, Assistant Secretary of War (Air), to Harry Hopkins noted, "You should know that all action on the British Flying School program, except planning is effectively blocked at present until a legal clearance is secured on the application of Lend-Lease funds to this enterprise." Carnegie noted another issue in a memorandum to the Air Ministry. "The lawyers have said that we can not put U.K. students into U.S. Army schools, but in spite of that General Johnson gave orders for 550 vacancies to be made available. He said he would get the legal side of it fixed somehow or other before they arrive."[6]

While the army staff dealt with questions concerning the Arnold Scheme, Carnegie had to contend with many aspects of the new civilian schools. In an early report Carnegie noted, "It has now been decided that we must buy the land and let the contracts but the army will supply the actual materials for construction. There are a lot of further complications which I am afraid may lead to delays especially as the sites for these new schools have only been tentatively selected but have not yet been approved."[7]

Actual procedural details, such as who would purchase materials, changed with frustrating regularity as rulings by various entities amended previous rulings by other entities. After numerous meetings with American military and civilian officials, Carnegie in his first lengthy situation report to Air Commodore Cochrane summarized the situation in the United States and added, "I know how upsetting this must be to you but you can rest assured that no stone is being left unturned at this end." Ever the optimist, Carnegie concluded his report, "All will be well, but it has been a bit disheartening these constant changes in official policy."[8]

Concerns over the various legal delays reached the highest levels and Prime Minister Churchill wrote to President Roosevelt. "I now understand there are legal difficulties. I hope, Mr. President, that these are not serious, as it would be very disappointing to us and would offset our arrangements if there were now to be delay."[9] Ten days later Roosevelt replied that all legal questions had been resolved.

Since the new British Civil Flying Training Schools were owned and operated by civilian contractors, the individual school locations had to be approved by the Civil Aeronautics Authority, as well as the Army Air Corps and the Royal Air Force. The Air Corps had gained valuable experience from the original civilian flight school program. As an example, Major Long's army contract school had been located at Dallas Love Field. The airfield had been developed in 1917 to train army pilots for World War I and had been turned over to the city after the war. When Long moved his operations to Dallas in 1926, the airport was a little-used grass field located six miles northwest of the city. By 1939 three hard-surface runways, a new terminal building, and a radio equipped control tower had been added to the field. In addition to Long's school, several other flight schools and three scheduled airlines, American, Delta, and Braniff, used Love Field.

After eighteen months of training it became apparent that Love Field could no longer accommodate the level of activity required by the army contracts. Long constructed a new army primary school in Brady, Texas, 180 miles southwest of Dallas and in the late spring of 1941 moved his army school from Love Field. From this and similar experiences, the Army Air Corps now required civilian schools to be located at airfields not served by scheduled airlines and off established airways.

Carnegie's hectic first weeks included meetings with various governmental officials, a meeting with General Arnold, and a Saturday evening meeting with the six civilian contractors. Carnegie found the contractors to be enthusiastic and ready to proceed, but hampered by delays in the official approval process. All of the contractors had tentative site plans and construction drawings for the proposed schools. These plans were basic in concept (with one exception) and based largely on their existing army contract schools. Carnegie reported that the contractors had assured him that construction could be completed within thirty to ninety days after the start of work. (Carnegie may have been overly optimistic in including the low estimate of thirty days.)

As paperwork piled up and Washington meetings continued, the Air Ministry send Wing Commander H. A. V. Hogan to join Carnegie. Hogan graduated at the top of his 1930 Cranwell class and received the prestigious Sword of Honor from the Air Ministry. Hogan commanded

501 Squadron during the Battle of Britain and had recently commanded an operational training unit.[10]

Squadron Leader Stuart Mills, the assistant air attache and the officer who had inspected the Refresher training schools, also joined Carnegie. The arrival of Hogan and Mills allowed Carnegie to leave Washington and embark on several extended trips to inspect the proposed sites for the new British schools, meet with the Army Air Corps commanders of the various flying training regions, and also visit the civilian contractors' army contract flight schools.

The initial plan called for two British Civil Flying Training Schools to be located in each of the army's three regional training areas, John Paul Riddle and Harold Darr in the South Eastern Air Corps Training Center with headquarters at Maxwell Field in Alabama, Major Long and Captain Maxwell Balfour of Spartan School of Aeronautics in the Gulf Coast Air Corps Training Center with headquarters at Randolph Field in San Antonio, Texas, and Major C. C. Moseley and T. Claude Ryan in the West Coast Air Corps Training Center with headquarters at Moffett Field, California.

Due to severe time constraints and tight budgets, the British flight schools were forced to search for locations that did not require extensive site work. This usually meant an area of about one square mile (640 acres) of fairly level, well-drained ground mostly free of obstructions or with obstructions that could be easily removed. The airfields would likely be grass covered without the benefit of hard surface runways.

The new schools had to be located near at least a medium sized town to provide housing and basic services, since the schools were designed to house only the British students. The British officers, as well as the civilian instructors and other school employees, would reside in town. The school location also needed to be served by utilities, all-weather roads, and a nearby rail line to insure the timely delivery of necessary supplies, equipment, fuel, and oil, as well as arriving and departing students and staff. Each school also required at least two auxiliary fields in order to maintain training efficiency and reduce congestion at the main airfield. These auxiliary fields needed to be located within ten to fifteen miles of the main airfield. And one last, but critical requirement: the site had to be reasonably priced. These ideal conditions had to be compromised in several instances.

On an early three-day inspection trip, Carnegie flew to Arcadia, Florida, and met with John Paul Riddle of the Miami based Embry-Riddle Company. Riddle had been an Army Air Service pilot and had operated an early civilian flight training school in Ohio before moving to Florida. Carnegie and Riddle toured the area around Clewiston, Florida, by air in Riddle's Fairchild. In earlier times this area located on the southwest shore of Lake Okeechobee, ninety miles north of Miami, had been used by native Seminole Indians as a fishing camp.

The town of Clewiston, located on Highway 25, a major east-west route between Palm Beach on the Atlantic coast and Fort Myers on the Gulf of Mexico, had a population of only 949 and had existed for less than twenty years. (Hendry County had only been formed in 1923.) Two enterprising developers, John O'Brien of Philadelphia and Alonzo Clewis of Tampa, purchased a large tract of land, laid out a new town (named for Clewis), and built a railroad, the Moore Haven & Clewiston Railroad, to connect the town to the Atlantic coast. Incorporated in 1925, Clewiston immediately became a favorite of sport fishermen in spite of hurricanes that regularly devastated the area. One particularly severe storm in 1928 killed several hundred residents around Lake Okeechobee, most from flooding. Construction of the Herbert Hoover dike around the lake in 1938 finally controlled the flooding and the region had been found to be ideally suited to growing sugar cane and citrus.

Carnegie also found the area equally suited for flight training. "The site consists of 2500 acres and the only work necessary can be done by a mower. Grass is sparse out here and there are small clumps of palmetto and scrub. The soil is a sandy loam . . . The only obstructions as far as the eye can see are clumps of palms and fir and the area is thus ideal for forced landing practices and for the establishment of auxiliary landing fields. A drainage ditch exists around three sides and from local statistics the ground should seldom if ever be out of action on account of rain."[11]

Returning from his meeting with Riddle and the inspection of the Clewiston site, Carnegie visited the Army Air Corps South Eastern Training Center at Maxwell Field. He found Brigadier General Walter Weaver, the army's regional training commander, to be "a great enthusiast and has a delightful personality, and who is 100% on our side as in fact is everybody in the Army Air Corps whom I have met."[12]

Shortly thereafter, Carnegie again traveled to the South Eastern training region to meet with Harold Darr. Darr had been an Army Air Service instructor during the war. After leaving the service Darr had become a successful banker in Illinois, but never lost his love of flying and had started his own flight school. Darr moved his flight training operations to Albany, Georgia, after his army contract school (one of the original nine army civilian schools) in Glenview, Illinois, had been taken over by the U.S. Navy.

Darr and Carnegie inspected two sites in South Carolina and Florida for his British flight school and both proved to be unsuitable for various reasons. Carnegie returned later to visit a third site which also had to be eliminated. Not until a later visit did Carnegie agree to a site outside of Aiken, in far western South Carolina, about twenty miles northeast of Augusta, Georgia, and the home of another Darr army contract school. This site had to be approved by the army, but Carnegie noted, "no further difficulties are anticipated."

Carnegie next journeyed to Texas where he met with Major Long at Dallas Love Field, the site of Long's civilian school with its Refresher students destined for the RAF, and soon-to-be-relocated army contract school. Long had also been an Army Air Service pilot during the war. After leaving the service, Long started his own flight school and co-founded Long and Harmon Airlines. Long and Carnegie traveled south to San Antonio to meet with Brigadier General Gerald Brant, commander of the Gulf Coast Training Center. Carnegie reported, "I found him most helpful in every way. We discussed training quite fully, and he is anxious to cut down the period of training and was most interested in a copy of our Syllabus which I gave him."[13]

Carnegie and Long, accompanied by army representatives from San Antonio, and Captain Price, a training staff officer from the War Department in Washington, traveled to Fort Worth, Texas, to view a site proposed by the army for Long's British school. This site did not impress Carnegie and he found it would involve considerable expense to purchase, then clear, grade, level, and provide adequate drainage. Carnegie had hoped that local municipalities might offer certain inducements to attract the British schools. Fort Worth, a large city with a population of 178,000, already contained numerous military, aviation, and other defense related facilities, including the new Consolidated Aircraft plant then under construction to produce B-24 bombers. City officials had no interest in contributing municipal funds to attract a small British flight school.

Fortunately another North Texas town, Terrell, located thirty miles east of Dallas, was very interested in attracting the British school. City representatives had called on Long at his Love Field office shortly before Carnegie's visit and Long had been impressed with the Terrell delegation's presentation and enthusiasm. But Long's primary concern involved the critical element of time. With the rejection of the Fort Worth location, the group traveled east to Terrell.

For several years Terrell civil and business leaders led by a committee from the Chamber of Commerce had tried to attract a new airport for the town without success. The prosperous town of 10,480 inhabitants was located on U.S. Highway 80, the main east-west route across the southern United States, which extended from Georgia to California. Downtown Terrell contained several banks, two theaters, a hotel, cafes, and various other retail businesses. Terrell also lay at the intersection of two major rail lines, the Texas & Pacific and the Texas & New Orleans.

The group arrived in Terrell and inspected a 526-acre site located one mile south of town leased by the local flying club. This field, much of it still planted in cotton, required minor grading and drainage work, the relocation of an electrical power line, and the removal of trees and several small houses. Although impressed with the site, the inspection team voiced concerns over the time it would take to acquire the privately owned property. County Judge Monroe Ashworth assured Long that the county could issue general warrants to purchase the land and thus avoid delay.

Two weeks later Major Long returned to Terrell with L. H. Luckey, his operations manager, and Squadron Leader Mills and met with city officials. The city agreed to lease the site to Long for one dollar per year, extend water, sewer, and electrical lines to the field, and provide free utilities (except gas) for ten years. The city owned the municipal water works and the local electric company. In return Long agreed to construct improvements estimated to cost $265,000 pending resolution of minor details.

Pleased with the site, Squadron Leader Mills commented prophetically, "I only hope that your extraordinary brand of Texas hospitality won't overcome our boys."[14] In fact, the enthusiastic display of friendship and hospitality soon to be shown to the young British students by local residents would become an enduring legacy, not only of the Texas school, but of each of the British Flying Training Schools.

After Long and the city reached a tentative agreement, the May 30, 1941, *Terrell Daily Tribune* banner headline proclaimed "RAF TO BASE HERE" and underneath in smaller, but still formidable letters, "300 Future British Flyers Coming." Although the announcement met with excitement and approval from local residents, one young woman reportedly exclaimed, "Oh my goodness! Foreigners in Terrell?"[15]

Soon after the announcement, county commissioners realized that general warrants could not be used to purchase property and the statutes dictated a countywide bond election. Bond elections required notices and public hearings, which would considerably delay the process and possibly void the agreement with Long.

At an emergency meeting held at the Terrell city hall, Walter P. Allen, president of the American National Bank, personally pledged $2,500 and another $5,000 from the bank to purchase the land, pending approval of the bond election. Other citizens joined in with additional pledges and in two days the $35,000 price of the property had been secured. Although opposition to the new airport surfaced from other sections of the county, the bond measure passed by 214 votes.

With the site selection process and preliminary negotiations proceeding favorably in Florida, South Carolina, and Texas, Carnegie next traveled to Tulsa, Oklahoma, to meet with Captain Maxwell Balfour of Spartan School of Aeronautics. Balfour had been an Army Air Service pilot in France during the war and remained as assistant air attache after the war. After returning to the United States, Balfour was severely injured in a fiery crash, which ended his army career and left him scarred for life.

Carnegie and Captain Balfour traveled to Ponca City, a town located in north central Oklahoma about seventy-five miles northwest of Tulsa, to view a site at the municipal airport. Surrounded by oil fields, Ponca City with a population of 16,800 was also the home of a large Continental Oil Company refinery, as well as numerous prosperous businesses. Two railroads, the Atchison, Topeka & Santa Fe and the Chicago, Rock Island & Pacific, served the town. A Chamber of Commerce committee headed by Colonel T. D. Harris, a Continental Oil Company executive, had been actively promoting the city to aviation interests and flight school operators. The site at the municipal airport proved to be well-suited for a training facility. In order to attract the British school, Ponca City officials, led by Mayor Frank Overstreet and Commissioner Guy Conner, were agreeable to favorable terms including free utilities and providing certain improvements such as extending the main runway. As in Terrell, the city owned the local water works and the electric company (which made enough profit that residents paid no city taxes).

In spite of the favorable inspection and the concessions, army representatives rejected the Ponca City site because Braniff Airways had two scheduled daily flights to the airport. The Chamber of Commerce recommended another location two miles away, but this site proved to be unacceptable due to drainage problems. Balfour explained the decision in a letter to Colonel Harris. "The south portion is much too low and would need a great deal of drainage. This type of soil becomes very sticky when soaked and we fear we could not operate without numerous runways." Balfour concluded his letter optimistically, "Perhaps we will have better luck next time."[16] As Carnegie departed for the west coast, Balfour promised to come up with another location, and in fact already had one in mind.

California, the home of Major Moseley's training activities, presented unique challenges. California already had an abundance of military bases, airfields, and defense installations, as well as numerous aircraft manufacturers such as Douglas, Lockheed, Consolidated, Vultee, North American, and Northrop. The state's varied geography presented the biggest problems.

Elevations much over 2,500 feet above sea level were not conducive to primary training due to the reduced performance of the lower-powered primary trainers at higher altitudes. Certain California coastal areas were often prone to the sudden formation of fog at various times of the year. Desert areas experienced temperature extremes during the summer and profitable agriculture already utilized much of the state's level ground, which made the land prohibitively expensive.

Moseley had been an army pilot in France during the war. In 1921 he had won the first Pulitzer Trophy Race at Mitchell Field in Long Island, New York. After leaving the service, Moseley remained in the Air National Guard and became involved in civilian flight training. Moseley's first choice for the new school Santa Ana, "a most delightful location," had to be ruled out because of the cost of the land, as well as soil and drainage problems, which Carnegie felt would require "matting" or oil stabilized runways. Because of the various limitations, primarily cost and geography, alternative sites proved to be scarce.

One 640-acre tract five miles west of Lancaster, fifty miles north of Los Angeles, proved to be, if not ideal, at least acceptable. The location in a high desert region at an elevation of 2,350 feet above sea level experienced high winds and blowing dust at certain times of the year, along with high summer temperatures, but did offer wide-open vistas, usually perfect visibility, generally excellent flying conditions, and freedom from the persistent fog that plagued many California coastal regions.

Lancaster, with 1,550 residents, lay along Highway 6 and the main Southern Pacific Railroad line in the Antelope Valley north of the San Gabriel Mountains on the western tip of the Mojave Desert. Alfalfa farming, along with a significant amount of gold mining in nearby Rosamond and Mojave, comprised the valley's major industries. Lancaster had grown from a train stop when the original Southern Pacific tracks were laid across the valley in 1876. The town quickly grew after the railroad drilled an artesian well to service locomotives. Hotels, schools, churches, and various businesses followed. The town barely survived several years of severe drought beginning in 1894, finally aided by the discovery of gold in the valley. During the mid-1930s, Lancaster had fielded several championship professional basketball teams.

With the site of the new British school tentatively chosen, Carnegie borrowed a Spartan Executive aircraft and visited two of Moseley's army primary schools in Oxnard and Ontario, which he noted were "very well run." Carnegie then visited the Douglas Aircraft Company where Donald Douglas provided a tour of the plant and the new XB-19 bomber, the largest aircraft in the world, soon to make its first flight.[17] After the tour, Carnegie met with T. Claude Ryan, the other west coast contractor.

Ryan operated an army contract flight school and his firm manufactured the PT-21, an all-metal low-wing primary trainer; an improved model, the PT-22, would fly a few months later. Ryan wanted to locate his British school in California's Imperial Valley, but Brigadier General Henry

Harms, the West Coast Training Center commander, opposed the idea because of the location's extreme summer temperatures, "which often reached 130 degrees." Other proposed sites in a fertile citrus growing region were eliminated due to the cost of the land. After other non-productive and frustrating searches, General Harms' staff suggested Phoenix, Arizona, an area still within the Army Air Corps West Coast Training Command. Carnegie described the area in a report to the Air Ministry. "Phoenix is in the middle of the Arizona desert but the town itself is a well-known winter resort and has every modern amenity including air-conditioned hotels."[18]

The Army Air Corps already had training facilities to the southeast and southwest of Phoenix and a civilian firm, Southwest Airways, operated an army contract primary school at Thunderbird Field northwest of Phoenix. The army allocated the area northeast of Phoenix for the new British school, which proved to be more difficult than it first appeared. After reconnaissance from the air and then on the ground by car, Carnegie and Ryan selected two sites. The army rejected the first site and the other turned out to be located on the edge of an Indian reservation, which Indian Bureau officials were not willing to lease on acceptable terms.

Carnegie and Ryan found a third site containing 720 acres located in the Salt River Valley a few miles from Mesa, Arizona, just east of Phoenix. This site met with everyone's approval, although a nearby airway radio range beacon almost eliminated it from consideration. Situated at an elevation of 1,330 feet above sea level, large orange groves bordered the field to the west. The city of Mesa had an option to purchase the property and Carnegie reported, "The field is entirely leveled, cleared and finished and has one 3,000 gallon permanent well installed and concrete irrigation ditches around the field. The use of this site will save from $75,000 to $100,000,"[19]

The Salt River valley had been inhabited by ancient Native Americans and later saw the passing of Spanish explorers. Mormon settlers began arriving in the valley in 1877 after the transcontinental railroad displaced many Mormons from Utah. At first these early settlers barely survived. Citizens incorporated Mesa City in 1883. After the first railroad arrived in 1895, the area experienced steady growth based on agricultural crops such as cotton, alfalfa, and citrus watered by an extensive system of irrigation canals, some dating back to prehistoric times. By 1917 Mesa was one of a small number of United States cities to own its own utility plant. During the Depression, Works Progress Administration funds paved streets and provided a new hospital, a new town hall, and a library. By 1940, Mesa, located at the junction of U.S. Highway 70 and State Highway 87 along the Southern Pacific Railroad main line, had a population of 7,224 and was home to numerous agricultural businesses, unusually wide avenues, and the Arizona Mormon Temple. During a later inspection tour, an unimpressed Squadron Leader Mills described the field as "just desert" and the town as, "a furniture store, food store and a couple of service stations and not much more."[20]

Before he left the area, Carnegie toured Thunderbird Field and came away impressed with the Southwest Airways operation. John H. Connelly, a former Army Air Service pilot and CAA engineering inspector, and Leland Hayward, owner of a Hollywood talent agency, owned and managed Southwest Airways, whose investors included several Hollywood celebrities.

On his way back from Phoenix, Carnegie stopped in Oklahoma and again met with Captain Balfour and an army officer from the Gulf Coast Training command to view another potential school site. This time Balfour presented a location in Miami (pronounced My-am-uh) in northeastern Oklahoma, "only a half hours flight from Tulsa and therefore convenient for Balfour."

A town of 8,340 inhabitants, Miami had grown from a trading post in Indian Territory into a prosperous regional financial center, aided by the discovery of lead and zinc deposits in the area shortly after the Civil War. Located on historic Highway 66 only fifteen miles from the Oklahoma-Kansas border, Miami was also home to Northeastern

Oklahoma Junior College, a two-year school with an annual enrollment of 300 students.

As Army Air Corps flight training gained momentum in 1939 and 1940, Miami had attempted to secure one of the new civilian flight schools. A committee from the local Chamber of Commerce led the effort. The initial contacts were disappointing and committee members were informed that all sites for the new schools had already been chosen. Responding to a suggestion, Chamber Secretary Harry Berkey traveled to St. Louis and met with the local Clayton Knight Committee and proposed Miami as a site for training British pilots. Although friendly, the representative informed Berkey that the selection of flight school locations was a little outside of the scope of the Clayton Knight Committee, but went on to suggest that Berkey prepare a formal presentation for the British Embassy in Washington.

After much work, the committee members, especially Berkey and W. J. Martin, chief engineer for the Northeast Oklahoma Railroad, prepared a leather-bound presentation, which included a site plan for the proposed airfield, details of individual properties whose owners had already agreed to donate or sell their land, and a list of possible auxiliary landing fields within a twenty-mile radius of Miami. The city also agreed to close an adjacent road to allow a sufficiently long runway. Berkey, Pop Root of Quapaw, Oklahoma, just north of Miami, and H. B. Coppan, president of the Northeast Oklahoma Railroad, traveled to Washington and arranged a meeting with Lord Halifax, the new British ambassador.

Halifax told the delegation that any plans for training British pilots in the United States depended on the proposed lend-lease legislation then under debate in the Senate. The three men from Miami left the ambassador's office and went directly to the Senate chambers where they were in time to hear Oklahoma Senator Josh Lee speak in favor of the proposed bill.[21]

Impressed with the Miami presentation, the British Embassy sent the proposal to Captain Balfour after passage of the Lend Lease Act. After the rejection of the Ponca City location, Balfour flew his Spartan Executive to Miami and met with city officials, led by Mayor M. M. DeArman, eager to present their site. After a thorough inspection of the property, Balfour had several additional meetings with Berkey, Chamber of Commerce President Walter Patterson, and attorney John Wallace. These meetings took place in both Miami and Balfour's Tulsa office before all of the various details were worked out and Balfour felt confident enough to present the site to British and Army Air Corps officials.

The proposed field lay just north of Miami along Highway 66 and the Kansas City Southern rail line. Group Captain Carnegie and an Army Air Corps inspection team found the site to be suitable in every way. A small flying club that used the field agreed to move and improvements would be minimal. The site also contained an unusual feature: a large three-story building built as a travel lodge along the historic highway, but never occupied because of the Depression. Constructed for $100,000 five years earlier, the boarded-up building, owned by Sinclair Oil Company and known as the Pennant Terminal, could be purchased for $10,000. After a thorough inspection, Carnegie reported, "This building will provide kitchen and messing facilities for 200 students and also a certain amount of accommodation for staff and will effect a great saving."[22] The army approved the site and Carnegie agreed to purchase the building.

This trip concluded the initial site selection process for the six British Civil Flying Training Schools. Carnegie stopped in Dallas to settle final details of the Terrell school with Major Long, then returned to Washington. Carnegie recorded in his diary that during this last trip he had flown a total of fifty-two hours, forty in army aircraft and the rest in aircraft provided by the various contractors and, therefore, "all at no cost to the government." Carnegie's hard work and persistence had resulted in definite progress. He probably felt that in his various dealings with the individual contractors, the local Army Air Corps commands, and the unique characteristics, considerations, and problems associated with each school site, that he had probably encountered every conceivable difficulty. That assumption would quickly prove to be wrong.

Shortly after Carnegie returned to Washington, T. Claude Ryan notified Carnegie that he had decided to withdraw from the program. Ryan felt that the risks associated with the new British training scheme were too great for him to continue. Ironically, after the expenditure of considerable time and much hard work, Carnegie now had an approved school site in Arizona, but no contractor.

Carnegie quickly recovered from the initial shock of this unforeseen development. Remembering his favorable impression of Southwest Airways and the Thunderbird Field operation, located only twenty-five miles from the new approved site, Carnegie placed a call to John Connelly. Impressed with the efficiency of the American phone system, "I got on to him by telephone which takes about two minutes in this country although the distance is 2,500 miles." Carnegie explained the situation and outlined the terms which had been negotiated with the other contractors. Connelly readily agreed to take over Ryan's position and construct the new school, then sent a telegraph confirmation a couple of hours later. The city of Mesa exercised its option and purchased the land from farmer Elias Habeeb for $28,740, then leased the site to Southwest Airways for two dollars per acre per year.[23]

With the site selection process almost concluded, Carnegie noted that the rules for lend-lease and the new British schools had once again changed, but this time favorably. With only a trace of sarcasm, Carnegie wrote, "Fortunately the A.A. [Air Attache] managed to reverse the decision on which I started off, to the effect that we had to purchase the ground and that the Army would supply the actual material for construction under Lease-lend and we pay the labor, as had this not been reversed some of the schools might have been ready to turn out pilots for the next war but they certainly would not have been of any value to us in this one. As it now stands we are advancing 60% of constructional costs to the operators and they will now be responsible for erection themselves."[24]

The 60 percent figure mentioned by Carnegie referred to an agreement whereby the British government would fund $250,000 to each school operator in order to speed construction and avoid delay. The operators would then repay this initial amount over a five-year-term at a 4 percent interest rate.

Carnegie penned the status of the various schools and assigned a number to each school. This is apparently the first time an official designation had been used for the individual schools. Carnegie also dropped the term "Civil" from the name of the program and shortened the title to just British Flying Training Schools. Carnegie's notes read:

No.1	Major W. F. Long —Terrell, Texas
No.2	Major C. C. Moseley —Lancaster, California
No.3	Captain Max Balfour —Miami, Oklahoma
No.4	Mr. J. H. Connelly —Phoenix, Arizona
No.5	Mr. Paul Riddle — Clewiston, Florida
No.6	Mr. H. S. Darr — probably Aiken, South Carolina

Carnegie's use of the word "probably" in his notes to describe the location of Harold Darr's school had an ominous ring, which proved to be prophetic. Several pieces of land made up the tentatively selected field outside of Aiken. At the last moment the owner of the middle piece, an old man who had farmed the land for fifty years, refused to sell. Darr raised the purchase price from $20 per acre (the land's value) to $300 per acre, but the farmer refused to sell at any price and the selection process had to begin all over again.

Carnegie traveled from Washington to Georgia on three separate weekends to view four tentative sites, which "nearly materialized" but all proved unsuited or had to be rejected for one reason or another. On another visit, Carnegie and Darr inspected another site in southwest Georgia that had been highly recommended by the army. "I was somewhat appalled at the amount of grading which would have been necessary and which it was estimated would cost $100,000. I discovered that sewage would be a further $50,000. To cut a long story short we managed to leave this alone without causing any offense and Darr agreed to look for another site."[25]

By the end of the summer, the other five school sites had been selected, approved, and construction had begun. British students had arrived and were now housed at the operators' nearby army contract schools. The lack of a sixth school went beyond frustrating; it disrupted the entire schedule of students en route from England to the United States. Carnegie had to consider a range of options, which included increasing the other schools' intakes in the short term until the last school became operational or possibly abandoning the sixth school altogether. The seemingly simple expedient of dividing the last school's students among the other five schools became complicated due to insufficient accommodations and changes required in the allocation of aircraft, Link trainers, and other equipment.

Carnegie hated to drop the sixth school since any future expansion would be easier with six schools instead of five. As Carnegie considered schedules and options, the real frustration fell on Harold Darr who genuinely wanted to make his British school a success. Darr had invested a considerable amount of personal time and expense in the project and had already hired many of the staff and instructors for his new school.

Even the Army Air Corps, which had to be involved in the selection process, shared in the frustration. Everyone finally agreed that the original concept of two schools in each of the army's three geographic training commands was not of paramount importance. The Gulf Coast Training Command had three locations in Texas, which they offered to Darr. All three sites were rejected for various reasons. Now truly frustrated, someone suggested the Ponca City, Oklahoma, location originally proposed by Captain Balfour. This site at the municipal airport had been considered an excellent choice except for the two daily Braniff Airways flights. The army waived its earlier objection and city officials agreed to expand the airport, lengthen the runway, and lease the northern portion of the airport for a rental payment of $100 per month. Ponca City, Oklahoma, became the home of Harold Darr's No. 6 British Flying Training School.

The site selection process for the new British schools, although time consuming and of primary importance, was by no means Carnegie's only consideration or frustration. From various conversations and meetings, Carnegie realized that one of his early tasks, which was to influence the Army Air Corps training program, could not be accomplished. Although helpful and eager to study British training methods, the army was not willing to alter its training program. A large part of this decision had to do with the very real possibility of disruption that changes would bring to a complex and rapidly expanding program.

Over time, however, both sides benefitted from these discussions. The Army Air Corps stressed precision maneuvers and taught the theory of flight at an early stage of training. The British flight training syllabus had never stressed precision maneuvers and the teaching of theory of flight had been reduced to a minimum due to wartime constraints. Early experience in the Arnold Scheme and the British Flying Training Schools demonstrated the value of both areas. A grasp of the theory of flight is essential to understanding how certain maneuvers are performed. Wing Commander Hogan noted in one of his early reports that RAF students in the Arnold Scheme "were posing ridiculous questions as regards flying, indicating their complete lack of knowledge about aircraft and theory of flight."[26] Carnegie recommended that British students receive this instruction in Initial Training Wings, which students attended in Britain before traveling to the United States, and added, "Many of the students did not know the difference between an aileron and a rudder, and as all American youths are so air minded, this has rather let us down."[27]

British officers also came to appreciate the value of certain maneuvers such as pylon eights, lazy eights, S turns across a road, and chandelles, which army instructors and the civilian BFTS instructors taught, although the British never fully adopted the army's strict precision flying techniques. In recommending these specific maneuvers that instilled proper control coordination, Carnegie remarked, "Many of my students at Grangemouth could not even execute a steep turn properly."[28]

For its part, the army came to appreciate the benefits of introducing instrument instruction early in the flight training program as in the British system. As production of Link trainers increased, all army primary schools were equipped with instrument trainers. The army, however, did not embrace the practice of night flying in the primary phase of flight training. Experiments with night flying in several army primary classes resulted in increased accidents, injuries, and damaged aircraft, and the army abandoned the practice. Night flying was left to the basic and advanced phases of flight training. Interestingly, the U.S. Navy introduced night flying in primary, but the practice was never popular with instructors.[29] In time both the British and the Army Air Forces (successor to the Army Air Corps) introduced changes in their respective flight training programs which reflected influences from the other service (but of course neither service ever credited the other service for the improvements).

At first glance it would seem an easy matter to tailor the new British Flying Training Schools precisely to British flight training methods. Several factors prevented this. The American primary training aircraft supplied to the British schools under lend-lease were not equipped for night flying or instrument flying. American primary trainers did not even have an air speed indicator in the student's cockpit. American students literally learned to fly "by the seat of their pants." Nor was it possible to simply order suitably equipped aircraft. American aircraft manufacturers were just beginning to approach quantity production. This production effort came as a result of a lengthy period of factory expansion, implementation of complex and expensive new machine tools, the creation of an elaborate system of subcontractors and suppliers, and most important, the standardization of aircraft types. Authorities felt that the introduction of changes to assembly lines would cause disruption and delays at a time when every aircraft was urgently needed for the expanding American flight training programs.

If properly equipped primary trainers could not be procured, then modifying the trainers which had been supplied would seem to be a relatively simple process since each British school had a civilian maintenance staff of licensed aircraft A & E (airframe and engine) mechanics. But delays resulted pending resolution of a legal question concerning ownership of the aircraft. This question boiled down to whether the British received title to the aircraft under lend-lease or were just leasing army aircraft. The answer to this question determined ownership and who had the authority to modify the aircraft. In time these questions were resolved and the aircraft were modified.

The availability of aircraft at this time also imposed constraints on the program. The British flight training system used two phases of instruction, elementary and advanced. The American system used three phases, primary, basic, and advanced. In both the British and American systems each phase of flight training used a different and progressively more sophisticated aircraft until the final or advanced stage, which utilized aircraft with the systems, equipment, and performance approaching operational types. Unfortunately, the shortage of advanced trainers, which had been mentioned in the earliest discussions concerning the possibility of British training in the United States, still existed. With insufficient numbers of North American AT-6 Harvard advanced trainers, the British schools were provided with Vultee BT-13 basic trainers to make up the difference. Therefore, the British schools were forced to use the two-phase British flight training syllabus modified for the American three-phase types of aircraft.

As American industry geared up for military production, aircraft were not the only equipment in short supply. Production of the Link trainer also lagged seriously behind demand. Carnegie constantly sought to balance the intricate pieces of a complex jigsaw puzzle made up of the arrival schedules of British students, the ever-changing construction status of the individual schools, and the availability of aircraft and Link trainers, while trying to find a way to modify the primary aircraft for night and instrument flying. Other smaller, even more mundane, matters also proved to be time-consuming and frustrating.

The Air Ministry shipped eighty-four crates of training materials to Carnegie for use in the first two schools. Unfortunately the crates were not packed in any order or labeled. Carnegie had to find enough warehouse space in Washington in order to unpack each of the eighty-four crates and then personally sort the contents by type of material and then repack and label the boxes for shipment to the individual schools. He also discovered that some small but essential items such as student logbooks were not included in the shipment. Carnegie tactfully suggested to Air Ministry officials that it might be more efficient if future shipments could be inventoried, packed, and labeled for each school before shipment.

Wing Commander Hogan departed Washington for an assignment as liaison officer to the army's South Eastern Training Command, since all of the Arnold Scheme schools and No. 5 BFTS would be located in that region. Hogan proved to be an ideal choice for the sensitive position at Maxwell Field. Hogan's wife Venetia joined him in Alabama and the young British couple became popular with the army officers and their wives, as well as with local political, professional, and business leaders.

Shortly after Hogan left Washington, Squadron Leader Mills also departed to become the chief flying instructor for the British Flying Training Schools in California (No. 2 BFTS) and Arizona (No. 4 BFTS). It is not surprising that Carnegie remarked, "I am finding it quite impossible to handle the work here; social activities do not interest me and all my time is therefore available for my work," but implementation of the Arnold Scheme, Towers Scheme, and the British Flying Training Schools, as well as supervision of the Refresher schools, "has made the volume of work such that I cannot keep pace with it."[30]

The Air Ministry recognized the need for a larger RAF administrative organization in the United States in light of the new training programs.

In July 1941 the Air Ministry formed the Royal Air Force Delegation in Washington. Air Marshal Arthur Harris, who had arrived in the United States earlier to head the British Air Commission, assumed command. The new organization, with the cable designation RAFDEL, was charged with supervising all RAF aircrew training in the United States and overseeing the RAF side of aircraft and equipment acquisition. In addition, RAFDEL also provided administrative support for the increasing numbers of RAF personnel being assigned to train and work in the United States.

Group Captain Carnegie became the Director of Training at the Royal Air Force Delegation. Carnegie would receive additional staff because now with the preliminary work completed, the real task of training British students to fly had begun.

CHAPTER 4

JOURNEY TO AMERICA

At the beginning of the war in 1939 young men across Britain rushed to join the armed services. These were joined by Englishmen living overseas who reported to British embassies, legations, and consuls around the world. Some faced arduous journeys just to enlist. Denys Rowland Ding lived in Kiangsi Province more than 400 miles into the interior of China. Ding traveled to the British Legation in Shanghai to volunteer for the Royal Air Force. The legation arranged for Ding to travel by steamship from Hong Kong through the South China Sea and the Indian Ocean, then around the southern tip of Africa, and back to England. Denys Ding had no trouble convincing a board of officers of his desire to become an RAF pilot.

This effort was not limited to Englishmen. Volunteers from Argentina traveled to Britain and enlisted in the Royal Air Force. Some of these young men later trained at No. 3 British Flying Training School in Oklahoma. Several hundred Argentinians eventually served in both the RAF and RCAF and formed the nucleus of 164 (Fighter) Squadron.

Personnel selection in the peacetime Royal Air Force had been governed by severe financial constraints that limited manpower levels and inherent prejudices that restricted recruitment to those with higher education and certain social positions. Only a limited number were selected for aircrew positions in the peacetime RAF. These constraints had to be hastily discarded in the rush to fill the increased manpower demands of war. The ingrained British custom of keeping to one's station in life had to be overcome with an intense recruiting effort to convince qualified young working-class men that an aircrew position in the RAF, which had previously been unattainable, was now possible.

Trevor Parfitt was one of ten children born in a small coal-mining community located in a remote valley. When war broke out Parfitt had never been far from home, had never driven an automobile, and had no more than a basic education. With some reservation, Parfitt responded to the recruiting effort and joined the RAF hoping to become an observer ("navigator" in the U.S.). During ground defense duties Parfitt learned that all observer courses were full, but it might be possible to go for pilot training. In spite of considerable apprehension, Parfitt applied and was accepted. Parfitt arrived in the United States with the second course at No. 3 BFTS in Oklahoma.

In spite of the recruiting effort, old habits sometimes died hard. Philip E. Mitchell, who later trained with Course 9 at No. 2 BFTS in California, provides an interesting insight into the RAF selection process. "The selection board consisted of three senior officers. Even in this enlightened age, I was asked if I hunted, shot, or fished. Seemingly, the hierarchy of the Royal Air Force had not yet realised the attributes required by aircrew were not necessarily only possessed by the landed gentry."[1]

One Sunday morning, Sydney J. Williams of London's Metropolitan Police Force directed traffic in the Strand outside Australia House. The air raid sirens sounded and above the noise of the traffic Williams heard bombs screaming down. Traffic stopped and people fell to the ground as a stick of bombs exploded. One bomb struck nearby Henekeys wine house and another bomb landed on the grounds of Buckingham Palace. The next day Williams requested to be released from his duties in order to join the RAF. Officials denied his request since policemen were a protected occupation. A few weeks later, however, police officer volunteers were allowed to join the RAF as pilots or navigators only. "As I had already applied, I was one of the first volunteer policemen to be accepted."[2]

The dire need for aircrew at the beginning of the war prompted the RAF to encourage ground crewmen and others to apply for aircrew training. The British Army also allowed qualified individuals to request a transfer to the RAF. Ronald Charles Lamb, who arrived in the United States with the second course at No. 3 BFTS, was in the Duke of Lancaster's Yeomanry training in Northern Ireland when an Army Council Instruction appeared on the notice board asking for volunteers to transfer to the RAF as aircrew. "About half the regiment volunteered and about 40 of us were finally accepted."[3]

Not all those who enlisted had a burning desire to fly. Ralph Stephen Trout, who would train with Course 12 at No. 5 BFTS in Florida, enlisted in the RAF just after the fall of France for general duties and was posted to RAF Sealand, Cheshire, on airfield defense. Trout later commented, "Fed up with the soul-destroying monotony, I applied for pilot training."[4]

The dramatic increase in manpower initially led to widespread confusion and disorder as the entire organization necessary to interview, examine, test, and process candidates had to be set up virtually overnight. In addition to the actual processing, a nationwide transportation network had to be arranged and then facilities created or commandeered to house and feed hundreds of young men waiting to be processed. These ranks quickly swelled to thousands.

From the beginning of the war, aircrew training vied with combat operations for the allocation of scarce supplies of men and equipment. Because of the large amount of individual training essential for every aircrew category, the training command was never sufficiently organized, equipped, or staffed to enable the immediate training of all the large numbers of volunteers. This led to delays in all phases of training and the situation existed throughout the war.

Due to the recruiting surge and limited facilities, many men who had been accepted for aircrew training were often placed in a deferred service status and told to remain at home until space at reception centers became available. These men were given special lapel badges so they would not be considered shirkers by those on the street. Even after training started, the demands of providing the correct number of men for each phase of training at each location proved to be impossible. As a result, until space became available in Initial Training Wings and flying training schools, many of the young men who emerged from short indoctrination courses were often posted for temporary duty to training and operational stations scattered throughout Great Britain. At these stations the aircrew volunteers performed domestic or ground defense duties until sufficient vacancies existed in schools providing the next phase of aircrew training.

Edward N. "Ted" Abbott, who trained with Course 23 at No. 1 BFTS in Texas, spent a long time in deferred service. "My headmaster at school was not too keen on the Air Force, so I left school and started work at an aircraft factory building Short Sunderland flying boats and joined the Air Training Corps in my spare time."[5]

After joining the RAF, Dennis Cash waited for eleven months before being called up from deferred service and it would be another nineteen months before he arrived in Oklahoma, with Course 19 at No. 3 BFTS.

Roger Mills, who trained with Course 14 at No. 3 BFTS, felt, like so many others, that much of his time after enlistment had been wasted. Much later, he evaluated his experience somewhat harshly. "For a country at war, with our backs to the wall, there was far too much waste of time between date of joining the R.A.F. and finally being posted for pilot training, in this case to the U.S.A."[6]

Sometimes the route to pilot training could be somewhat circuitous. David William Jones, who trained with Course 6 at No. 2 BFTS, joined the RAF as a wireless operator and reported to RAF Yatesbury in Wilshire to the Wireless Operators Training School. Toward the end of the course, each trainee went before a board to elect to be a ground wireless operator or to volunteer for aircrew and go on to do an Air Gunner's Course. Students could ask to be re-mustered for pilot training, but the chance of acceptance was slim. "When asked by the board, 'ground or air', I said I would like to be a Wireless Operator on an Air/Sea Rescue craft. Asked why, I pointed out that I had a fair amount of sailing experience." Jones then answered a number of further questions, then the board went into a huddle. "I rather think this was the first time anyone had made such a request. They came out of the huddle and asked me if I would like to be a pilot. I said, 'yes, please', unable to believe my luck."[7]

William Sydney Ellis, who trained with Course 12 at No. 1 BFTS, left his protected job as an Engineer Surveyor and joined the RAF in April 1941. Ellis was attested to several training camps and then trained as a aircraft engine mechanic. "During the course, I volunteered for aircrew and was told that I could go for pilot training as soon as a vacancy occurred." Ellis continued to work as an engine mechanic on Airspeed Oxford aircraft and during this time went aloft on his first flight. "I was transferred to a Service Flying Training School at Montrose, Scotland, again working on Oxfords. It was a bitter winter, and we spent a lot of time shifting snow. After about a month of this, my posting to aircrew training came through."[8]

Initially there were several small reception centers for new recruits until a large camp could be built. At the time of his enlistment in the Royal Air Force in December 1939, David William Jones, who would later join Course 6 at No. 2 BFTS, was living at home in Liverpool and employed in a paint company's laboratory. He arrived at the reception camp at Padgate, Warrington, where he spent several weeks during a severe freeze, which effectively shut off the water supply to the camp. Not only was there no water, but in those early days of the war, there were not enough uniforms to go around. Many of the new recruits wore light civilian clothes and many became ill.

The RAF built a large central reception center in Hyde Park, a royal park of several hundred acres with a zoo in the St. Johns district of

London. The park was near the famous Lord's Cricket Ground. Recruits were housed in a section of unfinished flats adjacent to the park and meals were taken at the zoo. Officially the RAF Aircrew Reception Centre (A.C.R.C.), recruits referred to the new camp as "arsey-tarsey."

Harry Pinnell arrived at the Aircrew Reception Centre at Hyde Park on 11 August 1941 and joined a flight of fifty men. The flight would stay together during training to become pilots. "We stayed in flats opposite Regent's Park and were fed in the London Zoo (we used to think we were an added attraction—see the monkeys feed, then see the RAF lining up with knife, fork, spoon and drinking mug). This lasted twelve days during which time we were kitted out—alterations to uniforms were made (if you found one to fit first time, you were obviously deformed) and tests such as night vision, inoculations, etc. were done."[9]

The British military services have a long tradition of establishing wartime administrative offices in private facilities and billeting service personnel in urban areas for set fees either in private dwellings or in sequestered hotels or guest houses. When permanent housing was unavailable, tents or other temporary structures were erected on public lands or on leased private green space.

Brian Davies joined the RAF on his eighteenth birthday and after passing the stringent medical and academic tests was accepted for pilot training. Davies arrived at the Aircrew Reception Centre at Lord's Cricket Ground in London in July 1941. The entire draft waited all day without food or drink until late in the afternoon and then marched through the streets of North London to Paddington Station. "Our rail destination was the Aircrew Reception Centre at Babbacombe, Devon. On arrival there, we were taken by truck to nearby Torquay to be fed prior to spending our first night at the Torquay United Football Ground where we slept in the stands on straw palliasses. Eventually, we were allocated beds in small hotels in Babbacombe which had been requisitioned by the RAF."[10]

Members of the various university air squadrons already had an introduction to service life. J. R. Sutton, destined to train with Course 4 at No. 3 BFTS, was an undergraduate at Keble College, Oxford University at the time of his enlistment. Sutton reported to the Aircrew Reception Center at Lord's Cricket Ground and was assigned to a flight composed entirely of University Air Squadron members from Oxford University, which included Denys Street, son of Sir Arthur Street, the then-Under Secretary of State for Air, and Maurice Bartlett, the son of a prominent English journalist of the time, Vernon Bartlett. "This fact was to have some significance to our subsequent career as Sir Arthur Street's son was consulted by the station commander here, and subsequently elsewhere, about our proposed postings. It was through him that we heard that our course was destined for training in the U.S.A."[11]

An underage Stanley Malcolm Robert Symons, destined to train with Course 16 at No. 4 BFTS, enlisted in the RAF in mid-December 1941. He was put on deferred service for eight months and when he reported to the Air Crew Reception Centre, St. John's Wood, London, he had just turned seventeen. Three weeks later, he reported to RAF Ludlow for basic training and "spent much time digging holes and filling them in."[12]

Several years later conditions had not changed much according to Ted Abbott. "I joined the RAF at the Aircrew Receiving Centre in London on 23 August 1943. Here we were given all our kit and generally introduced to the Air Force and its ways. It was a hectic happy time. A.C.R.C. was just near the London Zoo, and the public seemed to take as much interest in us as in the animals."[13]

The Aircrew Reception Centre at Hyde Park continued to be used until the end of the war. Peter Stugnell, destined to train with Course 26, the last course at No. 5 BFTS in Florida, later reflected on the first phase of his long journey to North America. "When we reported to the Air Crew Reception Centre in London, the 'doodle bug' blitz was at its height and we had to take turns on the roof on fire watching duties. I remember being terrified seeing these things coming over and always uttered the heart-felt prayer, 'Please keep going!'"[14]

After leaving either the initial confused and often chaotic reception centers or the new Aircrew Reception Centre, servicemen traveled to Initial Training Wings or ITW. Here the aircrew learning process began in earnest. ITW courses taught the demanding RAF initial ground school course, which included mathematics, navigation, Morse code signaling with buzzer and Aldis lamps, meteorology, aircraft recognition, RAF customs, drill and ceremonies, physical training, and a variety of other subjects designed to prepare young men for flight training.

Initial Training Wings were located in various areas of Britain and accommodations ranged from established RAF stations to universities such as Cambridge, St. Andrews, and the University of Wales, to hastily sequestered hotels and resorts such as Paignton, Torquay, Devon, and Newquay on the southeast coast, to Stratford-upon-Avon, to Scarborough on Yorkshire's North Sea coast.

Philip Mitchell reported to No. 8 ITW at Newquay in Cornwall. "At Newquay, we were billeted in what had been 'private hotels'. These had been stripped of all comforts and re-equipped with very narrow steel beds. I.T.W. was a happy time. We drilled; did P.T. on the beach, swam in the sea (even on Christmas day); attended classes in Navigation, signals, and other related subjects and after six weeks, having passed required exams, were re-classified as Leading Aircraftman."[15]

When Malcolm Thomas Sydney Davis, later to train with Course 4 at No. 2 BFTS, graduated from Cambridge, he joined the Royal Air Force. After doing some "square bashing [close order drill], queuing for meals, and cutting up national dailies into lavatory paper," he reported to an Initial Training Wing course at Torquay, Devon. "As an Aircraftman 2nd Class, even a Lance Corporal was God! We feared discipline, but found it to be essential—even square bashing became a pleasure much to all our surprises."[16]

Harry Lister of Course 5 at No. 3 BFTS recalled his ITW course. "ITW at Penrhos was a temporary measure introduced to deal with a glut of people who could not be accommodated at the established ITWs. Flights of 50 cadets were sent to certain selected Training Command RAF stations where they underwent ITW training by Station personnel. Penrhos was in a rather remote part of North Wales. Being a Navigation training School, most of us were able to get some air experience by flying as a supernumerary on training flights."[17]

Ted Abbott attended an ITW course at Newquay, Corwall, and recalled his unit and flight commander. "It was a very happy, very active unit. We had a wonderful Flight Commander, a Flight Lieutenant DeJong. He was a brilliant leader, an ex-army officer of 1914–1918 war experience. He had an equally brilliant Sergeant named Cunliffe. We all worked very hard at Newquay, but we were happy and all very much enjoyed our period of training there."[18]

Like many others, Peter Stugnell of Course 26 at No. 5 BFTS enjoyed his ITW course. "Initial Training Wing at Stormy Down was fun, as we were kept very hard at work and were only allowed off camp once a week —on Saturday afternoons—when we all made for the so-called fleshpots of Porthcawl in South Wales. We played a lot of sport and I was lucky enough to play Rugger for the station; in those days, if you were good at a sport, it was a great help in one's career and I feel that my rather meagre prowess on the Rugby Field helped me pass various courses."[19]

The ITW course proved more challenging for some students. Henry Ronald Preston, of Course 16 at No. 5 BFTS, joined the RAF in late 1941. After almost a year on deferred service he reported to the Aircrew Reception Centre and then, "After about three weeks, I went to No. 12 I.T.W. at St. Andrews in Scotland. The ground school course was for me, and many like me, hard going as I had left school at 14 to go to work in the Post Office as a messenger with no school between times."[20]

After his initial introduction to service life, Andrew L. Bayley of Course 17 at No. 1 BFTS arrived at No. 2 ITW, Pembroke College, Cambridge University for his ITW course. "Pembroke College was very old, built of stone, with narrow, spiral staircases and flag stone floors. The quadrangle had a nice lawn bordered by flower beds. The instructors were good and the work concentrated and difficult. Each day commenced at 0600 hours, and it was usually 1800 hours by the time we had finished tea. Meals were taken in the impressive old dining hall."[21]

Early experiences in overseas flight training schools revealed that a large number of failures were due to routine causes such as acute airsickness or an inability to coordinate the aircraft controls. This is not surprising considering that few of the British flight students had ever been in an airplane and most had never driven an automobile. In one of the more unusual incidents, two students arrived with the second course at No. 1 BFTS and after their first flight announced that they did not like flying! This came after the students had been recruited in England, attended an Initial Training Wing for eight weeks, and then traveled 6,000 miles to Texas. Nothing could be done but return the students to Canada for reassignment.

Students who were eliminated from flight training represented a considerable expenditure of resources. Early in the war training officers had recommended some form of familiarization flight before new flight students traveled overseas for training. Officials at first resisted this idea, but as eliminations rose the advantages became obvious. Beginning in November 1941 all flight students received a short introductory flight before going overseas. This introductory flight quickly expanded into ten to twelve hours of flight training at an RAF elementary flight school to determine a student's fitness for further flying training. Those found unsuited were reclassified to other aircrew duties.

Philip E. Mitchell of Course 9 at No. 2 BFTS recalled his grading course. "In early February, I was posted to No. 9 E.F.T.S., Anstey, a small grass airfield near Leicester. We flew in Tiger Moths, my instructor was Sgt. Mannering who, after some nine hours flying and a Flight Commander's test by F/O Hopkins, passed me as being suitable for further training."[22]

Frank C. Rainbird, destined for Course 11 at No. 3 BFTS, tried to join the RAF Volunteer Reserve as a pilot in early 1939 but had not completed enrollment by the time the RAFVR was mobilized on the outbreak of war. He was persuaded to join as a wireless operator (ground) with the aim of transferring to aircrew at a later date. This he did and was finally accepted for pilot training. After ITW, Rainbird reported for his grading course. "Now at last we could claim to be real airmen. What did it matter if the planes we were flying were only 'Tigers' and our flying time only reckoned in minutes. How proudly we told each other of our flying prowess 'Eleven hours (and solo)' looked disdainfully down on 'eight hours, 35 minutes (circuits and bumps and two spins)' who in turn, gave expert advice on landing and incipient spins, medium turns & stalls to poor 'one hour, 10 minutes' who was still very thrilled with his first attempt at straight & level flight."[23]

Ian Ferguson Glover described his flight grading course at No. 11 E.F.T.S. in Perth, Scotland as "intense cold, snow shoveling, and only 8 hours flying."[24] Somewhat fittingly, Glover went on to train with Course 9 at No. 4 BFTS located in the Arizona desert.

Memories of grading course were usually long-lasting as typified by Peter Stugnell, forty years after training with Course 26 at No. 5 BFTS. "Grading School at Sealand was fun. My first instructor was a Sergeant Brooker who took me to solo standard and I was sent solo by Flying Officer Jordan. Even now, I can remember the thrill, a great moment."[25]

Alan Watson, who would train at No. 6 BFTS in Oklahoma, arrived at his grading course at No. 3 Elementary Flying Training School at Shillingford, and noted the event in his diary. "The great day in my career as a pilot. I flew for the first time under training. It was super. The old Tiger bounced a bit, but otherwise she was O.K." Two weeks later Watson wrote, "THE GREAT DAY. I flew solo today, immediately after my Flight Commander's test. Am very happy and proud of myself. Very few men solo here so to solo after only 8 ¼ hours is jolly good."[26]

Sometimes the difference between flying and not flying could be razor thin. Derek A. J. B. Waterman failed the solo flight test at his grading course, which effectively ended any hope of flight training. After his last flight, Waterman was detailed to assist the flight commander with some routine paperwork. The flight commander asked about his flying and received the sad news of his failure. The sympathetic flight commander promised another chance and this time Waterman passed the test. He went on to graduate from No. 4 BFTS, flew Halifax bombers on operations, then C-47 transports in India and Burma. By the end of the war, Waterman had been commissioned and had been awarded the Distinguished Flying Cross.

The establishment of overseas training schools added enormously to the already complex logistics of trying to fill the necessary training schools with the correct number of men at the correct time. Before the war, the RAF had had to provide only limited accommodation and minimal transport for volunteers within Britain and small intakes from the Dominions. Now officials found it necessary to develop an organization to coordinate sea and land transportation with course intake schedules on several separate continents thousands of miles from Britain for increasingly large numbers of trainees. Delays and other problems occurred because the intake schedules varied at both ends of the training pipelines and because of the distances and hazards involved in crossing dangerous and often hostile oceans.

Students bound for overseas training sites received a short leave after completion of ITW and a grading course. Upon returning from leave, students reported to the RAF Personnel Dispersal Centre at Wilmslow, Cheshire, near the center of Britain. Accommodations at the early camp were basic, but the brief stay only included documentation and the issuance of essential clothing. In time a larger Dispersal Centre at Heaton Park, Manchester, replaced the small Wilmslow station. Even with the larger camp, delays soon occurred and the RAF developed several methods to keep recruits busy.

Peter Stugell trained with the last course at No. 5 BFTS. After ITW and a grading course, Stugell arrived at the Air Crew Reception Centre at Heaton Park to await further training. Trainees were detached onto various jobs where hopefully they would be of some use to the war effort. "I was sent to a bomber station at RAF East Kirkby in the wilds of Lincolnshire. We had a lot more freedom there and it was great fun. The station was very dispersed and our Nissen Hut was some 100 yards from the ablutions and a half a mile from the cookhouse. It always seemed to be raining, and I remember that our very large hut had only two stoves in it that were frequently out, as there was no fuel and it was very cold."[27]

Robert Hugh Brown of Course 20 at No. 4 BFTS spent ten weeks at the Embarkation Centre at Heaton Park after his grading course in which he did twelve hours of flying and soloed. "Up to this time, I had enjoyed my service career. I found I.T.W. hard at first, but as I got used to it, it got easier. A.C.R.C. at Heaton Park was wet, cold, and dismal, but looking back I think we expected too much. It was a place to wait; it could not have been any better."[28]

When the war broke out in 1939, Archie B. Venables, later to join Course 11 at No. 3 BFTS, was working in the sugar industry in his hometown of Peterborough. In May 1941, he was injured in an air raid, being buried alive for four hours and receiving a shell splinter through one foot. This injury, which he did not report to the medical officers, delayed his entry into the RAF, but it finally healed and he left for London in January 1942. Following an ITW course at Pembroke College, Cambridge University, Venables attended a grading course where he soloed. He then reported to Heaton Park Embarkation Centre awaiting transport to an overseas training station. "It was at Heaton Park that a very sad and dramatic parade took place, 'The following cadets have been re-mustered to other aircrew duties. Cadets will fall out as names are called!' My heart bled for old friends who fell out while the ranks were thinned. One old pal just stood stiff as if he had been shot. A sigh of relief from all those left standing."[29]

At the Dispersal Centre, Phillip E. Mitchell of Course 9 at No. 2 BFTS managed to learn more about his future training. The trainees were billeted in private homes and there were no organized parades. The code "A.T.T.S." had been stenciled on the trainees' kit bags. An older serviceman told Mitchell that if he visited a certain pub, frequented by engine drivers, and bought a pint for the right person, that person could interpret the code and tell Mitchell his destination and date of departure. "It worked! I was told I was going to the U.S.A. to one of six flying schools. Looking at the orders one morning, I noticed that I had to parade that afternoon with all kit. In the early evening, together with some hundreds of other airmen, I marched to the local railway station and boarded a waiting train."[30]

Trainees traveled from the Personnel Dispersal Center for embarkation on transports to overseas training stations. In order to avoid enemy air attacks, blacked-out night trains were used to transport aircrew pupils from a PDC in the English midlands to one of several ports on the west coast of Britain. The preferred ports of embarkation were Gourock or Greenock in the Firth of Clyde, Liverpool, and Avonmouth (Bristol), and at least one draft embarked from Milford Haven in southwestern Wales.

David Williams Jones trained with Course 6 at No. 2 BFTS. At the RAF Personnel Dispersal Centre, members of Jones' flight were issued their flying kits and overseas summer uniforms. "One night we were put on a train in pitch darkness without any idea where we were going. We had all marked our two kit bags with large letters ATTS/CHALK and put a blue band around the center (Later, we learnt ATTS stood for 'all through training scheme' and CHALK was the code name for our ship or party). When the train stopped finally, we were at Avonmouth, near Bristol, but we seemed to have been diverted half way around England to get there."[31]

Alfred W. Syrett, a postal worker living in Barking, Essex, who later trained with Course 13 at No. 3 BFTS, volunteered for the RAF in early 1941, but was rejected because of flu symptoms. He volunteered again several months later and passed the physical examinations for pilot training and was placed on deferred service for nine months. After processing at the Aircrew Reception Centre in London, Syrett attended No. 7 Initial Training Wing at Newquay, Cornwall, and then passed a flight grading course at Theale, near Reading. Syrett reported to Heaton

Park to await a posting overseas for further training. In October 1942 he traveled by train to Glasgow and there at Greenock boarded the *Queen Mary* bound for North America. At this stage Syrett remembered that he "had seen more bombing or danger as a messenger boy delivering telegrams in Fleet Street, and as a civilian living in London suburbs" than he had in more than a year of RAF service.[32]

Not all aircrew trainees had to go through deferred service and long waits. At the time of his enlistment in the Royal Air Force in August 1941, John A. B. Keeling, who later trained with Course 4 at No. 3 BFTS, lived at Hurst House, Sedlescombe, Sussex, and was an undergraduate at Oxford University reading Engineering. Since he was also a member of the Oxford University Air Squadron, he was not required to complete any basic military training or Initial Training Wing course. As a result, within a few weeks of enlistment, Keeling was posted to the embarkation centre at RAF Wilmslow where he joined an RAF draft for Gourock, Scotland bound for Canada.

James Fairlie trained with Course 26 at No. 4 BFTS. As an alternative to I.T.W., he attended a university short course of about six months' duration at Corpus Christi College, Cambridge University. He was also a member of the University Air Squadron and was able to complete ten hours flying on Tiger Moths. From Cambridge, he and his course mates reported to the Aircrew Reception Centre in London. After a few weeks there being kitted out, they formed into flights and were sent to Elmdon Airport, Birmingham for a flight grading course, now referred to as a P.N.B. (pilot/navigator/bomb aimer) course. Since he had already had some flying experience, Fairlie was able to solo in eight hours. Then, while awaiting assignment to further flight training, he spent the period from January to November 1944 on temporary assignments to various bomber stations. He and his course mates reported back to Heaton Park in December 1944 and embarked with some 15,000 other men bound for Canada.

Frank Rainbird of Course 11 at No. 3 BFTS completed flight grading and a period of leave, then went to Heaton Park, which he described as "a meeting place of friends and a holiday camp combined, with just a sprinkling of the RAF atmosphere for effect." Prior to embarkation the group received a final word from the camp's commanding officer. "C.O.'s speech was short & to the point. His opening remarks were greeted with enthusiastic agreement. They were, 'Gentlemen, I know I'll echo your own thoughts if I quote your own famous misquotation of a now famous observation 'Never in the field of human endeavour were so many buggered about by so few'. 'And now, I can only wish you speedy success in your course, happy landings and afterwards bags of good Germans—the only good Germans the RAF know being dead ones'. Then he merely wished us 'bon voyage' and 'good luck'."[33]

Late in the war, members of the last three courses to train in the United States faced even longer waits for postings to flight training schools, but the RAF came up with a novel way to fill the time. Each day squads of volunteers were taken into London to help clear rubble and rebuild areas of the city that had been devastated by V1 flying bombs and later V2 rockets.

Robin Howard, who eventually trained with Course 26, the last course at No. 4 BFTS, remembered the unusual duty. "I was in the first batch to volunteer for this enterprise (anything to get away from the monotony of Heaton Park)." At morning parade an officer asked for volunteers for various trades such as bricklayers, plasters, painters, and decorators. He then asked if anyone could drive a lorry. Howard thought this sounded like a "cushy job" so he and several others put their hands up. "The arrangements were that each Flight, with a Flight Sergeant in charge, was allocated a district which had suffered flying bomb damage and was given an empty house as its temporary HQ. Our Flight Sergeant was a fairly amiable alcoholic who didn't give us much trouble."[34]

Early drafts destined for Canada and the United States followed different routes across the Atlantic on whatever shipping happened to be available including smaller hastily converted freighters and ferries. Use of the smaller ships would be discontinued as larger converted cargo ships such as the *Highland Princess* and commandeered liners such as the *Pasteur* (an uncompleted French liner, which had been towed from Le Havre just as France fell and finished out as a troop ship) were placed in service. Finally large liners such as the *Queen Mary* and *Queen Elizabeth* were converted to troop transports.

Philip Sydney Smith trained with the first course at No. 2 BFTS. Smith and his 100-man contingent embarked on the Irish sea ferry *The Royal Ulsterman,* one of the early small hastily converted ships, destined for Canada via Iceland. "The privation and appalling conditions under which we spent our waking hours, or eating, etc., could not have been matched by the *Altmark,* the ill famed German prison ship. 800 other ranks shared one-half of one deck as a mess for sleeping and eating. The other half of the same deck were canvas-walled latrines for over 1,000 men."

Before the end of the first day, the latrines were blocked, and human sewage washed from port to starboard as the ship rolled from side to side. Meals had to be taken under these conditions, making sure that feet were lifted up every time the ship rolled from side to side. The only fresh air was on the poop deck which could not accommodate more than a hundred men. The deck contained one three-foot-square steel tank for washing pots and pans. "We queued for over an hour to get up to this deck, and on coming down we immediately joined the queue again to get back up."[35]

This group, like many of the first drafts, arrived in Iceland and went to a crude transient camp near Helgafell, twelve miles from the coast. The small camp had few facilities and the men lived in Nissen huts with no furniture, slept on the floors, and washed in a nearby mountain stream (the men did discover a nearby warm lake heated by Iceland's famed thermal energy). After several days, Smith and the rest of his draft sailed from Iceland to Halifax, Nova Scotia, aboard the armed merchant cruiser *Circassia.*

In another group in Scotland, Phillip E. Mitchel of Course 9 at No. 2 BFTS and his course mates left the Dispersal Centre and boarded a train for the British coast. After an uncomfortable overnight journey the trainees arrived at the Clyde estuary in Scotland and embarked on H.M.T. *Banfora*. "She was an ancient merchant vessel of some ten thousand tons. It was said that she had been captured from the Italians who had been using her as a prison ship! Our mess deck was C-3, which was the lowest deck in the after part of the ship, immediately above the propeller shaft. Some two hundred were packed into a space that would have been amply filled by sixty. We slept on the deck, on the mess tables with another layer suspended above in hammocks."

The ship left the Clyde accompanied by another troopship H.M.T. *Rangitiki* and two destroyers. The troopships flew barrage balloons tethered to the afterdecks as a defense against dive bombers. The seas rose and the weather deteriorated under lowering dark clouds. "On the first day out, the wind was so strong that both balloons broke their cables and disappeared into the blue. The next day, the destroyers turned back, presumably too rough for them, and the two troopships were left to complete the crossing on their own."[36]

After arriving at the coast, Frank Rainbird of Course 11 at No. 3 BFTS joined a queue for the tender, which after a long wait brought them out to the troopship. While waiting for dinner Rainbird reflected on the upcoming voyage. "For the first time when making any journey, I feel a little excited about it. I think everyone does. After all, not one of us does not realise that there is quite a bit of danger attached to this trip."

Once underway, Rainbird attempted to adjust to shipboard life. "Hammocks are favorites for first place on my list of pet aversions. The one I endeavoured to sleep in last night had a permanent list to port, and despite all my efforts at correcting this, my movements only seemed to make it worse & I was very often just on the verge of being tipped out. Washing is a problem, hordes of blokes seem to besiege the ablution rooms at all hours and a comfortable wash is an unknown luxury." Like virtually every other British trainee, Rainbird was appalled by the ship's heads. "Lavatory accommodation is rather medieval, to say the least. The pans are arranged in rows, with small partitions but no doors separating them. Hense the whole affair becomes rather a public occasion, and my shyness or bashfulness just had to go. To submit to bashfulness would be no less than to submit to constipation."[37]

John A. B. Keeling wrote home of his experience crossing the Atlantic on the *Pasteur*. "There is a most frightful crush on board and I sleep in a hammock in a room about the size of our drawing room with about a hundred other people. I can't think of words unpleasant enough to describe the sanitary arrangements on board, but, in compensation, the food is not at all bad and I think the trip will be short." After five days at sea Keeling wrote, "I am told that we have been very lucky to have such comparatively calm weather at this time of year, but I can't say I found it very calm myself. The ship seemed to pitch and roll about quite enough for me. Being right up in the very bows of the ship, the pitching was frightfully unpleasant." Keeling and many others suffered from seasickness. "The agony was made worse by the fact that there was nowhere to lie down and feel ill, one just had to feel ill from the bare deck to the lavatories and back again. To make things worse, one was not allowed to use the lavatories from 9:45 to 10:30 in the morning, but somehow I managed not to be sick during those periods."[38]

Aboard ship the RAF trainees performed many mundane tasks such as cleaning the heads, swabbing decks, and working in the kitchen. Some even guarded the water tight doors far below the water line. Ted Abbott explained, "We did not actually guard them, although that was the expression used. We sat either side of them to close them in an emergency, always hoping that the emergency would leave one on the right side."[39]

Even under the worst conditions, RAF aircrew trainees could show a certain creativity. John Hanbury Smith-Carrington, who trained with Course 4 at No. 3 BFTS, recalled his Atlantic crossing. "How to survive on a thoroughly overcrowded troopship, sleeping in hammocks in the hold, and on one meal a day. My solution was to volunteer as an officer's batman, where I served in the officers' dining room, and so got extra food, and we were excused the more unpleasant fatigues such as scrubbing out the lavatories and washing down the decks."[40]

David William Jones of Course 6 at No. 2 BFTS actually provided useful service on board the *Tamaroa*. Before sailing, one of the crew toured the troop decks asking if anyone knew the Morse code. Jones recalled, "Myself and another laddie said, 'yes, we were wireless operators.' We were hustled on to the bridge, given an Aldis lamp and told we were to serve as signalers throughout the trip. The ship's officers had forgotten all the Morse they had learned in peacetime. We coped quite well and received a friendly appreciation and a bit better treatment than the other troops below."[41]

Later in the war, transit across the Atlantic became faster and more comfortable after the addition of large converted liners such as the *Queen Mary* and *Queen Elizabeth*. These ships were still overcrowded, but offered some amenities and even a cinema. But not all drafts traveled on the large ships and the sea could still be formidable. In January 1944, Eric Gill, destined for Course 20 at No. 1 BFTS, boarded the *Batory,* a ship of 14,000 tons built in 1935. "It was a very rough crossing with terrible seasickness. Among the RAF passengers, there were men sleeping fitfully in hammocks, unable to eat, and there was the constant threat of U-boats and the impossibility of keeping clean on board a swaying ship filled with sick men."[42]

The sea was often no respecter of even the large ships. Alan Norman Watson, who trained at No. 6 BFTS, crossed the Atlantic on the *Queen Mary*. "This morning found us well under way with Ireland rapidly receding on our Port bow. The sea is getting pretty rough, the waves are already attaining a height of 30 to 40 feet and we are told that we are running—or sailing—with a gale and, believe me, I can quite believe it. The visibility is very poor today. The wind seems to be driving a mist before it, obscuring vision. I never imagined a ship of such tremendous dimensions as the 'Queen Mary' could roll so much as she is doing."[43]

Trevor Parfitt, destined to train with the second course at No. 3 BFTS, remarked philosophically, "seasickness banished all thoughts of U-boats."

Virtually all of the early drafts crossed the Atlantic in convoys. Later, fast troop ships, especially the large ones such as the *Queen Mary* and *Queen Elizabeth,* traveled independently and depended on their speed for protection against U-boats. These larger ships usually had cabins converted to multi-tier bunks instead of hammocks.

John C. Price of Course 17 at No. 6 BFTS recalled seeing the *Queen Mary* for the first time and his voyage to North America. "We saw an enormous liner out in mid-stream which someone said was the *Queen Mary.* Soon, we were alongside and looking up at the towering sides. We had all seen pictures of her in the papers before the war, but not much news after the war started. We climbed up a few steps and through wide double steel doors in the side of the hull, then along passageways and up more stairways to our accommodation. The cabins had been stripped of furniture and standing bunks had been installed."

Price remembered magazine pictures of the giant ship before the war and noted that while the opulent furniture had been removed and the decks covered with plywood, most of the "wall decorations and murals in veneered woods" had been left in place. The ship's food offered a pleasant surprise. "We saw white bread on the table and an abundance of butter. White bread had disappeared back in 1939 and as more and more of the grain was used, so the bread took on a distinctly brownish look over the years. Butter had also been rationed right from the start." Price learned that the reason for this "good living" was because supplies were taken on in the United States rather than using the rationed supplies in England. "So from now on, until we returned we were really living in the lap of luxury."[44]

John A. B. Keeling recalled the end of his voyage. "We sighted land at about 11 o'clock, and tugs had brought us up alongside the quay by 12.30. The first thing we saw through a slight mist were the fir trees. Our welcome was hardly what one would expect when a large liner comes alongside the quay. It was rather grim and solemn. The quay was completely deserted except for three Air Force officers there to receive us."[45]

Kenneth Henry Frere, destined for Course 12 at No. 3 BFTS, offered an enthusiastic comment upon arriving in Canada. "What a change in 12 months, from a small country town in the South to University in the North of Scotland; from riding a bicycle to flying an aeroplane, and then across the Atlantic to the New World."[46]

For the first several years of the war, Halifax became the main embarkation port on the eastern coast of Canada since ice on the Saint Lawrence restricted entrance to Montreal for much of the year and the fierce tides and tortuous channels of the Bay of Fundy made St. Johns less than ideal. Halifax had numerous modern docks, warehouse facilities, and a protected bay, which could accommodate large numbers of ships. Halifax also offered access to the Canadian rail network, which ran directly from dockside into the interior and eventually connected with the railway system in the United States.

In 1941, the province of Ontario offered the nearest accommodation capable of handling large drafts of arriving servicemen. British aircrew trainees disembarked from the arriving ships in Halifax directly onto waiting trains and immediately commenced a further 1,800-mile rail journey to the RCAF No. 1 Manning Depot in Toronto.

The long trip from Halifax to Toronto, which crossed the provinces of Nova Scotia, New Brunswick, Quebec, and much of Ontario, usually included a two- to three-hour stop and took about thirty-six hours. This circuitous route ran northwest from Halifax to the shores of the Gulf of St. Lawrence, then southwest through Levis past Quebec, through Montreal, and more than halfway across the Province of Ontario. On many of the early drafts, no provision had been made for food on the trip.

The westbound RAF trainees were worn out by the long train ride from Halifax to Toronto, but at the same time excited by the novel journey.

Most of these young men's experiences had been limited to an island nation in which a hundred miles constituted a long journey. They were thrilled by the sight of so large a country with seemingly endless forests broken by isolated farms and grazing lands, fast flowing streams, placid lakes, and occasional cities and villages.

As in England, the RAF learned from experience. After arrival, the troop ships were cleaned and sanitized before the return voyage and rail transport westward was significantly improved. Some trains even added a kitchen car.

Harry Witt, bound for the second course at No. 3 BFTS, reflected on his journey. "When we arrived in Halifax, we boarded a train at dockside; the train coaches were old time immigrant sleepers, made of wood, wooden pull down platform for the upper bunk, wooden seats padded with leather, heated with pot bellied stoves at the end of each car. One fellow from every group of ten or so would go to the kitchen car to pick up a tureen of something; another would get plates, tea, water, etc., and we would eat in situ. A very bedraggled group detrained in Toronto, unwashed and unshaven."[47]

Other improvements followed. The RAF Movements Group in coordination with the RCAF arranged for a small pay advance in Canadian dollars, as well as for sandwiches and pint cartons of milk to be distributed to the airmen when their train stopped at Truro, Nova Scotia, regardless of the hour. In addition to the snack, the local community also donated fruit and other items for free distribution to the young men. Harry E. V. Pinnell was amazed that "when the train stopped at Truro in the middle of the night, the platform was crowded with people giving us tea and cake, etc.—a marvelous welcome."[48]

John Keeling recorded the journey in his diary. "We got on train for Toronto last night, which will take nearly two days. Now going along South bank of St. Lawrence. Simply lovely. Masses of chocolates, cigarettes, sugar, milk, ham sandwiches and, above all, lights. We sleep along a coach in beds, which fold up in the day. Frightfully uncomfortable for sleeping in. Marvelous breakfast. Best since I joined up."[49]

On his train journey from Halifax to Toronto in September 1941, John Hanbury Smith-Carrington noted, "While traveling through the Maritimes and Ontario, crowds at every railway station heaped peaches and sweets on us. By contrast, whilst traveling through Quebec Province, reception was very cool."[50]

Later in the war many drafts traveled directly to New York or Boston. The trainees then traveled to the Canadian embarkation center for assignment to a flight school. Ted Abbott recalled his journey. "We crossed over to New York on the *Aquitania*, a four-funnel ship with direct drive steam turbines. Our sail down the Irish Sea was very rough, and I, for one, was very seasick. The ship made her way down across the Bay of Biscay. As soon as we started heading West the weather improved and we all took more interest in the ship. Our Westerly course took us past the Azores and by now the weather was excellent."

The voyage lasted ten days and a submarine warning provided a break in the monotony. "The guns on the ship were manned, and she zig-zagged a few times, the vibration was terrific and she really heeled over at the speed she was going. We saw nothing, and the cause of the incident was left to our imagination." Abbott learned to splice rope while on board and enjoyed talking with the crew. "I was really surprised as to how routine this sort of voyage was to them."

Abbott had one poignant moment on board. The ship carried American wounded as well as soldiers going home. One night while on guard duty, Abbott approached two soldiers who were talking on the restricted boat deck. "I went up to them and tried very politely to ask them to go to a lower deck. They turned round and, to my horror, they had no faces. I was very thankful that I had set out to be polite. I left them where they were, to enjoy the evening."[51]

In Canada, as in Great Britain, an entire system to transport, catalog, feed, process, and house vast numbers of trainees had to be created virtually overnight. This task fell to the staff of the Royal Canadian Air Force No. 1 Movements Group. The Movements Group established the RCAF No. 1 Manning Depot on the grounds of the Canadian National Exhibition on the south side of Toronto. It served as an RCAF recruit depot for that part of Canada and as an aircrew processing station for men assigned to the British Commonwealth Air Training Plan schools, which included the various flight schools in the United States.

Flight Lieutenant Paul Goldsmith arrived at the Manning Depot in May 1941 to head the fifty-man RAF detachment. By the middle of June the RAF unit had become the RAF Transit Section commanded by Squadron Leader J. F. Houchin, a veteran pilot of World War I and the 1940 Battle of France. Rejecting an early suggestion for temporary housing in tents, the unit instead set up several hundred multi-tiered bunks in the huge animal show arena of the Canadian National Exhibition Building, where the trainees slept, ate, and mustered for assignment, documentation, and shipment. Leonard G. Brookes, who would train with Course 4 at No. 1 BFTS, recalled being "billeted in the covered cattle market with an army of flies who seemed delighted to find some substitute for the cattle which had previously occupied the building."[52]

However the young RAF men might describe their billets, they were unanimous in their praise of the quantity and quality of the food. John A. Cook described the food in a letter home. "They certainly feed us well here, and there are second helpings for anyone who can eat them. And what's more the food is always well cooked, in fact, I haven't had such good grub since I was at home."[53]

In spite of the good food, there were also problems. As incoming drafts swelled in size, personnel eliminated from flight training in the United States and Canada returned to Toronto for reassignment. The failed students returned to a routing system still under development. This exacerbated the already overcrowded conditions and also led to morale problems as the dispirited eliminated aircrew mingled with the newly arriving personnel with negative stories about the new training programs. Officials began to segregate the eliminated students, but the situation only improved when the Canadian facilities were able to process the returned students quickly onto other assignments.

Based on the experience with the overcrowded temporary processing facilities in Toronto, construction began on a new camp that would house 8,000 men. In order to eliminate the long and exhausting train ride from Halifax to Toronto the new camp would be located in Moncton, New Brunswick, 250 miles west of Halifax on the main Canadian rail line, which also linked with the American rail system. The new camp would serve as the official entry and departure station for all RAF personnel in North America.

By mid-October 1941, the first completed portions of the new camp were ready to receive both westbound and eastbound RAF drafts. The new camp would ultimately include four squadron areas, each of which had lecture rooms, stores, a hangar-like drill hall, large two-story barracks blocks, a dining hall, a recreation hall, and a canteen. The camp also included three parade grounds, three outdoor sports areas, and a hospital. The RAF Transit Unit left the RCAF No. 1 Movements Group in the buildings of the Canadian National Exhibition and moved to the new station, now designated No. 31 RAF Personnel Depot. Squadron Leader Houchin assumed temporary command of the station. The RCAF decided to build its own No. 2 Station on land adjacent to the new RAF depot in Moncton so that the two stations might share some facilities and personnel.[54]

Leonard Trevallion had served for six years in the Metropolitan Police and survived the London Blitz before joining the RAF. Trevallion arrived in Moncton with an early draft destined for the United States just after the camp opened. "The whole camp was knee deep in mud and we walked between barracks and mess rooms on duck boards, and the weather continued to be awful. However, our gloom was soon dispelled when we entered the mess room and were faced with more food than we had seen in years. I think many of us had guilty consciences when we remembered the folks back home."[55]

Whether first in Toronto or later in Moncton, Canadian citizens offered abundant welcome and hospitality to the newly arrived young men from Britain. In addition to new service facilities, local residents invited the young trainees to their homes for Sunday meals or evening gatherings. In Moncton there existed great concern over the ability of the small Canadian town to entertain large numbers of young men since there were no Public Houses (pubs) and very rigid laws governing the sale of alcoholic beverages in Canada. Moncton's aldermen made every effort to provide essential services and to encourage citizens, churches, and other institutions to prepare for the large influx of servicemen. Despite the shortage of facilities, the entire town of Moncton made extraordinary efforts to accommodate the transient visitors. Churches enlarged or developed recreation facilities for servicemen and the local Y.M.C.A. underwent renovation and enlargement.

The young men were overwhelmed by their greeting and the hospitality. Both the YMCA and Salvation Army hostels were popular places for the young airmen. Many of the transients found in these institutions warm smiles, a hot cup of tea, a place to write letters, read, and play table tennis, cards, or other games. The Salvation Army hostel even operated an outdoor ice rink in winter and offered other sports in season. If the airmen remained in Moncton very long, they soon discovered regular entertainment such as Friday and Saturday night dances, as well as the hospitality of individual families. As Christmas 1941 approached and the weather became bitterly cold, the RAF student population increased at a phenomenal rate. The local newspaper called on residents to make special efforts to entertain servicemen during the holidays and individual families from Moncton and nearby communities responded by taking the airmen into their homes.

The hospitality only increased as the weather warmed. John McKenzie-Hall graduated from an Arnold Scheme school in the United States, then after further training in Canada, received a posting to No. 1 BFTS as the gunnery officer. McKenzie-Hall reflected on his first stay in Moncton. "I met up with a local family who owned a jewelry business in Moncton, and during my stay, I fear their profits must have slumped as we were out every day. [We had] picnics in the forests, swimming, canoeing on still lakes, parties in the evening and barbecues all night long."[56]

After the camp in Moncton opened, additional recreation facilities continued to be added to the station. Sports activities such as regular boxing shows and a five-team basketball league occupied large numbers of men, while nightly motion pictures shown in two of the recreation halls proved very popular. Impromptu musicals were organized and all of these activities supplemented the inevitable table tennis and card games.

Spending a few weeks in what was perceived as almost a wilderness environment, many of the British students suffered from culture shock. Not only was the dialect different, but so was everything else. Among the obvious differences were lights rather than blackouts, large quantities of fresh fruit, which had all but disappeared from greengrocer shops in Britain, and the quantity and quality of all foods, most of which were now severely rationed or unavailable in Britain. The young men were surprised to see lighted shop windows filled with consumer goods rather than the boarded up blacked-out shops common in British cities.

Other fascinating things included the amount of land, the variety of trees, and huge train engines and rail cars, which one walked into "up steps" rather than tiny cars which one boarded at station platform level. At this time in Britain there were few vehicles, except military ones being driven on the left side of narrow roads and lanes. The young British flight students were fascinated that most people, even the working classes, owned large automobiles and drove on the right side of the surprisingly wide roads.[57]

Lee Randall arrived in Moncton in May 1941. His first day involved the usual filling out of forms and settling into his eighteen-man billet with double bunks and a locker for each trainee. The next day after a filling breakfast and a pay call, Randall left camp to explore the town, which he described as "very different from any English town of the same size." Randall noted, "Hardly any house is built of brick, but they are well laid out in wide streets with grass verges running along either side. There are no fences at all and the electric cables running overhead tend to make the place ugly when it could be very pretty. There are no 'pubs' which makes the town seem rather incongruous." Randall found the local YMCA and spent a good deal of time there and then commented on another establishment. He found a "colossal number of so called 'drug stores' and 'grills' which are similar to milk bars and ice cream parlours cum restaurants at home. The food in these establishments is good and reasonably cheap."

Randall summarized his first impressions of Canada, "Now a word about Canada; we have been on its soil for 48 hours and I like it—it's great! In Great Britain, as the war has progressed and various restrictions and rationing have slowly been imposed, we tend to forget what peacetime was really like. You can imagine what surprise is caused by coming to a land like this apparently flowing with milk and honey and with so few restrictions." Randall could not help noting the contrast between Canada and the England he had so recently left. "In England because of shortages of labour and materials, buildings and towns are beginning to look very dull, but here the colours are amazing. There is no camouflage of buildings or cars, petrol stations still sell various brands of gas with their vari-coloured signs, whilst goods for sale in shops add to the scene."[58]

Gordon Davies, who trained with Course 10 at No. 4 BFTS, arrived in Moncton and wrote home describing some of the same differences the other trainees had noted. "A drugstore is THE place to go on this side of the Atlantic; it is an institution that has no parallel in the British Iles —don't ask me why!—to all outward appearances, a chemist, yet inside one looks twice; on the counters down one side is everything one would get from a chemist; medicines, soap, pills, cosmetics, whilst opposite is a long milk bar selling fruit drinks, milk shakes, ices, whilst at the back of the shop is a small restaurant with tables. One can, in fact, purchase most of one's small needs in the one shop."[59]

No matter how fascinating the trainees found the new Canadian sights, military discipline still prevailed in Moncton as one British student noted shortly after his arrival. "I have had my first fatigue on Canadian soil today as a punishment for whistling on parade. With unusual initiative, I reduced my sentence to sweeping out the orderly room and left the camp with all speed by 6.0 p.m."[60]

John Roberts Davies in a 19 April 1942 letter to his future wife described the Canadian hospitality. Davies and two other trainees had hitchhiked ninety miles to St. John with a Mr. Poole who gave the young men his address and invited them to his home. After a short sightseeing tour, Mr. Poole took Davies and the others home to a scrumptious dinner with his family. "After the meal, we sat round a log fire and talked about everything, mainly about the RAF and Great Britain. The whole of the Poole family were there and Mrs. Poole's mother was very English— in fact, everyone I have met out here is very patriotic and thinks very highly of Great Britain."[61]

Regardless of how fascinating the young trainees found Canada, Moncton, even with its improvements, remained a holding camp. The day finally arrived for sorting and assignment to individual flight schools. While some trainees had been designated for specific flight schools while still in Britain, for others the selection occurred in Canada. The actual selection process varied.

Sydney Urch, who trained with Course 11 at No. 6 BFTS, noted the form soon after he arrived in Moncton. "I remember hundreds of airmen assembled at Moncton for the picking of who would go where, and I had already learnt roughly the procedure. The first groups would go to Canada, and the end groups to the U.S.A. so when it was 'line up in lots of 50's', I hung around until it got to the BFTS as I definitely wanted to go to the USA not the frozen north of Canada."[62]

Seventeen months after joining the RAF, J. K. Ellwood arrived in Canada and described the selection process for a BFTS at that time. "The sergeant in charge said we were going to 5 schools & if we liked to get into 5 groups with our friends. We had to gather in areas marked on the hangar floor, Clewiston, Terrell, Miami, Ponca City, Mesa—no mention of states. A few of us dived into the Miami group thinking of that glamour place & imagine our dismay when we were sent off to Miami, Oklahoma. However, we had no regrets in the end as the Middle Western people were the most hospitable in the world."[63]

Phillip E. Mitchell found the decision already made. "After some days, those of us who were in the A.T.T.S. Scheme were told to which school we were posted. To my delight, I was to go to No. 2 B.F.T.S., Lancaster, California. This meant farewell to friends made on the ship, none of whom were posted to Lancaster. In spite of our request, no changes were made to the nominal rolls."[64]

Students destined for training in the United States received special attention. Charles George Waller, destined to train with the first course at No. 2 BFTS, remembered the process: "The first 100 of us selected for training in U.S.A. were specially interviewed before being sent for training in America."[65]

Those selected also received a small blue book which contained specific instructions and advice from a service obviously concerned with the realities and pitfalls of training in civilian schools in a neutral United States. The book included the following cautions:

> Airmen should realise that they have been specially selected for training at this particular centre as individuals whose conduct and bearing at all times will bring credit to their Service. They will be relied upon to foster the good relations, which already exist with the people among whom they will live during training, and in particular, should refrain from criticism of local conditions, school

organization, or of individuals. Any difficulties or misunderstand-ings should always be addressed to the head of the training school. These points are emphasized since the airman will not be subject to Air Force discipline when at the training centre, and as a conse-quence, they must be placed on their honour to conform strictly with the school regulations, and outside the school to speak with discretion and conduct themselves with propriety.[66]

Following assignment to individual British Flying Training Schools, students underwent documentation and processing, which included photographs, fingerprinting, and filling out visa applications, then boarded trains bound for the United States. The first contingent of 100 students destined for the temporary home of No. 1 BFTS in Dallas, Texas, and the temporary home of No. 2 BFTS in Glendale, California, boarded a train on the grounds of the Canadian National Exhibition and left Toronto on the evening of 31 May 1941. Dressed in gray civilian suits, blue shirts, black ties, and black shoes, each student also had a temporary visa for entry into the neutral United States. An RCAF or RAF officer armed with rosters, schedules, and meal and travel vouchers accompanied each group.

The train carrying the first course for the first two British Flying Training Schools entered the United States traveling south toward the first stop in Chicago, Illinois. Following a meal and a layover, which allowed a brief tour of the city, the students changed trains and continued south to St. Louis, Missouri, known as the Gateway City and another brief stop. One British student recalled the journey, "We were in American trains now, the Pullman coaches were excellent—lovely sprung adjustable seats, the trains are like traveling hotels."[67]

The remainder of the first draft destined for the first four schools in the United States did not leave on time. Due to the danger posed by the German battleship *Bismarck,* then reported to be at sea in the North Atlantic, the 100 students destined to form the first course at No.3 BFTS temporarily in Tulsa, Oklahoma, and No.4 BFTS temporarily in Phoenix, Arizona, were delayed for two weeks in Britain.

British officials, with American concurrence, abandoned the gray civilian suits about a month before the United States entered the war. Some British students, therefore, entered a neutral United States in uniform.

Evan Bumford left Canada with Course 5 destined for No. 3 BFTS. Just after leaving Montreal, the Canadian conducting officer told the trainees that they could change into the civilian clothes that had been issued. The students chuckled when they told the officer that the civilian clothes had been taken back by stores. The officer replied doubtfully, "You're the first bunch I've been asked to take across the border in uniform." At Chicago the next morning, the young men left the train in uniform for a short layover. An American matron approached the group and asked, "Say, what military academy are you boys from?" Bumford remembered the incident, "Mustering our dignity we replied rather huffily that we were members of the ROYAL AIR FORCE and showed our cap badges to prove it. She seemed more bewildered than impressed."[68]

Later trains traveled directly to the individual schools without carrying contingents for two schools. As the British students traveled into the United States, they marveled at the sheer size of the new country and the ever changing scenery. John Roberts Davies recorded his impressions as he and his course mates traveled to No. 2 BFTS in California. "Just after passing Omaha, we saw the Rockies. The train kept to the valleys with the peaks rising thousands of feet on either side. The Gore Canyon was beautiful—cliffs rising sheer on either side of the track. It is utterly impossible to describe the grandeur of this scenery—mountains with their peaks flashing snow in the sun thousands of feet above and green slopes beneath." The train passed through the Rockies and then through Salt Lake City. The young men were particularly interested in the Bonneville Salt Flats where Englishman Sir Malcolm Campbell had garnered the world land speed record in 1935. The train passed through San Francisco and the students marveled at the Golden Gate Bridge and Alcatraz, the well-known American prison located on an island in the bay. "We then came down through the Californian Valley. This too was lovely—green fields, wheat, eucalyptus trees, apple and lemon trees. The sun was hot and always those snow capped mountains on the horizon; we reached the Mojave Desert where Lancaster and the flying field are situated; the field is in a sort of hollow surrounded by mountains."[69]

These first journeys south marked the beginning of a continual stream of trainees from Canadian depots to the British Flying Training Schools. Depending on the Manning Depot location (either Toronto or Moncton) and the individual school destination, trains traveled into the United States through Chicago or Detroit and then down to St. Louis or into the northeast to New York City and on to Philadelphia and Washington, D.C.

These trains carrying at first hundreds and ultimately thousands of young British trainees south at regular intervals would continue unabated for the next four years. This would be the stage the British aircrew trainees had waited for, labored toward, and dreamed of for so long, flight training.

Figure 1. Map of BFTS locations.

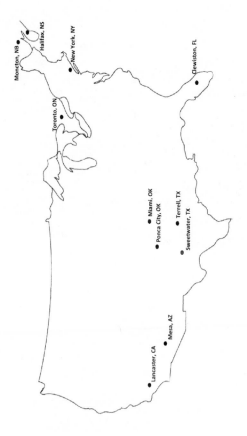

Map by Nicole Shortes
The British Flying Training Schools were located across the southern United States. British students arrived in North America via Halifax, Nova Scotia, and later New York City. Personnel reception centers were located temporarily in Toronto, Ontario, and later at a new center in Moncton, New Brunswick.

Figure 2. The first course at No. 1 BFTS in temporary quarters at Dallas Love Field.

No. 1 British Flying Training School Museum, Inc.
Note the news photographers in the foreground.

Figure 3. Unauthorized aerial photograph of No. 4 BFTS and Falcon Field by a British student.

Author's collection
Note the extensive runway pattern, which was unusual for a BFTS.

Figure 4. Aerial view of No 5 BFTS.

Embry-Riddle Aeronautical University Archives
Note the diamond-shaped ring road.

Figure 5. A portion of Course 17 at No. 6 BFTS.

10 DEC 43 - PONCA CITY — SAME AS NUMBERED PHOTO, BUT SHARPER IMAGES

Author's collection
Note the American AAF cadet kneeling second from the left.

Figure 6. Instructors and dispatcher at No. 6 BFTS.

From *The Ponca City News*

The first civilian flight instructors and a flight dispatcher at No. 6 BFTS in front of a Stearman PT-17 primary trainer. Henry Jerger, the chief flight supervisor, is standing second from the right. Jerger was killed in the crash of an AT-6 on a maintenance test flight in June 1943.

Figure 7. The entrance to Polaris Flight Academy at No. 2 BFTS.

Author's collection Note the stylized RAF wings on the wall to the right of the entrance.

Figure 8. Even instructors had to take flight checks.

No. 1 British Flying Training School Museum, Inc.

Figure 9. Fairchild PT-19 primary trainer used at No. 3 BFTS.

Northeastern Oklahoma A&M College

Figure 10. Gun camera image taken from an AT-6 Harvard.

Terrell Heritage Society

Figure 11. Saturday morning parade at No. 5 BFTS, Riddle Field.

Embry-Riddle Aeronautical University Archives

Figure 12. Aerial view of No. 3 BFTS just after the school opened.

Author's collection

Historic Hightway 66 is in the foreground. Note the unique Pennant Terminal building purchased with the site.

Figure 13. Cartoon by British student

No. 1 British Flying Training School Museum, Inc.
One British student's humorous view of the three phases of flight training.

Figure 14. The first and only course at No. 7 BFTS.

Author's collection

Figure 15. Vultee BT-13 Basic Trainer

Author's collection

Figure 16. AT-6 Harvards in formation

Terrell Heritage Society

Figure 17. Wings Parade at No. 5 BFTS

Clewiston Museum

Figure 18. Link Trainer

Clewiston Museum
The operator sat at a nearby desk with a control console.

Figure 19. British graves in Arcadia, Florida.

Author's collection
The plot contains twenty-two BFTS students, one Arnold Scheme student, and John Paul Riddle.

Figure 20. Interior of the Bass Drug Store

Margaret Bass photograph collection located in the Riter C. Hulsey Public Library The Drug Store was a favorite Terrell hang out of the British students.

Figure 21. Fatal AT-6 crash in Texas

Margaret Bass photograph collection located in the Riter C. Hulsey Public Library

Figure 22. Ground School classroom

Terrell Heritage Society

Figure 23. Damaged Stearman primary trainers

No. 1 British Flying Training School Museum, Inc.
The Stearmans were damaged by a storm which struck Thunderbird Field and No. 4 BFTS on August 1, 1945.

Figure 24. Lord and Lady Halifax

No. 1 British Flying Training School Museum, Inc.
Lord and Lady Halifax dedicate a small monument in the RAF section of the Oakland
Memorial Park cemetery in Terrell, Texas.

Figure 25. Primary flight line, No. 1 BFTS

Terrell Heritage Society

CHAPTER 5

NEW SCHOOLS

No. 1 BFTS

At ten o'clock on Monday morning, 2 June 1941, a Southern Pacific passenger train pulled into Dallas Union Terminal under a low gray overcast sky threatening rain. The train contained the first contingent of 100 Royal Air Force students destined for the British Flying Training Schools. Fifty of those on board, designated for Major Long's No. 1 BFTS, stepped down from the high cars and onto the station platform. Each student wore the same gray civilian suit and the only discernible difference within the group was that several of the young men wore hats while several others smoked pipes.

After a short time, a tired conductor called out the traditional "all aboard" and with several short blasts of its whistle, the train started to move. Many of the fifty British students remaining on board hung out of the open windows and called "cheerio" to their recent traveling companions, now standing awkwardly on the platform. They then started to sing "Bless 'em All" as the train pulled out of the station, continuing westward to Major Moseley's No. 2 BFTS in California.

On the platform to greet the British students were the two Royal Air Force officers assigned to the new school, Wing Commander Fredrick Hilton, the chief flying instructor, and Squadron Leader Andrew Beveridge, the chief ground instructor. The two RAF officers looked as much out of place as the students because they too wore similar gray civilian suits in accordance with United States neutrality laws. Also at the station to greet the British students were several local newspaper reporters, which not only surprised the RAF officers, but would prove to be a harbinger of things to come.

The reporters departed after eliciting several newsworthy tidbits from the British arrivals such as surprise at finding no cattle on the railroad tracks and no cowboys at the Dallas station. Also, the students had not been overly happy about training in Texas while their traveling companions were destined for glamorous California, that is, until someone on the train mentioned that Texas had the prettiest girls in the nation.[1]

. After the reporters left, the students boarded buses for the temporary school at Dallas Love Field. Since the site selection process had taken longer than originally anticipated, these first students arrived in Dallas before Major Long had concluded his negotiations with the city of Terrell and before construction of the new school had even begun.

The British students moved into the Dallas Aviation School facilities recently vacated by Long's army contract primary school. The school buildings located at the north end of Love Field were basic and consisted of a long barracks, a ground school building, and a dining hall with a canteen. All of the buildings were single-story wood construction with corrugated metal roofs. The ground school building contained two classrooms with little more than a blackboard and individual seats with a small writing surface much like those found in local public schools. The barracks had been divided into small rooms for four students each, but the partitions seriously restricted ventilation. Many of the British students had difficulty sleeping in the hot stuffy barracks in the Texas heat. The barracks and ground school building were located more than

500 yards from the hangars along a road undergoing extensive repairs. The officers noted that the school contained "no room where pupils can congregate, read, and talk together."[2]

The bright spot in the otherwise drab facilities turned out to be the dining hall and canteen. The dining hall offered a wide variety of good food in abundance, which delighted the British students after coming from a nation plagued by severe shortages and food rationing. The canteen offered delightful treats such as soft drinks, candy, and other small items. The students quickly developed their own special drink, two scoops of vanilla ice cream in a glass of orange juice.

The school offered no medical facilities and little in the way of recreation. Small uniform replacement items such as caps and belts, as well as clothing and shoe repairs, were unavailable. Each student had one regulation RAF uniform to be worn at the school and the gray civilian suit with two pairs of trousers for occasions away from the school. The RAF officers looked into a group membership at the local YMCA, but a lack of transportation and the tight training schedule made this idea impractical.

The two officers had arrived only days before the students and had taken rooms in the local Dallas Athletic Club, but since the cost exceeded their housing allowance, they had decided to look for a nearby house to rent.

Hilton, a former bomber pilot with considerable combat experience, and Beveridge, who had previously served in various training commands, had received a verbal briefing from Air Ministry officials in Britain after being selected for the new American program. The two officers were told that they would act only in an advisory capacity and should not attempt to alter the civilian school training program. The civilian operators were said to be extremely sensitive regarding their authority and course curriculums. The officers were also warned to avoid any discussion of the war, or the possible entry of the United States into the war, because isolationist sentiment was strongest in western states such as Texas. The two officers were also warned to avoid any adverse publicity that might offend local citizens.

Due to the novelty of the new program, Hilton and Beveridge found that there were no manuals, ground school supplies, or other training publications available. (This was before the Air Ministry assembled and shipped the eighty-four crates of materials to Carnegie.) Hilton and Beveridge returned to their previous commands at No. 11 Elementary Flying Training School at Perth and operational training units at Heston and Upper Heyford and gathered an assortment of materials, which they brought with them to the United States.

As soon as they arrived in Dallas, Hilton and Beveridge met with Major Long, L. H. Luckey, the school director, and other staff members. Luckey had originally met Long in Oklahoma in the early 1920s when he traded a Packard automobile to Long for an airplane. Luckey left Braniff Airways to become director of the new British school, which had been incorporated as the Terrell Aviation School.

Hilton and Beveridge quickly realized that much of what they had been told by Air Ministry officials was incorrect. The RAF officers were pleasantly surprised to find the staff of the new school to be not only experienced and cooperative, but also eager to incorporate RAF training methods into the school curriculum. The staff included E. Van Lloyd, a former airline pilot and army instructor, as the chief advanced flight instructor, R. D. Griffin, the chief primary flight instructor, I. V. French, the chief ground school instructor, and Jimmy Hayden, the maintenance supervisor. These men wanted to build a strong school spirit since this school had been designated the first, or No. 1 British Flying Training School.[3]

After the initial meeting, Hilton flew with the two flight commanders. Although not impressed with the technique used to execute a slow roll, Hilton commented, "All instructors here—far from insisting on their own methods—are very keen to see and discuss our ways of training. They have decided to use our terminology in their teaching, and it seems our system will be adopted almost entirely."[4]

The RAF officers were also surprised to find an abundance of pro-British sentiment in North Texas. Many local residents who greeted the RAF officers openly expressed the opinion that the United States should join Britain in the war. The previous month, the Terrell newspaper had reported on local opinion. "In cafes, department stores along Moore Avenue and in private homes the average Terrell citizen thinks it will be only a matter of months or weeks until the United States becomes involved in the war which is now raging in most parts of the world."[5]

Little in the way of equipment for the new school had been delivered. Even so, ground school classes started the day after the first students arrived. The Army Air Corps delivered the first seventeen Stearman PT-18 primary trainers three days later, but heavy rains, high winds, and low clouds delayed the start of flight training. As torrential rains fell from leaden skies, local creeks and rivers rose and then overflowed their banks. The rains prompted the RAF officers to comment that an earlier assertion by Major Long that Texas had 364 days of flying weather per year, "erred on the side of optimism."[6]

Construction of the Terrell school got underway as soon as Major Long completed his negotiations with Terrell city officials. The parties signed the various documents on Flag Day, 14 June, which many local residents saw as symbolic. The initial school facilities consisted of two large hangars and seven buildings, including an administration building, dining hall and canteen, two barracks, two ground school buildings, and a building to house six Link trainers. Trucks as well as mule-drawn wagons delivered materials to the construction site.

From the administration building, located just inside the entrance to the airfield, a single wide sidewalk divided the school buildings. The dining hall was located on one side of the sidewalk, followed by the two ground school buildings, one on either side of the sidewalk, and then the two barracks, again on either side of the sidewalk. The barracks, influenced by the Love Field experience, had twelve-foot-high ceilings and were open on the inside with numerous exterior windows for ventilation. Two-tiered bunks were arranged along each of the long exterior walls and small lockers provided space for uniforms and personal items. Each of the barracks housed two courses with each course of fifty students occupying one end of the barracks. The center section of each barrack contained common shower and toilet facilities. The hangars and Link trainer building were set apart from the main buildings.

With the exception of the two steel-framed hangars, all of the school buildings were single-story frame construction built on concrete slab foundations and painted white with green composition roofs. The Link trainer building was the only air conditioned building due to its sensitive electronics.[7] The buildings were located at the northwest corner of the airfield close to the dirt road leading into Terrell. The remainder of the airport land angled to the southeast for approximately one and one-third miles. The wide grass-covered area allowed takeoffs and landings in any direction from north-south to northwest-southeast, which conformed to the prevailing winds. When the RAF officers complained about bare areas on the airfield left from the grading and leveling process, Luckey agreed to sod these areas. But the concerns proved to be well founded. Bert Allam, an early British student, later described the Terrell field as, "a dust bowl when dry and a glue pot when wet."[8]

The only disagreements concerned the ground school buildings and the recreation building. The RAF flight training syllabus included more ground school instruction than comparable Army Air Corps schools and Long had patterned the ground school buildings after his army schools. The RAF officers were able to persuade Long to enlarge the ground school buildings in order to increase the number of classrooms.

Major Long had also deleted the recreation hall, which had been included in the original plans, since he felt that students could use the barracks or canteen for any after-hours activities such as studying and letter writing. The RAF staff, however, felt that a recreation hall offered positive benefits and Long had originally agreed to build the school in accordance with RAF preferences. Long put the recreation hall back into the construction schedule, but the design now included a dispensary at one end. The dispensary had a waiting room for daily sick call and six beds. The school had retained a local doctor to provide medical services. Minor illnesses were treated in the school dispensary, while more serious cases were taken to the doctor's clinic in town, which included a surgery.

When completed, both the recreation hall and the canteen had interior walls finished in an oiled natural knotty pine and both included wide screened-in verandas that allowed the passage of cooling summer breezes and the nocturnal noises of rural East Texas. The still country nights carried sounds such as the far off barking of a dog, the occasional low rumble of a car passing in the distance, and the forlorn lament of a retreating train whistle mingled with the nearer sounds of night birds, the constant chirping of crickets, and the steady drone of insects. These sounds, blended with the fragrance of jasmine, honeysuckle, roses, and other native plants, would leave an indelible impression on the young British students destined to train in Terrell.

Whether located in subtropical Florida, the rich agricultural areas of Texas or Oklahoma, or the arid desert regions of the American west, the distinctive sights, sounds, and fragrances indigenous to the various regions would become an enduring legacy of each of the British Flying Training Schools.

Although the school facilities were neat, well arranged, and generally above average by the military standards of the day, the British students were surprised by the open lavatories. Sinks and toilets were arranged in long lines with no partitions and showers were taken in a large open area with shower heads spaced along the walls, again with no partitions. Almost all British students later remarked that inhibitions quickly became a thing of the past in Terrell and echoed the sentiments of Brian Latham of Course 19. "It (the barracks) really was very comfortable, but there was absolutely no privacy. Even the lavatories were in a row and you were shoulder to shoulder, chatting and straining amiably! It was no use being bashful."[9]

By mid-August the first two courses were training at Dallas Love Field, which filled the school to capacity. The first course completed primary and went on a week's leave. When this course returned from leave the permanent facilities in Terrell were nearing completion and the third course was en route by rail from Canada to Terrell. The move to the new school took place over the weekend of 23–24 August to avoid interrupting the training schedule. Instructors flew thirty Stearman PT-18 primary trainers and five Vultee BT-13 basic trainers from Dallas to Terrell. Before landing, many of the instructors performed aerobatics over the new airfield, which thrilled the local residents who had come to watch the move. The canteen's soda fountain did a brisk business in the summer heat as the newly installed juke box played popular tunes.

The first courses experienced disruptions and delays caused by the temporary facilities, the move to a new location, a shortage of critical maintenance parts and supplies, a lack of ground school materials, and numerous other problems associated with a new and complicated venture. When the first course finished training on 30 October the RAF officers reported, "Mr. Luckey, Mr. Van Lloyd and the flying instructors have displayed praiseworthy energy and keenness in achieving results in the face of the aforementioned difficulties."[10]

No. 2 BFTS

In the early morning hours of 4 June 1941 the same train that had deposited the first British students in Dallas pulled into the Los Angeles suburb of Glendale, California. The remaining fifty students left the train and boarded buses for the temporary home of Major Moseley's No. 2 British Flying Training School. Until the new facilities in Lancaster could be completed, the British students commenced training at Glendale's

Grand Central Airport alongside the school's American Refresher students.

Squadron Leader Thomas G. Whitlock, the RAF chief ground instructor, had arrived in Glendale just two days before the first British students. The next day, Squadron Leader Stewart Mills, the former assistant air attache, arrived in Glendale after being reassigned as the school's chief flying instructor. As with their Dallas counterparts, these RAF officers found Major Moseley and his civilian staff competent, enthusiastic, and eager to begin the new program. In fact, Moseley proposed an idea unique to military flight training. He would guarantee that every member of the first course would successfully complete flight training if humanly possible. In order to accomplish this, any additional training time required by slower students, who would have normally been eliminated from the program, would be done at Moseley's expense. Although skeptical, the British officers readily agreed to the experiment.

Despite the extraordinary effort and additional contractor flight time, one student in the first course washed out in the primary phase of flying, having failed to solo after seventeen hours of dual instruction. British student Charles George Waller of Course 1 remarked, "As the first course, I believe the American instructors did their best to get everyone up to the required standard; and, I believe that on my course we had 49 people who gained their wings out of the original 50. Some record."[11] Actually, this record represented a phenomenal success rate. Unfortunately the experiment could not be repeated for other courses due to the expense and the disruption to the necessarily fast-paced training schedule. Later courses experienced elimination rates normal for military flight training programs of the period.

Due to a housing shortage in Glendale, students were initially housed in a former road house that dated from the Prohibition era. Charles George Waller commented on the accommodations: "We were quartered in what used to be a night club, which once belonged to 'Bugs' Moran. Our beds were in what was the gambling casino; one wall slid up to allow the gaming machines to be hidden when the place was raided, and the ceiling had paintings of women all over it."[12] P. S. Smith remembered the quarters as "luxuriously appointed" and Joseph S. Ekbery of the second course remembered being "billeted in an ex-night club [with] nude women painted on the ceiling!"[13]

As in Dallas, the first students found the facilities at Glendale primitive. Ground school classes were taught in small, poorly ventilated rooms close to the noise of the maintenance shops and the flight line. Another major problem in both the Dallas and Glendale schools turned out to be logistical. Both schools lacked aircraft, parachutes, equipment, supplies, and support facilities. Not only had equipment not arrived, apparently no system had been implemented for procuring equipment and supplies.

On 6 June 1941, the U.S. Army Materiel Division at Wright Field in Dayton, Ohio, issued a memorandum authorizing regional Army Air Corps supply depots to issue equipment to the British schools. This memorandum provided that "The use of Air Corps equipment and supplies, airplanes, engines, parachutes, spare parts, gasoline, oil, etc. required for the operation of these schools is authorized under Lend-Lease procedures. All equipment and supplies with the exception of food and medicine will be provided by the Air Corps thru normal supply channels."[14] As with any new military program, implementation of this directive at the local level took time.

In spite of the lack of equipment and limited facilities, ground school classes began the day after the first students arrived. Several days later the army delivered the first Stearman PT-13 primary trainers to Glendale. Primary flight training began immediately under the direction of H. G. Reynolds, the civilian chief flight instructor. Owing to early morning fog and air traffic congestion at the Glendale airport, flying commenced from a grass auxiliary field at nearby Newhall, California.

Joseph Ekbery recalled the daily trip to the remote field. "We flew from a satellite aerodrome at Newhall, a few miles away in the San Fernando Valley; to get there by bus, we passed the huge Lockheed works every day. The little Spanish kids working in the fields used to throw melons at the bus and we caught them through the open windows ... all good fun."[15]

These first students inaugurated a training schedule typical of military flight training programs of the day. Each class was divided into two flights. Each flight spent half of each training day in ground school and the other half flying. While one flight flew in the morning, the other flight attended ground school; in the afternoon the schedule reversed. This practical and efficient system remained in effect throughout the operation of the British Flying Training Schools.

Besides the limited facilities and lack of equipment, another minor, but troubling, problem surfaced in Glendale. The students experienced an unusually high number of colds, sore throats, and ear trouble. Both the civilian doctor retained by the school and the army medical officer assigned to the army contract mechanics course were mystified by the problems. These upper respiratory ailments apparently stemmed from the heavy smog surrounding Glendale because the problems disappeared when the school moved to the dry desert air of Lancaster.

About the same time that work commenced on the Terrell school, Glendale contractor Victor J. Nelson arrived in Lancaster and started work on No. 2 BFTS. The new school buildings included administration, operations, a dining hall with a recreation room, a ground school building, and two Link trainer buildings, as well as two large hangars, each capable of holding forty-five aircraft, and another small hangar.

Work progressed despite labor problems with the local carpenters union, which resulted in pickets outside the main gate. The contractor filed an injunction against the strike citing a new California law which prohibited strikes that interfered with defense projects. A lower court issued the injunction, but was overturned on appeal. Despite the legal aspects, the strike failed because the local Teamsters Union representing truck drivers refused to honor the picket line. Trucks continued to deliver a steady stream of supplies and building materials to the work site.

The airfield, named War Eagle Field, located five miles west of Lancaster, benefitted from two deep wells that provided ample water for the school. Another deep well provided water for the auxiliary field. There were, however, differences in the facilities at Lancaster, both good and bad.

The ground school building, with three classrooms, which Major Moseley had patterned after his army schools, proved to be inadequate. While the RAF officers in Terrell had been able to influence Major Long to expand the original ground school buildings at No. 1 BFTS, that did not occur in Lancaster. After the first students arrived, the school had to convert a small office into another classroom.

After the RAF added an administrative officer and an armament NCO to the school staff, Flight Lieutenant Green commented that Flight Sergeant Woodcock's armament course, "became something of a moveable feast, until a form of out-house was finally converted into a permanent armament lecture room."[16] Major Moseley belatedly built additional rooms onto the ground school building.

Due to the intense desert heat, the British officers requested a swimming pool at the new Lancaster school, but Major Moseley refused to install a pool and justified the decision by stating that the Army Air Corps did not allow swimming pools because they caused ear infections. The flaw in this argument became clear when the army took over the school at the end of 1942 and immediately began the construction of two swimming pools.

One interesting footnote concerning swimming pools is found in contemporary documents. Often when requesting the inclusion of a swimming pool on a military base, whether British or American, officers frequently justified the expenditure to parsimonious budget officials, not as a recreational or morale benefit, but as a potential fire-fighting reservoir.

The good news at Lancaster concerned the student housing. The school offered a radical departure from the standard barracks found on virtually every military base of the time. At No. 2 BFTS students were housed in twenty-four stucco cottages, each containing four bedrooms and a bath. The cottages were arranged in pairs with another bath connecting the two buildings. Each cottage and the ground school classrooms also featured evaporative cooling, an amazing luxury in the desert heat. John Roberts Davies, who trained later with Course 9, commented on the housing. "The bungalows are set around a green lawn. The rooms are pleasant, two to three beds in each of the four rooms—lovely coloured curtains on the windows and cream-coloured venetian blinds. Also in the room are two writing tables with modern adjustable reading lamps."[17]

The first two courses were training at Glendale when the third course left Canada by rail destined for California. Since the facilities at Glendale could not accommodate three courses and the new facilities in Lancaster were not complete, officials made a difficult decision. Course 1 moved from Glendale into the incomplete facilities at Lancaster and started basic training, while Course 3 arrived in Glendale to begin primary training alongside Course 2.

On 20 August 1941, flying instructors flew the newly arrived Vultee BT-13 basic trainers to War Eagle Field with the students as passengers. The aircraft arrived in the midst of high winds and a dust storm, which almost obscured the airfield. Fortunately the aircraft landed without mishap. Basic training began under the direction of Flight Lieutenant Green and Flight Sergeant Woodcock.

At Glendale, the primary instructors under the supervision of Squadron Leaders Mills and Whitlock continued with Course 2 and the newly arrived Course 3. The division between Glendale and Lancaster continued to cause problems until everyone moved to Lancaster a month later. Even after the move the school continued to be plagued by blowing dust and problems with the sewage disposal system. Several weeks passed before grass began to grow around the buildings and the sewage problems were solved.

The new school offered little in the way of recreation facilities. The recreation building contained a limited number of games and furnishings consisted of hard wooden chairs and two radios, one a gift and the other purchased by the students. The school library contained books donated by Lancaster and Los Angeles residents. A promise by the contractor to build two tennis courts never materialized. For swimming and athletics the RAF students were occasionally able to use the swimming pool and other sports facilities at the Lancaster High School when they were not in use.

In spite of these limitations, the school fielded a cricket team and entered a team in the Los Angeles Soccer League by October 1941. Soon afterward the students began to play both cricket and soccer in the city every Sunday. Eventually the school fielded three soccer teams. At Christmas 1941 one of the RAF soccer teams traveled to San Francisco where it defeated two local teams.

After the full complement of four courses had arrived and started training, and the initial construction problems had largely been resolved, another complication arose. The American Refresher students had been left in Glendale when the British students moved to Lancaster. When the United States entered the war in December 1941, the Army Air Forces appropriated the Glendale airport and the Refresher students had nowhere to go. Major Moseley asked if these students could be accommodated in Lancaster. Squadron Leader Mills had little choice and reluctantly agreed, but the addition of fifty extra students resulted in overcrowding and complicated the training schedule.

Besides the overcrowding, Mills and the other RAF officers expressed concern over mixing the American Refresher students, who were essentially civilian volunteers who could resign at any time, with the RAF students who were part of a military service. These fears proved to be unfounded. When the last Refresher students graduated in June 1942, the RAF officers reported that the American students had been treated the same as the other students, had stood their turn at duty, took part in drill, and much to the officers' surprise, had even mastered the British salute.

No. 3 BFTS

The initial organization called for each RAF chief flying instructor to supervise two British Flying Training Schools. Wing Commander Hilton commanded both No. 1 BFTS and No. 3 BFTS. Soon after Hilton and Beveridge arrived in Dallas, met with Major Long and his staff, and settled into their new quarters, the two RAF officers traveled north to Tulsa, Oklahoma, to inspect the Spartan School of Aeronautics. Beveridge had to be pressed into service since No. 3 BFTS did not yet have a chief ground instructor. The RAF officers reported on their tour of the school: "We visited with Mr. Max Balfour and saw around the Spartan School. We were most impressed by the layout, the keenness and apparent efficiency of the instructors, the condition and cleanliness of the hangars, shops and aircraft, the good food, and the general air of all-around efficiency."[18]

In the early morning dawn of 16 June, the train carrying the second contingent of students for the British Flying Training Schools arrived in Tulsa. Forty-seven students left the train destined for the first British course at Spartan (joined later by three students who had been delayed). This contingent of British students had been scheduled to arrive at the same time as the first contingent, but had been held in Britain for two weeks by reports of the German battleship *Bismarck* rumored to be at sea in the North Atlantic. As with the first train to enter the United States with British students, this train also carried the initial students for two schools. After leaving Tulsa, the train continued westward to Phoenix, Arizona, with the first students destined for the temporary home of No. 4 BFTS.

The travel-weary students stepped down from the train in Tulsa wearing the "wrinkled uniform like gray double breasted suits." On hand to greet the students were William Skelly, owner of Spartan School of Aeronautics, Captain Balfour, and Squadron Leader Beveridge. Also on hand to greet the new arrivals were local residents who had braved the early morning hour and several newspaper reporters. Wing Commander

Hilton arrived in Tulsa the following day to be on hand for the start of training.

The students had been warned to be very careful in answering questions (for "security reasons") and the reporters were probably disappointed by their responses. One student when asked about his trip across the Atlantic and unsure how to answer, replied, "yes our trip was all right" and another said simply, "jolly good." The reporters fared little better with the short, stocky, and balding Skelly who commented, "nice looking bunch of boys." Thirty minutes later, viewing the Spartan facilities for the first time, the tired students again responded to newsmen's questions with, "jolly big" and "looks right."[19]

The reporters had better luck with Royal Canadian Air Force Pilot Officer W. C. Clements who had escorted the students from Canada and Captain Balfour. Clements, a native of Saskatchewan, told the reporters, "They had a pretty rough time of it. On the decks across the Atlantic. Landed at Halifax the tenth of the month. Two days in Toronto. On down here—in day coach all the way. These boys have been in a bed only two nights out of the past two weeks." Balfour explained to the newsmen that the students "would be given twenty weeks of training at Spartan first in Tulsa and then in Miami, Oklahoma, where construction of a special school has begun" and then added, "We will give both primary and advanced training. It will be somewhat similar to the training American air corps cadets receive."[20]

Most British Officers were uncomfortable dealing with the American press. Beveridge noted, "Captain Balfour seems to have the press much more under control than does Major Long at Dallas, and reporters were allotted one and one-half hours on Monday afternoon to meet the pupils and get stories and pictures."[21]

The first course began training the day after the students arrived in Tulsa. Due to an initial shortage of equipment and flight instructors, each instructor had five students. (Normally each instructor would have four students, but this was not always possible in the early courses.) Since the arrival of the first course had been delayed, the school inaugurated an accelerated training schedule, which put considerable strain on instructors and students alike. Also, the newly arrived Fairchild PT-19 primary trainers were not equipped for instrument or night flying and Spartan had no Link trainers in Tulsa.

Spartan did offer several advantages over the other British schools. The staff of the army contract primary school at Spartan included an army supply officer. Beveridge and this officer agreed that the flight clothing issued to the British students was unsuited to the Oklahoma summer heat. The supply officer immediately issued light-weight flying gear to the British students from the army supply. Also, and somewhat surprising to the British officers, the commander of the army detachment offered assistance to the new school, which included providing the services of both the army medical officer and the army physical training instructor to the newly arrived British students.

Spartan also had a cutaway aircraft engine that had been supplied by the army as a training aid. This engine so impressed the RAF officers that they pressured Major Long to get one for the Terrell school. The army responded by providing No. 1 BFTS with two cutaway engines, an inline engine and a radial engine.

There were still minor but annoying issues. Certain ground school supplies had not arrived and the instructional Dalton navigation computer used by Spartan was not the same model used by the RAF. Ground school supplies would be delivered to all of the British schools over the next several months.

The newly arrived British students were housed in the Spartan Aeronautics barracks and ate in the large stone cafeteria with the various other Spartan flight students (a considerable improvement over the temporary facilities in Dallas and Glenview). Here the British students first observed the Army Air Corps rigid form of discipline. The less experienced army flight cadets known as lower-classmen were constantly hazed by the more experienced or upper-class cadets. Any infraction of the numerous rules resulted in demerits, which had to be worked off by marching around the flight line with an infantry rifle. The British students developed a distinct distaste for the strict army style of discipline, which they found to be petty and offensive, although, as one British student admitted, "we were full of admiration for the finished product."[22]

The British students did not interact to any great extent with the army aviation cadets undergoing training at Spartan. Both groups were reserved and found it difficult to bridge their service and cultural differences. The British students associated more with the American Refresher students. Since these young men were destined for the Royal Air Force, the Refresher students were full of questions about the British aerial service and the British students were happy to oblige. In return, the more experienced American students, who were already pilots, reciprocated with flying tips and advice on flight training.

The British students arrived in Tulsa and started training before the permanent RAF chief ground instructor had arrived. This placed a tremendous burden on Squadron Leader Beveridge who had to supervise both the Dallas and Tulsa schools. Squadron Leader A. C. Kermode, the newly appointed No. 3 BFTS chief ground instructor, arrived in Tulsa one month later, just before the first course moved to Miami. Kermode, a veteran of World War I, had served in the RAF for twenty years and had written several books on flight training and the theory of flight.

By comparison, when the first Army Air Corps contract primary school at Spartan had opened in 1939, the army assigned a permanent on-site staff of five officers to the school. This organization included the commanding officer (a captain), officers to oversee administration, ground school, and flight training, as well as a medical officer. Another officer later joined the staff. And the army contract school covered only primary training; the British schools included all flight training from primary through advanced.

On 27 June a short ground-breaking ceremony in Miami, Oklahoma, led by Mayor M. M. DeArman and George Coleman, a local retired mine operator who made much of the new school site available through his philanthropy, marked the beginning of construction on the new Spartan school. Construction workers from Waller-Wells construction company in Tulsa quickly began work on the ten-acre portion of the 300-acre cornfield surrounding the Pennant Terminal, the vacant travel lodge that had been purchased with the site. The travel lodge, which fronted Highway 66 along the eastern edge of the airfield, became the administration building with a lobby and reception center, numerous offices, recreation hall, a soda fountain, and even a barbershop. Motel rooms on the building's third floor were retained for visiting personnel and overnight stays, which Balfour explained, "will save us money in hotel bills or rent."[23] The unused service station in front of the travel lodge became the school's gate house.

Behind the administration building, workers constructed the other school buildings around and facing a landscaped courtyard traversed by walkways. The courtyard also included two transplanted twenty-foot evergreen trees, which Balfour described as "my emeralds" and explained, "I like trees." The school buildings arranged around the courtyard consisted of a large T-shaped barracks on the south side, a modern dining hall that could seat the entire complement of 200 students across from the barracks on the north, and a ground school building with numerous classrooms on the western side of the courtyard. To the northwest of the main buildings, workers cleared an area for a recreation field, which included a volleyball court and two tennis courts. Further to the west of the main complex, workers constructed a large hangar that included maintenance shops, equipment storage, a parachute loft, and the Link trainer facility. Workers also updated the field's small existing hangar into a machine shop. Except for the hangars and the original travel lodge, the school buildings were white single-story frame structures with wood shingle roofs stained green. After the first two British courses moved into the new facilities, the school started construction on a 3,200-square-foot gymnasium.

As construction of the school buildings commenced, the city of Miami contracted for improvements to the city-owned airfield as part of the agreement with Spartan. These improvements included a 4,000-foot-long by 100-foot-wide, hard surface runway and a wide aircraft parking apron. The school also leased two grass auxiliary fields from local farmers, one located several miles north and the other several miles west of the main airfield.

By the middle of July, rain had delayed construction in Miami, the Tulsa facility had received more army cadets, and the second British course was en route from Canada. The Tulsa airfield experienced considerable congestion, exacerbated by the accelerated training schedule due to the late arrival of the first course. The RAF officers noted, "flight congestion at Tulsa is very bad and will become dangerous after course 2 arrives." On Sunday, 13 July 1941, in order not to disrupt the training schedule, the first course moved from Tulsa to Miami. Since the new school facilities were incomplete, the students were temporarily housed in the Northeastern Oklahoma Junior College men's dormitory, now vacant due to summer vacation. The British students also ate in the college cafeteria.

Only forty-eight of the original fifty British students moved from Tulsa to Miami. One student had been eliminated due to flying deficiencies. On 11 July, the Friday before the course moved to Miami, the other student, nineteen-year-old Ronald "Dennis" Harrison of Sunderland, England, became the first casualty of the British Flying Training Schools when his primary trainer spun in from low altitude and crashed near Collinsville, Oklahoma, fifteen miles north of Tulsa, killing Harrison.

Great Britain had an extensive history of foreign wars and numerous colonial conflicts associated with its vast empire. Considering Britain's small land area at home, officials had long before decided that servicemen would be buried where they fell. In accordance with this policy, Harrison was buried in the Tulsa Memorial Park cemetery. At the funeral, six members of his course carried the casket, draped with a Union Jack, past an American Legion honor guard. Mrs. W. Dickinson, a local woman who had befriended young Harrison, stood in for his mother. Mr. and Mrs. Dickinson had been born in Harrison's hometown of Sunderland and had emigrated to the United States in 1908. Mrs. Dickinson later related that Harrison had a premonition about his own death and once told her, "you know, I have the strangest feeling I'll never see England again."[24]

At 11:00 pm on 17 July the second course of fifty tired British flight students arrived in Miami. After a short address by Squadron Leader Kermode, these students boarded buses and went directly to the vacant women's dormitory at Northeastern Oklahoma Junior College.

Captain Balfour appointed Charles Reynolds as the school director and Tony Ming, a pilot with twelve years' experience and a former Spartan instructor, as the school's chief flight instructor. Reynolds served in Tulsa and then moved to Miami when the new school opened, but left after one month and Ming became the school director. When the school opened, Balfour transferred Spartan flight and ground school instructors from Tulsa to Miami. In addition to the instructors, twenty-six Spartan aircraft maintenance employees, a welder, a parachute rigger, four flight dispatchers, two men for the school office, and a grounds supervisor also transferred to Miami. Spartan employed more than 200 workers at No. 3 BFTS. Following the British decision to assign a chief flying instructor to each school, Wing Commander D. H. Lee arrived in Miami on 13 August and assumed command.[25]

Course 4 arrived in September, which brought the school up to its full complement of 200 students. New student John A. B. Keeling gave his impressions of the dining hall in a letter home. "The food is still marvelous, and not only good and well cooked and plenty of it, but served up to look nice, as in any good restaurant. We all dine in one room at tables for six with everything laid already for us, and sauces and everything. It works on a cafeteria system. We each collect a tray and pass down a long counter, taking exactly what we want."[26]

Several months later British student Roddy Robertson arrived in Miami and commented on the school. "We arrived on 30th April [1942] and were favorably impressed by the camp. Accommodation was in single storey barrack blocks, clean and airy. Meals were taken in another block on a cafeteria system. The food was very good, varied and plentiful, especially after the austerity of wartime Britain." Robertson also noted, "The camp had a gymnasium and a sports field. In addition to the usual exercise programme in the gym, we all became very keen on basketball. The main game in the sports field was soccer. In town, there was a good open air swimming pool where on one occasion we had an inter-flight swimming competition."[27]

The third week in October 1941 Spartan held an open house at the new school. Local residents and dignitaries got a first look at the recently completed facilities. The open house also coincided with the graduation of the first course. Thirty-six students completed training and departed from Miami with little fanfare.

No. 4 BFTS

After leaving Tulsa, the train carrying the remainder of the second contingent of British students traveled westward and the next day delivered the first course for No. 4 BFTS to Phoenix and the Southwest Airways contract Army Air Corps primary school at Thunderbird Field. As with the other British schools, construction of the school in Mesa had not even begun when the first students arrived. Unfortunately, Thunderbird Field was one of the later contract flight schools in the army expansion program and many of the facilities were still under construction.

Due to the delayed arrival caused by rumors of the German battleship *Bismarck* in the North Atlantic, British officials accelerated the flight training program for No. 3 and No. 4 BFTS in order to keep the schedule in line with No. 1 and No. 2 BFTS. Course schedules for the first four British Flying Training Schools would be the same. Due to the lengthy site selection process and construction delays, No. 5 BFTS would be one course behind and No. 6 BFTS would be two courses behind the first four schools.

Although located on the same field, the training regimens for the British and American flight students at Thunderbird Field were conducted separately. One of the American students, however, later commented that a "friendly rivalry" existed between the two groups. The British and American students shared the constant confusion caused by the hurried construction activity, a massive invasion of crickets swarming over the field, and the notorious extremes of the Arizona climate. Although only the middle of June, afternoon temperatures were already consistently above 100 degrees (which restricted flying).

As in the other schools, the first British students encountered many small, but still frustrating, problems. They arrived in Arizona with only one wool uniform, and no small uniform items such as badges, caps, or belts were available to replace lost items. No provision had been made for other mundane items such as shoe repairs, and the Army Air Corps supply depot designated to support the new school had been unable to implement the recent directive to issue parachutes, flight suits, helmets, goggles, gloves, and other items necessary for flight training. In order to commence training, Southwest Airways personnel scrounged, begged, or borrowed a minimum number of these items from other schools.

No RAF chief ground instructor had arrived in Phoenix, nor had one even been appointed for the new school. Squadron Leader Mills, the chief flying instructor at the temporary home of No. 2 BFTS in Glendale divided his time between the schools in California (which included American Refresher students) and Arizona, and also supervised the last American Refresher school run by Plosser and Prince Air Academy in Bakersfield, California. Squadron Leader Thomas Whitlock, the chief ground instructor in Glendale, also had to be pressed into service in Phoenix. This work load placed a tremendous burden on these officers, especially considering the start-up nature of the two schools.

The No. 4 BFTS flight training program, headed by Southwest Airways' chief pilot, Al Storrs and his assistant, J. G. Coulter, began with twelve instructors. With the rapid expansion of flight training facilities across the United States, Southwest Airways experienced problems hiring sufficient instructors, especially those qualified on advanced aircraft. Only three days after the start of training, ten of the initial instructors traveled to the Army Air Corps airfield in Stockton, California, for a three-week course on advanced aircraft. Other civilian instructors from Southwest's army courses filled in with the first British class.

When the training course ended, the army hired five of the instructors from No. 4 BFTS for the army school. The British resented this, "but as a matter of policy, protests were not pursued." When the remaining five instructors returned (joined by other recently hired instructors, which brought the complement back to the original twelve), they trained other instructors on the Vultee BT-13 basic trainer as the first British course approached the basic phase of training. Later this small core of instructors trained other instructors on the North American AT-6 in time for the first course to begin advanced training.

Group Captain Carnegie's fortuitous enlistment of Southwest Airways following T. Claude Ryan's abrupt departure from the program allowed the construction of the new school in Mesa to proceed only a couple of weeks behind the school in Miami and about a month behind the schools in Terrell and Lancaster. Following the signing of the various legal documents, John Connelly and Leland Hayward, owners of Southwest Airways, selected architect Millard Sheets to design the new school facilities and the Stover Company of Claremont, California, to be the general contractor.

On 16 July, Mesa mayor George Goodman and Arizona governor Sidney Osborn presided over ground-breaking ceremonies for the new school. Visitors arriving for the ceremony noted that outlines of most of the school buildings had already been staked out and other preliminary work had begun. The local newspaper held a contest to name the airfield and Mesa city engineer E. B. Tucker won the prize of an airplane tour of the Salt River Valley for two by submitting the winning name of Falcon Field.[28] An appropriate name in every way since the falcon is a British sporting bird of prey, the name also complemented the Southwest Airways contract school at Thunderbird Field.

Construction proceeded rapidly and by the end of the first week in August the local newspaper reported, "construction was well underway, workmen were progressing on concrete footings and floors, and two carloads of materials had arrived for the big buildings."[29] The new school consisted of four L-shaped single-story barracks arranged around a central quadrangle. Sidewalks across the quadrangle connected the buildings. The ground school, dining hall, and other school buildings (also single-story frame) were clustered together to the east side of the quadrangle. Just to the north of the building complex, two massive steel-framed hangars and a flight operations building topped by a glass-enclosed control tower were located on an expansive aircraft parking apron.

Due to construction delays in Mesa, the first three British courses arrived at Thunderbird Field and began training. Since the first course had arrived two weeks late, students had to catch up by flying on weekends and days off. With more British students and army cadets arriving at Thunderbird Field, basic training for the first British course had to be conducted from one of the auxiliary fields, which the British officers described as, "dusty, hot, and generally uncomfortable." The long hours and primitive conditions, however, served as a stimulus and the British officers noted, "these disadvantages were greatly overshadowed by the enthusiasm and co-operation of both cadets and instructors."[30]

British students of the first three courses started moving to Falcon Field on 25 September, even though the new school was still under construction, and were joined the next day by the arrival of Course 4 from Canada. Soon after they arrived, the new students formed next to the incomplete hangars; names were called out and assigned to instructors. Newly hired instructor Ray Corn remembered that day: "After meeting my students, I went to Phoenix to the Maricopa County Courthouse to marry Nell Marie Seay. I paid two dollars for the license and found Justice of the Peace Harry Wesfall in his office where he married us at no charge. It was the best deal I ever got!"[31]

Students and staff found the new school far from complete and students had to be initially housed in the unfinished hangar. A visitor noted, "the kitchen is not completely equipped but functioning." A newly hired ground school instructor reported to Falcon Field and found "a few semi-finished buildings, a few foundations being laid, and carpenters, painters, plumbers, and electricians dashing wildly around looking efficient. But then who could work up any enthusiasm when the temperature was one hundred and twenty degrees and the nearest shade was seven miles away, in Mesa."[32]

Ground school classes were held in the unfinished barracks with students sitting on the floor. Workmen swarmed everywhere, tools and building materials cluttered every space, and the sound of construction permeated all of the buildings. Water faucets emitted a trickle of milky brown substance when turned and dust, heat, and swarms of insects aggravated the situation.

In the distance, swirling dust devils moved across the dry desert landscape of sand, rocks, low scraggly vegetation, and dry washes. Stately Saguaro cactus, which grew to heights of more than fifty feet and lived to be more than two hundred years old, dotted the desert floor. Heat thermals caused the distant stark reddish-brown mountains to shimmer on the horizon. Rather than being depressed by the bleak surroundings, the British students were captivated by the austere beauty of the desert landscape and enthralled by what they considered to be their American wild west adventure.

When the school opened, takeoffs and landings were conducted from the hard desert sand. It would be several weeks before workers completed laying asphalt on the apron and runways. Falcon Field would eventually have five wide, hard-surface runways.

The unfinished facilities at Falcon Field were not the only problem. Aircraft deliveries to the new school were consistently behind schedule. The late deliveries only aggravated an already difficult situation since the first two courses were flying an accelerated schedule. The RAF officers commented on the situation: "The intensive flying placed an obvious strain upon the students and particularly upon the School Staff giving up their leisure hours, and their support and efforts is considered to be commendable."[33]

A shortage of some routine maintenance items such as tachometers for the Stearman primary trainers and a lack of tail wheel tire inner tubes seem trivial, but still rendered aircraft unserviceable and caused disruptions to the training schedule. Although twenty Vultee BT-13 basic trainers had been delivered prior to the start of basic training, only five were serviceable due to leaking fuel tanks. Vultee supplied repair kits, but the repairs proved to be lengthy and frustrating. Most of the Course 1 basic training was carried out on five aircraft. The first AT-6 Harvards did not arrive in Mesa until ten days after the scheduled commencement of advanced training. Link trainers also arrived late and students of the first two courses graduated with considerably less than the prescribed number of instrument hours.

British training supplies also arrived late. Since the school's civilian ground school instructors lacked experience in certain British subjects, students with service experience were used to prepare lesson plans and in some cases actually taught classes. The early use of British students in ground school subjects also occurred in other BFTS schools.

Recreation facilities were virtually nonexistent when the school opened, but slowly improved. The school added "two billiard tables, two table tennis tables, and badminton sets." The RAF staff later reported, "Every effort was made to provide recreation, games were played on the grounds of Mesa and Tempe Colleges, the authorities of which kindly placed their flood lit fields at the disposal of the pupils." By the time Course 2 neared the end of training another report stated, "Work is progressing at high pressure on sports grounds which will include football and cricket pitches and two tennis courts."[34]

The RAF staff situation slowly improved. Squadron Leader William T. Holloway arrived as the school's permanent chief ground instructor. Flight Lieutenant E. C. Metcalf reported to the school as the administrative officer four months after the first British students arrived in Arizona. Metcalf had been an investment banker in London before the war and also a top-ranked tennis player who had played on several British teams in international matches. He commented to a local reporter, "I joined the RAF because I thought I should do my part."[35] The officers were joined by Sergeant J. G. McCowan, the armament NCO.

The final class report for Course 1 listed the numerous problems encountered by the new school and then catalogued in graphic detail the numerous flying deficiencies of the first course. This extremely negative report, which faulted virtually every phase of the early training at No. 4 BFTS, concluded on a positive note. "The manner in which No. 1 Course pupils overcame the numerous difficulties with which they were confronted from the commencement of training is deserving of very high praise."[36]

In spite of the early problems, or maybe as a reward for the numerous hardships, Southwest Airways staged a gala graduation party for the first course. The dinner dance was held in the just completed east hangar, which had been decorated and featured a live orchestra. Guests that night included Southwest Airways executives and twenty-five-year-old Hollywood film star Dorothy McGuire. One of the school's office workers commented on the party: "All sorts of dignitaries—civilian, military, the socially prominent and their daughters from around the valley were invited."[37]

Following graduation, the first course departed for Canada, the construction chaos diminished, new aircraft and equipment, as well as new courses arrived in Mesa, and the training activity accelerated. The final report for Course 2 concluded, "a considerable improvement has been made in the flying instruction generally."[38]

No. 5 BFTS

On 17 July 1941 the first British students destined for No. 5 BFTS arrived at Carlstrom Field in Arcadia, Florida, the home of John Paul Riddle's Army Air Corps contract primary school. Besides the army cadets, this school also housed British students in the Arnold Scheme. The first course would be one course behind the first four British Flying Training Schools. The first two No. 5 BFTS courses began training at Carlstrom Field until the permanent school in Clewiston, Florida, could be completed.

Riddle's contract school at Carlstrom Field had been designed for the fairly standard complement of 250 Army Air Corps flight cadets, but the design also allowed for future expansion. By the time the first No. 5 BFTS students arrived in Arcadia, construction had begun to enlarge the school to 650 students. The expansion activity and the arrival of the BFTS students only exacerbated existing problems at the school.

The British students training at Carlstrom Field under the Arnold Scheme were subject to the Army Air Forces rigid form of discipline, which included hazing by upper-classmen and myriad rules and regulations. The British Arnold Scheme students also had to discard the RAF form of drill (140 steps per minute, arms swinging shoulder high, and rifle on the left shoulder) and learn the American close order style drill (120 steps per minute, natural arm swing, and rifle on the right shoulder). Infractions of the rules resulted in demerits, which were worked off by long tours marching around the flight line in the hot sun. Most of the RAF students, now labeled "cadets" (a term the British disliked), viewed the army system as petty and offensive. These young men were fresh from a nation at war and their overriding desire was to learn to fly as quickly as possible and return to help their beleaguered country. Most of the British students endured the army system out of an overwhelming desire to learn to fly, but a certain resentment remained, especially among those students who had been on active service.

The addition of British students destined for No. 5 BFTS highlighted the differences between the British and American flight training systems. The British Flying Training School students were learning to fly under the RAF flight training syllabus, supervised by RAF officers, and under a different and more relaxed form of discipline. This only added to the Arnold Scheme students' resentment. Also adding to the tension and congestion, cadets from another unfinished Embry-Riddle army contract primary school also came to Carlstrom Field until their school could be completed. Due to the construction delays at Clewiston, the second course of British students destined for No. 5 BFTS also arrived at Carlstrom Field to begin training, adding to the congestion.

The differences in the flight training systems, the disruption caused by the construction activity, and the congestion at Carlstrom Field, which resulted in seven-day-a-week training schedules, all led to heightened resentment. The Florida weather also conspired against the school. Russell Cooke, a member of the first No. 5 BFTS course, described a typical occurrence in a letter home: "It's raining. Fifteen minutes ago the sun was shining brightly and now it's a terrific storm. Half the boys are down at the hangars where they thought that they would be flying, but as it happened yesterday afternoon as well, it's all off for today. The rain is coming down in sheets, the camp is now like a lake and the palm trees are tearing at their roots."[39]

Even the food, usually a delight to the British students, proved disappointing at Carlstrom Field. A British student described the situation. "The food is getting quite a problem. We just can't eat all the macaroni and noodles, asparagus and spinach and the stuff they call meat or fish. We don't even get our rations equivalent. Have never seen any cheese, only small pats of butter and very rotten bacon. So that's why we like to get out on the weekends and get some good food in a hotel for a change."[40]

In spite of the best efforts of the American and British officers, and the civilian staff, the situation at Carlstrom Field eased only when the Clewiston facilities neared completion and the first two No. 5 BFTS courses moved to the new school in late September.

Even though the Clewiston location had been one of the first sites to be approved, the No. 5 BFTS facilities took longer to construct, cost considerably more to build, and opened later than the other schools, except for No. 6 BFTS in Oklahoma. By the middle of July, when construction of the first four schools was well underway, the local newspaper reported on recent rumors: "Although no official announcement has been made in Washington it appears virtually certain that a civil contract flying school will be established by the J. P. Riddle Corporation on a site eight miles west of Clewiston."[41]

The reasons for the delays were many. The final site negotiations were prolonged (the state of Florida owned 140 acres of the site and other portions required foreclosure to clear title defects), adverse weather plagued the construction, and the school experienced the typical building material shortages. All of these added to a final factor unique to this school.

All of the school operators in the new British program, except John Paul Riddle, saw the British Flying Training Schools as a matter of wartime expedience. The various schools were competently designed and constructed, efficiently laid out, and provided training facilities comparable to other American military installations of the time (and considerably better than many of the temporary facilities in England), but the operators envisioned only a wartime use for the schools.

Riddle, however, envisioned his schools, the army contract schools, the Arnold Scheme school, and No. 5 BFTS, as having a postwar use. Riddle believed that there would be a need for advanced aviation training facilities after the war in order to adequately train a new generation of civilian pilots and mechanics in the complex technological advances generated by the war. Riddle also believed that a flight student's performance improved by training in a pleasant learning environment.

Not only did the Army Air Corps not fully agree with Riddle's views, some army officials actually felt that Riddle's ideas were too radical and might not be compatible with army training methods. Riddle persisted, however, and hired famed Miami, Florida, architect Stefan Zachar to design his schools with the twin goals of creating a pleasing learning environment and with Riddle's postwar vision in mind. The final cost to build the new British school in Clewiston would be more than $1.3 million, three to five times the amount required to build the other British schools. Riddle's long-term goals, although commendable, would cause serious short-term financial problems for his firm.

Stefan Zachar had set new architectural standards for flight schools when he designed John Paul Riddle's two contract schools in Arcadia and continued the same high standard at No. 5 BFTS. Clewiston's newly named Riddle Field consisted of two major grass takeoff and landing areas arranged in a V pattern. This arrangement allowed takeoffs and landings according to the prevailing winds, which largely negated the adverse effects of cross winds. The conventional gear trainers flown by students with limited experience were highly susceptible to mishaps in cross winds, especially strong gusty cross winds.

A large 90 x 31-foot swimming pool formed the centerpiece of Zachar's school design. Major buildings, including two large barracks with individual rooms each housing four students and the administration building, were arranged around the swimming pool. Other buildings, including several smaller barracks, a large dining hall, a U-shaped recreation hall, flight operations building, a ground school building, and an infirmary, were arranged around the landscaped campus located inside the V formed by the two runways. In a departure from the standard frame buildings found on other bases, the No. 5 BFTS colonial-style buildings were built of haydite block covered with white stucco. Outdoor recreation facilities included four tennis courts, a basketball court, and volleyball courts.

A characteristic of Zachar's other school designs had been a distinctive ring road, which formed a border around the buildings and afforded excellent access. In one Arcadia school Zachar utilized a circular ring road and in the other school an oval ring road. Zachar selected a diamond-shaped ring road for the Clewiston school, which blended aesthetically with the V pattern of the runways. Only the large hangars and the aircraft parking apron were located outside the ring road at the apex of the V formed by the runways.

As soon as the various site issues were resolved, C. W. McSheehan, supervisor for the Miami-based construction firm of C. F. Wheeler, arrived in town and immediately began hiring local laborers. As construction activity intensified, an early observer commented that the grounds were "filled with piles of lumber, concrete blocks, building steel, etc., which the poor defenseless pedestrian must go over, around or under all the while dodging the literally thousands of trucks, steam shovels and tractors which go charging madly all over the place."[42]

Besides the normal construction delays caused by a shortage of building materials experienced by all of the new British schools, No. 5 BFTS encountered its own unique problems. The construction activity dislodged numerous large rattlesnake dens, Clewiston experienced several days of record high temperatures (along with oppressively high humidity) in August, and heavy rains in September slowed progress. John Paul Riddle often visited the construction and urged the workers to greater efforts. Instead of generating resentment, most of the workers came to embrace Riddle's infectious enthusiasm. On the construction site Riddle often repeated a familiar phrase. "The quicker we get this job done, the faster we can train those British kids to fly."[43]

John Paul Riddle selected G. Willis Tyler an Embry-Riddle employee at Carlstrom Field to be the general manager of the new Clewiston school. Tyler, a native of Manchester, England, had a varied aviation career that included barnstorming throughout the western United States during the 1920s, flying for a California airline, and working for the Civil

Aeronautics Association. In addition to his other pursuits, Tyler had also operated his own flight school. As Tyler and other personnel for the new school, including C. E. Bjornsen, the chief ground instructor, arrived in town, many of the employees took rooms in the Clewiston Inn.

The inn had been built by Southern Sugar Company in 1926 to house visiting company officials and dignitaries. The inn, which had survived several hurricanes, burned in 1937. Rebuilt in 1938, the classical revival style hotel served as home to many Riddle employees throughout the war. John Paul Riddle incorporated the new school as a separate entity, the Riddle-McKay Aero College, but most people continued to refer to the school as Embry-Riddle.

The civilian employees were soon joined by the RAF staff. Wing Commander K. J. Rampling, who had completed a tour of operations with Bomber Command, arrived as the chief flying instructor and Squadron Leader George Burdick arrived as the chief ground instructor. When the BFTS staffs increased, these officers were joined by Flight Lieutenant G. W. Nickerson, the administrative officer, Flying Officer William Reinhart, the navigation officer, and two enlisted personnel, Sergeant J. Henley and Sergeant T. Pullin.

As construction of the school buildings proceeded, the local phone company extended the phone line five and a half miles to the school site. The new line accommodated the five new circuits required for the school. Although school personnel would staff the school switchboard, the phone company announced that now two operators would be on duty in Clewiston each day from 8:00 a.m. to 8:00 p.m. (except of course during lunch time).

On 25 September the eighty-nine remaining students of the first two No. 5 BFTS courses boarded buses in Arcadia and arrived in Clewiston later that day. Even after the first two courses had moved to the new school and had been joined a week later by Course 3, the school facilities remained very much under construction. Ground school classes were conducted in several makeshift areas, the recreation building remained unfinished, and even the swimming pool had yet to be completed. When Course 4 arrived in Clewiston in early November, the school offices were operating temporarily out of the last vacant barracks building, and the administration building and recreation hall were only then nearing completion.

The newly arrived students at least found the food situation in Clewiston much improved over that at Carlstrom Field. One student described the meals: "The food is beyond imagination. The caterer says he just works to make us feel at home and is truly a great chap at heart. He gets just what we like and although we have been here a week we have had nothing twice for any meal. Fresh pineapple and lime drinks, salads beautifully prepared, etc."[44]

As the initial confusion began to subside, a hurricane in October stopped both construction and training. Instructors and students flew the aircraft 200 miles north to Ocala in deteriorating weather to escape the storm. British students were assigned to fly the primary trainers, while the instructors flew the twenty basic and four newly arrived advanced trainers to safety. Russell Cooke of Course 1 had just entered basic flight training when the storm approached. "All we had was a shaving kit plus the uniform we wore. I was given a P.T. to take solo and I am glad to say I kept it all the time and have brought it back unhurt."[45]

The training schedule continued along with the hurried construction activity and weather interruptions. Course 3, the first course to travel directly to Clewiston, set an almost unheard-of record when all fifty members completed primary training without a single wash-out. One student, A. D. Rigg, bailed out of his Harvard advanced trainer at the incredibly low altitude of 500 feet after a propeller blade separated in flight and the resulting vibration tore the engine loose from its mounts. Rigg miraculously survived with only a small broken bone in his ankle.

Conditions at Riddle Field were graphically illustrated in a letter by a member of the first course, destined to take the final ground school exam, known as the Wings Exam, in two weeks and graduate in less than three weeks.

> We are now having five hours Ground School a day as well as flying and P.T. The latter we are now having before sunrise. Next week I have two large cross countries to do. The latter is a six hundred mile trip, the equivalent of a flight from home into the heart of Germany. Great news this week was the opening of our canteen complex with soda bar and lounge. Our first hangar is now springing up. Our Ground School is now complete though the painters are still working in the rooms during class. Our administration building is just in use and provides a home for the typists and our two R.A.F. officers.[46]

As the school buildings neared completion, large palm trees were hauled in and planted. The first prefabricated hangar, designed to house sixty aircraft, ordered from Starr Manufacturing Company in Oklahoma City, neared completion in late November. Construction of a second hangar started shortly after the first hangar had been completed.

Also toward the end of November, as the school facilities neared completion, the thirty-seven remaining members of the first course graduated. There was little ceremony except for a dinner at the Quarterback Club in Miami. No wings had been sent to the school and no decision had been made concerning commissions. The entire class graduated as sergeants, bade goodbye to the residents of Clewiston and returned to Canada where about one-third of the class belatedly received commissions.

No. 6 BFTS

By midsummer 1941, each of the British schools, except No. 6 BFTS, had received their initial complement of students and had begun training at the operator's nearby army contract facilities. Because of the delayed site selection process, and the fact that No. 6 BFTS finally located in

Oklahoma, far from Harold Darr's other flight training facilities, students destined for this school started training literally amidst the construction of the new school.

Harold Darr and Ponca City mayor Frank Overstreet signed the contract for the use of the municipal airport and the thirty-acre school site at the north end of the airport on 4 August 1941. Under the terms of the agreement, the city agreed to expand the airport property, make certain improvements, extend utility lines to the school site, and construct a hard-surface aircraft parking apron adjacent to the school along with taxiways from the apron to the existing airport runways.

On 13 August, work finally commenced on the new school. The local newspaper announced, "all competent carpenters reporting to the work site, north end of the municipal airport, will be hired by the contractor building the Darr School of Aeronautics hangars, barracks and other buildings." The paper quoted P. W. King, the construction supervisor, "we can use 125 carpenters if we can get them."[47] King had previously supervised construction of Darr's contract army primary schools in Georgia and Florida.

Local architect Joe Cannon designed the new school facilities, which included an administration building, a ground school classroom building, a dining hall, a combination recreation hall and library, Link trainer building, and four barracks. Each barrack housed fifty students and had two wings separated by lavatories and an area for relaxation, which contained a ping pong table, radio, and piano. The initial work concentrated on the first two barracks, which were rushed to completion. Work also commenced on the first large 206-foot by 124-foot steel-framed hangar.

Local general contractor Dick Sherbon experienced the now familiar construction delays resulting from the nationwide shortage of building materials. In particularly short supply was the water line required for the school. City officials, as well as Oklahoma congressman Ros Rizley, had to be called upon to exert influence to speed delivery of the water pipe from the Alabama steel mill. Even though the Ponca City school held the highest wartime priority rating for the procurement of critical materials, virtually every other project in the country held the same rating, which effectively rendered the priority system meaningless.

The first students arrived only two weeks after the start of construction. The first fifty tired students disembarked from the Santa Fe Streamliner on the night of 26 August in a light drizzle of rain. Even though the arrival had not been announced, the RAF students were greeted by school officials and a small group of local residents. Buses transported the students to the Ponca Military Academy, a private military school, located four and a half miles from the airport. The Academy had offered the new British school the use of its facilities, now vacant due to summer vacation.

Squadron Leader H. F. Suren, the newly appointed No. 6 BFTS chief ground instructor, arrived in Ponca City earlier the same day as the first British students. Suren, a former cavalryman, was the only permanent RAF officer assigned to the school. Wing Commander Hilton from No. 1 BFTS, three hundred miles to the south, had to fill in as the school's chief flying instructor. While some records referred to Hilton as the school's commanding officer, another reference, somewhat uncharitably, only mentioned that Hilton, "visited the school at intervals."[48]

Flying Officer M. O'Callaghan arrived as the school's administrative officer two and a half months after the first students, followed two months later by Sergeant H. Gray, the new armament NCO. Wing Commander C. A. Ball, the school's permanent chief flying instructor and commanding officer, did not arrive in Ponca City until May 1942, eight months after the first students.

Before the first students arrived, six Stearman PT-17 primary trainers had been delivered to the Ponca City airport from the Boeing plant in Wichita, Kansas. Four more primary trainers were delivered the day the first students arrived and nine more were delivered two days later, in time for the start of flight training.

The students of the first course were given two days' rest then started the flight training program. Ground school classes were held at the Ponca Military Academy, students ate in the Academy dining hall and buses transported students to the airfield where flight training commenced. The primary trainers took off and landed alongside the hurried construction activities at the north end of the airfield.

Harold Darr promoted DRoss Ellis from his Albany, Georgia, school to be director of the new Ponca City school. Ellis originally came from Stillwater, Oklahoma, had graduated from Oklahoma A&M College in 1930, and held a reserve commission in the Army Air Corps. Three instructors, Henry "Hank" Jerger, B. G. Dewit, and Paul F. Victor organized the flight training program, while Herbert Glasser, another Darr employee from Georgia, arrived in town to head the maintenance department. V. L. "Casey" Jones, previously with Darr's Augusta, Georgia, army contract primary school, became head of the ground school department. Jones arrived in Ponca City the day after construction commenced and immediately started hiring ground school instructors and Link trainer operators from temporary office space in the First National Bank building. Ellis arrived in Ponca City two days later.

The school encountered difficulties hiring trained flight instructors due to the rapid expansion of training facilities across the United States. Ellis estimated that the school would initially need forty instructors. In response to this urgent need, the school offered to hire pilots without an instructors rating. Ellis explained the process to a local reporter: "We will give them a course and prepare them to pass the regular civil aeronautics administration exams."[49] The pilots were paid a salary during this training period and then immediately hired as flight instructors after passing the required tests.

Course 2 arrived in Ponca City on 30 September and went directly to the Ponca Military Academy. Several days later the newly arrived students, along with the first course, moved into the first two, almost completed, school barracks. The move had been slightly delayed until the large dining hall could be completed and fully equipped.

As in other locations, linguistic differences between the British students and their American cousins quickly became apparent. A new student observing the hurried construction activity approached an elderly carpenter with a question. "This place has been shot up, hasn't it?", meaning the school had been built quickly. The workman looked puzzled, then replied, "Waal, the Indians did kinda shoot a bit in the old days, but that were some time ago."[50]

By the middle of October the school buildings were nearing completion and the contractor entered the final stage of construction, an extensive landscaping of the campus to include more than forty trees of varied types along with numerous plants and shrubs. The first large prefabricated steel-framed hangar neared completion in late November, while construction started on two additional hangars. At the entrance to the school both the United States and British flags flew from adjacent flagpoles.

The remaining members of the first course graduated without ceremony and departed from Ponca City on 23 January 1942. The school Operations Record Book noted simply, "29 Pupils of No. 1 Course posted to Moncton, N.B., Canada, on completion of Flying Training."

During the year following the initial construction, the school added a recreation center, library, and tennis court. In September 1942, local oilman and philanthropist Lew Wentz generously donated a swimming pool to the school. The swimming pool became an instant hit in the summer heat.

No. 7 BFTS

After the initial six British Flying Training Schools opened, British officials began to consider expansion, although by early 1942 it had become apparent that the various training schemes, both in the United

States and around the world, were producing pilots at a rate that would soon exceed Royal Air Force requirements. The Air Ministry reported a slow down in the expansion of front-line strength which "would lead to our having a considerable surplus of pilots during the whole of 1942."[51]

Large differences of opinion still existed concerning future require-ments and especially projections of future losses. In order to meet any contingencies (and, some have suggested, to take full advantage of readily available lend-lease funds), British officials requested another flight school in the United States. Documents pertaining to the British request or even the true motivation for requesting another school are virtually nonexistent. American officials obviously agreed, even though Army Air Forces and Navy expansion continued to take many of the suitable training sites.

British officials selected Plosser and Prince Air Academy to operate the new British school. Joe Plosser and Charles Prince operated an Army Air Forces contract primary school in Bakersfield, California, known as Aeronautical Training Centre, and another school in Seeley, California, which housed American Refresher students destined for the RAF. After the United States entered the war, the government commandeered the Seeley school for Marine Corps expansion. Officials, however, recommended an alternate site in Texas where Plosser and Prince could locate the new British school and continue Refresher training.

The citizens of Sweetwater, Texas, led by city manager R. C. Hoppe and the usual consortium of city officials, local business leaders, and the Chamber of Commerce, had sought a flight training school for their city for some time without success.

Sweetwater is located forty miles west of Abilene, Texas, and 400 miles east of El Paso on Highway 80. The town is also at the intersection of the east-west main line of the Texas & Pacific Railroad and the north-south line of the Santa Fe railroad.

Sweetwater had been founded in the late nineteenth century on the banks of the Sweetwater Creek by traders following buffalo hunters and government surveyors. The settlement grew from a single dugout store in 1877 in spite of weather extremes, which included a severe drought in 1886–87 and a devastating blizzard in 1885. The Texas & Pacific Railroad arrived in 1881.

By 1940 Sweetwater had 10,848 inhabitants and had grown into a shipping center for local ranching and agriculture. The town also had two oil refineries and several large plants to process recently discovered nearby gypsum deposits. Sweetwater also had the advantage of an excellent, but little used, municipal airport.

Local residents began to realize the town's strategic importance when the record-breaking Army Air Service around-the-world flight stopped in Sweetwater for fuel and minor repairs in September 1924. The next month the U.S. Navy airship USS *Shenandoah* flew over Sweetwater on the first nonstop cross-country flight. Virtually all activities in town stopped as enthralled citizens watched the giant airship cruise majestically over Sweetwater at sixty miles-per-hour.

Early itinerant flyers and barnstormers had used an abandoned polo field on the outskirts of town. With interest in aviation running high, Sweetwater built a new municipal airport five miles west of town. The official dedication, held on 10 August 1929 drew thousands of spectators and featured speeches, demonstrations by army flyers, parachute jumpers, and various other aerial performers. After mayor C. W. Bryant proclaimed "the city of Sweetwater, Texas, was officially launched into the Air Age," the mayor and other dignitaries boarded a Southwest Air Fast Express Ford Tri-motor for the inaugural flight to Tulsa.[52]

The new airport formed an important stop during the early period of transcontinental airline travel when passengers traveled by a combination of air and rail due to the risky nature of aerial night flights. The onset of the Depression severely limited travel in general and especially air travel. With declining revenues, airlines discontinued the Sweetwater service and the airport fell into disuse.

Private flyers, including several notables such as famed aviator Wiley Post, continued to use the airport, but the condition declined until one source described the airport as "a liability."[53] A 1935 Works Progress Administration grant authorized $45,700 for much-needed improvements, but the Sweetwater airport continued to be little used.

After war broke out in Europe and the Far East, an October 1940 congressional act appropriated federal funds to improve certain municipal airports that in the future could be deemed "as necessary for national defense."[54] The city of Sweetwater implemented plans to qualify for funds under the new legislation. In return, the United States government allocated $190,000 for airport improvements. Contractors completed the majority of the work by the end of 1941.[55]

Considerable efforts by city leaders to secure an army basic flight school failed and the city found no civilian flight school operators interested in the site. In the spring of 1942 an inspection team from the Gulf Coast Training Command recommended the airport as a possible site for the new British school.

Plosser and Prince traveled to Sweetwater and found the location at the municipal airport to be completely satisfactory. The city agreed to lease the site to the Defense Plant Corporation (which in turn leased it to the new school) for ten years at one dollar per year. The city also agreed to lay a new water line to the airport boundary and then split the cost of extending the water line to the school site.[56] In return, Plosser and Prince agreed to construct the new school facilities estimated to cost around $300,000. Relieved after the earlier disappointments, the local newspaper announced, "Sweetwater finally has been assured of a flying school."[57]

Plosser and Prince hired California contractor Victor Nelson to build the new school. Nelson had been the general contractor for Major Moseley's No. 2 BFTS and was familiar with the procedures and general construction requirements for the British flight schools. Nelson arrived in Sweetwater and construction started four days after the initial announcement.

As work on the new school got underway, the local newspaper sponsored a contest to name the airfield. Mrs. Grace Favor, a junior high school teacher, won the fifty-dollar War Bond prize with her suggestion of Avenger Field.[58] Her submittal also included the following poem, which accurately reflected the national mood in the months following the attack on Pearl Harbor.

> Built on a Texas hillside in a land
> Of proud tradition, filled with tales of brave
> And stalwart men who gave their precious lives
> Wrongs to avenge, that Freedom's flag might wave—
> Avenger Field, your sons shall issue forth
> Through troublous skies in peril to prevail,
> The Tyrant to subdue to make right the wrong
> On mighty wings these heroes shall not fail.
>
> Sleep on martyr'd dead, you have not died in vain!
> The torch we'll bear . . . nor to the despot yield
> 'Til all is safe for peace throughout the world.
> Your purpose shall be served, Avenger Field![59]

Work proceeded rapidly on the fairly standard single-story white frame buildings built on concrete foundations. The buildings included two barracks, administration, ground school, dining hall, recreation hall, Link trainer, and a theater in addition to two large metal hangars. At the end of one of the hangars workers constructed a two-story frame operations building with outside stairs leading to a glass control tower surrounded by an open walkway. Across the front of the second story of the operations building large black letters proclaimed "Plosser-Prince Air Academy" and centered underneath in slightly smaller letters "Avenger Field" and below that a blue circle enclosed a white star with stylized wings reaching upward.

A new access road from Highway 80 and a 500-foot railroad spur were constructed to serve the flight school. Little in the way of outside recreation facilities were included in the initial construction except for a large open area for calisthenics and group sports. Plosser and Prince also leased two 640-acre auxiliary fields located ten miles and fifteen miles west of the main airfield.

In early June 1942, with construction progressing in spite of a shortage of certain materials, Group Captain Carnegie, Joe Plosser, and Charles Prince inspected the new school. The trio expressed satisfaction with the progress, although they did note that not all of the construction would be completed before the first course arrived. The first students were scheduled to arrive in Sweetwater sometime after the middle of the month.

With construction well underway, the civilian staff for the new school, which included manager R. E. Olin, director of training C. W. Seaton, advanced flight instructor Kenneth Freidkin, and maintenance supervisor Charles Jenkinson, began arriving in town. Olin, Seaton, and Freidkin, along with several ground school instructors and other employees, had been with Plosser and Prince for some time and transferred from California. Building maintenance, cafeteria, and custodial workers were recruited locally. As with the other British schools, the school facilities housed only the students. Staff members, both civilian and RAF, found lodging in town. Sweetwater, like its sister cities with new flight schools, experienced a housing shortage.

The main construction delay resulted from a shortage of building materials common in a nation faced with unprecedented construction activity. In particularly short supply was the six-inch water line which proved impossible to secure. The first British students arrived and began training before completion of the water line. In order for the school to open, water had to be trucked from town each day, resulting in a strict water rationing program. The contractor finally located a supply of nine-inch pipe, which was substituted for the original specification.

Wing Commander Frederick W. Moxham, the school's chief flying instructor and commanding officer, arrived in Sweetwater on 11 June. A native of Deel, England, Moxham had been in charge of training Polish pilots for the RAF before coming to the United States. Moxham told a local reporter that as a small boy he had dreamed of coming to the United States and especially to Texas, "where I thought I would like to be a Texas Ranger."[60] The other RAF officers and enlisted men assigned to the school arrived in town shortly thereafter. These staff members included Squadron Leader Ralph Edwards, the chief ground instructor, Flight Lieutenant James Lewis, the administrative officer, Sergeant James Roland, the armament NCO, and two corporals.

The first course arrived in Sweetwater by train on Saturday afternoon, 20 June.[61] They were joined by the displaced American Refresher students transferred from the Plosser and Prince school in California. Some of the American students drove to Sweetwater in their own automobiles, which fascinated the British students. Since the barracks had not been completed, the first students were temporarily housed in the elegant seven-story Blue Bonnet Hotel in Sweetwater.

Wing Commander Moxham hired Mary Curry to be his secretary. Curry, a young woman in her early twenties with a husband in the army, became the only woman at the school. She found the British students to be "just kids away from home and homesick" as well as "very polite compared to Americans." Curry's duties included the daily afternoon ritual of preparing tea for the British staff. She also recalled one of the British noncommissioned officers as "a cockney which required an interpreter to understand anytime I talked to him."[62]

As with the other British Flying Training Schools, the first students began the new realm of flight training against a background of unfinished facilities, novel sights and customs, broad landscapes, limitless skies, plenty of fresh food, and an abundance of unreserved hospitality. During their limited free time, the British students were invited to local homes, attended church services, swam in the municipal pool, were guests at local ranches and attended picnics, barbeques, and dances, often arranged in their honor.

With flight training underway at Avenger Field, the city of Sweetwater staged the largest local celebration ever held to commemorate the 1942 Fourth of July. At the opening ceremony held in the high school athletic stadium, horsemen carried the flags of twenty-six of the Allied nations, while Boy Scouts in uniform formed a giant "V" for victory. The all-day event included parades, fireworks, patriotic speeches, picnics, and an abundance of flags, as well as an open house and official dedication at Avenger Field.

The patriotic crowd that came to the airfield thrilled to aerobatic displays flown by the new school's flight instructors followed by a demonstration of formation flying and precision maneuvers by army pilots from Midland Army Air Field. High-ranking officers from the Gulf Coast Training Command along with officers from several West Texas army bases attended the celebration. The USO entertainment unit from the 395th Infantry presented an hour-long musical comedy show, the Sweetwater high school band performed, and a contingent of British students sang a variety of songs, which concluded with a stirring rendition of "Deep in the Heart of Texas" delighting the local crowd. Everyone pronounced the event a huge success. Sweetwater, Texas, had finally joined the national war effort.

Several days after the elaborate Independence Day celebration, and less than three weeks after the first British students arrived in Sweetwater, both the school and the city received official notice that No. 7 British Flying Training School would close.

City officials, as well as local residents, were stunned. No one seemed to have any information. Wing Commander Moxham said only that he had received instructions "to move his contingent of RAF students from Avenger Field in early August" and added that he did not even know where he was to go.[63] In the short time that it had taken to construct the school, Army Air Forces officials faced with unprecedented expansion had decided to take over No. 2 BFTS in Lancaster, California, as well as No. 7 BFTS. The Sweetwater school would train USAAF primary flight cadets while the Lancaster school would be expanded into a civilian contract basic flight school.

Flight training continued while questions regarding the future of the British students and the RAF staff remained unanswered and army personnel arrived to prepare for the transition to an Army Air Forces contract primary school. Each morning half of the first (and now only) course assembled on the flight line while the other half reported for ground school. As classroom lessons began, dispatchers armed with clipboards and numerous forms scurried about the flight line calling out aircraft assignments, while instructors and students discussed the day's session. As the West Texas sun rose higher, the Stearman engines slowly turned over, then one after another coughed into life amidst clouds of blue-gray smoke. The trainers formed a long line taxiing to the end of the runway and then the airfield reverberated to the sound of engines advanced to full power as the planes took off and fanned out over the semiarid rolling plains.

The British students soloed, studied, sweated ground school exams, flew periodic check flights, were introduced to the mysteries of the Link trainer and instrument flight, then began to venture out on cross-country flights. Students began night flying with the natural apprehension associated with taking off into a black sky aided by only a few instruments, a flickering flare path, and limited ground references. Unfortunately, some of those who had arrived in Sweetwater were eliminated from flight training and returned to Canada for reassignment. But the remaining students were becoming pilots.

Toward the end of the first week in August the first USAAF aviation cadets arrived in Sweetwater and moved into the unused portions of the school barracks. The army cadets began flight training alongside the British students who were completing primary training. A classmate of British student Jimmy Gill took a snapshot of Gill standing in front of the school barracks. Gill wrote on the back of the photo, "August 1st 1942 Temperature 112 in the shade."

The British students of the only course at No. 7 BFTS finished the primary phase of flight training and then left Sweetwater on 15 August. Local residents gathered at the train station to say goodbye. Only one British student remained behind. Frank Ashworth had been injured in a serious auto accident, which had claimed the life of a Sweetwater resident. Ten days after the other British students had departed, Ashworth left the local hospital and boarded a train for Canada.

As the British Flying Training Schools were conceived and constructed, British officials, either in Washington or in London, exercised little control over the design and layout of the various schools. In some cases the local RAF officers were able to influence the school design and in other cases officers had little or no influence.

Each school reflected the philosophies and business practices of the individual operators and most were influenced by the austerity of the Depression years. For the most part the schools were utilitarian in design and some had unique features such as the Pennant Terminal at No. 3 BFTS and the bungalow-style housing used at No. 2 BFTS. The one exception, No. 5 BFTS, reflected John Paul Riddle's vision for a postwar aviation school. As the war progressed, enrollments increased, staff levels rose and considerable improvements, as well as additional amenities, were added to each school.

When the new schools opened, British officials were more than satisfied. In spite of individual differences, and some disagreements, all of the schools were modern, adequately equipped, and well organized; the civilian staffs were competent and enthusiastic, and the food abundant and nutritious. This more than satisfied the urgent need to train pilots. In fact, according to contemporary student comments, these schools represented a definite improvement over many of the makeshift facilities hastily thrown together in Britain.

In October 1941 a high-ranking delegation including Air Marshal A. G. R. Garrod, British Air Member for Training, Group Captain Carnegie, and Lord Douglas Hamilton, along with a group of American Army Air Forces officers led by Brigadier Generals G. E. Stratemeyer and C. L. Tinker toured each of the initial six new British schools. By all accounts, these officers came away from their inspection tour favorably impressed.

Chapter 6

Training

Within a few days of their arrival, British students assembled on the school flight lines, met their instructors, and had a first look at the aircraft in which they would learn to fly.

All of the British Flying Training Schools, except No. 3 BFTS, received the Stearman primary trainer. Officially the Boeing Kaydet, the trainer had been designed by the Stearman Aircraft Company before the company became a division of Boeing Aircraft and would forever be known simply as the Stearman. The Army Air Corps accepted the trainer in 1935 and production included several models that differed only in the engine and minor details.

To the first British students, most of whom had never been in an airplane, and even later students who had been through a grading course on the RAF Tiger Moth elementary trainer, the Stearman, an open cockpit fabric-covered biplane, presented an imposing sight. With a maximum loaded weight of 2,717 pounds, the Stearman towered more than nine feet to the top of the upper wing.

Even though noted for its rugged construction and easy handling in the air, the Stearman could be difficult to land, especially in a stiff cross wind, due to its narrow conventional landing gear. The Stearman had a tendency to ground loop if not properly handled. A ground loop is a fast, rather violent, rotation in a small circle on the ground. Most ground loops resulted only in damage to the pilot's ego and possibly a scraped wing tip as long as the pilot held the control stick firmly back and the propeller did not strike the ground. In extreme ground loops, however, damage to the propeller, engine, and even broken wing ribs and spars could occur.

Spartan's No. 3 BFTS received the Fairchild PT-19. A low wing monoplane with an inverted Ranger engine of 175 horsepower, the Fairchild had a pleasing streamlined appearance, but retained the open cockpits and tubular steel frame, fabric-covered fuselage of earlier trainers. Because it sported a wide conventional landing gear, instructors and students generally found the Fairchild to be more forgiving and less prone to ground looping than the Stearman.

Four or five British students were initially assigned to each of the civilian flight instructors. After a short introduction, the instructor took his students on a walk around the aircraft pointing out the various aspects of the primary trainer. The flight instructors were mostly young men, many not much older than the British students. Although some of the schools had to hire newly licensed instructors, the majority of the instructors had considerable flying experience; some had learned to fly as teenagers, others with the army, and many had earned a living as crop dusters or in other risky aerial pursuits. Many of the instructors were from the southern United States and spoke in a slow drawl almost unintelligible to the young British students. The students also spoke in a variety of regional accents that added further confusion. One early student thought that Hollywood movies had better prepared the British students for the southern accent and that the instructors were the ones at a disadvantage. Anthony Payne, who trained on the first course at No. 3 BFTS, voiced a common opinion: "The quality of flying instruction seemed to us to be supremely good and we all had high admiration for our instructors."[1]

Besides the unfamiliar speech, terminology offered further confusion with terms such as "fuel" or "gasoline" instead of the British "petrol," "landing gear" instead of "undercarriage," "propeller" instead of "airscrew," and "landing patterns" instead of the British term "circuits." The aircraft were even referred to as ships, which seemed strange indeed. One BFTS graduate, who had just returned to England from training in the United States, encountered a senior RAF officer who told him with "strong feeling" and some exasperation, "In the RAF we fly aircraft, not ships."[2]

After the walk around, the first student climbed into the rear cockpit (regardless of whether the trainer was a Stearman or a Fairchild), a cavernous hole in the large fuselage with a metal bucket seat and wide restraining belt. The seat had no cushion; each student sat on his own low-slung parachute. An instrument panel in front of the student contained only basic instruments. The early primary trainers did not even have an airspeed indicator in the student's cockpit. The instructor's cockpit contained an airspeed indicator, altimeter, and turn and bank indicator, as well as the standard oil pressure and oil temperature gauges, magnetic compass, tachometer, and a magneto switch. As soon as possible, instruments including an airspeed indicator were added to the student's cockpit to allow night flying and instrument instruction in the primary phase.

Since the primary trainers had no electrical system, a ground crewman started the engine with a hand crank. In some schools this chore fell to the students. When the engine started, an oil residue in the cylinders quickly burned, producing an initial cloud of blue-gray smoke, which blew back and dissolved into the slipstream of the spinning propeller.

The student's first flight involved a kaleidoscope of emotions, sights, and sounds, beginning with the roar of the engine advanced to full power. After an incredibly short takeoff run, the primary trainer did not seem so much to fly as the runway appeared to fall away from the aircraft and objects on the ground grew smaller and smaller. As the trainer climbed away from the airfield, the wings framed an ever-expanding horizon of blue sky above a varied and almost mystical landscape. The landscape as seen by a student on his first flight climbing away from one of the British schools varied depending on the locale, but the sensation of flight remained the same. After a short time, the wings tilted, or rather the horizon seemed to slant, as the aircraft banked for the first time. These sights and sounds were forever indelibly imprinted on the students' mind, even more so than he realized at the time.

One comment on the American primary trainers common to almost all British students who had been exposed to the RAF Tiger Moth, had to do with the seatbelt. The Stearman and the Fairchild both used a single wide lap belt. The Tiger Moth used a three-point restraint system of seatbelt and shoulder harness. Designed to offer the occupant more protection in the event of a crash, the Tiger Moth system also offered more confidence during inverted maneuvers in the open cockpit.

After a distinguished career in the RAF, David Green, an early student at No. 3 BFTS, reflected on the American lap belt. "With the uncovered cockpit and absence of shoulder harness one felt sort of unguarded and exposed, rather like sitting on a dining room chair at 5,000 feet. It took quite a bit of getting used to. Indeed, when stalling, spinning and aerobatics were the order of the day, it was essential to tighten the solitary lapstrap to the point of a double leg amputation before one felt reasonably confident of remaining in the aircraft at all."[3]

The communication system in the primary trainers consisted of a flexible rubber tube called a gosport. The gosport allowed only one-way communication (usually garbled) from the instructor in the front cockpit to the student in the rear cockpit. Even though instructors usually (but not always) discussed the flight session before takeoff, once in the air the student had no means of replying or asking questions. One early student vividly remembered the crude communication system. "What to me was a serious impediment to learning was the incredible difficulty in conducting any worthwhile form of airborne communication. To ask a question about an aspect of flight in urgent need of clarification one had to wait until the flight was over—and by that time my instructor was normally too speechless with rage to answer."[4]

With the roar of the engine, the noise of the slipstream around the open cockpit, the limitations of the gosport, the apprehension experienced when inverted and held to the aircraft by the single belt, and the use of unfamiliar terminology spoken in a slow southern drawl, it is amazing that so many students actually learned to fly. Both the Stearman and the Fairchild, despite certain shortcomings, proved to be excellent trainers.

A typical training day began when the instructors along with the first students walked from the school buildings to the flight line and the long rows of trainers. Dispatchers armed with clipboards and various official forms scurried about calling out aircraft assignments. Moments later, as the engines turned over and started, blue-gray smoke poured from the exhausts and the trainers formed a line taxiing to the end of the takeoff area. As the field reverberated to the sound of engines advanced to full power, the trainers took off and headed for the practice area. Practice areas were designated for each phase of training to keep from mixing the slower primary trainers with the faster advanced trainers. The remaining students boarded some form of transportation to the auxiliary field. These fields were used to ease congestion at the main airfield and again were segregated according to types of aircraft. The primary trainers used one auxiliary field, while the basic and advanced trainers used another practice field.

Old school buses were the usual form of transportation to the auxiliary fields. These buses rumbled down dirt lanes, rattling over wooden bridges or crossed western dry washes according to the locale, accompanied by the laughter and group singing of the British students, along with the frequent grinding of gears in the old transmissions. The songs ranged from patriotic, to sentimental, to bawdy bordering on obscene.

When the first flight session ended, the instructor and first student landed at the auxiliary field and the second student climbed into the aircraft. The instructor and his last student flew back to the main airfield at the end of the day. This system increased efficiency and the only problems occurred when a thunderstorm or sudden change in the weather sent all of the trainers scurrying back to the main airfield. Then the hastily improvised landing pattern became a long drawn out melee of trainers jockeying for position. Accidents were surprisingly rare during these scrambles.

The first hours of primary instruction introduced the student to the new, and often bewildering, realm of flight. The student first learned to fly straight and level while attempting to hold a steady course and maintain a constant altitude, then began making gentle turns, climbs, and descents. Once the student could reasonably control the aircraft, steeper turns, stalls, and basic maneuvers were introduced and then spins. An early RAF publication defined stalls. "Stalling occurs when the aeroplane is flying at such an angle (more loosely speaking, so slowly) that its wings fail to give it support. The aeroplane then stalls."[5]

Aviation accidents from inadvertent spins after stalling an aircraft at low altitude resulted in many deaths. In response to this trend students practiced spin recovery early in training. Spins were begun from an altitude that allowed for recovery, at least 3,000 feet above the ground.

After basic aircraft control and maneuvers had been introduced, students progressed to rudimentary aerobatics. These initial maneuvers consisted of loops, slow rolls, stalled turns, half rolls (half of a slow roll to inverted and then the bottom half of a loop to pull out), and a half roll on top of a loop.[6] Students also practiced precautionary landings (using engine power to control the descent) and power-off forced landings to simulate an engine failure.

Students shot endless takeoffs and landings, usually at one of the auxiliary fields. Landings presented a unique challenge to the neophyte because of the coordination required to reduce power, slow the aircraft, and then establish a glide from pattern altitude (usually 800 feet above the ground) while maintaining the proper airspeed and executing several turns (the civilian schools used a rectangular traffic pattern) down to an exact spot on the airfield, arriving just above the ground in the correct attitude, and at the proper airspeed, just above a stall, but not too fast, while correcting for winds that were often contrary. Some of the British Flying Training Schools utilized large open fields that allowed all initial takeoffs and landings to be conducted into the wind. Even these schools soon introduced cross wind takeoffs and landings, which required fine control harmony and quick reflexes to avoid a ground loop.

None of this learning process required superhuman skills, but learning to fly involved a high degree of control coordination and an intrinsic feel for the aircraft. The entire program was also geared to an inflexible schedule. This fixed timetable introduced an added element of stress. Many students simply could not master the myriad tasks in the time allocated and had to be eliminated from the program. To be eliminated or "washed out" was a devastating blow to a young man who had dreamed of nothing else than becoming a pilot.

Kenneth Stott washed out at No. 1 BFTS because he could not seem to judge height on the landing approach. "After elimination, I was very depressed. At nineteen the world seemed to be at an end! I was not alone, as within a week a further eight had joined me."[7]

Thomas William Reece trained on Course 10 at No. 3 BFTS and recalled the process. "My impression of the scheme of training was that it was very thorough & spared no effort to produce pilots of a very high calibre. At the same time, there was an on-going system of checks. Those who did not pass were posted to Navigation, Gunnery or Wireless Operators School. Cadets were so keen to earn their wings that many of those who were 'washed out' broke down and cried."[8]

One dramatic case illustrates the emotional aspects of being washed out. In December 1942, a student eliminated from training at No. 2 BFTS left a suicide note then took off in a primary trainer on an unauthorized flight. As soon as school officials realized what had happened, an instructor took off after the student and finally persuaded him to land at another airfield. Many eliminations occurred after a failed check ride, while others were more dramatic. John Roberts Davies of Course 9 at No. 2 BFTS and a fellow student were night flying. The other student approached the field for a landing, but stalled about twenty feet in the air and the Stearman's left wing hit the ground. Davis described what happened next: "he probably panicked then and jammed on full throttle. The force knocked his right wing into the ground and he had to attempt to take off again, missing some telephone wires by inches. I'm sure the instructors were quite scared when he was flying around the field, as they expected his wings to fall off any minute. Two crash trucks and fire engines were waiting near the landing strip in case he cracked up on landing—luckily, he landed safely and got out unhurt."[9] The next day the student was given a check flight and eliminated from flight training.

The first training milestone came with the student's first solo flight. The first solo consisted of several circuits (takeoffs and landings), while the student's apprehensive instructor watched from the ground. The student remained in the traffic pattern usually at one of the auxiliary fields. The next flight occurred with the instructor, followed by both solo and dual flight sessions in the designated practice area. By the end of the seventy-hour primary phase of training, the student had logged approximately half of the time with his instructor and the other half flying solo.

Following solo, instructors introduced additional maneuvers. Even though the school courses followed the standard RAF flight training sequence, the American instructors invariably added maneuvers from their civilian experience. These maneuvers usually involved some form of pylon eight or S turns across a road. In a pylon eight the aircraft traces a figure 8 at low altitude around two fixed objects on the ground such as trees or grain silos. With the wind at right angles to the figure 8 the purpose of the maneuver is to maintain a fixed distance from the objects on the ground while constantly turning the aircraft. In order to maintain the prescribed distance from the objects on the ground, the student must continually vary the angle of bank to compensate for the wind. Turns that traced a figure S across a road with the wind again at right angles to the road accomplished the same purpose. These maneuvers taught the proper coordination of the aircraft's rudder, elevators, and ailerons.

After mastering a variety of maneuvers and flying both dual and solo in the practice area, students embarked on cross-country flights. The first cross country was a dual flight with the instructor. The following solo cross-country flights represented a maturing of the student who was no longer restricted to the practice area or under the constant scrutiny of his instructor. As in all phases of flight training the first cross-country flights were short affairs. Bert Allam, an early student, reflected on his first solo cross-country flight: "Had I known where to look, it would have probably been possible from about 2,000 feet to have seen all the way round the route without leaving the vicinity of the Terrell field."[10]

Navigation on these cross-country flights relied on dead reckoning using the magnetic compass and an aeronautical chart, since the primary trainers had no electrical system, radios, or navigation aids. Railroad tracks became known as the "iron compass" and students quickly learned that most southern and western towns had the name of the town painted on the water tower, although this method was not foolproof. One British student, unsure of his position, descended and circled a small town water tower only to see the words, "Go to Church on Sunday." Most of these cross-country flights were triangular courses in order to keep from flying over the same terrain and to gain experience compensating for local winds on different headings.

Ken Bickers flew the first leg of an early cross-country flight, arrived approximately on time, and circled the small grass field just outside of his first destination. Several students were flying the same cross country that day, and although not flying together, students usually glimpsed other aircraft, especially at landing fields. The absence of any other Stearmans on the field apparently did not concern Bickers. After landing and shutting down the engine, Bickers walked to the small airport shack to get his logbook signed as proof of the flight. Two grizzled old timers sat on the porch. Before Bickers could speak, one of the men raised a hand and with an air of disdain said, "Ah know, don't tell me, y'all British and y'all lost."[11]

Arthur Ridge became lost on one of his first cross-country flights and decided to land when his fuel ran low. Ridge landed in a field soft from recent rains and the Stearman bogged down. Looking for assistance, Ridge approached a nearby farmhouse and knocked on the door. A large, rather formidable-looking, black woman appeared complete with a red bandanna on her head. Ridge, whose total knowledge of southern racial norms probably came from the movie *Gone With the Wind* (the black woman even resembled Hattie McDaniel who played Mammy in the movie), straightened to his full five-foot seven-inch height and asked politely, "Is the master at home?" The woman stepped back and slammed the door without a word.

Ridge then gave a farmhand a dollar to hitch his mule to the landing gear of the Stearman. When the mule failed to make any progress, a new idea occurred to Ridge. He started the Stearman's engine in order to aid the effort, but the noise only terrified the animal. The mule bolted forward, the reins slipped up the landing gear and were promptly cut by the propeller, which dumped the mule on his nose in the mud. The offended mule took off in full flight toward the next county. Ridge finally succeeded in extricating the Stearman, determined his location, and returned to Terrell.[12]

The British believed in introducing instrument flying in the primary phase of training. The early courses were limited due to a lack of suitably equipped aircraft, but after the primary trainers had been modified, all of the British students undertook instrument training in primary. This consisted of flying under a crude hood, which blocked all outside references (and obviously only with an instructor). Even after modification, the primary trainers offered only the barest of instruments. Instrument training occurred in small increments throughout training and "in earlier stages preferably on every dual flight."

Douglas Roman Byrne of Course 15 at No. 6 BFTS described instrument training around Ponca City. "One of the more painful memories is of learning instrument flying in these conditions (hot rough air at low altitude in Oklahoma) sweating under a canvas hood and trying to control a bucking aircraft by reference to rudimentary instruments (needle, ball, airspeed and altimeter, no artificial horizon, gyro or rate of climb indicator) while being bawled at by the instructor and having no way of answering back—there was a voice-tube one-way only."[13]

A significant portion of instrument training took place, oddly enough, on the ground in a strange contraption known as the Link trainer. Edwin Link designed the first synthetic trainer, a forerunner of the modern flight simulator, to teach the basics of instrument flying while on the ground. Link completed the first crude model of his trainer in 1929 and continued to make improvements to his machine throughout the 1930s.

The Link trainer consisted of a small enclosed plywood structure, with no outside visual reference. The inside of the Link replicated an aircraft cockpit complete with fully functioning instruments and flight controls. The plywood structure (complete with small mock wings and tail surfaces) was mounted on a short pedestal. Electrical inputs from an operator seated at a nearby control panel operated a system of air bellows that gave the Link full 360-degree turning movement, as well as limited pitch and rolling movement.

Despite its appearance, the Link trainer was no toy. Students practiced straight and level simulated flights on specific compass courses, precision climbs and descents, and timed turns at various angles of bank. Link operators could input various scenarios, vary cross winds, render the airspeed indicator and/or artificial horizon inoperable, and simulate rough air. An operator's fiendish manipulation of the Link could leave a student, wrestling with the controls in the darkened enclosure, shaken and sweating. A graph recorded the results of the Link session for later study. Toward the end of the war, specialized Link trainers became available that even included simulated aerial gunnery. As with actual instrument flying, the British schools scheduled student sessions in the Link trainer in short intervals throughout flight training.

Students in the first courses received around ten hours of instruction in the Link. As additional trainers were added to the schools, time in the Link increased to nineteen hours and finally students in the later expanded courses were averaging twenty-eight to thirty hours in the Link.

Toward the end of primary training students began night flying. This was one of the major differences between the British and American flight training programs. Although the first courses in the new British schools experienced little night flying in the primary phase due to a lack of suitably equipped aircraft, all later primary courses included night flying. At first, night flying consisted of dual instruction only, but students in later courses soloed at night and some even undertook short dual night cross-country flights.

No amount of ground instruction could adequately prepare a low-time student for night flying. The first takeoff into a black sky was fraught with apprehension. Takeoff and landing areas were outlined by small smudge pots like those used to mark highway construction areas. One U.S. Navy instructor commented, "The flare pots illuminated nothing, but they did enable a pilot to judge his altitude—with a little practice."[14] During a night landing approach, descending into the darkness toward a dimly flickering row of smoky smudge pots, with the landscape and its associated hazards shrouded in darkness, a student experienced a sense of foreboding that could quickly develop into fear and then panic if not controlled. Later courses had the benefit of a light bar installed at the end of the runway. A visible amber light indicated a high approach, a green light indicated a correct approach, and a red light indicated a low approach.

Jonathan Smalley trained with Course 16 at No. 5 BFTS and commented on the apprehension of night flying that continued into advanced training, "Sitting all alone in that Harvard and telling myself that I could land without incident between those dim, flickering flares didn't really help.

The entirely unpredictable space of time that elapsed between the moment I first expected to touch down and the actual moment of impact was usually long and terrifying."[15]

Learning to fly an aircraft represented only half of flight training. Often overlooked in histories or later accounts, students spent the other half of each training day in ground school. As flying progressed, ground school classes covered a diverse range of subjects such as navigation, meteorology, airmanship, principles of flight, engines, armament, parachutes, signals, and aircraft recognition. A major portion of ground school involved navigation and meteorology.

Navigation included the use of aerial charts, plotting wind triangles to determine course correction for the effects of winds aloft, exercises involving application of bearings, measurement of distance, latitude, longitude, as well as great circle and rhumb line calculations. Navigation instruction also relied heavily on the use of the Dalton computer (known to the British as Navigation Computer Mk. III). A portable circular slide rule, the Dalton solved time and distance problems, provided ground speed over a course, true airspeed, fuel consumption, and determined course corrections based on local winds.[16]

Meteorology delved into the mysterious world of air masses, frontal systems, winds aloft, cloud types, formation of fog, pressure and temperature variances, and various reports and forecasts, as well as the effects of ice, snow, hail, and even lightning strikes on aircraft. Even though this section dealt with considerable theory, meteorology lessons were always based on the practical application of weather relative to aircraft flight. One British publication advised ground school instructors to "make every endeavour to get away from dull scientific explanations, and put his subject over in a practical way. Whenever possible references should be made to local conditions, and lectures illustrated by weather observations of students and staff at the airfield."[17]

Engine classes covered both the theory of four-stroke internal combustion engines and practical operating procedures for all types of engines, air-cooled radial engines, liquid-cooled inline engines, and the unique British sleeve valve engine. Besides engine theory and operating procedures, students had to be proficient in supplemental systems such as lubrication, ignition, fuel, cooling, and the operation of variable pitch propellers.

Signals training included sending and receiving Morse code with both keys (buzzers) and signal lamps (know as Aldis lamps) at six words per minute. Other classes included armaments, principles of flight, the use of parachutes, aircraft recognition, and airmanship, which involved "proficiency in knowledge of handling and operating aircraft on the ground and in the air."

Anthony Payne trained with the first course at No. 3 BFTS and recalled the ground school classes: "With temperatures up into the hundreds and a generous and varied menu in the canteen some of us found great difficulty in keeping awake during the alternating afternoon sessions." Squadron Leader Kermode, the chief ground instructor, taught theory of flight at No. 3 BFTS. Kermode had written the standard book on theory of flight used by the RAF, so students knew "it behooved us to keep awake during his classes." Payne recalled an afternoon class taught by Kermode: "I had the distinction of putting up a major black; asked what happened to the centre of pressure over the top of the wing at the moment of stall I gave as my opinion that it 'fell off the front edge', whereas of course it moves smartly backwards. I am convinced that my failure to be awarded a commission at the passing out of the course dated from that moment!"[18]

Many of the British students saw little value in armament training, especially the operation and intricate assembly and disassembly of the Browning machine gun. Even American students, who had a reputation for familiarity with firearms, found the standards challenging. Paul G. Charbonnet, Jr. a USAAF cadet, and Tulane University graduate, trained with Course 15 at No. 3 BFTS. "In our flying, we were not given any gunnery work and no shooting except skeet on the range. Then when we studied about the Browning machine gun and how to take it apart, etc., it was all Greek to me. In one test, they put the pieces back together 'incorrectly' and told you to change them properly. Well, I just could not do it all; some, yes, but not perfectly."[19] Most students reasoned that there was little a pilot could do to clear a machine gun stoppage in flight.

Tests in the various subjects were taken throughout ground school and at the end of the course students took a comprehensive written test known as the Wings Exam. In early courses when pilots were desperately needed, ground school failures were still allowed to graduate. As pilot production rose throughout the various training schemes, ground school failure became a cause for elimination from flight training. In order to graduate, students were required to pass individual sections of the Wings Exam, as well as achieve a certain overall grade. Students were allowed to retake failed sections.

In an early review of the British school's civilian employees, Group Captain Carnegie noted a wide disparity in salaries between flight instructors and ground school instructors. While flight instructors were well paid, ground school instructors were usually paid considerably less. Carnegie felt that this was not sufficient to retain experienced personnel. At first the salary discrepancy did not cause undue difficulties, but as flight training became a major portion of the war effort, a shortage of qualified ground school instructors (as well as some other key positions) became a major problem in the civilian schools.

John A. B. Keeling trained with Course 4 at No. 3 BFTS. Keeling praised the flying instruction in America. "It takes five weeks longer [than in England] and we get more flying and I think very probably a better flying training with greater facilities." But Keeling expressed his misgivings about the ground instruction in a letter home. "The ground training, which is equally important, is not nearly as well taught as I think it would be in England. The subjects are taught by civilian instructors who have never done the subjects before and really know little more than we do. The man who teaches us navigation is next to hopeless at teaching, even if he knew his stuff, and the man who teaches us aircraft recognition couldn't tell a 'flying fortress' from a starling or a blackbird."[20]

The quality of the civilian ground school instruction improved with time. The Royal Air Force Delegation in Washington also recognized the inadequate level of the initial RAF staff at the new British schools, and over time added specialized service personnel to each school. These new personnel included an armament NCO, a navigation officer (these officers usually had operational experience in either Bomber Command or Coastal Command), and later assistant navigation officers, a signals warrant officer, and toward the end of the war, a gunnery instructor. The increased RAF staff augmented the school's civilian instructors.

After the primary phase of flight training students in the first courses progressed to the basic phase and an entirely new aircraft. For basic training the army supplied the Vultee BT-13 Valiant, also referred to (not always affectionately) as the Vultee Vibrator. Accepted by the Army Air Corps in 1939, the Vultee was designed to be a step above the primary trainers, both in terms of equipment and performance, but also in the crucial area of developing a flight student's skill.

Equipped with a more powerful 450 horsepower, Pratt and Whitney, radial engine, the 4,360 pound BT-13, a low wing monoplane, featured all metal construction (except for the fabric covered control surfaces), a long sliding plexiglass canopy that enclosed the cockpit with its two tandem seats, a two-position adjustable propeller, manually operated wing flaps, and a fixed conventional landing gear. The BT-13 had an electrical system that allowed amenities such as an engine starter, navigation and landing lights for night flying, and a radio, including two-way communication between the student and the instructor. The rotund Vultee cruised at 140 miles per hour and landed more than twenty miles per hour faster than the primary trainers. Vultee produced another variant of the Valiant, the BT-15, the only difference being the substitution of a Wright engine of equal horsepower. Official records are sketchy, but a limited number of

BT-15s appear to have been used at No. 4 BFTS and possibly in other British schools.

John Roberts Davies of Course 9 at No. 2 BFTS, recalled the basic trainer: "There's a terrific lot to do in them, for example, on entering the circuit, I have to change pitch to fine, mixture rich, put down 20 degrees flaps, keep my revs at 2,100 and airspeed at about 110, and glide down to 1,000 feet at the same time I have to radio our control tower and go through a lot of rigamarole for landing."[21]

Even though it was produced in greater numbers than any other American primary or basic trainer (11,537), opinions regarding the Vultee varied widely and the BT-13 never achieved the popularity of the Stearman. Al Storrs, the director of training at No. 4 BFTS, thought the Vultee was actually too easy to fly.[22] Most instructors, however, disagreed. Many instructors found the BT-13 to be underpowered, while others questioned the trainer's stall characteristics. The wildest rumors maintained that when stalled, the Vultee would always roll inverted. Actually, stalls in the Vultee were normal when performed at altitude with the wings level. When stalled out of a turn, however, the Vultee would snap toward the high wing and the nose would pitch sharply down.[23] A stall in a Vultee at low altitude, such as on a landing approach, especially out of an uncoordinated turn, could be deadly.

Bert Allam, an early student at No. 1 BFTS and later an RAF instructor in England before joining Bomber Command toward the end of the war, found that his basic instructor flew the Vultee straight and level during dual flights and never demonstrated aerobatics in the aircraft. Allam thought that the instructor actually feared the Vultee. In contrast, Allam, who regularly performed aerobatics in the Vultee during his solo flights, enjoyed flying the basic trainer.

In spite of the negative opinions, the Vultee provided an important step in transitioning a student pilot from the low powered, forgiving primary trainers to the higher performance service aircraft. As one instructor told his student, "This plane is bigger and heavier than you've been flying. It has more torque. It is a *safe* airplane. But it differs in one most important way. This airplane is *unforgiving*. Get careless with it, and it will kill you."[24]

Another early student summed up the BT-13. "The Vultee BT-13 was yet another character. Bigger still, metallic and dramatically noisy, it seemed to be a warning to the overconfident that there was yet a great deal to learn."[25] An experienced Royal Air Force pilot may have had the ultimate pithy comment regarding the Vultee. "It has a tendency to snap roll on landing, which can be rather disconcerting. Other than that it isn't very dangerous."[26]

The new basic phase of flight training represented a continuation of the maneuvers and skills first introduced in primary training. Students gained experience flying a heavier, faster, and more sophisticated aircraft. Instructors also introduced formation flying in the basic phase of training. The British did not stress precision formation flying as taught to Army Air Forces aviation cadets, instead preferring training in smaller, looser formations. Instrument flying and night flying continued, as well as ever longer cross-country flights. As in primary, the student flew about half of the basic phase solo and the other half with his instructor.

In the basic phase of flight training students combined two previous skills by flying certain cross-country flights on instruments. The student took off under the hood and the instructor positioned the aircraft over the airfield. The student then navigated the triangular course by flying time and distance by reference to the instruments, the objective being to arrive back over the original airfield. Russell Cooke described the results of two instrument cross-country flights he took on the same day in a letter to his parents. "You then take the hood off and consider yourself lucky if the field is within sight. Luckily I was only three miles off in one and 5 in the other. I was quite pleased. One of my pals, one of the originals from Paignton was washed out yesterday owing to his inability to master the B.T."[27]

In November 1942, the British schools eliminated the basic phase of training and the Vultees were removed as more advanced trainers became available. This brought the British Flying Training Schools more in line with the standard two-phase RAF flight training curriculum. After this time students transitioned directly from the Stearman or Fairchild primary trainer to the AT-6 Harvard advanced trainer.

Along with the new basic or advanced trainer, students were usually assigned a new instructor (but not always, especially in some early courses in several schools). Authorities believed exposure to different instructors enhanced the learning experience. In the years between the wars, both the military and civilian flight schools had worked to develop better training programs. These efforts resulted in improved training syllabuses, but little had been done to develop the profession of instructing. Most authorities still believed that a good pilot would naturally be a good instructor. The RAF came close to understanding the proper role of the instructor when it noted, "The potential instructor must obviously be a keen and sound pilot who can persevere, and be patient and restrained under the tedium of long hours of repetitive work."[28]

The civilian flight instructors had no common economic, educational, or social background. They came in all physical descriptions and from all backgrounds. Some were quiet and soft-spoken, while others were gregarious or even flamboyant. Away from the flight line the instructors represented the complete spectrum of American society. Many of the instructors were married and led lives devoted to their families. Many drank only socially or not at all. Other instructors, however, engaged in endless partying, hard drinking, womanizing, and could be accurately described as exhibiting the lowest moral standards. The common thread that bound the instructors was a passionate love of flying.

Bert Allam is probably representative in describing his instructors. Allam credits much of his later success as a pilot to Bill Brookover, his primary instructor. Brookover combined patience with a genuine desire to see his students succeed. Allam's basic instructor, on the other hand, proved to be silent and uncommunicative, combined with a quick temper and little patience. Allam even took the unusual step of requesting a change of instructor, which the school denied. Allam's advanced instructor, J. L. Isabel, proved to be entirely different from either of his earlier instructors. Isabel, a small man with a fierce reputation, could be critical and demanding, but Allam always found him to be fair.[29]

Each school had unique policies regarding changing instructors. As Allam's experience illustrates, some schools did not allow changes in instructors, while other schools routinely granted student requests for a different instructor. David Green and his primary instructor did not get along. "It took a lot of courage, I discovered, for an eighteen year old student, trailing badly behind the field, to form up in front of the Chief Instructor to ask for a change of instructor. Desperation urged me on. He was sympathetic, and assigned me to one Al Donahue. Tall, sun-tanned, graying, quiet and good-humoured, I took an instant liking to him. The result was predictable, I went solo within the hour. From that day onward my development as a pilot went smoothly if not meteorically."[30]

Joseph Ekbery, a member of the second course at No. 2 BFTS temporarily quartered in Glendale, commented on the nature of the instructors in California. "The base aerodrome at Glendale/Los Angeles figures in almost all the flying films from Hollywood. Our instructors came from all walks of life in America. There were army men, navy men, bush pilots, civil instructors, crop dusters, test pilots and more than one, especially 'Straight and Level Brown', had done stunt flying and crashes for the films."[31]

Although most of the instructors were young, others could be described as almost elderly. Joe Lievre, a fifty-three-year-old native of France and an instructor at No. 1 BFTS, had taught Major Long, the school's owner, advanced aerobatics at Kelly Field in San Antonio during World War I. More than twenty-five years later Terrell residents watched enthralled as Lievre performed early morning aerobatic routines, which lasted up to forty-five minutes, high over the town.

Robert DeWald graduated from U.S. Army flight training at Kelly Field in 1924. After serving as a primary flight instructor with the army, DeWald flew as a pilot with National Air Transport between 1928 and 1931, and then engaged in private flying. When Spartan Aeronautics hired DeWald as an instructor in 1940, he listed his experience from 1935 to 1940 (the depths of the Great Depression) as "mostly unemployed."

At the beginning of the war the army deemed Harold Morgenstern, born in Bremerhaven to a German sea captain and a Texas mother, to be too old to fly. He had soloed in an OX5-powered Eaglerock in 1929. Spartan, however, hired Morgenstern and assigned him to No. 3 BFTS as a deputy Basic/Advanced flight commander. Morgenstern's family joined him in Miami. "As my family, one wife, three children, ages 2 to 12 was there with me, we did not have much time to socialize with the boys, but did have some of them over for afternoon tea. They were properly horrified as my little daughters graciously offered cream, sugar, or lemon to add to the tea. Anyhow, we became the best of friends, in spite of mutilating their tea." Many of the civilian instructors routinely used foul language, which offended many of the British students. Morgenstern noted, "Being one of the non-cussers, I drew all the washout candidates. Out of 35 managed to save 30."[32]

Alfred Syrett of Course 13 remembered Morgenstern four decades later, "An ex-Air Mail pilot who flew Curtiss Jennies. I had great empathy & confidence in this man who taught me to fly the aircraft as a pilot." After ferrying aircraft, including Hawker Hurricanes and American P-47 Thunderbolts, throughout India and Southeast Asia, Syrett's logbook received a "green endorsement" for flying without an avoidable accident. Syrett's comment, "due to Mr. Morgenstern."[33]

Andrew L. Bayley trained with Course 17 at No. 1 BFTS and enjoyed flying the Stearman. "I found them a delight to fly, and their open cockpits were a godsend during the hot weather." Bayley was among the British students who were not offended by the language. He found the civilian instructors "efficient and friendly" and his primary instructor "swore admirably, and his favorite expression was 'son of a bitch' which he used frequently." Bayley and his instructor got on particularly well, especially after one incident. "He was instructing me on my first low flying excercise when we were (correctly) flying along and keeping to the right of a road we were following, when suddenly I spotted another aircraft flying towards us at the same height and heaved back on the stick while the other craft whizzed by underneath. My instructor exclaimed, 'I never did see that son of a bitch!'"[34]

Flight instruction sought to develop in students both an intrinsic feel for the aircraft and confidence in themselves. Instructors approached these goals in different ways. Dennis John Mason of Course 4 at No. 2 BFTS remembered his primary instructor, "A piece of good advice from Mr. Marvin, which I shall always remember, was: 'Damn it Mason, fly by the feel of your ass!'"[35]

Don Stebbings and his primary instructor Bill Stewart, described as a "bronzed and lanky Old Gold smoking Texan," departed one day on an early dual cross-country flight. After takeoff Stebbings got out his chart and notes, not realizing that Stewart had little use for formalized flight plans and believed in a more fundamental style of flying. Stewart suddenly rolled the Stearman inverted and Stebbings watched his chart and notes disappear below. Stebbings somehow completed the fight successfully and later described Stewart as, "The greatest and indisputably the most colorful of all the instructors with whom I flew."[36]

Archie B. Venables of Course 11 at No. 3 BFTS remembered Mr. Stevenson, his primary instructor, as "a quiet, courteous man who inspired confidence and dedication, a superb instructor. Forty years on, I remember him with gratitude and great affection."[37]

L. J. Taylor trained with Course 17 at No. 5 BFTS and enjoyed the primary phase of flight training flying the Stearman. At first Taylor did not do as well in advanced. "When we moved to advanced from primary training, I had difficulty, but fortunately Mr. C. W. Barclay, my instructor, had the patience of Job and saw something in me that caused him to persevere until I got it right. I was eternally grateful to him for the rest of my career in the RAF because of his ability to teach. Thanks to Mr. Barclay, I qualified for my wings with distinction and a rating of excellent, which stood me in good stead in later years."[38]

Instructor Bill McGallard had an unusual experience when he took a British student up to do slow rolls. After reaching altitude, McGallard called for the student to execute the first roll. The Stearman rolled inverted, then the nose dropped. McGallard called for the student to 'keep the nose up' but when nothing happened, McGallard rolled the Stearman back level, then noticed that he was flying alone. No one was in the rear cockpit. McGallard made a quick bank, looked below and saw a white parachute slowly floating toward earth. The student later explained that he had forgotten to fasten his seatbelt.[39]

Mead Barker of Course 10 at No 1 BFTS returned from a night cross-country flight without his instructor. According to Barker, the instructor ordered an altitude of 5,000 feet over the first check point and became upset when Barker replied that the flight plan called for an altitude of 7,000 feet. The instructor slammed the stick violently forward, then back, at which point the trainer stalled and entered a spin. Barker, at first thinking the instructor was still flying the AT-6, rode the aircraft down to 1,000 feet, then managed to regain control. Realizing the instructor had bailed out, Barker flew the Harvard back to Terrell. The instructor maintained Barker had been sightseeing and not paying attention to his altitude. The instructor claimed he had pushed the stick forward in order to make a point, not realizing he had removed his seatbelt, and hit his head on the canopy. Dazed and finding the aircraft in a spin, the instructor bailed out. School officials believed Barker and dismissed the instructor.[40]

Several deficiencies in the schools' civilian staffs became evident. While the school operators found it relatively easy to recruit qualified primary flying instructors, advanced instructors were not so easy to find. Advanced instructors had to have experience flying higher performance, sophisticated aircraft equipped with controllable pitch propellers, flaps, and retractable landing gear. These aircraft carried radios and were equipped for instrument flight and night flying. At this time, advanced aircraft types were not readily available in American civil aviation. Civilian pilots with commercial licenses and instructor ratings could amass considerable flying experience and still not have experience on advanced trainers.

Fortunately time worked in the school operators' favor. When the initial schools opened, the first British students would not progress to the advanced stage of flight training for several months. During this time the army offered a short course in nearby army training facilities to update the civilian instructors on advanced aircraft. While some of the older instructors resented being taught to "fly the army way" especially by young "wet behind the ears" army officers, few failed to complete the army courses. These instructors returned to the British schools and in turn instructed other instructors on the basic and advanced trainers.

When No. 4 BFTS opened in Mesa, the RAF officers noted some of the difficulties, "Due to the geographic position of the school, being situated in Arizona, together with expansion of local Army Schools, experienced instructors were difficult to secure and training of instructors had to accompany the training of students."[41]

North American AT-6 trainers started arriving at the first four British schools toward the end of September 1941. Designed to approximate the characteristics of operational aircraft, the streamlined, low wing, all metal (except for the fabric covered control surfaces), AT-6 mounted a 550 horsepower Pratt and Whitney radial engine (rated at 600 horsepower for takeoff), enclosed cockpit, full instrumentation, retractable landing gear, hydraulic wing flaps, landing lights, and a Hamilton Standard constant speed propeller. Weighing more than two and a half tons, more than twice the weight of the primary trainers, the AT-6 offered a top speed of 210 miles per hour and cruised between 155 and 185 miles per hour depending on the power setting.[42] The British named the AT-6 the Harvard. Even though technically army property and officially named the Texan by North American in 1943, the AT-6s used by the British schools in the United States were almost always referred to as Harvards in contemporary sources.

When the selected civilian instructors from the British schools first received a short course on the AT-6 from regional Army Air Corps flight centers, some of the army instructors had less than favorable comments about the advanced trainer, especially regarding its stall characteristics and its tendency to ground loop. British commanders such as Wing Commander Hilton attempted to allay these concerns by relating the favorable experiences of British flight schools that had operated the Harvard for some time. Hilton even demonstrated various maneuvers in the aircraft to the No. 1 BFTS civilian instructors.

Although regarded as a forgiving and pleasant flying aircraft and ultimately the favorite aircraft of almost every British student, the Harvard presented a formidable challenge to low-time students due to its higher operating speeds and sophisticated systems. The landing approach in the primary trainer had required little more than retarding the throttle, setting up the appropriate glide speed, and aiming the aircraft at the runway. The AT-6, however, required lowering the landing gear, lowering the wing flaps, adjusting the trim, setting the propeller controls, insuring the proper mixture and carburetor heat settings, and the selection of the reserve fuel tank (the AT-6 had two main fuel tanks and a reserve tank, each of which could be selected individually), all while maintaining the correct approach speed. In an era before printed check lists, students repeated the acronym TMPFF, which stood for trim, mixture, pitch, fuel, and flaps before each takeoff, and UMPFF, for undercarriage, mixture, pitch, fuel, and flaps, before each landing.

Several decades after training with No. 3 BFTS, David Green remembered the Harvard. "It was an almost perfect advanced trainer. It was certainly admirably suited to World War 2 days. The cockpits were spacious, the aircraft steady, the visibility superb (except from the back seat at night—which was the instructor's problem)." Concerning comments that the Harvard was overly sensitive and difficult to fly, Green answered, "the Harvard would give the ham-fisted student plenty of warning that all was not well. Of course, if the warnings were ignored, then quite violent retribution would ensue—but a good fright in the flying business is often an equally good lesson."[43]

The advanced trainers flew the landing pattern at an altitude of 1,000 feet, as opposed to the 800-foot pattern flown by the other trainers. This allowed the student additional time for the numerous tasks and to compensate for the higher speed of the Harvard. Jack Bolter received a final briefing from his instructor before his first solo in the AT-6. The instructor, in the typical slow southern drawl, attempted to reassure an apprehensive Bolter. "Now see here Bolter, you're gonna find this here AT a bit faster and a bit more of a handful than that little old PT, so give yourself plenty of room. Go out a bit wider on your approach, for sure as hell, you're gonna be as busy as a cat covering up shit."[44]

American aviation cadet William Watkins, who trained with No. 6 BFTS, described his first flight in the AT-6 in his diary. "Boy! What a beautiful ship—handles with finger tip control—bags of power and unlimited visibility! Really a dream ship after the PT's—great speed too! Fly mostly from the front cockpit and really have a thrill sitting and flying up there."[45]

The student had to monitor the fuel system of the Harvard and manually select the correct fuel tank. Advanced flight students on long cross-country flights sitting serenely contemplating the passing scenery and their considerable piloting skills were sometimes startled when the engine suddenly quit without warning. Fortunately students had been taught to switch to the auxiliary fuel tank in the event of an engine failure. Usually the engine roared back to life in a few seconds and the humbled student realized he had forgotten to switch fuel tanks and had run one tank dry.

The advanced phase of flight training consisted of more than just manipulating the controls of a faster aircraft. John Roberts Davies trained with Course 9 at No. 2 BFTS and offered insight in a letter to his future wife. "I started advanced navigation this afternoon. We have lectures in the afternoons and flying in the mornings and since 6 this evening I've been trying to solve the problems of convergency and conversion angles as applied to loop bearings, I still don't get the hang of it."[46]

When the British Flying Training Schools opened, RAF and Air Ministry officials were well aware that the flight training syllabus of 150 hours was a wartime expedient. Earlier, when the war situation for Britain had been desperate, flight standards for student pilots had been lowered to 130 hours (and as low as 100 hours in some overseas schools). By comparison, students in the Army Air Corps peacetime pilot training program (including British students in the Arnold Scheme) graduated with around 240 hours of flight time. In December 1941 RAF officials increased the flight time in the British Flying Training Schools to 200 hours and the course length to twenty-eight weeks. Toward the end of the war, flight times were raised to 210 hours and finally 220 hours in a thirty-two-week course.

Accidents were an unfortunate aspect of flight training where young men were learning to fly sophisticated military aircraft in a fast-paced environment. Accidents covered a wide range of incidents all the way from emergency or precautionary landings that resulted in little or no damage or injury, to deadly mishaps in the air. The airfield itself, especially the crowded flight ramp, could also be deadly.

On 13 February 1942, No. 2 BFTS experienced high winds and limited visibility due to snow flurries. Striding across the flight line with head down, British student M. B. Himelstaub walked into the propeller of a taxiing AT-6 and died instantly.[47] In a similar incident, as the first course at No. 3 BFTS neared the end of training, the senior student, Freddy Tufft, an older, married ex-schoolteacher, walked into a propellor one night and was killed."

Not all accidents resulted in fatalities. Some could even be almost comical. One British primary student at No. 1 BFTS landed his Stearman on top of another Stearman waiting to take off. Both students escaped unharmed, but the Stearmans were destroyed. Asked about the accident, the landing student reportedly replied that the other student, "was sitting on my spot." With that explanation, the landing student washed out of flight training.

A similar accident occurred at No. 4 BFTS when a landing Stearman flown by K. Hermiston landed on top of another Stearman flown by D. Maxwell, which was taking off at night. Miraculously, this accident also resulted in no injuries. Officials found no fault with either student (the primary trainers modified for the British schools did not even have landing lights). In fact, Hermiston and Maxwell both graduated, both were later commissioned, and both were awarded the Distinguished Flying Cross.[48]

Among the most tragic accidents were those that resulted in multiple fatalities. On the cold morning of 20 February 1943, a flight of nineteen Harvards with thirty-eight students from Course 12 took off from No. 1 BFTS on a low-level cross-country flight to No. 3 BFTS. A gray misty overcast obscured the sky. One source remembered the civilian instructors recommended canceling the flight, but were overruled by the RAF commanding officer. Several of the school staff watched with an ominous sense of foreboding as the planes took off.[49]

As the day progressed, the weather continued to worsen and the school issued a recall to the aircraft now approaching the Kiamichi mountains in southeastern Oklahoma. Many of the planes did not hear the recall. Kenneth Dean and his navigator Reg Flanders knew they were approaching rising terrain, but were still startled by the sudden appearance of mountains immediately ahead in the mist. Flanders let out a loud expletive as Dean applied full power and climbed steeply into the clouds on instruments. Once they broke out on top of the clouds, Dean and Flanders conferred and decided to return to Terrell.[50]

Most of the Harvards returned to Terrell and six others that did not hear the recall message reached Miami. But three of the planes were missing.

In one of the Harvards, pilot John Wall and navigator Gordon Wright (nicknamed "Wilbur" Wright) found themselves trapped in a valley surrounded by heavily wooded hills which extended upward into the dark gray overcast. Noticing a small clearing, Wall pulled the power, banked the Harvard steeply to remain within the narrow confines of the valley, lowered the landing gear and flaps, and made a perfect precautionary landing.

After calling the Terrell school, Wall and Wright were advised to remain with the plane until the weather cleared. A young couple, Mr. and Mrs. E. F. Jordan, who lived next to the field, took the two students into their home. The next day Wall and Wright joined searchers from nearby communities, parties that had arrived from Terrell, and several search planes from Miami, led by Wing Commander Roxburgh, to search for the two missing planes.

That afternoon searchers found one of the missing Harvards and recovered the bodies of Vincent Cockman and Frank Fostic. The following day searchers found the other Harvard along with the bodies of Michael Hosier and Maurice Jensen. Both Harvards had crashed into the mountains obscured by haze and thick low clouds.[51]

On a hot August morning just outside of Chanute, Kansas, two Vultee BT-13s from No. 3 BFTS collided in midair during a formation cross-country flight. The four students on board the two aircraft, Alan Brown, Harold Burman, Herbert Hacksley, and Donald Harfield, were all killed. Two days later the four students were buried in Miami following a funeral attended by the Course 9 students, Wing Commander Lee and other RAF officers, Mr. Ming, the school director, and many of the flight instructors.

Two students from Course 17 at No. 6 BFTS, R. D. W. Eyres and T. G. Gray, were in the Ponca City traffic pattern flying solo at night and preparing to land. For some unknown reason, the two aircraft closed and the propeller of Gray's aircraft sliced through the tail of Eyres' trainer. Eyres spun into the ground and was killed instantly. Gray's plane crashed nearby and he was taken to the local hospital in critical condition. John

Price, another member of the course, recorded the incident in his diary and added, "I know that tomorrow we will all have our eyes skinned in the traffic pattern."[52]

As the war situation improved, the RAF detached veteran pilots to visit the British schools in the United States. The visitors gave talks on service conditions and lessons learned in combat. One of the notable visitors, Wing Commander Edward M. Donaldson, included a low-level aerobatic display in an army Curtiss P-40 fighter. Donaldson performed his aerobatic exhibition, which included a slow roll on takeoff, at No. 1 BFTS.

Ten days after Donaldson's visit, Kenneth W. Coaster ran out of fuel on a solo flight, landed in a field, and called the Terrell school for assistance. His instructor, M. B. McDonald, brought fuel to the site, but both McDonald and Coaster were killed when the Stearman failed to clear the trees at the end of the field on takeoff. Rumors persisted that McDonald attempted to emulate Donaldson's slow roll just after takeoff and stalled. There is no firm evidence to support this rumor and the exact cause of the accident will probably never be known with certainty.

A slow roll at low airspeed, such as just after takeoff, requires a tremendous amount of power to pull the aircraft through the maneuver. It is hard to believe that an experienced instructor such as McDonald would have attempted a dangerous low-level maneuver at minimal airspeed in a 220-horsepower Stearman simply because he had seen the same maneuver performed in a 1,200-horsepower single seat fighter. Jim Millward of Course 14, another of McDonald's students, always doubted the rumors. Millward remembered McDonald as "a quiet and unassuming man and certainly not an exhibitionist."[53]

Not all of the hazards came from aircraft (either in the air or on the ground). In early March 1943 the RAF reported, "A serious hanger fire at No. 4 B.F.T.S. which destroyed all the parachutes and many records together with other material. The aeroplanes, however, were all saved owing to prompt action by the cadets."[54]

The No. 3 BFTS Operations Record Book for 24 April 1943 reported another fire. "Fire at gasoline installation on Flight Line at 0315. Pump house destroyed. R. Wilson, Maintenance Chief, and A. Dahl, Night Mechanic, extinguished blaze from two 10,000 gallon tanks by backing a lorry with staging, up to the tanks and using C.O.2 apparatus. This after Miami Fire Department had used all their chemical appliances, as gasoline was boiling over from both tanks. This was a fine job on part of Wilson and Dahl."[55]

Despite official prohibitions, as well as constant warnings and threats, many young men learning to fly military aircraft could not resist the urge to show off. Unauthorized dog fighting and low flying provided an almost irresistible thrill. Common targets were farmhouses, trains, cars on roads, even buses, and the ultimate allure of flying under a bridge. But the ground held many hazards. After one fatal crash in Kansas, British officers offered a terse explanation, "Apparently shooting up a train and dived into ground."[56]

William Sydney Ellis of No. 12 Course at No. 1 BFTS had a fright one day. Ellis and his buddy Stu Barter were doing some unauthorised dog fighting and extreme low flying when Ellis spotted electrical wires immediately ahead and just managed to fly under the wires. Barter flew through the wires. Barter limped back to the airfield and instructor Ed Smith saw the Stearman coming in with bits and pieces hanging from it. After Barter landed, Smith drove up to the damaged Stearman and asked, "what the hell you been doing, boy?" Barter replied, "I hit a bird, Sir!" To which the incredulous Smith snorted, "What was it a goddam Pterodactyl?" Barter washed out of flight training, returned to Canada and remustered as a navigator.[57]

Some students under stress could show amazing creativity. Two students returned to No. 6 BFTS from a cross-country flight in a badly damaged AT-6. The wing leading edges were dented, the landing light lens broken, the radio mast had been torn off and remains of the aerial were embedded in the tail. Obviously the aircraft had been flown through telephone or electrical wires and the students would certainly be washed out. Asked by school officials to explain, the two students replied that after takeoff from a high altitude field the propeller had suddenly gone into fine pitch and due to the full fuel load, altitude, and warm temperature, they could not maintain altitude and selected an emergency landing field. They only saw the electrical lines across the end of the field when it was too late and hit the lines, which caused the propeller to go into course pitch. The propeller in course pitch enabled the Harvard to climb and maintain altitude and they returned to the field they had just left. After mechanics inspected the aircraft, the students continued to Ponca City.[58]

This inspired story is barely plausible and the facts could be true. Harvards did experience problems with the propeller pitch control and a consequence of the prop failure would have been an inability to maintain altitude, especially with the full fuel load, high altitude, and warm temperature. Hitting the wires, which would have been hard to see, could have caused the prop to go back into course pitch. School officials gave the low flying students, who had barely avoided killing themselves, the benefit of the doubt. Instead of being washed out, the students were congratulated on their sound thinking and good flying skill. The British officers, as well as the American civilian school staff prided themselves on being fair; if the story was to be accepted, then congratulations were in order.

Blaine H. Schultz, an American cadet with the first course at Riddle Field to include both RAF and Army Air Forces cadets, recalled flying low in Florida. "Every cadet at Clewiston must remember the low flying episodes. We would fly down the canals so low that you couldn't look over the banks. I recall a man fishing from a boat in a canal. We came down in a deep dive and saw him lie down in the bottom of the boat as we roared over. We chased the Brahman cattle all over the landscape. The British cadets would play chicken with cars on the highway. One RAF flier flew so low he touched the road surface, bending the tips of his prop. To avoid being caught, he landed with his wheels up, thereby really bending (or re-bending) his prop."[59]

Students were not the only ones tempted to show off. One day primary student Don Ashby heard his instructor, J. W. Talley, a former crop duster, say, "I've got it." Talley, obviously bored, then descended over one of the county farm-to-market roads. At flying speed, the main wheels touched down on the narrow road and the instructor held the stick forward to keep the tail in the air as the Stearman drove down the road. An old car appeared in the distance and confronted the aircraft head on. Talley held the Stearman on the pavement until the last possible moment and then eased back on the stick. The Stearman hopped over the car and then settled back onto the road. Ashby looked back to see the shaken farmer emerge from the car that now rested at an angle in the ditch alongside the road.[60]

Toward the end of the war the expanded flight curriculum allowed for longer cross-country flights in the advanced stage of training. After several dual and solo cross-country flights in the Harvard, including two low-level flights at 500 feet, students set out on long cross-country flights that lasted for several days and crossed several states. Students were paired on the longer flights. On each leg of these long cross-country flights one student flew while the other navigated. On the next leg of the flight, the roles reversed. The student navigator removed the control stick in the rear cockpit and used a board to spread out charts, flight plans, and various instruments.

Pilots on these long flights took devilish delight in waiting until the student in the rear seat was engaged in some navigation task and then rolling the aircraft inverted or pushing the stick violently forward, inducing negative g's. On one cross country, Alan Bramson suddenly slammed the stick forward only to hear his navigator Bryan Baker snicker, "Well laugh that off." Bramson turned around to find Baker's leather helmet, goggles, and headset stuck in the broken plexiglass canopy. Baker had removed his seatbelt to retrieve a pencil just as Bramson slammed the stick forward. Baker hit the canopy with enough force to break the plexiglass. Bramson, the top cadet in the senior class, contemplated a dismal future in the infantry. After landing, mechanics had to remove the jammed canopy in order to free Baker from the rear seat. Summoned before the chief flight instructor, Bramson assumed an innocent demeanor and told of having to take sudden evasive action after being bounced by a P-51 Mustang (a common enough practice among newly commissioned army fighter pilots). The chief flight instructor looked skeptical, but the barely plausible story could not be refuted by the fictional army pilot. Several days later Bramson graduated from No. 1 BFTS as the top cadet of Course 16.

Later courses enjoyed camera-equipped AT-6s, which provided photos of simulated aerial combat. At first only about 25 percent of students in the advanced course had a chance to fly the Harvards with gun cameras, due to a shortage of suitably equipped aircraft. In the last courses all students were able to train on gun camera-equipped Harvards. This training tool was especially valuable in evaluating a student's possible future role as a fighter pilot.

Throughout advanced training, ground school classes continued, along with periodic examinations. The final Wings Exam contained a comprehensive evaluation of all the material covered in ground school. This final test contained questions designed to reflect practical operational situations and were often quite detailed. The final navigation examination included one and a half hours of written theory questions and a two-hour simulated flight over enemy territory in the Link trainer.

After the first courses graduated, later students were given a pamphlet titled "Flying Regulations and Procedure used by the R.A.F. in England." This pamphlet attempted to introduce students to some of the differences between flying in the United States and operational flying in England. One of the major differences had to do with airfield regulations. The United States schools taught a rectangular landing pattern, but in England the RAF used a circular pattern entered at 1,000 feet above the ground. In

England many airfields operated under conditions of radio silence due to the threat of enemy action. These airfields employed an elaborate system of signals displayed on the ground in a forty-foot hollow square ("always very easily seen from the air") located adjacent to the airport watch office. Examples of these signals, as well as other differences, were explained.

At the end of training, most students in the early courses graduated with little fanfare. One exception occurred at No. 2 BFTS when the graduation of the first course coincided with a visit by Air Marshal Garrod, British Air Member for Training. The school held a formal march past and salute, followed by an address by Air Marshal Garrod. Another exception occurred when Southwest Airways staged a gala dinner and dance party for the graduates of the first course, along with invited guests and dignitaries.

The other schools celebrated early graduations with nothing more than a small informal dinner in a nearby hotel or restaurant. These dinners were usually attended by the graduating students, along with a few members of the RAF staff and school personnel. Some early courses had no formal recognition at all.

Raymond Stanley trained with Course 3 at No. 1 BFTS. "My last flight on the course was a night flight which ended in the very early hours of the morning. There was a light covering of snow on the ground and I finished the flight with a burst tail wheel tyre. After taxiing to the hangar, I was informed the course had ended. There was no graduation ceremony. A very few days later, we were paraded, bid goodbye and entrained for Moncton. I was now a qualified RAF pilot with the rank of Sergeant."[61]

An unusual early graduation occurred when Jan Ciechanowski, the Polish Ambassador to the United States, attended the graduation parade for Course 6 at No. 2 BFTS. The ambassador not only delivered the keynote address to the graduating students, but awarded RAF wings to his son, who also received the Moseley Award as the top student of the course.

Not only were ceremonies scarce for early graduates, several schools did not receive items such as pilots' wings and sergeants' chevrons (apparently one or two schools received these items from the beginning). No wings or chevrons were available for the first two courses at No. 2 BFTS, but graduates of these courses somehow obtained Royal Canadian Air Force wings. Wearing these wings back to Canada, the graduates dubbed themselves members of the "Royal California Air Force."

David Green on the first course at No. 3 BFTS described his graduation. "Very low key. Under cover parade when, Squadron Leader Kermode, read out the order promulgating our new status as pilots, with promotion to Pilot Officer, or Sergeant. (Two-thirds of us, including me, remained non-commissioned). One pair of wings pinned to shirt of student first in order of merit (Shackleton—killed within the year)."[62]

Graduates of these schools traveled back to Canada and received their wings and sergeant stripes from the supply depot in Moncton. In several incidences these early graduates arrived in Canada and were denied entrance to the local NCO club because they had no proof of rank or proof that they were pilots.

Philip Mitchell and four of his course mates at No. 2 BFTS also encountered confusion. Mitchell and his friends graduated as sergeants and returned to Canada. "Reporting to the Adjutant at No. 1 Manning Depot, we were reprimanded for wearing Sergeant's stripes; did we not know that we had all been commissioned and were now Pilot Officers?"[63]

In time, all of the schools held formal Wings Parades. These elaborate ceremonies included a march past of all students and speeches by dignitaries from the RAF Delegation in Washington or the Army Air Forces Training Command, usually accompanied by a band from a nearby army base. Selected civilians from the local community were invited to the Wings Parades through a formal printed invitation. Each graduate received his wings personally from the owner of the school, the RAF commanding officer, or the visiting dignitary. (Course 3 graduates at No. 6 BFTS, received their wings from the mayor of Ponca City.)

Each school also presented some form of memento. At No. 1 BFTS, Major Long presented a silver cigarette case to the top student in each class. Graduates of Spartan School of Aeronautics at No. 3 BFTS and Embry-Riddle at No. 5 BFTS received formal diplomas from the school, and the top student in each course at No. 5 BFTS received a gold wristwatch. At No. 2 BFTS each graduate received a leather wallet and a metal disk designating that student as a graduate of Polaris Flight Academy and the outstanding cadet received the Moseley Award, a gold identification bracelet. At No. 4 BFTS, Jack Connelly, president of Southwest Airways, presented a gold and silver bracelet to each graduate.

A day or two after the graduation ceremony the class assembled at the train station. Local residents were on hand to say goodbye and often presented small presents to the departing students, now qualified Royal Air Force pilots. The journey back to Canada and then on to Great Britain in many ways mirrored the students' original journey to the United States, but so much had transpired in so short a period of time.

On arrival back in Britain, the new RAF pilots received additional training in an Operational Training Unit on service type aircraft. After OTU, pilots were posted to an operational squadron, assigned to other duties, or received additional specialized training.

CHAPTER 7

AMERICAN HOSPITALITY

British flight students arriving in Canada had experienced generous and abundant hospitality. This much-appreciated warm welcome, although surprising, was still understandable because Canada was a Dominion country, a member of the British Commonwealth, and totally engaged alongside England in a devastating war with a common and deadly foe. Nothing, however, could prepare those British students destined for the British Flying Training Schools for the overwhelming hospitality soon to be encountered in the United States.

Ever mindful of Anglo-American relations, British officials gave each student a small blue book. The book began, "You are going to America as guests" and then explored various aspects of American life, defined the different geographical regions of the United States, recommended several books on American history, and offered tips on conduct. The small blue book described America as a "great, friendly, yet different nation" and warned students, "you will not be expected to tell your hosts and hostesses what is wrong, in your opinion, with them and their country." Students were also advised to be careful when asked about American aid to Britain, or to compare the relative merits of British and American aircraft. The book ended on a lighter note by advising students to "mingle freely with the people and partake generously of their natural hospitality."[1]

Even before reaching the individual British flight schools, students were not only captivated by this new land, but immediately encountered American hospitality. Some encountered this hospitality from fellow countrymen. On the journey south from Canada to No. 2 BFTS, the train carrying John Roberts Davies stopped in Chicago for a five-hour layover and the students toured the city. Davis wrote to his future wife, "I saw Lakeside Drive [sic: Lake Shore Drive]—a beautiful road on the shore of Lake Michigan. I went into Marshall Field's store, the largest in the world and then met an Englishman who, I believe, was the under manager, his name was John Barclay and he played the role of the Mikado in the film; we had quite a chat." The Marshall Field department store had a large restaurant with a fountain in the middle. Davis enjoyed "a huge ice cream covered with strawberries—free—on the house." The city of Chicago had a lingering notoriety from the days of Al Capone and other mobsters, and Davis added a final comment to his letter, "There were no gangsters to be seen and we were told that it is just about the most peaceful city in the world now since the days of prohibition when the gangsters simply ran the city."[2]

Two years later on the east coast, John Broome and his course mates on their way to No. 5 BFTS also encountered American hospitality before reaching their destination. "On our train journey we had a pleasant surprise at Lake Wales, Florida. Instead of our customary breakfast on the train, we were greeted by a fleet of cars at the railway station. All fifty of us left the train, piled into the various cars, and were taken to homes of the local townsfolk for a sumptuous breakfast. Hospitality on this scale was strange indeed to us, but what a warm feeling it generated! We got back to our cars and found in each compartment a sack of oranges— something that we had not been able to enjoy for years."[3]

L. J. Taylor traveled with Course 17 to No. 5 BFTS. The train made a routine stop in Sebring, Florida, and local ladies invited the British students to a nearby hotel for breakfast. The hotel dining room included a pianist. Taylor and his course mates were enjoying the food and the hospitality as the pianist played several melodies; "suddenly she broke into a tune very familiar to us cadets. There was a clattering of cutlery and dishes as we all jumped to attention. I don't know who was most embarrassed, we or the pianist, when it was explained to us that the melody was a popular tune in the United States. The pianist at Hotel Sebring was playing 'My Country Tis of Thee'—the same tune as 'God Save the King' the British national anthem."[4]

Even though the British students encountered cordiality and friendliness as soon as they entered the United States, true American hospitality manifested itself when the train arrived at its destination. Local residents were on hand to meet the trains and greet the arriving students. Early students were often interviewed by reporters and posed for photographs. This attention occurred in spite of the fact that some of the initial arrival schedules had not been published and other arrivals occurred late at night or in inclement weather. Nor did this interest wane with time. As long as the schools existed, local citizens met each arriving train and later at the end of training assembled again at the station to say goodbye to each departing course.

This intense interest in the British students took the RAF officers completely by surprise. Accustomed to an obscure service existence these officers were at a loss as to how to handle the attention. The meager official records contain questions from RAF officers assigned to the new British schools asking the Royal Air Force Delegation in Washington for guidance in handling the numerous requests for invitations, statements, and interviews. From the temporary home of No. 1 BFTS in Dallas, Wing Commander Hilton and Squadron Leader Beveridge reported, "Tremendous interest has been shown in us, and we have been overwhelmed with hospitality and offers of hospitality for ourselves and the pupils."[5]

Hilton and Beveridge attempted to handle the numerous invitations from local residents with tact and diplomacy, but were often unsuccessful.

A young couple from the affluent North Dallas suburb of Highland Park invited the entire first course to a cookout and swim party at their home. The RAF officers replied that, regrettably, the new school in temporary quarters had no transportation equipment and thought that explanation sufficient to end the matter. The following Saturday morning, fifteen Dallas taxicabs hired by the couple arrived at Love Field and transported the entire class to Highland Park.[6]

The British students and the RAF staff were the usual focus of local attention, but all aspects of the new British schools created interest. Aircraft for the schools usually arrived unheralded, but one group arrival in Terrell broke up the summer monotony and provided an unexpected diversion for the community. On the afternoon of 13 August 1941, as construction of the school facilities neared completion, Terrell residents heard the sound of approaching aircraft. The sound grew louder and louder until a formation of twenty-three Vultee BT-13 aircraft appeared in the blue summer sky and flew low over the town. The aircraft were the first contingent of basic trainers for the new school. Eleven of the planes were destined for No. 1 BFTS; the other aircraft came to take the pilots back.

On streets across the town, cars and trucks stopped or pulled over to the side of the road, merchants left shops and stores, and women abandoned household chores, picked up babies and went outside. Nearly everyone in town gazed upward into the clear sky. Each Vultee trainer sported the standard army dark blue fuselage, bright yellow wings, and alternating red and white horizontal stripes on the rudder. The entire town reverberated to the sound of twenty-three low-flying trainers, each mounting a powerful Pratt and Whitney radial engine. The engines produced a distinctive throaty roar from their short exhaust stacks. People instinctively headed for the airport as each aircraft turned over the town and entered the standard army line astern descending circular landing pattern.

Vehicles and pedestrians choked the narrow dirt road leading to the airport and created the worst traffic jam in Terrell's history. Since the airport had no fence, arriving cars pulled off the road and parked in nearby fields and the townspeople walked out onto the field as the aircraft landed. The still rough and uneven grass field had no defined runways or taxiways.

On the ground, the BT-13, with its conventional landing gear, sits with the nose in the air and the tail on the ground. This position, and the round cowling enclosing the radial engine, obscures the pilot's forward visibility. In order to see ahead while taxiing, the pilot must constantly S-turn the aircraft.

As each plane landed, the pilots alternately craned their heads from side to side to see around the high round noses, stabbed the rudder pedals and brakes to S-turn, while applying bursts of power to taxi over the uneven ground as local residents walked around to get a better look at the airplanes. After much jockeying the twenty-three trainers taxied into a rough line and the pilots shut down the engines. The silver propellers slowly came to a stop, fortunately without inflicting any injury. The next day, L. H. Luckey, the school director, diplomatically admonished Terrell residents through the local newspaper, "Please be careful around the aircraft."[7]

British students arrived in the United States from a land ravaged by war and subjected to nightly blackouts and constant food shortages. Students marveled at the seemingly endless expanse of the American landscape. On a visit to No. 1 BFTS, Squadron Leader Mills commented, "It's hard to become accustomed to so much space. We feel keenly that it is possible to put the whole of England and Scotland in this part of Texas—and still have space left over."[8]

Regardless of the school location, students were dazzled by the brilliant city lights and amazed by the abundance of consumer goods and food. Varieties of meat, along with fresh vegetables, fruit, butter, and especially white bread were all plentiful. The students were introduced to new foods such as fried chicken, chicken-fried steak, hamburgers, hot dogs, okra, and corn on the cob. (The English used corn mainly for animal feed.) Asked to describe corn on the cob one student replied, "Well it was cylindrical with little things pasted all over it and it was yellow."[9]

British students in the western schools discovered chili, tamales, frijoles, tortillas, and enchiladas. Most students developed a fondness for iced tea, especially in the summer heat, and any number of eggs were available for breakfast. In England, eggs were rationed at one egg per person per week. Pancakes and maple syrup quickly became breakfast favorites.

The students had never seen anything quite like a jukebox and everyone in America seemed to own an automobile. Someone had even invented an outdoor theater "where you stay in your car!"[10]

Although the British students in each school were the recipients of the overwhelming American hospitality, the locale presented some interesting variations. Charles George Waller arrived with the first course in Glendale, California, the temporary home of No. 2 BFTS. "As the first fifty RAF students in Los Angeles, we received many invitations. We were treated royally and given a tour of the film studios at a time when it was difficult to get in. Charles Laughton invited all of us to a party at his home. At the party were Edward G. Robinson, Deanna Durbin, Greer Garson. We had a passing [graduation] party at a place called Ella Campbell's, and I have a photo of Lionel Barrymore at the party—an uninvited guest as I recall."[11]

Phillip Mitchell of Course 9, the next to the last course to train in Lancaster, encountered the same interest from the Hollywood community as the earlier California students. Mitchell and two fellow students, Jimmy James and Johnny Lyle, "got mixed up with the French, to be more precise, Charles Boyer and his friends." Boyer invited the three British students to his home on several weekends. "We arrived for lunch time drinks to be followed by fun and games in the pool or a trip to the beach, aperitifs at five-thirty; dinner at six. Dinner being served in the typically French fashion lasted until eleven-thirty or twelve, when the party split up and we crept to bed. After a late breakfast on Sunday, we made our way back to Polaris ready for parade on Monday morning."[12]

Although California offered glamor, film stars, and studios, other schools also presented unique experiences. Chief Victor Griffiths of the Quapaw Indian tribe made an official visit to No. 3 BFTS in Miami, Oklahoma. The chief, accompanied by his wife and entire family, received a royal welcome, toured the school facilities, and then ate lunch with the British students and school staff in the cafeteria. Chief Griffiths and his family were particularly intrigued by the strange movements of the Link trainers.

In Ponca City, Oklahoma, the RAF officers assigned to No. 6 BFTS, Squadron Leader H. F. Suren, the chief ground instructor and Flight Lieutenant George Shea, the administrative officer, were both honored as sub-chiefs of the Kaw tribe. Chief Little Standing Buffalo made the presentation. Later that evening, the RAF officers and about one hundred British students attended a tribal victory dance.[13]

The weekend after the first course arrived at the short-lived No. 7 BFTS, the citizens of Snyder, Texas, located forty miles northwest of Sweetwater, invited the entire class to be honored guests at the sixth annual Scurry County Rodeo. This popular event drew crowds estimated at between three and four thousand. The city of Snyder provided buses to transport the British students to the rodeo, accompanied by the British officers and a group of Sweetwater residents. The British students and RAF officers, along with the other spectators, delighted in the novel display of authentic cowboys, bucking broncos, calf roping, and bull riding.

When the buses from Sweetwater arrived in front of Wimpy's café in Snyder, a local reporter described the meeting as "booted west Texans met their khaki clad British allies for the first time."[14] The locals had assembled approximately thirty-five horses and the more adventuresome of the British students, with some encouragement and a limited amount of instruction, mounted awkwardly. The students then rode around the town square several times to the delight of the local crowd before riding to the nearby rodeo grounds. One British rider "lost his saddle" when his horse became skittish and another horse slipped down on the slick paving. Neither riders nor horses suffered serious injury, but the first student returned to Sweetwater with "a patch of adhesive tape across his nose." Many others walked gingerly for some time from saddle sores. British student Duke Martin remarked to a local reporter, "until we get enough instructions on riding a horse we better stay up in aircraft where it is safe."[15]

Alastair Michie, the top cadet on Course 3 at No. 5 BFTS, commented on his time in Florida. "We had wonderful weekends in Miami, courtesy of the always generous drivers offering transportation. The town of Fort Myers played host to us one weekend and lavished upon us great hospitality. Throughout our time in Florida, generosity knew no bounds. I acquired a snakeskin belt from a Seminole Indian and thereafter never flew without it, to a point that I became deeply superstitious concerning it."[16]

Along with the hospitality, British students could not help but notice the differences between things in America and back home. John A. B. Keeling of Course 4 at No. 3 BFTS recorded some of the differences in his diary. "The girls round here wear skirts shorter than in England. There are so many things over here that are so new and odd. The first floor is called the second floor, light switches are on when up, 3/9/41 is 9th of March, and in every bar there is one of those machines with a long list of the latest gramophone records, and you put in a nickel and a loudspeaker blasts out the tune."[17]

Wherever they went, the British students received not only hospitality, but often adulation. Keeling again remarked, "On Saturday, I got a lift into Joplin in Missouri, 35 miles, and back again. I was twice asked to make a speech in beer cafes when tunes were sung in our honour. Some boys who went to a cinema were asked if they could arrange for some of the English boys to go there every night, and go on the stage and answer questions from the audience."[18]

Ronald Charles Lamb arrived in Oklahoma with the second course at No. 3 BFTS and was amazed by the welcome. "I will never forget our reception by the people of Miami, as we walked down the sidewalks in the main street on our first day there. They clapped as we walked by. I think that it was probably reflected glory from the Battle of Britain, which had ended but a few months before. But nowhere in this world have I ever had a reception like that either before or since."[19]

J. R. Sutton of Course 4 at No. 3 BFTS had been a member of the Oxford University air squadron before arriving in Oklahoma. Members of the early courses wore civilian suits away from the schools. After the Japanese attack on Pearl Harbor in December 1941 the British students wore RAF uniforms out of camp for the first time. During an extended period of leave between primary and basic training, Sutton and four friends visited New Orleans, "where we were the cause of much interest, as most Americans had not previously seen RAF uniforms. Needless to say, we had a superb holiday."[20]

On October 2, 1941, the Brooklyn Dodgers defeated their arch cross-town rivals, the New York Yankees by a score of three to two in the second game of the World Series. This tied the Series at one game apiece. Radios in businesses and private homes across the nation were tuned in to the game and conversation abounded on the relative merits of each team, as well as discussions of individual players who were all well known. Throughout the existence of the British flight schools, the British students and RAF staff could never understand the American obsession with baseball and the World Series. The Yankees went on to win the Series four games to one.

Of course Americans would never understand the British game of cricket either. (Many Americans didn't think the British even understood the game.) Soccer was popular on both sides of the Atlantic and the British schools frequently fielded teams against local American teams and participated in local soccer leagues. The British students developed a fondness for basketball even though they sometimes tried to play the game like rugby, even to bouncing the ball off the wall (one American Army Air Forces cadet's comment, "hilarious").

As the first summer waned and autumn arrived in the cities that hosted the British schools, local women formed committees to see that each British student received an invitation from local families for the Thanksgiving and Christmas holiday season. This tradition continued throughout the existence of the schools except when preempted by the flight schedule.

In Dallas, Mr. and Mrs. Leslie Kye entertained three British students from Course 6. The Kye family had emigrated from Chichester in Sussex, England, to Vancouver, British Colombia, in 1914 when Mr. Kye was a small boy. The family later moved to Texas. The three British students, Sid Clark, Ken Crowther, and Bob Watson, were captivated by the couple's young daughter Phyllis. The three students continued to be guests in the Kye home and four months later on Phyllis' tenth birthday they pooled their meager funds and bought her a new wristwatch, which they left under her pillow. The three students would often fly low over the Kye house as a greeting (strictly against regulations). All three British students graduated from No. 1 BFTS, but none survived the war.[21]

Alan Norton Watson arrived in Ponca City with Course 13 in November 1942. He and a fellow student spent Christmas Day with the Taft family and recorded the experience in his diary. "Gordon, Charlotte and I stayed in the small park near their home and played like a trio of kids, but then we were very happy. It's Christmas and a time to have fun." After a large, typically American, Christmas meal of turkey and all the trimmings, "we just couldn't move so we all sprawled around and talked." After a walk around the neighborhood and afternoon tea, Mr. Taft drove Watson and his friend back to camp. Watson entered a final note in his diary, "I wrote a letter home telling mum all we had done. Very Happy."[22]

After that first Christmas, Squadron Leader Beveridge wrote an open letter to the community to express

Our gratitude and appreciation for the kindness and hospitality shown by people in Terrell and the neighborhood to our pupils over the Thanksgiving and Christmas periods.

In Britain, as in America, Christmas is the Festival of the Home, and it has meant a very great deal to our pupils so far from their own homes to have the opportunity of participating in your Christmas festivities. They came back to barracks, laden with gifts and eatables and one and all spoke of the good time they had.

May I add the thanks of the R.A.F. staff here to their thanks for a Christmas which could have been bettered only by one spent at home.[23]

Once in America, some linguistic differences required explanation. British students were told not to go into a store and ask for a rubber, "the correct term in the United States is eraser." Grits is an English term for a combination of sand and gravel. Students in the southern schools must have been confused to hear the term for road surfacing material used in connection with breakfast. After being introduced to the southern collective "y'all," more than one British student on leaving a store heard the owner say "y'all come back now" only to turn around and reenter the store to see what the owner wanted. Many students after an excellent meal or weekend visit referred to the lady of the house as very homely. The strange look in return must have confused the student. In England the term homely is used to describe a particularly neat and efficient housekeeper and is considered a compliment. British students were surprised by the sudden hostility after telling a young lady that they would be around at a certain time to "knock her up," meaning to pick her up for a date. Considerable embarrassment ensued when the American meaning of the term was explained.

The British students also came into a measure of national prominence through the American medium of advertising. Even though one British administrative officer described the taste of Coca-Cola as closely akin to "brown shoe polish," most of the British students liked the drink. The Coca-Cola company responded with a national magazine ad featuring a caricature of two RAF cadets enjoying Coca-Cola. Part of the ad copy read, "One of the things you read about in the news is how R.A.F. boys training in this country enjoy Coca-Cola. Many of them have discovered its goodness for the first time. Like you, they welcome that distinctive taste." And for only five cents a bottle.

British students arriving in Canada had encountered the myriad and often confusing liquor laws in North America. Entering the United States only heightened the confusion. John Hanbury Smith-Carrington commented on his journey south from Toronto en route to Miami, Oklahoma. "Again we found the licensing laws on the train most confusing, the bar being shut or open or beer only depending on the States we were passing through."[24]

Students couldn't understand why towns such as Terrell would be dry while Dallas only thirty-five miles away openly served alcoholic beverages. Students became aware of the existence of the local bootlegger, but with Dallas so close, the British students probably did not partake of the illegal commodity to any great extent. British students at No. 3 BFTS faced the same situation in a dry Miami, but found nearby Joplin, Missouri, only thirty-five miles away, to be a wet community. Joplin quickly became a favorite weekend destination for socializing and parties.

Not all of the British students were enthralled by their American adventure. Although John A. B. Keeling of No. 3 BFTS felt that the "training here is very good (and so is the food)," he felt that in other ways "we seem to be very unlucky." Keeling was dismayed that both Oklahoma and Kansas to the north were dry states, although he had discovered Joplin, Missouri. Keeling was not impressed with the town of Miami and confided in his diary, "Miami itself is very much a one-horse town, and very holy. The only way of meeting anybody is to go to church, of which there are millions, though no Catholic, and there is no dancing and only one cinema. Absolutely 'damn all' to do, even if we had the time off to do it in."[25]

Most of the British students who trained in Oklahoma would disagree with Keeling's assessment. William A. Cory of Course 9 at No. 3 BFTS recalled his experience. "Any misgivings we had about the so-called midwestern isolationist attitude were soon dispelled. We were welcomed by all the local people and from people farther afield. Each weekend, there would be a line of cars outside the camp to pick up cadets of courses already in training and offering hospitality to the newcomers. During my stay, I spent several weekends away from Miami, with two families in particular. I also enjoyed several meals with an elderly couple in Miami itself as a guest in their home."[26]

David McClymont trained with Course 13 at No. 3 BFTS. McClymont got to know the Reverend Curtis of the First Presbyterian Church in Miami who introduced him to Madeline and Bill Hall and their small daughter, Anna Laura. This introduction resulted in a friendship that was still strong forty years later.

After Alan Norton Watson spent Christmas Day with the Taft family in Ponca City, he continued to be a regular guest in their home. Watson met the family for lunch at the Continental, a downtown restaurant, and then added a comment in his diary, "I'm certainly having a grand time. Mr. and Mrs. Taft have been wonderful, words can never express my gratitude to them, I shall never forget them and their hospitality."[27]

Geoffrey Cunliffe arrived at No. 3 BFTS with Course 12. The first several days were spent exploring the school and getting to know the staff. One of the cafeteria workers Cunliffe first met was "the lady who would insist on putting large quantities of pancakes and maple syrup on one's breakfast tray, and that was just for the starter! Known to the students as 'Mama', her name was Cordelia Powell, and she always took a great interest in the students." Cunliffe and his fellow students soon ventured into Miami. "Some of us had an open invitation from a family in Miami to visit whenever we wished. These very kind people were

Mr. & Mrs. Sheldon and their young daughter Anne (known to one and all as 'Peaches')."[28]

Frank Rainbird trained with Course 11 at No. 3 BFTS. In his diary Rainbird described an active social life which included church parties, USO functions in various cities, rodeos, Indian ceremonies, and visits to Joplin and Tulsa. He liked Miami and its people where he received many invitations to dinners, dances, and parties. He described American girls as, "lovely, charming, intelligent, good dancers, etc." Rainbird was distressed because of all the invitations that he and his classmates did not have time to accept. "The American people have been really wonderful to us, and I believe that had we had six times as many boys in the camp we still could not have accepted half the invitations we received."[29]

A good conversationalist with an outgoing personality, Rainbird met prominent people socially and was introduced to the elite of Oklahoma society. On one occasion Rainbird attended the Chamber of Commerce meeting at the Tulsa Club where he was introduced to the meeting and then met William Skelly, the founder of Spartan School of Aeronautics, who joined Rainbird's party for lunch.

Another time Rainbird went to Oklahoma City on leave and visited the state capitol while the legislature was in session. Members asked Rainbird to say a few words to the assembled House of Representatives. Rainbird then met Robert Kerr, the newly elected governor. In answer to a question, Rainbird told the governor, "I just came to see how your government works in Oklahoma." Not to be upstaged by the young man from Britain, the new governor quickly replied, "If you find out come back and tell me."[30]

David Stewart of No. 5 BFTS and his course mates made numerous trips into Clewiston, usually accompanied by the school mascot, a dog named Queenie. The students felt that Queenie knew the local bus schedule as well or better than they did. When the students received weekend passes they often ventured to neighboring towns such as West Palm Beach. Stewart's favorite destination was Sebring, until one day a driver giving him a ride said, "I'll tell you, son, you ought to go to Fort Meade, it's a great town for uniforms." Stewart took the suggestion and never regretted it. "I made friendships there that have weathered the years. Sitting on the ground with two maidens peeling oranges as fast as I could eat them, interrupted only with time out for swimming, I thought, 'This is the way to spend a war!' Anita Oakes's father would drive me out on the highway, and I would get a ride to Riddle Field, usually from the first car that came along."[31]

Robert H. Tilney trained with Course 26 at No. 3 BFTS, one of the last courses, which did not graduate in Miami, but returned to Britain at the end of the war. After four years the intensity of the American hospitality had not diminished. "A friend and I decided to go to Tulsa. We would go to a service center in Tulsa and they would look after us. We were met there by some charming ladies—do you have any place to stay? We were told to sit down and wait. We were there for half hour, then a couple came in, took us to their home, and said, 'as long as you are in America, this is your home!' We were given keys to their door, and given a room to share." Tilney and his friend continued to visit the family whenever they could, "we were like two sons to them; we became a part of the family, met their friends, had dates arranged for us (the girls had cars, always)." Tilney and his friend also accompanied the family to the local Methodist Church on South Boston Street, "we attended church, and people shook hands with us, while another queue formed to shake hands with the minister—our line longer than the minister's."[32]

At first glance, Mesa, Arizona, the home of No. 4 BFTS, seemed a lonely outpost in the desert. But Mesa residents went all out for the British students. One student, Cecil Bridges, had joined the RAF in 1935 and trained at the technical school at Halton. Bridges had considerably more service experience than most of the British students when he arrived with Course 8. Bridges found that Arizona, "was to my young but slightly war-weary eyes almost a place of enchantment—the palm lined streets of the Phoenix suburbs, the sun-drenched acres of orange and grapefruit trees, the clear cut outlines of Camelback and Superstition Mountains and, best of all, the thought of flying those azure skies above what was indeed Paradise Valley." Bridges and his course mates encountered the same unbridled American hospitality in Mesa. "Our reception by citizens and field personnel was incredibly generous. The British War Relief Society held open house—perfect strangers offered their homes for holidays—to pay for a beer in a bar was almost impossible. Weekend garden parties, swimming at the Camelback Inn and the Jokake Inn or the local Country Club—all these things were a far cry from England in March 1942."[33]

As Bridges mentioned, Phoenix offered abundant entertainment opportunities. Mrs. Elizabeth (Libby) Maguire, a young British bride who had moved to Phoenix with her husband in 1938, provided a perpetual open house for the British students. She and her husband took many of the students on picnics, swimming in the Salt River, and on long walks to various Indian ruins. And Arizona is located next to California. For the British students, California meant Hollywood. Even after two years of war, one student remembered Hollywood fondly. "Once in town we found that, in 1943, wearing a uniform was exactly the same as waving a magic wand. Doors opened all over the place, invitations came easily, and we had to fight really hard to pay for our own drink in a bar. Get back into bed on the same day in which you got up and you were labeled a dead-beat."[34]

Andrew Bayley of Course 17 at No. 1 BFTS recalled the hospitality of one Dallas family. "Dr. and Mrs. Guessner of Dallas afforded three fellow cadets and me generous hospitality and sleeping accommodation on Saturday nights when we could visit Dallas. They also fed us on Sundays and often we accompanied the doctor on his rounds on Sunday mornings. They attended our wings presentation, drove us back to Dallas and took us out for a meal and entertained us for the rest of that weekend. I shall never forget them!"[35]

John Jeffrey of Course 6 at No. 2 BFTS later commented on his stay in California. "The people treated us like royalty, came out 70 miles offering accommodation in L.A., even driving us each way by car, and often taking us on trips to the Mexican border through the mountains, and to the many beaches."[36]

John Broome trained with Course 18 at No. 5 BFTS. On an early leave, Broome and his friend Charlie Holliday went to Palm Beach. The two students were gazing wide-eyed at the beautiful large homes with immaculate gardens when a car pulled up and a charming lady invited Broome and Holliday to visit her at an address just around the corner. "She and her husband became 'Mom and Pop' Feek to Charlie and me all during our stay at Riddle Field. They made us most welcome, opening their home on Chilean Avenue to us. They also gave us much encouragement in our studies to become aviators and, above all, provided close bonds of friendship when we were without our families." To celebrate the students' graduation, Mrs. Feek decided to prepare a traditional English meal of roast beef and Yorkshire pudding. But no one knew how to cook it, the British students were no help, and a search of recipes proved fruitless. Mr. Feek offered a solution, "The British embassy in Washington will have the recipe for Yorkshire pudding—That's part of their job." After several telephone calls, the embassy staff, from the ambassador on down, put their collective talents to work and came up with a detailed recipe, the results of which were described as "a smashing success."[37]

Joseph S. Ekbery who trained with the second course at No. 2 BFTS had an interesting comment on California hospitality. "The life attached to the studios and the cinema was very artificial, so most of us were glad to be entertained by the real natives of Los Angeles. These people came forward in droves to take parties of us for outings, and sometimes for the weekends."[38]

In each community there were ladies who opened their homes, organized events, made sure the British students had places to stay or invitations to dinner, and generally organized the local hospitality. In Clewiston, honors were shared by Mrs. Rubert Smith, Mrs. Beryl Bowden and others. In West Palm Beach, Florida, that lady, more than any other, was Mrs. Florence Nesmith, a wealthy socialite and Canadian national. Mrs. Nesmith's favorite nephew had been killed in action flying with the Royal Canadian Air Force. Nesmith also sent crates of warm clothing and other much-needed items to Britain. "Florence Nesmith thought nothing of calling social register luminaries for contributions to what friends jocularly labeled the FFFF, Florence's Friendly Fund for Fliers."[39]

Hospitality and offers of help were not confined to individual Americans; the British schools were literally adopted by the local communities. When it became obvious that No. 1 BFTS would not include a gymnasium or a swimming pool, the nearby Texas Military College, a private school with classes ranging from elementary school through high school and junior college, offered the British students the use of their facilities. The city of Terrell installed a bench on Moore Avenue with a sign exhorting drivers to give a student a ride to Dallas. British students never waited long for a ride. Volunteers from the Terrell Junior Chamber of Commerce took one hundred of the first British students to the Majestic Theater in downtown Dallas to see the opening of the movie *A Yank in the RAF* starring Tyrone Power and Betty Grable and also arranged for one hundred Southern Methodist University coeds to attend.

Clewiston residents transported the British students of No. 5 BFTS ninety miles to Miami, Florida, to see the opening of the same movie. The theater featured a profusion of Union Jacks and a giant model Spitfire mounted on a sign welcoming the Clewiston students. The mayor of Miami greeted the students in the theater foyer and autographed the plaster casts of two of the young men with broken legs. The movie began only after several speeches and the British students had been introduced and asked to stand. Russell Cooke of Course 1 described the film as "very good indeed, though the fighting over Dunkirk was rather overdone [the course included a British army veteran who had been one of the last to be evacuated from Dunkirk]." Cooke commented, "We arrived back at camp in very good spirits about 2am, to be flying again at 6:30am."[40]

When the first students of No. 3 BFTS arrived in Miami, Oklahoma, before the school barracks had been completed, Northeastern Oklahoma Junior College offered the use of their dormitories, which were vacant due to summer vacation. In Ponca City, the Ponca Military Academy, another private school, housed and fed the first British students until the barracks and dining hall at No. 6 BFTS were finished. The private school also allowed the use of its classrooms so ground school classes could start immediately. Afterwards the academy continued to support the school in various ways. When No. 4 BFTS opened with few recreation facilities, nearby Mesa and Tempe colleges offered the use of their "flood lit fields" to the British students.

Ponca City residents took eighty of the British students from No. 6 BFTS to Bartlesville, Oklahoma, in a mile-long caravan escorted by the Oklahoma Highway Patrol. Once in Bartlesville, the students enjoyed a visit to a dude ranch complete with deer and buffalo, then on to an old-fashioned square dance at the local lodge where dates had been arranged for each student. The students then ate dinner at the American Legion Hall and afterwards, "An excellent orchestra played for ballroom dancing, which finished all too quickly." The Ponca City residents then conveyed the British students back to the school in the early morning hours, again escorted by the Oklahoma Highway Patrol.

In several cities local corporations with cafeterias and auditoriums generously made these facilities available to the British schools. In Ponca City, Continental Oil Company (Conoco) offered the use of its considerable facilities. Conoco hosted a Wings dinner and dance for most graduating courses at No. 6 BFTS. United States Sugar Company, the leading corporation in Clewiston, offered the use of its auditorium to No. 5 BFTS for graduation parties and dinner dances, as well as special events staged by the school.

The United Service Organization (USO) opened service clubs in many cities across the United States. The opening of No. 7 BFTS in Sweetwater, Texas, also coincided with the opening of a new USO club located on East

Third Street across from the Sweetwater Post Office. The local newspaper reported, "Sweetwater citizens turned out en masse Saturday night to welcome students of the British air school of Avenger Field." Opening ceremonies included American soldiers from Camp Barkeley in Abilene, piano and accordion music, and songs performed by a group of the newly arrived British students. Several high-ranking army officers from West Texas bases, as well as the British officers, were introduced and the proceedings were broadcast live over local radio station KXOX. Following the thirty-minute radio broadcast, a square dance team entertained the crowd.

Some of the smaller cities without a USO opened their own clubs. The city of Clewiston opened a club in the town's community center, which had a lounge room, "tastefully furnished and completely equipped with a kitchen, radio, victrola, library, and every facility of a well appointed club." The club was made possible through the efforts of a committee of local women headed by Mrs. Elbert Stewart and Mr. and Mrs. Ira Nesmith of Palm Beach, who called for donations of money, furniture, and equipment from the people of that city. An instant hit when it opened in March 1943, the club operated during all open post hours and featured dancing and a floor show on Saturday nights.

Citizens in Miami, Oklahoma, opened a service center after the Dobson family donated a vacant building downtown. Donations by churches, civic groups, and private citizens furnished the center. Activities included reading, playing games, and dancing. Specially selected local girls, approved by a community committee, served as hostesses, but with very strict rules of behavior.

In Mesa, Arizona, citizens opened another servicemen's club with "telephones, showers, books, and card tables" billed as an "International Club." In addition to the British and Army Air Forces cadets training in the area, Thunderbird Field also hosted a contingent of Chinese flight students. The British War Relief Society in Phoenix also opened a club largely through the efforts of Mrs. Herbert Mosse, an energetic lady originally from New Zealand. As in other areas, local residents provided donations to equip the club.

In August 1942 Mr. and Mrs. George Brett along with their daughter Ellen opened their Ponca City home as an unofficial servicemen's club. Rooms in the home were furnished as game rooms and other rooms were converted into reading rooms. The floor of the porch received a special coat of wax for dancing and the lawn provided areas for croquet and shuffleboard. Volunteer hostesses were on duty, the home featured light refreshments, and entertainment was provided on special evenings.

In addition to the USO or special clubs, businesses in each town became favorite meeting places for the British students. Probably the most popular were the local drug stores with their delightful soda fountains, and after these were eating places and cinemas. In Terrell, the Bass Drug Store and its flamboyant owner Margaret Bass became a favorite place to relax, as well as Chris' Café. In Ponca City, students quickly found Cuzalian Drug Store and the three cinemas, the Roxie, Murray, and Poncan Theater. Also in Ponca City the British students enjoyed horseback riding at Wetump's stables. So great was the demand that Mr. Wetump had to purchase additional horses. For night life in Ponca City, the Club Lido featured dancing every night except Monday and offered a live orchestra on Saturday night, all for an admission price of fifty-six cents. In Clewiston, the Seminole Drug Store became a favorite hang out. In Miami, students frequented the Coleman Theater.

Officials at Camp Crowder, a large U.S. Army Signal Corps training base located in Neosho, Missouri, fifteen miles south of Joplin, often invited the British students from No. 3 BFTS to dances and other special events. The camp had its own band, as well as a large movie theater.

Movies became an important part of the British student's social life in the United States. Even small towns such as Clewiston had a movie theater and medium-sized towns usually had two or three theaters. At this time there were many Hollywood films playing for short runs. A person could go to the theater every other night and always see a different film. Movie theaters were an inexpensive place to take a date and the British students enjoyed a wide range of films, westerns, mysteries, dramas, love stories, comedies, and musicals. British students became astute critics and their diaries and letters often contain commentaries on particular films, plots, and actors' performances. Even the American flight cadets who later trained at the British schools recorded similar comments. William Watkins, an AAF cadet in Ponca City, wrote in his diary, "Went to town and saw 'The Gangs All Here' again. Just love Alice Faye in that picture."[41]

No. 3 BFTS proudly displayed an autographed, studio portrait of M-G-M starlet Susan Peters. In addition to the autograph, the picture included a hand written greeting, "My sincere thanks to the boys of No. 3 British Flying Training School." The picture had been sent after Course 18 voted Peters "The girl we'd like most to have waiting for us on the flight line."[42]

Even though Clewiston residents went all out to entertain the British students, Clewiston was still a small town. Other nearby Florida towns, especially Fort Myers, Sarasota, Fort Meade, and Arcadia, also took it upon themselves to entertain the British students. An Embry-Riddle employee described Arcadia: "It is a typical small central Florida town with its lovely old houses, large moss hung live oaks and friendly people."[43]

One Saturday afternoon after the conclusion of the training day, residents of Fort Myers traveled to Clewiston in forty private cars and conveyed the British students back to Fort Myers in a lengthy motorcade. The cars arrived to blaring auto horns and signs proclaiming "Welcome British Cadets." Staging out of the local Elks Club, students were assigned to private homes for the weekend and a local girl accompanied each British student to the planned festivities, which included sightseeing, an outdoor fish fry, dinner, and a dance. Most of the students did not get to bed until 2:00 the next morning and one student's experience is typical. Returning to his room, "I found a lot of home made cookies and a bowl of grapes awaiting me." The next morning most of the students accompanied the families to local churches. "I went to the Methodist with the family. After being publicly welcomed by the vicar we each had to stand up and announce our identity and hometown. It's funny how they all want to shake hands with you over here. I nearly broke my arm that weekend."

Following church services the students were taken to a local lake, "where a grand lunch was awaiting to be served up by more of the town." The afternoon was spent swimming, eating, and talking. Russell Cooke described the weekend in a letter to his parents and concluded, "About 5 pm we bid farewell to our now many great hearted and charming friends of Ft. Myers and we were driven back to camp in another motorcade. Everyone is looking forward to a speedy return to Ft. Myers where we have a permanent invitation for any weekend."[44]

Hospitality also worked both ways. Throughout the existence of the British schools the students returned the hospitality of their American hosts. The British flight students participated in local events, patriotic parades, and war-bond drives. They appeared on radio programs and staged special performances for local audiences. The students also introduced Americans to songs and dance steps that were popular back home such as the Palais Glide and Lambeth Walk.

British students from No. 3 BFTS participated in a Tulsa radio quiz show in competition with a team of American Aviation cadets from Spartan School of Aeronautics. As a result of that experience and a victory for the RAF team, the RAF commanding officer asked the successful students to write an inter-flight quiz to be held the next week. They wrote numerous amusing multiple choice questions for use in the quiz. On another occasion, RAF students were asked to participate in an unsponsored radio broadcast in Dallas titled *Wake Up America*, described as a show "of a patriotic nature intended, amongst other objects, to promote the sale of defense bonds and stamps and generally to aid morale."[45]

Just after the United States entered the war, Flight Lieutenant Palmer, the new administrative officer at No. 1 BFTS, organized an elaborate New Year's musical show. The two-hour presentation in the Terrell

High School auditorium included comedy skits, patriotic tunes, and the song "We're the Boys of No. 1 BFTS" written by Palmer. One of the cadet performers, Leonard Blower, had been a member of the British Broadcasting Corporation (BBC) chorus before the war. A *Dallas Morning News* reporter described Blower as "a British songbird." The show ended with stirring renditions of "God Save the King," "There'll Always be an England," "The Eyes of Texas," and "The Star Spangled Banner" accompanied by the British and United States flags on stage. The RAF cast presented the well-received show again the next day to another sold-out crowd (admission twenty-five cents going to the RAF recreation fund), and again the next week in Dallas and nearby Kaufman. The British students presented a slightly revised show the following year.

Blower, a lay preacher, later preached the evening service in the local Methodist church. Blower titled his sermon "Jesus Is All the World to Me." Three weeks after his sermon, Blower's AT-6 collided in midair with another AT-6 flown by Raymond Berry. Both students were killed in the crash and are buried in the Oakland Memorial Cemetery. When Blower's voice, which had graced so many musicals and church services, had been stilled forever, the entire town of Terrell mourned.

British students from No. 6 BFTS presented several talent shows in Ponca City. One of the most popular shows, titled "Grand Vaudeville in 1943," contained songs and comedy skits. In February 1944, just months before the school closed, the students staged another show, styled a review, titled "Wakey-Wakey" in the Ponca City high school auditorium.

The British officers were often asked to speak to local civic organizations and to participate in local events. In Sweetwater, Texas, Wing Commander Moxham, the No. 7 BFTS commanding officer and a former Boy Scout leader in England, officiated at the investiture of Eagle Scout rank on Billy Nichols of local Troop 47 and then spoke to the assembled residents about scouting in England. Squadron Leader Edwards, the No. 7 BFTS chief ground instructor and a former schoolmaster, spoke to the local Rotary Club about education in England.

In Florida the return hospitality took an unusual form. The area around Clewiston had few physicians and after the U.S. Army added a small hospital to each BFTS school, the army doctor at No. 5 BFTS regularly offered routine and emergency medical services to local residents. Captain Murray Cash, M.D. served as flight surgeon at Riddle Field from 1943 to 1944. "My memories of Clewiston and 5 BFTS are very fond ones. In establishing a rapport with the British, I had an advantage over other Americans because I had been a British subject. I was born in Toronto, Canada, and later became an American citizen. As a matter of fact, it was because of my background that I was assigned to Riddle Field."[46]

Apparently no aspect of the American experience escaped the British students. The Miami, Oklahoma, Junior Chamber of Commerce invited the students from No. 3 BFTS to be guests at a local donkey softball game in which the players were mounted on donkeys, a beast noted for obstinate mannerisms. The students enjoyed the game so much that the Junior Chamber of Commerce asked if they would like to participate next time. They would. In fact, Course 10 fielded its own donkey softball team. The British students won the resulting game, but one has the impression that the score was less important than the spectacle itself. And the image of softball played astride Oklahoma donkeys is probably best left to the imagination.

Every town celebrated the uniquely American holiday of the Fourth of July. These celebrations invariably included parades, numerous flags, patriotic speeches, fireworks displays, and outdoor picnics. The picnics featured an abundance of hotdogs, hamburgers, fried chicken, potato salad, baked beans, watermelon, cold drinks, and assorted condiments, along with a variety of desserts, such as pies, cakes, and homemade ice cream. The British students participated in the local festivities and marveled at the celebrations. During the festivities many of the students suddenly realized, "Hey, they're celebrating independence from us!"

Each school, except the short-lived No. 7 BFTS, promulgated some form of unit publication. No. 1 BFTS published several issues of a book, similar to a high school or college yearbook, titled *Detached Flight*. Each issue contained a message from the RAF commanding officer and the school director, as well as photographs of each individual student, group photos of the school staff, and routine activities around the school. The school published the first *Detached Flight* in March 1942. Six issues were eventually published and each issue included three courses. The title originated from a feeling of remoteness felt by the RAF personnel assigned to the Terrell school.

In March 1942, No. 2 BFTS published the first of six issues of the student magazine titled *SALUTE*. This publication resulted from the efforts of F. J. Gobelle, an employee of the school, and his wife, the school's RAF secretary. The January 1943 *SALUTE* marked the last issue, as well as the closing of the school.

Both Spartan School of Aeronautics and Embry-Riddle published school-wide newsletters and each issue had a section devoted to each individual school. In addition to the company newsletters, both Spartan's No. 3 BFTS and Embry-Riddle's No. 5 BFTS compiled their own publications. Each course at No. 3 BFTS issued an official journal, titled *Open Post*. This publication contained literary pieces written by the British students with additional articles contributed by the school staff. No. 5 BFTS published a newsletter titled *Roger Out*. The Embry-Riddle company publication may have had the most original title, *Fly Paper* and the catchy subtitle, *Stick to It*. Beginning in March 1942 the students in Mesa published their own book, *Peregrine*. It too followed a literary format, but in a more humorous vein much like *Punch* back home.

No. 6 BFTS published a school magazine titled *Tails Up* with the first issue dated Christmas 1941. It too followed a literary format written by the students. The first issue contained a Foreword by Flight Lieutenant Suren, at the time the only permanent RAF officer at the school, and welcome messages from Frank Overstreet, the mayor of Ponca City, and Dan Morgan, the president of Continental Oil Company. Morgan reiterated a common impression of the British students. "Since coming here, your personal conduct, high morale, and studious application to your arduous task have been exemplary."

All of the school publications carried advertisements to help defray the cost of printing. Local businesses took out ads and many of these carried words of welcome and greetings to the British students. The support of local businesses was a tangible demonstration of the close ties between the local community and the individual schools.

Flight Lieutenant Palmer warned arriving students not to drive an automobile while in the United States "because Americans drive on the wrong side of the road." Palmer's humor aside, British students were forbidden to drive an automobile during training. This prohibition appeared in the schools' Routine Daily Orders, but seems to have been selectively enforced. There are records of students being brought up on charges for driving, but the punishments were minor. Other schools apparently ignored the infractions. American families who befriended British students were often happy to teach a young man to drive. In some schools it became a source of pride for a student to drive the family, in the family car, to his own graduation ceremony.

Renting a car was usually too expensive for students' limited resources, but one group of British students pooled their funds to hire a car for an extended trip during leave. One of the students had a British drivers license. At this time a British citizen could obtain a driving license without any form of test (the same as in the United States). Using the student's British license, the group hired the car and set out on leave even though the student with the license had never driven a car. He apparently learned on the way.

The British students enjoyed periods of leave during flight training. The first leave usually occurred after primary and students took the opportunity to see various sections of the United States. Before the United States entered the war, students could travel by air, but after Pearl Harbor restrictions limited commercial air travel to priority military and civilian passengers. Even though students received reduced fare passes for rail and bus travel, accommodations were often limited. But hitchhiking was an accepted mode of travel.

John Hanbury Smith-Carrington of Course 4 at No. 3 BFTS described one of his leaves. "In between the Primary and Basic Stages, we had a ten-day holiday. I and a friend went hitch hiking around the Southern States and visited Houston, Dallas, New Orleans, etc. We had wonderful hospitality, rarely had to pay for anything and arrived back at Miami with almost the same amount of dollars we started out with."[47]

Peter Brannan started with Course 25 in Clewiston but was put back to Course 26 due to illness. One morning, Brannan and a friend left Riddle Field "with our thumbs in the appropriate position" and with a squeal of brakes the first car that approached stopped and picked up the two students ("this was typical") and drove to West Palm Beach. "Our beacon was the home of Mrs. Nesmith, who greeted us like long-lost sons and despatched us to the winter home of the Countess Apponyi on Everglades Avenue.[48] At the proper address, we found that the countess was not in residence at the time, but we were to be guests of the house. Countess Apponyi's Filipino manservant catered to our needs—cooking, making our beds, and keeping the fridge well-stocked with beer and assorted goodies."[49]

William Sydney Ellis and Frank Fostick along with their Course 12 mates were on the train destined for No. 1 BFTS. Feeling bored, Ellis and Fostick wandered to the observation car and struck up a conversation with an amiable gentleman. Apparently the observation car was out of bounds for the British students and they were ordered back to their own car, which upset the gentleman. He said if they couldn't talk in the observation car, then he would go to their car. He did, and the three resumed their conversation. During the conversation the gentleman said he lived and worked in Houston and if the two ever got to Houston they should visit him and could contact him at the Gulf Oil building. The students received seven days' leave after primary and "Frank and I decided to get to Houston to look up the gentleman who had been so kind to us on the train." Ellis and Fostick hitchhiked from Terrell to Houston and spent the night in a motel. The next morning, the two located Judge John E. Green, corporate attorney for Gulf Oil Company at his office in the Gulf Building. Judge Green packed up work and took Ellis and Fostick to his home on Lazy Lane called "Green Pastures." Mrs. Green was entertaining when they arrived, and amongst the guests was Madame Chiang Kai-shek. "We were treated like royalty, we had the blue guest room, were made honourary members of the Country Club, so we could use it when our hosts were otherwise engaged and were taken to the stables, given horses to ride, and introduced to the art of Trotting in those very flimsy carts. And to cap it all, John insisted on booking us reservations on the 'Sunbeam Special' (a streamlined express train) for our return to Dallas, so that we could stay till the last hour without having to hitch back."[50]

Roger Mills of Course 14 at No. 3 BFTS used his leave time to advantage. He first hitchhiked to Albuquerque, New Mexico, on the historic Route 66 westward from Miami through Tulsa, Oklahoma City, and Amarillo, Texas. In Albuquerque, some American Army Air Forces personnel suggested that Mills might catch a ride by air from the nearby army air field. He succeeded in getting a flight on a B-24 Liberator from Albuquerque to Sacramento, California. From there, he paid for an airline flight to Burbank where he stayed with the pilot of the plane while in the Los Angeles area. Near the end of his leave, Mills caught a Greyhound bus to Oklahoma City and hitchhiked back to Miami, arriving in time to continue training.

Taking leave after primary training at No. 1 BFTS, Harry Hewitt and Stan Marshall hitchhiked south to Waco. While exploring the town, they met the local sheriff, complete with large Stetson hat and cowboy boots. After hearing that Hewitt and Marshall had been constables in England, the sheriff gave the pair a tour of the county jail and offices, complete with several bullet holes in the walls and ceilings. The affable sheriff even lowered his trousers to show the pair an old bullet wound in the buttocks he received while arresting a particularly recalcitrant suspect.

Upon leaving the jail the sheriff hailed a passing station wagon and asked the couple inside to give Hewitt and Marshall a lift further south. The students spent several days at the couple's south Texas ranch, swimming and enjoying a new experience, steaks cooked on an outside grill. After traveling on to the state capital in Austin, the two students hitchhiked back to Terrell and resumed training.[51]

William I. Davies and two friends were headed back to Riddle Field after a weekend pass in Palm Beach. The British students had little money and were almost out of time. The three had just reached the highway to Clewiston when a police car drove up and stopped. "We found it fascinating to see those massive men with big guns in holsters with real cartridges around the middle." The big policeman asked, "Where you boys headin?" and when they answered, "Clewiston, sir" he replied, "sit tight." The students waited until the policeman spotted a large car and waved it over to the side of the road. "The big officer with the big gun gently told the driver, 'Now you be sure that you set these here boys down safely in Clewiston, you hear now.' 'Sure do, sir,' replied the driver as we three gave our profuse thanks to the big cop. It seemed that we were home in no time!"[52]

The allure of Hollywood extended beyond California and Arizona. Taking leave from No. 1 BFTS, Gordon Wenham, Ronnie Ward, Stan Wildman, and Jim Millward of Course 14 hitchhiked to Hollywood in two and a half days. The young men were briefly arrested in El Paso by Texas Rangers, unfamiliar with RAF uniforms, who thought the students might be escaped German prisoners of war. In California the students met actress Carole Landis on duty at the Hollywood canteen and spoke to actor Peter Lorre, who took an interest in their flight training. The group split into pairs for the return trip, which took three and a half days.[53]

John Hanbury Smith-Carrington recounted his experience with American hospitality. "As we were only paid one dollar a day, we had to rely on hitch-hiking outside the base. There was always a queue of cars offering to take us out for a meal or hospitality. Joplin was the nearest town, but many of us headed for Kansas City at weekends where there were a number of families who would ask us to stay for the weekend. After coming from food rationed U.K., we were amazed at the amount of food offered. In particular, it took us some time to get accustomed to the American breakfast!"[54]

Among the families in Kansas City whom Smith-Carrington mentioned, one became particularly well known. Mrs. Lucille McPherson Jenkins, a personal friend of Eleanor Roosevelt, who became known as "Mama Jenks," maintained a perpetual open house for the British students on leave. In addition to her home in Kansas City she frequently visited Miami and Ponca City to host parties and gatherings for the British students, usually at local hotels. Mrs. Jenkins maintained a visitors log in her home and one entry is representative: "This house and those in it holds a section of my heart for ever. There is no place like it—there are no people like you. You are tops and I will never forget you."[55]

Some of the British students were fortunate to have family in the United States. Sometimes these relatives were distant relations that parents had mentioned; others were more recent emigrants to the United States and therefore known to the student. In either case the students attempted to get together for reunions during periods of leave. Before the United States entered the war and travel became a matter of priority, early students could travel by air, and those who did marveled at the experience. An uncle of John A. B. Keeling of Course 4 at No. 3 BFTS paid for Keeling to visit relatives in Los Angeles. After a short fuel stop in El Paso, where passengers could see the lights of Mexico, the flight continued westward. "There was a brilliant moon, and at midnight we were flying not over the Rockies but through a pass. It was simply lovely. The planes are marvelously comfortable and they each have a pretty stewardess who looks after you and cooks your meals. I fell asleep during the evening and when I woke up, my seat was tilted back, I was wrapped up in a blanket and had a pillow under my head, That's what I call service!"[56]

Archie B. Venables, who trained with Course 11 at No. 3 BFTS, learned a great deal about his family history in a very unusual way. Shortly after his arrival at the school, a local Judge Venables sent his car to pick up Venables for a weekend visit. "It was in his house that I learned more about the Venables family than I ever heard in England. I knew that my father & grandfather were born in Cheshire, England. It was in Oklahoma that I learnt that the family had been there and documented since 1066. I learned that Abraham Venables settled in Virginia in 1680, that John Venables was a staff officer to Washington and many other members of my family had played a distinguished part in the early days of your country. I was indeed an honoured guest in Oklahoma."[57]

The lasting friendships that developed between the British students and local residents resulted in considerable correspondence long after the students graduated and left the United States. Former students as well as their families continued to convey news back to the United States. The father of Ken Bickers wrote to Mr. and Mrs. A. H. Boyd in Terrell to let them know his son had been awarded the Distinguished Flying Cross. Bickers, one of the youngest flight commanders in the Royal Air Force, successfully flew his severely damaged Lancaster bomber back to England after an attack by two German night fighters that killed one of the crew and wounded several others.

The news from the families of former students was often tragic. The wife of Flight Lieutenant Harold Taylor wrote that her husband had been shot down on his first mission over Europe. A. D. C. Jenkins died in the crash of his Royal Mail flying boat on a flight from Cairo to London. Jenkins' father wrote to friends in Terrell to let them know how much Jenkins had enjoyed his time in Texas.[58] Len Chapman became an instructor upon his return to England. Chapman and his student were both killed when a German night fighter shot down their trainer.

The mother of Andy Wright wrote to let Mr. and Mrs. J. J. Maresh know that Wright had been killed on a bombing mission to Stuttgart, Germany. "I thank you very much for the love and kindness you showed Andy, and especially for the lovely photos you sent of him. I have him near me and always will as long as I can see him in the photos you sent. They are so lifelike, better than any we can get done here."[59] Wright was on his last mission before a well-deserved rest. Wright's death had been reported six months later by the German commandant at Stuttgart. The Germans had given Wright and the other members of his bomber crew a military funeral.

The popular first commanding officer of No. 5 BFTS, Wing Commander Kenneth Rambling, had returned to Bomber Command after leaving the United States. Residents of Clewiston and the surrounding towns were saddened to learn that Rambling had been killed in action.

Carolyn Wadlow and her family in Palmdale, Florida, regularly entertained the British students from Riddle Field. She stayed in touch with many of the students after graduation and regularly reported to the Embry-Riddle company newsletter on the latest postings and news. In one report, Wadlow supplied a news clipping and a birth announcement. The news clipping noted the death of Pilot Officer W. H. Marshall during a bombing mission over Germany on February 24, 1945. The announcement reported the birth of Christopher Harold Marshall, born March 30, 1945 to Pilot Officer and Mrs. W. H. Marshall.[60]

Even officials stayed in touch with friends. In September 1944, Air Commodore Carnegie, now Director of Training at the Air Ministry in London, wrote to let Al Storrs at Southwest Airways know that Dick Medhurst, the top student of Course 17 at No. 4 BFTS, was missing in action. Medhurst had been assigned as a copilot on a Dakota transport for the ill-fated Arnhem resupply mission in which British casualties were high. Carnegie concluded his letter optimistically, "We are hoping that Dick managed to get away with it." Sadly that was not to be; Richard Medhurst was reclassified as killed in action on 19 September 1944.[61]

Not all of the messages were tragic. Terrell residents were relieved to learn that Wing Commander Hilton, the first commanding officer of No. 1 BFTS, who had also returned to Bomber Command, successfully bailed out of his stricken bomber after being shot down over Europe. Hilton survived and became a prisoner of war. Clewiston residents were proud to learn that Flying Officer Donald McIntosh, a graduate of Course 11, had received the Distinguished Flying Cross for a dangerous attack on the German battleship *Tirpitz* then sheltered in a heavily defended Norwegian fiord. Pilot Officer J. C. Weller wrote from England to let friends in Terrell know that the recent stories of his death were "a bit exaggerated".[62]

Because of Great Britain's lengthy history of foreign wars and colonial conflicts, along with a small land area at home, British officials had long ago decided that servicemen who died on active service would be buried where they fell. British flight students who died during training at the British Flying Training Schools are buried in local cemeteries.

Individuals, the American Legion, the British War Relief Society, or committees of local women tended to the care of the graves of the British students. Although customs varied between schools, most of the families of those who died in the United States received a photograph of the grave and often a photograph of the service.

After the first two fatalities at No. 4 BFTS, the local American Legion Post sent a telegram to the families that read in part, "the boys are resting in the most beautiful little city in the Valley of the Sun. A bit of England where the trees and the shrubs are forever green."[63]

Family members wrote to express their appreciation not only for the photographs, but for the obvious care the graves would receive in the future. Most of these families knew they would never have a chance to visit the graves of sons or husbands.

Mrs. Molly Campbell of Plymouth, England wrote to the local American Legion commander in Mesa. "It is very consoling to a mother who is thousands of miles away from her dear son's grave to know that it will be always honoured by your Legion, together with the resting places of your comrades who have also given their lives for the cause of freedom." Mrs. Campbell concluded, "One of my greatest regrets is that my beloved son did not live to finish his training in Mesa as he was so happy out there and his letters were full of all the interesting people he had met and how kind everyone was to him."[64]

Mrs. Mollett, the mother of the first student fatality at No. 1 BFTS, wrote after receiving a photograph of the RAF section of the local cemetery: "It looks extremely nice, and the graves well kept. We cannot express our gratitude to the ladies of the Terrell War Relief Society in mere words, but we find consolation in all they have done and this is what our boy Dick would have wished for most. My husband and daughter join me in heartfelt thanks."[65]

Residents of Lancaster, California, and Terrell, Texas, were proud to learn that a graduate of their British school had been a recipient of the Victoria Cross, Britain's highest military decoration for valor. Both William Reid of Course 2 at No. 2 BFTS and Arthur Aaron of Course 6 at No. 1 BFTS received the award after being wounded during attacks, which severely damaged their bombers. Reid recovered from his wounds, but the notice received in Terrell failed to mention that Aaron died of his wounds.

Mrs. O. I. Cole, the hostess of the Terrell USO, stayed in touch with many of the British students she came to know. John J. T. Johnstone of Course 17 later wrote, "I shall never forget the wonderful times we used to have, just chatting over a cup of tea or sitting around the piano singing the old songs. You know, you were more than just a hostess to the English fellows, for you filled the place of those ladies who were most dear to us, but were 7,000 miles away. I don't think you could ever know how grateful we and hundreds of mothers and fathers in England are to you."[66]

Francis M. Keen trained with Course 18 at No. 3 BFTS and his memory of his experience in the United States is interesting.

We all came back with an American accent, we learnt to spell "night" and "light" as "nite" and "lite" and using the symbol # for number. The Wings Cross Country to El Paso, signing forms for "gas"—Lend Lease, crossing into Mexico for the evening, Juarez was the border town. Meeting the American cadets for the first time, and asking what their medals were for? Evenings on camp discussing whether "the South will rise again" with cadets from Georgia and Alabama. Graduation Day, what a day to remember, the American cadets all as 2nd Lieutenants resplendent in their "pinks" and crushed hats, they slept on them to get the "operational" look.[67]

In a written thank you from Course 24, the last course to graduate from No. 5 BFTS, the British students specifically mentioned Mrs. Nesmith in Palm Beach and the ladies of Clewiston, "who have worked so hard on our behalf."

In the pages of the No. 6 BFTS publication *Tails Up*, students frequently offered special thanks to local residents such as Mrs. L. O. Fuller, Mrs. McCoy, the McDowell family, Mr. and Mrs. C. Thomson, and Peggy and Frank Ramsey for their unfailing hospitality. On first meeting Mrs. McCoy, the British students were surprised to find her knitting thick woolen socks in the Oklahoma summer heat and a pile of completed wool garments on her couch. The items were destined for British destroyers on convoy duty in the freezing North Atlantic. In cities across America, local women or the local British War Relief Society knitted or collected items to be sent to Britain for use by both British servicemen and civilians.

After each British course graduated, local residents assembled at the train station to say goodbye and to see the departing graduates away. J. R. Sutton graduated with Course 4 at No. 3 BFTS. "When our course finally left for Canada on our way back to the United Kingdom, we were seen off by the town band, and the Mayor of Miami who offered one hundred dollars to the first member of our course to shoot down a Messerschmitt!"[68]

A former student wrote to Una Pierce Kilpatrick of Dallas who had maintained a virtual open house for the British students who helped in her garden and kitchen and came to regard Kilpatrick as a second mother. "When we left Texas last Monday we really knew how much it had meant to us. There wasn't a cheer as the train pulled out. Our hearts felt empty and it was a sorry day for us."[69]

A few of the British students continued to experience American hospitality after graduation. A limited number of British graduates were retained in the United States as flight instructors assigned to Army Air Forces schools. Philip Mitchell graduated with Course 9 at No. 2 BFTS and then attended an instructors course at Kelly Field in San Antonio, Texas. Mitchell then received an assignment to the army basic flight school at the Waco Army Airfield in Waco, Texas. Now an officer, Mitchell recalled American hospitality while he was an instructor. "My weekend relaxation was taken mostly in San Antonio, where John Smith (who was stationed at Alamogordo) and I had been adopted by the Martindale family. One of the perks of instructors was the use of an aircraft when not on duty; this made travel very easy and very cheap. Depending on whether one was night flying on Friday, I flew either Friday evening or Saturday to Kelly Field to be met by my friends. The weekends were much the same as in California—swimming, tennis, eating and drinking."[70]

Philip Mitchell's tour as a flight instructor with the USAAF ended in August 1943. "Before leaving Texas, John Smith and I had a wonderful holiday with the Martindales in Mexico City. At last came the tearful farewells and promises and yet again a train to Moncton."[71]

Many of the British students maintained contact with American friends long after the end of the war. Even after victory, British citizens at home continued to experience hardships. Rationing remained in effect for food and consumer goods, while many parts of the country continued to experience housing shortages due to wartime damage. Many Americans who had befriended British flight students while training in the United

States sent food parcels and other rationed or hard to obtain items to Great Britain for several years after the war.

British student William Sydney Ellis had met John Green, corporate attorney for Gulf Oil Company, on a train and then enjoyed Green's hospitality in Houston. After Ellis graduated, the two stayed in touch. Green even sent food parcels and other rationed items to Ellis' parents in England. When Ellis got married, he wrote the joyful news to Green, who "wrote to say that I must take my new bride to America to visit Lazy Lane and 'Green Pastures'. I sent the wedding photos John had asked me for, and my plans to visit him. Instead of a reply from him, I was shocked to receive a letter from his secretary saying that John had been killed in a fall from his horse and enclosed his obituary and funeral service booklet."[72]

After the war many of the former British students made pilgrimages back to the United States to renew old friendships. Some of the British students even returned to the United States to live. The strong ties and long continuing friendships formed between Americans of all walks of life and all social standings and the young British students they befriended during training is one of the most enduring legacies of the British Flying Training Schools.

CHAPTER 8

CHANGES

The British Flying Training Schools began from the simple concept of utilizing American civilian flight schools to train pilots for the Royal Air Force. When the first schools opened in 1941, Britain stood alone against Nazi Germany, the war news was anything but good, and the need for trained aircrew acute. The schools opened in an atmosphere of haste and urgent need. The British Air Ministry had to create a new organization in the United States, the Royal Air Force Delegation in Washington, abbreviated RAFDEL, to administer the new training programs. Staffing for the Royal Air Force Delegation, staffing for the individual schools, and the school facilities all reflected this expedience.

As the war progressed, the Royal Air Force Delegation and the contract flight schools never remained static and in fact continued to grow and evolve. In many ways this evolution mirrored the changing war situation. As the Allied·war effort slowly gained momentum around the world, the role of RAFDEL expanded and its staff increased. Enrollment in the British Flying Training Schools also increased, staffing levels rose, bolstered by combat veterans, the flight training curriculum expanded, and the individual school facilities were enlarged and improved.

Soon after the first schools opened it became obvious that the authorized staff for the new schools was totally inadequate. The Air Ministry had allocated only nine officers, a chief ground instructor for each school, and a chief flying instructor for each pair of schools, to supervise the six British Flying Training Schools located across the southern United States from Florida to California.

When the first schools opened, not even this inadequate staffing was available. When the first students for No. 5 BFTS arrived at the school's temporary home in Arcadia, Florida, no chief ground instructor had been appointed and the BFTS students attended ground school with the school's Arnold Scheme students. Both No. 4 BFTS in Arizona, and No. 3 BFTS in Oklahoma, opened before the chief ground instructor had arrived and the chief ground instructors from the California and Texas British schools had to supervise these additional schools, which were located several hundred miles away. Squadron Leader Thomas Whitlock, the newly appointed chief ground instructor at No. 2 BFTS, arrived at the school's temporary home the day before the students arrived. Squadron Leader Andrew Beveridge, the No. 1 BFTS chief ground instructor, along with Wing Commander Fredrick Hilton, the chief flying instructor for No. 1 and No. 3 BFTS, arrived in Dallas only two days before the first students. Squadron Leader H. F. Suren, the chief ground instructor for No. 6 BFTS, arrived in Ponca City on the same day as the first students. In all of these schools, training had been scheduled to begin the day after the students arrived. This placed an almost impossible burden on these first officers.

This situation was so acute that when No. 4 BFTS opened with no chief ground instructor (one had not even been appointed) several students with service experience were utilized assisting the civilian ground school instructors. In several cases these students actually taught classes. Nor were these incidences confined to the Mesa school. Many of the British students in the early courses had service backgrounds and were used in various ways to assist in ground school.

The chief ground instructors were intended to supervise the ground school program and also teach subjects in which the civilian instructors were not proficient such as Royal Air Force law and procedures, signals, aircraft recognition, and armament. The chief ground instructors were also expected to maintain the school records. The initial work load with the available staff proved to be overwhelming and only the most essential items could be accomplished.

At the time the schools opened, RAF personnel strengths were strained at all operational levels. Realizing the inadequate nature of the initial school staffing, as well as the reality of the available personnel, Group Captain Carnegie at first only expressed his concern. "I am very worried about the non-appearance of all the C.G.I's . . . We actually need one C.F.I. for each school, including the three refreshers . . . an administrative officer is also essential at each School . . . but knowing the position at home, I have not asked for these." Carnegie did suggest to the Air Ministry that if any surplus instructors were available or even "tired pilots" they would be invaluable at the schools, "as they are all very anxious to learn all about our methods."[1]

Officials originally felt that the school records would be minimal given the civilian nature of the schools. This expectation quickly proved to be naive as the Air Ministry in London and the new Royal Air Force Delegation in Washington required more reports and training statistics. After four months of operation, Squadron Leader Beveridge wrote to Group Captain Carnegie: "It is becoming quite impossible to keep abreast of the various P.O.R.'s returns and reports asked for by your Headquarters with only one stenographer."[2]

Carnegie quickly overcame his reluctance to ask for more staff and requested a chief flying instructor for each school, as well as an administrative officer. "The C.G.I's are spending practically all their time dealing with administrative matters, which include all the forms which are now necessary . . . This is naturally hindering the work for which they have been sent out, and I am only hoping that the administrative officers may soon be available."[3] Carnegie also requested an armament noncommissioned officer (NCO) for each school. The armament NCO would supplement the civilian instructors in subjects such as armaments, signals, and aircraft recognition and also act as the school's disciplinary sergeant major.

The Air Ministry approved Carnegie's request for additional school staff, as well as increased staff for the Royal Air Force Delegation in Washington. But the changes took time. Flight Lieutenant M. W. Palmer, the first administrative officer assigned to No. 1 BFTS, arrived two months after the school opened, followed a week later by Sergeant C. E. Moffat, the new armament NCO. Squadron Leader George Greaves, who had supervised Refresher training, reported to No. 2 BFTS as the CFI and Squadron Leader Mills became the CFI of No. 4 BFTS (which he had previously supervised together with No. 2 BFTS). Flight Lieutenant Martyn Green, a well-known prewar singer-actor with the D'Oyly Carte Opera Company, became the No. 2 BFTS administrative officer and Flight Sergeant L. W. Woodcock arrived in Lancaster as the armament NCO. Wing Commander D. H. Lee arrived in Miami as the CFI at No. 3 BFTS. Squadron Leader William Holloway arrived in Mesa as the school's CGI and Flight Lieutenant E. C. Metcalf reported to the school as the administrative officer four months after the first British students arrived in Arizona. These officers were followed by Sergeant J. G. McCowan, the new No. 4 BFTS armament NCO. Although now officially responsible only for No. 1 BFTS, Wing Commander Hilton had to be pressed into service at No. 6 BFTS (three hundred air miles north of Terrell) when that school opened without a chief flying instructor. Wing Commander Charles A. Ball, the permanent CFI, did not arrive in Ponca City until eight months later.

The Operations Record Book is the official record of each RAF unit. When Flight Lieutenant Palmer sought to bring the No. 1 BFTS ORB up to date, he began with the following introduction: "this station record is being compiled 12 months after the opening of the Station, and must of necessity present in outline only the history of the unit. On a unit with such a small staff as was available for the first year, it was quite impossible to contemplate keeping anything else than a simple diary of outstanding events, and most of what follows has been compiled largely from memory by the two officers still remaining on the station."[4]

The No. 6 BFTS ORB for December 1942, sixteen months after the school opened, offered a brief generic introduction, then an explanation. "Due to a lack of records, no information can be given of the early days of the School."[5] The No. 3 BFTS ORB introduction offered no explanation or even attempt at reconstruction. "Detailed operation logs were not kept until 1st May 1942 by which time 4 courses had graduated."[6]

The addition of a chief flying instructor at each school, along with an administrative officer and armament NCO, considerably improved the efficiency and the service atmosphere of the British schools. As the war situation slowly improved, and combat veterans became available, the Air Ministry added a navigation officer to each school. These officers usually had operational experience in Bomber Command or Coastal Command. Flight Lieutenant E. J. L. Robb, one of the first of the new appointments, had served as a Wellington bomber navigator before arriving at No. 1 BFTS as the station navigation officer. This unique operational experience, when incorporated into the school's curriculum, enhanced the civilian instructors' lectures. These officers began arriving about a year after the schools opened.

The initial command structure at the British Flying Training Schools has led to some confusion. Since the chief ground instructor was at first the only permanently assigned RAF officer at each school, many sources, both contemporary and later accounts, often refer to the chief ground instructor as the school's commanding officer. In some cases the chief ground instructors signed certain reports and documents as "commanding officer" apparently feeling the frequent absence of the chief flying instructor justified the title. Even with the initial responsibility for two schools, the Air Ministry intended the RAF chief flying instructor to be the commanding officer of the British Flying Training Schools.

The actual status of the first British students in the United States has also caused confusion. The Air Ministry fully intended that these students would be civilians during training. An early order contained the following directive: "(2) On reaching the transit camp [Canada], action will then be taken to effect their temporary release from the Air Force, from which date they will assume civilian status and retain that status throughout the period of their stay at the training centre (3) On the return to the transit camp en route to the U.K. on completion of their training they will be recalled to the Air Force and resume their normal Air Force service."[7] In fact, the system never worked as intended.

From the beginning, British officials in Washington and London required numerous RAF forms to document all phases of training. The students wore RAF uniforms at the schools (the gray civilian suits issued to the first students were worn away from the school). The school's RAF officers requested public funds to cover minor expenses such as shoe repairs and uniform replacement items that would have been available on RAF stations. With the increasing role of RAF personnel in the operation of the schools, several of the RAF officers openly questioned the "civilian" status of the students. The issue quietly went away. Even the first British students in the United States never had any doubt that they remained members of the Royal Air Force.

In the early days, besides the very tangible everyday problems associated with new unfinished facilities and limited staff, there were other more subtle difficulties. The RAF officers assigned to civilian flight schools in a foreign country thousands of miles from home found themselves in a situation totally alien to their previous service experience. Not only were the sights, sounds, and customs in the United States different and often confusing, but these officers no longer had the comfort of the Royal Air Force support system behind them. With little official guidance, these officers coped with their new situation and environs in different ways.

Due to the civilian nature of the schools, the RAF officers had to use persuasion to achieve results rather than commands. While some officers adapted well, others did not do as well. Wing Commander Hilton and Squadron Leader Beveridge in Dallas were able to influence Major Long concerning certain physical aspects of the new school in Terrell. Squadron Leader Mills did not fare as well with Major Moseley in certain design elements for the new school in Lancaster.

Most of the early officers accepted the civilian nature of the schools even though they realized that the British students "had little chance to absorb a true Service atmosphere."[8] Others sought to change the nature of the schools. Nowhere was this more evident than at No. 2 BFTS. Even though Squadron Leader Mills had been unable to convince Major Moseley to add a swimming pool or additional ground school classrooms, he apparently did much better at influencing the school's operation.

From the beginning, the British students at No. 2 BFTS were told to salute when reporting for duty and to address their instructors as "sir." The British officers also persuaded the school to add a form of rank badge on each instructors' shirt and the instructors were to be considered the same as officers. The instructors were warned of the "dangers of undue familiarity" and reminded that in matters of appearance they should set an example. The British officers reported, "Eventually all these arrangements bore fruit, and the post began to resemble something of a military station."[9]

Measures at the other schools did not go as far as those at No. 2 BFTS. Most of the RAF officers assigned to the other BFTS schools seem to have adapted better to the civilian nature of the schools. But even with the intense effort to mold the Lancaster school into a facsimile of an RAF station, not all of the initiatives were successful. "Other expedients tried were the creation of a daily duty officer (instructor) and the formation of an officers' mess. In these two items the same degree of success was not obtained."[10]

The RAF officers at No. 2 BFTS also experienced frustration over the staffing differences (or limitations) between the school and an established RAF station in the United Kingdom, as well as the general California lifestyle. Obviously the RAF staff could not do everything and had, at times, to rely on civilian personnel. And in this lay a difficulty. "Requests for information and for minor jobs, e.g. transportation of pupils, frequently proposed an almost incredible degree of delay and forgetfulness. Often the officers would be found doing the job of an A.C.H. runner." The British officers specifically commented on the nonchalant attitude in California. "It would seem that there must be a 'je ne sais quoi' in the Southern California air, for similar difficulties were experienced with the local tradesmen, e.g. laundryman, barber, shoemaker and the representative of the Southern Pacific Railway at the depot. Furthermore it was an almost impossible job to get the civilian guards to take the 'booking in and out' system seriously."[11]

Regrettably, the frustrations did not end there. The RAF officers assigned to No. 2 BFTS set up a messing committee to advise the school cafeteria staff on proper British cooking methods (other schools had messing committees, but apparently did not go so far as teaching cooking methods). The messing committee strongly recommended the removal of apples from the green salads, which was duly accomplished. Changes in the cafeteria staff unfortunately resulted in the frequent return of apples to the green salads, in spite of the most earnest and persistent efforts at elimination. The frustrated RAF officers must have longed for a more normal assignment.

The British schools in the United States readily adopted the RAF flight training syllabus, but there were some changes. Royal Air Force flight training included engine air starts, which consisted of shutting down the engine in flight. After the engine died and the propeller stopped, the student learned to dive the aircraft in order to build sufficient airspeed to turn the propeller, then restart the engine. The American trainers with larger engines and higher compression ratios were not as well suited to this procedure as the RAF's elementary trainer, the de Havilland Tiger Moth with its smaller four-cylinder engine. After some initial trials in the United States, Wing Commander Hilton reported, "restarting a stopped airscrew in American type trainers is almost impossible." Air starts were eliminated from the American flight training curriculum.

The Royal Air Force Central Flying School is where RAF flight instructors learned their craft. Along with aerial maneuvers, the CFS taught a very precise "patter" to new instructors. The patter was a clearly defined explanation of each maneuver. Instructors learned to recite the patter virtually verbatim along with demonstrating the maneuver. An RAF instructor explained the procedure, "Taking off into wind, and landing. You have to describe what's happening exactly as it does happen, not a second sooner or later."[12]

Another instructor commented, "The 'patter' for recovering from a spin is one of the things that you have to learn by heart. A spin is a damned quick thing, and in all these demonstrations you've constantly got to be gaining and keeping height, so you want to do as few turns as possible and therefore spend no time thinking of what to say."[13]

The official patter came to the American schools along with the RAF flight syllabus. The schools readily embraced the RAF syllabus, but the official patter never found favor. Royal Air Force officers who had been trained under the Central Flying School system despaired that the laid-back American instructors would ever master the RAF patter. Most of the civilian instructors never even tried.

When the schools opened, a shortage of advanced trainers forced the British to modify the two-stage RAF flight training syllabus to conform to the three-stage Army Air Corps syllabus, which consisted of primary, basic, and advanced. This change necessitated the use of the Vultee BT-13 basic trainer. British officials had never been happy with the basic phase of flight training. Toward the end of 1942 the supply situation had reversed and the AAF experienced a shortage of basic trainers and an ample supply of advanced trainers. Army officials asked if the British would consider trading their Vultee basic trainers for North American AT-6 Harvard advanced trainers. The British were delighted with the change because the training syllabus could now conform to the RAF elementary and advanced phases of flight training. The Vultees were removed from the British schools in November 1942 and students now progressed from the Stearman or Fairchild primary trainer directly to the Harvard advanced trainer.

The original 150-hour training schedule had always been considered the bare minimum required to train a pilot and a temporary measure dictated by the urgent need for aircrew early in the war. Carnegie noted, "Whilst, under the stress of dire necessity, we had a year ago drastically reduced the length of our flying training courses, it was essential at the earliest possible moment to reverse the process and lengthen the courses again. Experience had shown that the amount of flying the pupils got under the existing arrangements was not nearly enough, and that they reached Operational Training Units insufficiently experienced."[14]

Air Vice Marshal L. D. D. McKean, OBE, Air Liaison Mission, Ottawa, Canada offered a further explanation. "It is not that pilots have been inadequately trained, but that their training has not provided a sufficient background of experience. They are therefore constantly meeting fresh situations during the early part of their operational tour—situations which we should endeavor to face them with while they are still under training."[15]

As the Empire Air Training Scheme and the American training programs began to gain momentum and pilot production increased, officials revised the training syllabus. In December 1941, the RAF announced an extension of flight training in the British Flying Training Schools to 200 hours. Course lengths were increased from twenty to twenty-eight weeks. Both the primary and advanced phases of flying training would be extended to fourteen weeks' duration. Flying hours for the primary phase of training increased from 70 to 91 hours and the basic-advanced phase of training was extended from 80 to 109 hours. The change would be implemented gradually.

Students in the first two courses graduated with around 150 hours of flight time. Courses 3, 4, and 5 were transitional courses. Course 3 received a total of twenty-two weeks of training, Course 4 received twenty-four weeks, while Course 5 underwent a total of twenty-six weeks. Later courses received the new total of twenty-eight weeks of training.

After the change had been implemented, officials realized that students gained little from the extension of primary training from 70 to 91 hours. The real benefit of the extended flight training syllabus came from the increased experience in the sophisticated advanced trainer. While retaining the new total of 200 flight hours, the RAF amended the primary phase back to the original 70 hours and increased the advanced stage to 130 hours.

In addition to the increased number of flight hours, the RAF also raised pilot training standards. Schools and training commands were notified to wash out those students who had not soloed in ten and a half hours. Holdovers, except for illness, were discontinued. Previously, slower students who had not progressed as fast as other students, but still showed promise, were held over and joined the next course to finish training. For the first time ground school failures were to be eliminated. Before the new rules, local commands had been allowed more leeway in working with individual students.

The British Flying Training Schools were initially hampered by unfinished facilities, lack of equipment, and the limited staff. As the facilities and equipment improved, staff levels increased and the training tempo accelerated. In only eighteen months since the first schools opened, the staff at each school had steadily grown and now would be increased even further to twelve officers and enlisted men. The new staff included the chief flying instructor, two assistant flight supervisors, the chief ground instructor, two navigation officers, an administrative officer or adjutant, three armament NCOs, an accounts corporal, and a physical training instructor.

As the worldwide training schemes turned out more aircrew and the trend of the war news grew more favorable, combat veterans became available. RAF observers with operational experience served as school navigation officers, which allowed them to aid in ground school instruction and fly on formation cross-country flights. Before being posted to the civilian schools many of the armament NCOs had been wireless operators or air gunners in Bomber Command or Coastal Command. By the last year of the war the school's RAF staff included an assistant ground instructor, a signals officer, and a gunnery instructor.

Over time the make up, not just the numbers, of the RAF staff changed. Few of the first officers sent to the United States had combat experience. Many positions were filled with older officers, some of whom had served in World War I. As younger officers became available, they were added to the BFTS staffs. The September 1942 staff at No. 3 BFTS is representative of the changes. Wing Commander H. A. Roxburg, AFC, of Henley on Thames, Oxfordshire, the CFI, had been in the RAF for twenty years. Squadron Leader A. Addrley, the CGI from Wynsham, Oxfordshire, joined the Royal Engineers as a dispatch rider in 1915 before transferring to the Royal Flying Corps. After the war, Addrley rejoined the RAF in 1929. Flight Lieutenant E. C. Pitam, DCM, the administrative officer, served in World War I as a regimental sergeant major. Flight Lieutenant Albert Bonning, the navigation officer, joined the British army in 1937 and then transferred to the RAF and underwent observer training in 1941. The youngest officer, Flying Officer J. D. Morrison, actually graduated from No. 3 BFTS then attended a Canadian gunnery course before returning to Miami as the school gunnery instructor.

The schools' civilian staffs also changed. Not only did the number of personnel increase, as could be expected with the increased course enrollments and the expanded training curriculum, but the composition of the civilian staffs also changed. When the schools opened, the civilian staffs reflected the hiring practices common in American businesses of the time. The staffs were predominantly male except for a limited number of women in clerical positions or service jobs such as cafeteria workers. As the rapidly expanding draft took eligible young men for the various armed services, an acute shortage of workers in the burgeoning defense industries resulted. The schools had no choice but to actively recruit women for formerly male positions.

When Pauline Bond graduated from Baylor University, teaching in public schools for eighty dollars a month did not seem appealing. Born and raised in Kaufman, Texas, twelve miles south of Terrell, Bond had met several of the RAF students at various social functions and one of them, Brian Smith, suggested that she apply for a job as a Link trainer operator. Bond decided to apply for the job after Smith explained the purpose of the Link trainer and the role of the operator. Harding Lawrence, the head of the No. 1 BFTS Link department, hired Bond, but only after explaining in the strongest terms that she would not date any student. The Link operators graded the student's instrument proficiency, a task too important to let personal feelings possibly interfere. Bond later remarked, "We were very formal in those days, even though we were both twenty-one, I called him Mr. Lawrence and he called me Miss Bond."[16]

Louise Sacchi grew up in Pennsylvania with a love of flying. After receiving her pilots' license Sacchi realized that finding any flying job for a woman would be virtually impossible, so she traveled south to Texas and became a navigation instructor at No. 1 BFTS. In Terrell she joined Jane Howell, another navigation instructor who later became a Link trainer operator. Elsee "Dee" Dutton became one to the first female control tower operators in the United States when she went to work for Darr School of Aeronautics at No. 6 BFTS. These stories are typical of the personnel changes in all of the British schools.

Ultimately women worked in expanded administrative and personnel jobs, as well as ground school instructors, Link trainer operators, supply clerks, parachute riggers, and control tower operators. Women also worked in the schools' aircraft maintenance department, as engine mechanics, doing dope and fabric work, sheet metal repairs, and as instrument overhaul specialists. The Spartan School of Aeronautics magazine noted, "Women are especially adapted to instrument repair work since it is delicate and precise and their fingers are more nimble" and then echoed a popular theme that "the feminine touch will play an important part in winning the war."[17]

At times some personnel rules had to be modified to accommodate the changes. Dress codes at the various schools usually specified skirts for women. But the control tower at No. 1 BFTS could only be accessed by a tall outside ladder, so the rules were relaxed to allow women control tower operators to wear slacks. Women mechanics wore the same style overalls as the male mechanics. At Spartan Aeronautics, singing by the British students (common for the British and uncommon for Americans) had to be banned. Apparently the lyrics of these "ditties" were often obscene and Spartan officials observed, "each course tries to outdo the others while singing and marching" and reminded everyone that "there are young ladies working at the school."[18]

At the inception of the British Flying Training Schools, Air Ministry officials anticipated that these schools would attract large numbers of American volunteers to the RAF. Early projections set aside one BFTS school to be used exclusively by American volunteers and some officials thought that Americans might make up the total enrollment of two BFTS schools. Plans were developed to add an Initial Training Wing in one of the British Flying Training Schools for the American volunteers. These plans never materialized due to several factors including the inability to advertise, the Clayton Knight Committee's efforts for so many Canadian and British programs, implementation of American selective service rules requiring young men to register and be subject to the draft, and ultimately the American entry into the war.

Some American volunteers did enter the program and were admitted to BFTS schools in limited numbers. Although detailed records are sketchy, these Americans usually trained in Courses 6 through 10. For example, at No. 2 BFTS there were ten Americans, three Englishmen, and one Polish student who were direct-entry civilians. Of the ten Americans, three left the program at their own request, one washed out for flying deficiencies, and one was called up by his draft board for service in the US Army. Unlike any other military program of the time, these civilians were apparently allowed to join a BFTS school without joining the RAF. Training as civilians, these volunteers were free to leave at their own request and were still subject to selective service. Of the nine volunteers who completed training in Lancaster (five Americans, three Englishmen, and the one Polish student), three (two Americans and the Polish student) were the top cadet of their courses. After graduation, all nine joined the RAF in Canada and were commissioned pilot officers.

The No. 5 BFTS officers were surprised to see two Americans arrive with an early course and asked if they knew this was an RAF school. They did. Gifford Rossi had lived in England for six years and had even attended Oxford. The other American, William Watkins, was the son of an Army Air Corps lieutenant general and his two brothers were in the air force. Watkins did not want his father's prestige to influence his training. Around nine Americans trained in Clewiston.[19]

When Lord and Lady Halifax visited No. 1 BFTS in April 1942 a picture appeared in local newspapers showing Lady Halifax on the flight line speaking to an American volunteer. According to the caption, the young man had been rejected for military service because he had contracted infantile paralysis as a child. The young man wrote directly to President Roosevelt (who had the same disease) and received permission to join the RAF. No name appeared in the news story. Once again the official records are unclear, but it appears that around ten American volunteers trained at No. 1 BFTS.

At No. 4 BFTS ten students were listed as "civilian pupils." (The last arrived rather late with Course 13 in November 1942.) At No. 3 BFTS and No. 6 BFTS in Oklahoma, around the same numbers of American volunteers trained at those schools.

While the American volunteers trained in obscurity and little information is available, one revealing comment from No. 2 BFTS survives. "This experiment of including civilian trainees was a great success. Although some of them had had no military training at all, and all lacked I.T.W. training, they evinced such keenness and enthusiasm that this lack of military background was very quickly obscured by their outstanding achievement. In all courses and at all times they were very popular among their fellow cadets."[20]

The British Flying Training Schools also received other additions. British students in the Arnold Scheme found the Army Air Corps system of discipline, which included hazing and punishments for minor infractions, to be distasteful. Most endured out of an overriding desire to learn to fly. Others did not fare as well and this dissatisfaction may have led to some eliminations. Early in the program and with an urgent need for pilots, washed out students from the Arnold Scheme (and even a few from the Towers Scheme) were interviewed in Canada and some were allowed to resume training at a British Flying Training School. There is no accurate record of former Arnold Scheme students who joined a BFTS, but there were apparently several at each school. No. 5 BFTS probably received the largest contingent when ten ex-Arnold Scheme students joined Course 2. The practice ceased when flight training production rose and the urgent demand for pilots diminished.

During the first years of the war various US government agencies vied for control of the nation's manpower resources. At the heart of the struggle lay the conflicting requirements for men for the various combat services versus the need for skilled workers in defense industries at home. When it appeared that the priority of draft boards had been established, the Army Air Forces, fearful of losing trained personnel such as those employed in the contract flight schools, came up with a novel solution. In July 1943, key civilian workers at the schools, such as flight instructors and maintenance personnel, were sworn into the inactive army reserve. This action precluded the workers from being drafted, unless they left the school.

From the inception of the BFTS program, RAF officers had misgivings about Royal Air Force students training in civilian schools so far away from any established RAF commands. Officers felt that students "had little chance to absorb a true Service atmosphere" at these schools due to the small initial RAF presence.[21]

In response to these concerns, the RAF implemented a system of student leadership in the schools. The new system divided each class into flights and appointed students as cadet officers and enlisted ranks to oversee the daily administration and discipline of the flights. The ranking student in the senior course held the rank of cadet wing commander. Cadet officers supervised daily activities such as reveille, working parades, color hoisting and lowering, reporting defaulters, punishment drills, lights out, and bed checks. Cadet officers also handled minor disciplinary matters and could impose limited punishment such as confinement to camp during open post, polishing all boots in the barracks, scrubbing the barracks floor, and tours of extra drill.

The RAF staff handled more serious breaches of discipline such as being absent without leave or failure to report back to camp on time. The RAF commanding officer had considerable leeway in these cases, as one example from No. 5 BFTS illustrates. In April 1943 seven students were brought up on charges of being absent without leave. The reasons given by three of the students were judged to be legitimate and the commanding officer dismissed the charges. One student, whose explanation failed to impress the CO, was confined to camp with the loss of privileges for seven days. The other three students' absences were considered serious enough to warrant an indefinite confinement to camp, loss of privileges, extra drill, forfeiture of one days' pay, and "other duties as ordered." At No. 4 BFTS one student had been absent without leave for seven days and another had been gone for two weeks and the ORB noted, "both these cadets were of a poor type." Both were confined to camp and then washed out of flight training.

Serious violations of flight rules such as unauthorized stunting or low flying often resulted in elimination from the program, especially if the violation resulted in an accident. Less serious violations of flight rules were noted in a log book entry, which followed the student throughout his RAF career. Minor infractions during training were often handled in more creative ways. At No. 3 BFTS instructors imposed a fine of fifty cents for minor lapses of rules (posted on a blackboard labeled "Dumbell Roll") such as taxiing with the flaps down, leaving the aircraft with the controls unlocked, or leaving a parachute in the pilot's ready room instead of checking it in. The fines were used to purchase war bonds, which were then raffled off.

Another, although exceedingly minor, point bothered RAF officers. British students in the Arnold Scheme had always been referred to as "cadets" in the normal US Army parlance. British officers disliked this term, preferring the term "student" or "pupil," but could do little about the army schools. In time the term "cadet" also came into normal usage in the British Flying Training Schools.

At the beginning of the BFTS program, students who washed out of flight training were returned to Canada for reassignment to other flying duties. A selection board in Canada made the decision, but the system was inefficient and entailed delays, which also caused morale problems. In time, a panel of officers at each BFTS (who were more familiar with the individual student) made the decision before the student returned to Canada. Kenneth Stott was devastated when he washed out of flight training. "I had a Selection Board which consisted of the RAF Wing Commander and a Flight Lieutenant who were sympathetic and asked me my preference for another aircrew category. I said I wanted to be an air gunner, but looking at my record from ITW where I came second in navigation, they persuaded me to take a navigation course back in Canada, to which I agreed."[22]

In the summer of 1942 the Army Air Forces training command notified the Royal Air Force Delegation that owing to unprecedented expansion and a shortage of training sites the army intended to assume control of both No. 2 BFTS and the just opened No. 7 BFTS. Since only one course had started training at No. 7 BFTS, that school's British function ceased in August 1942 with the completion of primary training. No. 2 BFTS also received an eviction notice, but Wing Commander Greaves, the school's chief flying instructor, adamantly refused to vacate the school until the last course graduated in December 1942.

The USAAF reluctantly agreed and training continued for RAF students at No. 2 BFTS while army engineers arrived to enlarge the school facilities and convert it into an army contract basic flight school. For the last six months that RAF students trained in Lancaster, they shared the school and field with construction activity and increasing numbers of Army Air Forces aviation cadets. At the Wings Parade for Course 10 on 31 December 1942, seven flights of American aviation cadets marched with the RAF flight for the graduation of the last British students and one group of American flight cadets.

As long as it existed, No. 2 BFTS had only a small staff: a chief flying instructor, a chief ground instructor, an adjutant, a navigation instructor, an armament NCO, and an accounts corporal. As the staffing levels in the other British schools increased, No. 2 BFTS never received the specialized staff such as a physical training instructor, assistant flying instructors, assistant navigation officers, or a signals officer, nor did the school become involved in camera gunnery with a designated RAF gunnery instructor.

Despite the early problems at No. 2 BFTS such as limited facilities and civilian instructor turnover, Squadron Leader Whitlock received a message from the Royal Air Force Delegation praising the school's achievements. From Course 1 through Course 10, RAFDEL noted that No. 2 BFTS had "the steadiest average, the highest mean average, the highest number of cadets graduated, and the lowest number of examination failures." The take over of No. 2 BFTS and No. 7 BFTS left five British Flying Training Schools in the United States.

The most radical changes to the British flight schools occurred in 1942. Realizing the value of the program, British officials decided to increase the enrollment in each school from 200 to 300 students. Instead of four courses of fifty students, the schools would now have three courses of one hundred students. The first expanded course was scheduled to arrive in November 1942.

Estimates of future personnel requirements for a vast and complex service such as the Royal Air Force in wartime are fraught with uncertainties. The lead times for implementation of plans and the construction of facilities are lengthy, estimates of future casualties are difficult to project, and these are by no means the only considerations. Several factors reduced the demand for aircrew after the decision had been made to expand the British flight schools. British officials decided that the new four-engine heavy bombers, the Handley Page Halifax and the Avro Lancaster, just entering service in large numbers would be flown by only one pilot instead of a pilot and copilot.[23] Another crew member, usually the flight engineer, would be trained to aid the pilot in routine flight matters and in case of an emergency. This decision alone drastically reduced the demand for pilots. The diversion of aircraft to Russia had also temporarily reduced the numbers of service aircraft.

The immediate demand for aircrew had eased at a time when expansion of the schools had already begun. At the same time the US Army Air Forces' unprecedented expansion still could not keep up with the demand for pilots. Army officials inquired about space in the British Flying Training Schools.

The Royal Air Force Delegation reported the army inquiry to the Air Ministry and offered a suggestion:

> Consideration is being given to the question of justifying the existence of the B.F.T.S's in American eyes. According to American

standards the B.F.T.S's are not being used to their fullest capacity. The population of most American schools is greater and the number of pupils per aircraft is also greater. It is understood that they do not intend to ask for this training capacity to be handed over but would, of course, welcome any offers that we might make. It is felt that the best course of action would be to offer to train a certain number of U.S. Army Air Forces Cadets in each of the B.F.T.S. Such an offer would probably be accepted and be of great value in furthering co-operation and inter-change of ideas between our services.[24]

For the first time, US Army Air Forces aviation cadets would be trained in British schools, alongside British students, using the RAF flight training syllabus. The various parties decided that the new course enrollment of 100 students would consist of eighty-three British students and seventeen American aviation cadets. In later courses the ratio changed to eighty (later ninety) British and twenty American students.

The USAAF sent flight cadets to train in the British Flying Training Schools beginning with Course 13 (Course 12 at No. 5 BFTS and Course 11 at No. 6 BFTS), which arrived in November 1942. Army officials at first decreed that army cadets would be segregated from the British students and march in separate formations. Officials quickly rescinded this shortsighted order and American army cadets and British students were arranged in alphabetical order and trained side by side with no problems. Army cadets trained in seven courses with the British Flying Training Schools from November 1942 through June 1944.

Army officials also wanted to make sure the American cadets did well in the British schools. A memorandum dated December 8, 1942, to a Colonel Price, an officer on the US Army Air Forces training staff, is illuminating:

> In connection with the BFTS schools, it is General Yount's desire that our Training Centers be informally advised, perhaps it could better be handled by telephone, to be very careful in the selection of American students to attend these schools. We have been

somewhat critical in the past of British students. We do not want to leave ourselves open to any criticism from them. This information should be given to Training Centers unofficially and the British should not be aware of its existence.[25]

This concern resulted in the decision that all Army Air Forces cadets selected for training in BFTS schools would have prior flying experience. Most of these army cadets had trained in the Civilian Pilot Training Program and had at least a private pilots' license. Several army cadets, such as L. G. Bue from Minnesota and William Watkins from California, had commercial pilots' licenses, while Ralph Breyfogle had been a CPT instructor. It is not surprising that the American cadets at BFTS schools did well in the flight training program. The American cadets, however, did not fare as well with ground school subjects. This discrepancy probably stems from the fact that British Initial Training Wings, which potential flight students attended before entering flight school, emphasized ground school subjects such as navigation, meteorology, and mathematics and the British schools included more ground school instruction. Army Air Forces cadets who failed the RAF ground school were allowed to complete flight training at an army facility.

British officials were also sensitive about image. A note in one of the fortnightly reports from the Royal Air Force Delegation in Washington to the Air Ministry seems almost petty, but is nonetheless revealing. "The tropical kit of British cadets in this country has been increased by one shirt, and as a result they are better turned out and no longer show up so unfavorably against American cadets." Another memo from the Royal Air Force Delegation criticized an aircraft recognition film made in Britain for use in overseas flight schools. The film used model airplanes and appeared amateurish. "It is desired to emphasize that the distribution of poor material such as this in the U.S.A. has a most deleterious effect on the attitude of the U.S. forces to the R.A.F. training organisation."[26]

Army cadets trained in the British schools were destined for either ferry or transport command after graduation. It is unclear why the army made this decision, especially since these cadets had prior flying experience and could be expected to be among the best students in their classes. This led to some resentment and disappointment among army cadets who trained at BFTS schools even though army training officials insisted the policy was known up front. Some later sources have attributed the army decision to a respect for the British emphasis on navigation training. Due to a lack of documentation, it is impossible to disprove this theory, but the reasoning appears thin.

The only friction that occurred from the mixing of British and American flight students came from several of the American officers assigned to the British schools to supervise a small staff who administered the army cadet records. These officers were service pilots and felt that they commanded not only the army administrative staff, but also the American flight cadets, and any decisions regarding the American cadets, such as flight standards and washing out a cadet, required their approval. This discussion went all the way to Major General Barton K. Yount, commanding officer of the Army Air Forces Training Command. General Yount issued several memorandums that confirmed the authority of the RAF commanding officer at each school. The last memorandum concerned proficiency standards. "It is desired to reiterate that the RAF commanding officer has complete charge of training and is responsible for establishing levels of proficiency."[27]

Ralph A. Bass, an Army Air Forces cadet, who trained with Course 15 at No. 3 BFTS, remembered his first meeting with the British students. "We (the American students) arrived at the Flying School a day or so ahead of our British counterparts, and when they did arrive, our first question was 'what part of England are you from?' Needless to say, we were promptly informed that while some of the 85 cadets were from England, the rest were from Cornwall, Wales, Scotland, and Ireland, and didn't really somehow appreciate being called 'English'."[28]

British student Alfred Syrett remembered training with USAAF cadets in Miami. "The people and the food were wonderful. It was a great lark—

coke, candy, great weather & open space. U.S. type uniforms, and Army Air Corps Cadets, who dwarfed us in maturity & physique. [Syrett's nickname was "Shorty."] 13 Course, I believe, was the first course to be mixed with U.S. cadets who did our navigation. We beat them at soccer & they killed us at basketball."[29]

American aviation cadet Douglas Moore trained at No. 5 BFTS. "I was assigned to Course 18, along with nineteen other U.S. cadets, mixed in with ninety British cadets of varying ages and backgrounds. My squadron included an older former policeman, a few cadets from upper-class universities (such as Cambridge), and all kinds of youngsters. I was the ripe old age of twenty-one and my Embry-Riddle flight instructor was twenty-nine."[30]

When the first course of British and American cadets graduated from Riddle Field, the school publication *Roger Out* carried a summation of the recent student mix. "British and American cadets have worked together, flown and played together, shared the same rooms, eaten at the same table, argued, laughed at and with each other, and have found that they have a great deal in common."[31]

As the expansion plans were being implemented, another major change occurred: the United States government purchased the British Flying Training Schools.

The Reconstruction Finance Corporation had been created by the Hoover administration as one of the first government agencies created to deal with the Depression. Although its early efforts at fiscal stimulation through aid to state and local governments and low-interest business loans were largely ineffective and generated considerable controversy, newly elected President Franklin Roosevelt kept the agency and expanded its efforts and its influence.

One division of the RFC, the Defense Plant Corporation, funded the construction of new plants for war-related industries at a time when private sector funds were limited and development time was critical for the nation's rearmament programs. Besides new plants, DPC funds were also used to purchase the sophisticated and expensive machine tools necessary for these facilities. At the inception of the British Flying Training Schools the Defense Plant Corporation did not fund civilian flying schools. That policy changed and in June 1942 the agency began the purchase of all contract flight schools in the United States (around sixty schools) including the six initial British Flying Training Schools. The British contract schools retained their names and civilian operation, but became the property of the US government. The operators were paid for the physical assets of each school and then entered into a lease for the use of the facilities. Construction of the last school, No. 7 BFTS in Sweetwater, Texas, began under the auspices of the Defense Plant Corporation.

The British government benefitted greatly from the purchase of the schools. To all outward appearances the schools remained the same; the school operators and civilian staffs, with which British officials had developed a close working relationship, remained in place, the schools retained their individual names and identities, and the British contracts were honored. But now the schools had access to US government funds for improvements.

Although a simple process in theory, the actual purchase of the civilian flight schools was complicated and time consuming. The purchases were begun in June 1942 and the process continued for more than six months. The DPC first conducted a detailed inspection of each school and made an inventory of all assets, including individual buildings and miscellaneous items such as tools, kitchen fixtures, and maintenance equipment. The description of each building included physical dimensions, type of construction, mechanical systems, and utilities. Following the detailed inventory, each item received a value based on original cost less depreciation. After considerable review and negotiation, the operator received the total value of the school's facilities, less any amounts owed to the British Government from the initial construction advances.

A complication to the complex purchase process occurred because the operators had already begun construction to enlarge the schools from 200 to 300 students (except Major Moseley's No. 2 BFTS, which was slated to be taken over by the army). A value had to be placed on work in process as of the effective date of the purchase and then amendments to the purchase contract were issued for additional improvements. For example, Major Long's Plancor 1483 states that the Terrell Aviation School was purchased by the DPC on 30 June 1942, "Using funds allocated for Reverse Lend-Lease, the U.S. government purchased the contractor's leases and other property and equipment for $287,327.00." Over the next several years, with DPC approval, additional improvements were added to the school in five amendments, raising the total cost to $706,422.[32]

For the initial school assets, Major Moseley received $322,296, Spartan School of Aeronautics received $424,426, Southwest Airways received $264,330, and Darr School of Aeronautics received $236,723. Riddle-McKay Aero College received the largest sum, $1,314,757, because John Paul Riddle's school design embodied certain amenities and he had a vison of a continued postwar role for the school. All of the initial improvement amounts, except Major Moseley's, were substantially raised by additional amendments.

In order to enlarge the schools for the new enrollment of 300 students, each school contracted for the new construction or enlargement of barracks, dining halls, Link trainer buildings, and ground school classrooms. Additional hangars and maintenance facilities also had to be constructed or expanded since the school complement of training aircraft had been increased from 75 aircraft to 103 aircraft. The construction activity again encountered shortages of building materials, which resulted in delays and inconveniences reminiscent of the initial school construction. With the increased enrollment and allotment of aircraft, the schools also leased additional auxiliary fields to handle the increased training activity.

A beneficial and welcome addition to No. 4 BFTS did not come from the operator or the US government. Leland Hayward and John Connelly of Southwest Airways had close ties to Hollywood and the film industry. Several well-known Hollywood celebrities, such as Jimmy Stewart, Henry Fonda, and Cary Grant, were investors in Southwest. It is not surprising that several movies were filmed at Thunderbird Field and Falcon Field. William Wellman directed the first movie, *Thunder Birds, Soldiers of the Air,* starring Gene Tierney, Preston Foster, and John Sutton. A fairly decent film of the time in spite of a hokey plot with an unlikely romantic triangle and improbable exploits, the Technicolor film features magnificent aerial photography, as well as various shots of the British students at Falcon Field. In return for the use of the spectacular location, Twentieth Century Fox donated a large swimming pool to the school. The pool became the key recreational feature at No. 4 BFTS. When the DPC purchased the physical assets of the school, however, it did not value the swimming pool since it had been a gift.

Along with the new government ownership, with its associated funds and benefits, also came government bureaucracy. On the eve of expansion, a memo from RAFDEL to the Air Ministry summarized the current status: "The building programme is being held up whilst getting the necessary sanction for materials by the War Production Board."[33] In October 1942 with Army Air Forces flight cadets scheduled to arrive with the first enlarged British class in mid-November, RAFDEL again reported on the status: "Building to meet the expansion, has not yet started at any of the five B.F.T.S.'s. The delay is due to the administrative ramifications of lend-lease, contracts and the Defense Plant Corporation consideration of plans etc. This will mean that there will be a period after 12th November during which accommodation will be very cramped, pupils having to sleep in tents, recreation halls, etc. It is hoped, however, that these conditions will not prevail for more than three or four weeks."[34] The various communities offered help. In Miami, Northeastern Oklahoma Junior College again extended the use of its dormitories to No. 3 BFTS during the construction. Some students at No. 4 BFTS were temporarily housed in the El Portal Hotel in Mesa.

The individual British flight schools recorded virtually nothing of this aspect of dealing with the government bureaucracy, with one exception. The RAF adjutant at No. 6 BFTS entered a brief, but illuminating, note in the school's Operations Record Book. "Mr. Darr, the operator, incensed at the delay in approving the extra buildings, to accommodate the increased population, started to construct the buildings without approval."[35]

Another major change occurred to the school's medical facilities. When the schools opened in 1941, each school had a small infirmary and each school retained a local doctor to provide medical care for the students. The doctor presided over daily sick call and minor illnesses were treated at the school. More serious cases were taken into town to the doctor's clinic, which had a basic surgery. The school negotiated a list of set fees for medical expenses. These fees included items such as a day flight surgeon, a night flight surgeon, other professional services, prescriptions, and hospital stays. Extra fees included providing a medical kit, and/or doctor, along with an ambulance (usually provided by the local funeral home) on site during hazardous times such as night flying at the auxiliary fields, since these fields were often remote and had no telephone.

The initial temporary locations of the British schools increased the makeshift nature of the medical arrangements. Some schools fared better than others. In Dallas the RAF officers retained a Dr. Williams for $450 per month to provide a qualified doctor for the school. Dr. Williams contracted with Dr. Oliver A. Fulcher, a newly licensed physician, whom he paid $300 per month. Dr. Fulcher proved to be not only competent, but also popular with the students. The RAF officers noted that a good medical officer was beneficial to morale and students would often tell the doctor things which they would not discuss with their officers. Since he had no established practice, Dr. Fulcher agreed to move with the school to Terrell. Not only did the RAF retain the services of an excellent and popular physician, but the move also saved the RAF Dr. Williams' $150 per month override fee.

After No. 1 BFTS moved to Terrell, Dr. Johnson, the new civilian doctor hired by the school, offered a summary of services. He also noted the status of the auxiliary fields. "An ambulance or converted vehicle for carrying two patients remains at the field all times flying is carried out, permanent equipment at each field is first aid bag with supplies, blankets and one crash board." But Dr. Johnson concluded with a sobering note. "Most of the roads in areas surrounding all fields are poor and practically impassable in bad weather."[36]

When No. 3 BFTS opened temporarily in Tulsa, the commander of the Spartan Aeronautics Army Air Corps detachment graciously offered the services of the army physician assigned to the school to the newly arrived British students. This offer greatly simplified the medical arrangements for the new school while in Tulsa. The other British schools were not so fortunate and Royal Air Force officials in Washington commented, "medical arrangements have been a difficulty since the opening of the schools."[37]

The medical limitations are graphically illustrated by one incident. The official report of a non-fatal accident at a No. 3 BFTS auxiliary field involving a Harvard advanced trainer included a commendation. "F/O J. Morrison alone at the practice field, did a fine job of work in putting out fire which broke out in the aircraft, extricating the pilot from the damaged plane and driving the ambulance back to Camp—15 miles."[38]

Student dental services were handled in the same manner. A local dentist provided care according to a list of previously negotiated fees (for example, a simple extraction: $2.25, and a wisdom tooth extraction: $3.00), billed on a monthly basis. Billings for medical and dental care frequently exceeded expectations, reflecting the often poor health and dental condition of British youth during the interwar years. Captain Balfour of Spartan Aeronautics once commented, "One student arrived with no top teeth."[39]

The army found the British schools' medical arrangements to be woefully inadequate. The Army Air Corps staff of officers assigned to the civilian contract primary flight schools had always included an army physician at each location. Since the army had responsibility for the British schools under lend-lease and also because Army Air Forces cadets were scheduled to train at the British schools, army officials, along with the DPC, decided to add an army hospital to each British flight school. These hospitals were small ten-bed facilities, but fully equipped and staffed by two army physicians and six enlisted male orderlies.

The army simplified the change in medical facilities at No. 4 BFTS by simply swearing in Dr. Bayard L. Neff, the school's contract civilian doctor, into the Army Medical Corps with the rank of captain. Another army physician and several orderlies soon arrived to complete the school's new medical contingent.[40]

In addition to the changes in major facilities such as buildings and hangars resulting from the increased student enrollment and the addition of an army hospital, the Army Air Forces and DPC added many smaller utility items at each school. Fire trucks and a crash truck were added, new fuel trucks and aircraft tugs appeared on the flight lines, and the new hospitals included an ambulance. The schools also received a number of army vehicles for ground transportation. No. 1 BFTS received one of the more unusual items, a utility aircraft.

Little known today, the Army Air Forces acquired considerable numbers of the Canadian-built Noorduyn Norseman aircraft. Originally designed as a bush plane to serve the vast outlying wilderness areas of Canada, the Norseman served with the Army Air Forces in the United States, Alaska, India, and Europe. A large, high-wing, strut-braced, fabric-covered cabin monoplane, with a cavernous fuselage, powered by a single 600-horsepower radial engine, the Norseman was designated by the army as the UC-64. No. 1 BFTS used their Norseman, which the Terrell staff dubbed "Jumbo," to pick up parts, run errands, and ferry personnel. It is not clear why the Terrell school received a utility aircraft, but the RAF commanding officer at No. 4 BFTS also received a personal aircraft.

Wing Commander A. V. Rogers, AFC, requested a twin-engine aircraft to keep his multi-engine rating current and to provide a suitably fast aircraft for official trips. The army apparently agreed and supplied a Beechcraft AT-10. The all wood AT-10 did not impress Rogers. The aircraft lacked performance, had maintenance related problems (the AT-10 even had wooden fuel tanks with plastic liners), and parts were hard to obtain. Rogers simply declared the AT-10 surplus and requested another aircraft. This time the army supplied a Beechcraft AT-7, a derivative of the popular civilian Model 18 and the military C-45 series. This twin-engine, all metal, low wing aircraft with retractable landing gear offered impressive performance, good handling, and excellent range. Rogers enjoyed flying the AT-7 until he departed from Mesa to return to England.[41]

Although the British schools experienced extensive construction activity during the fall of 1942 and early 1943 due to the increased student enrollment, the Defense Plant Corporation continued to fund improvements well after this time. In 1943, the DPC added a new two-story operations building and an expansive concrete aircraft parking apron at No. 1 BFTS. The operations building contained offices, briefing rooms, a student ready room, and a supply room for flight gear, as well as a new glass-enclosed control tower. The Terrell control tower operators no longer had to scale the outside ladder to reach the tower. The next year the wide grass-covered airfield at No. 1 BFTS received a new 3,000-foot hard surface runway. The advanced trainers used the new runway while the Stearman primary trainers continued to use the grass alongside the runway for takeoffs and landings. Later, the DPC added another hard surface cross-wind runway to the airfield. Griffin Field, the satellite field used by the advanced trainers, also received a small operations building that included a control tower and space for several Link trainers so students could practice instrument procedures while waiting to fly.

The Army Air Forces had rectified the early supply problems by adding a small army contingent at each British school to coordinate supply needs and ensure maintenance supplies were on hand when needed. When the first army cadets arrived to train at the British schools, an army administrative staff arrived to maintain the cadet records. The army also added a flight supervisor and an engineering contingent to each school to supervise the aircraft maintenance. The various army personnel at each British school were organized into a separate unit designated an Army Air Forces Training Detachment, later changed to Army Air Forces Base Unit, usually with an army captain as the commanding officer.

The British had added a stores unit to each school to provide small replacement items such as uniforms, caps, badges, belts, and miscellaneous items. An absence of these items had caused considerable inconvenience when the schools opened, even though Group Captain Carnegie suspected that many of the "lost" badges and caps had in fact been given to, using his word, "admirers" (i.e. young ladies). Each school also received a small library with material covering the latest service issues. "It is hoped that cadets using this room will increase their service general knowledge appreciably and usefully."[42]

As the recreational activities became more organized, the RAF added a physical training instructor to each school and included activities such as archery and skeet shooting. Both the American and British aerial services felt that skeet shooting improved hand-eye coordination, essential in aerial gunnery before the advent of computer gunsights. As the emphasis on physical training increased, the RAF adopted the army system of grading the physical fitness of arriving students and continued to monitor each student during training. The enterprising physical training instructor at No. 3 BFTS, Corporal Mervyn Richardson, a former professional bike racer, created an obstacle course for the school. In time other British schools added obstacle courses.

An example of the diversity of additions to the individual British schools occurred in June 1944 when the army added a weather station at No. 1

BFTS. The weather station occupied space on the first floor of the new operations building. Originally staffed by one officer and eight enlisted personnel, in time the staff expanded to three officers and nine enlisted men. The army later upgraded the station to a Type A weather station and the staff began taking twenty-four-hour weather observations.

The British Flying Training Schools enjoyed a continuity of civilian ownership and management throughout the war years with two exceptions. J. Paul Getty, an eccentric oil millionaire, gained control of the parent company of Skelly Oil and Spartan School of Aeronautics through a series of complicated stock manipulations. In early 1942 Getty ousted Bill Skelly and took over control of Spartan. Several security agencies led by the FBI had investigated Getty for possible Nazi ties. An Office of Naval Intelligence investigation concluded that "Getty has been indiscreet in his choice of associates and naive in his interpretation of the political scene, rather than an avowed supporter of the Nazi or Fascist regime."[43] Another report noted, "Subject reputedly disorganizes and upsets every organization to which he had gained access."[44]

It does not appear that Getty's personal problems or his often bizarre management style (while in Tulsa Getty lived in an underground bunker and received his small salary in nickels for use in the Coke machine) had any adverse effect on Spartan School of Aeronautics. In fact, many former employees remember Getty as a tireless worker who took pains to learn every aspect of Spartan's business. The change in ownership had no effect on Spartan's flight training programs, which remained firmly under the control of Captain Maxwell Balfour throughout the war.

John Paul Riddle had long been enthusiastic about the aviation training possibilities in South America. Riddle formed a division of Embry-Riddle to conduct training in Brazil, a key Allied nation in South America (with U.S. Army and government approval). Riddle saw this cooperative wartime venture as the beginning of a postwar training opportunity in South America. John McKay did not share Riddle's vision. Their differences led to a dissolution of the partnership, unfortunately with hard feelings and negative repercussions for the company. John Paul Riddle sold his interest in the company to John McKay in June 1944.

The last major change in the British Flying Training Schools came in the spring of 1944. By this time the immense training programs around the world were turning out aircrew at rates undreamed of just a few years earlier. Although the Allies had scored notable victories, much hard fighting still lay ahead, especially in the skies over Europe. But the Axis powers were on the defensive. With an ample supply of pilots, graduates of British flight schools encountered delays in holding centers waiting for operational postings.

The Army Air Forces also experienced the same surplus of pilots and notified the Royal Air Force Delegation in Washington that USAAF aviation cadets would no longer train in the British schools after June 1944. This decision generated additional space in the British schools at a time of surplus aircrew.

British officials decided to close one of the five remaining British flight schools in the United States. The reasons for choosing No. 6 BFTS are unclear and official records are scarce. Rumors persist that the reason had to do with poor aircraft maintenance at the school. Some, including former staff members from Ponca City, vigorously deny that aircraft maintenance had anything to do with closing the school.

Whether or not maintenance issues led to closing the school, No. 6 BFTS did experience maintenance problems. Aircraft serviceable rates, especially for the advanced trainers, were consistently below the levels at other schools. At one point in February 1943 the availability of advanced trainers fell to only 35 percent of strength and for many months the availability remained less than 50 percent. In April 1943 two USAAF maintenance officers visited the school to investigate an unusually high number of primary trainer engine failures. Three months later the USAAF sent twenty-eight mechanics to temporarily assist the school's maintenance department.

John Price, a British student at No. 6 BFTS, commented on the maintenance situation in his diary: "There seem to be a hell of a lot of ships in dock at the moment. Maintenance doesn't seem to be all it should to my mind."[45] Comments on aircraft maintenance by a flight student are very unusual.

One tragedy highlighted the maintenance situation at Ponca City. On 21 June 1943, Henry Jerger, the school's chief flight supervisor, and mechanic E. Murray were both killed in the crash of an AT-6 on a maintenance test flight. The advanced trainer spun in from low altitude. Jerger bailed out too low for his parachute to open. Witnesses said Jerger waited too long to bail out, trying unsuccessfully to make sure the mechanic got out of the aircraft. The cause of the crash was determined to be a broken elevator torque tube. The fatal crash occurred just one week after a RAFDEL memorandum concerning No. 6 BFTS. "The outstanding blot on an otherwise attractive picture was the very bad state of the maintenance at Ponca City. The serviceability has been very low and the state of the aircraft generally appalling. The matter has been discussed with the operator and with U.S.A.A.F. Flying Training Command, who will assist the operator in improving this unsatisfactory state of affairs."[46]

The Ponca City school also had recurring problems with poor sanitation in the cafeteria. At one point the army medial officer closed the cafeteria until corrective measures were implemented.

Regardless of the reasons for selecting the Ponca City school, on 15 April 1944 the students of No. 6 BFTS marched to the last Wings Parade for the graduation of Course 16. The remaining students were transferred to other BFTS schools to complete their training. Students flew the school aircraft to the other schools, each making a final low pass over Ponca City as they departed. The RAF staff and the U.S. Army detachment briefly remained. The British staff packed the various service materials for shipment to other schools or to RAFDEL in Washington, while the USAAF personnel inventoried the school assets for disposition. By the middle of May the No. 6 BFTS school buildings had been locked and all personnel had departed.

As the individual British Flying Training Schools underwent numerous changes throughout the war, the Royal Air Force Delegation in Washington also grew and changed. The Royal Air Force Delegation officially came into being in July 1941. The organization existed to supervise and support the various training schemes in the United States. These training schemes, the Arnold Scheme, the Towers Scheme, the Pan American Airways navigation school, the British Flying Training Schools, and Refresher training, required a considerable North American organization to provide logistical support, financial accounting, coordination of personnel movement orders, and interaction among the Royal Air Force, the American military services, and the civilian flight school contractors.

Group Captain Carnegie arrived in the United States in May 1941 and immediately tackled the immense problems associated with the implementation of the various training programs. With no staff, little support, and from a borrowed desk in the War Department, Carnegie provided liaison between the Air Ministry in London and the British Air Attache, the US Army Air Corps, US Navy, American State Department, and other assorted government departments. A considerable portion of his early time involved the site selection process for the six initial British Flying Training Schools. Even with help from newly arrived Wing Commander H. A. V. Hogan, DFC, and Squadron Leader Stuart Mills, DFC, the task of implementing the various training schemes proved to be daunting.

The Air Ministry had seized the opportunity afforded by the necessity to install an organization to administer the new American training schemes to establish what in essence became a mini-Air Ministry in the United States. The Royal Air Force Delegation expanded to include directorates of Equipment, Supply, Intelligence, Signals, Finance and Administration, Movements, Personnel, and Accounts. In addition, RAFDEL officers sat on boards and committees concerned with a wide range of wartime issues.

In spite of the expanded responsibilities, RAFDEL remained essentially a training command and Group Captain Carnegie became the Directorate of Training in the new organization.

Air Marshal Arthur Harris, the first commanding officer of RAFDEL, saw the new organization expand beyond its first offices on the second floor of the American Trucking Association building (the union occupied the first floor) to offices in nine Washington, D.C. locations, a technical unit assigned to the US Army's flight test center at Wright Field in Dayton, Ohio, and an RAF Operational Training Unit in the Bahamas funded by lend-lease and constructed by US Army engineers.

Air Marshal Harris returned to Britain in February 1942 to assume command of Bomber Command and Carnegie and his expanding training staff moved into new offices on K Street. This organization evolved into a miniature training group headquarters, which supervised the various training programs located across the United States and also provided assistance to the U.K. Director of Training.

As the staff of the Royal Air Force Delegation increased, a steady stream of RAF officers temporarily assigned to the United States or awaiting permanent assignments rotated through the RAFDEL offices and added experience. Wing Commander Kenneth J. Rampling, DFC, arrived in the United States, reported to Washington, then traveled south to the South Eastern Air Corps Training Center in Alabama to act as assistant to Wing Commander Hogan. Rampling became the first CFI at No. 5 BFTS after completion of the new Clewiston school.

Among the new RAF officers assigned to the expanding Washington office, Wing Commander Wilfred E. Oulton took charge of navigation training at all schools in the United States in which British personnel were being trained. Wing Commander A. A. de Gruyther arrived to serve as Deputy Director of U.K. Training in Washington. Wing Commander Priest, an expert in armaments, worked closely with BFTS instructors, as well as the USAAF schools. Group Captain Lord Nigel Douglas Hamilton reported to Washington and joined the staff to assist Carnegie in liaison with a number of political offices and service headquarters.

As early as October 1941 famed Battle of Britain ace Wing Commander Robert Stanford Tuck and a number of other British pilots flew with American pursuit groups during the US Army's Carolina maneuvers. Group Captain Harry Broadhurst came to the United States to demonstrate fighter tactics to USAAF officers and Wing Commander Edward M. "Teddy" Donaldson was assigned to duty as an expert in gunnery. Broadhurst, Tuck, and Donaldson also test-flew various models of American aircraft and visited many factories, as well as USAAF and RAF training stations.

When the USAAF established a system of aerial gunnery schools in each geographic command, Donaldson became a major advisor and a strong influence on gunnery training at the American as well as the British schools in the United States. Before he moved to fame in the Western Desert, Group Captain Broadhurst brought an extensive knowledge of European fighter combat operations to the discussions held at various flying training commands and in the USAAF School of Applied Tactics, which had been transferred from Maxwell Field in Alabama to Orlando, Florida.

As the war situation improved, it became standard practice to send experienced RAF pilots to the United States to talk to flight students about actual combat operations. Squadron Leader Beveridge commented on these visits, "Talks by ex-operational pilots are considered here to be of the greatest value to instructors and cadets alike, situated as this Unit is so far from actual operations."[47] Besides the instructional value, these visits could also be inspiring. Squadron Leader James MacLachian, DSO, DFC, visited the British schools and the No. 3 BFTS Operations Record Book described his talk: "A talk of over two hours which was probably the most interesting ever given at this school."[48] After his talk MacLachian performed a precision aerobatic display in a Curtiss P-36 fighter despite the loss of one arm in combat over Malta.[49]

Newly promoted Group Captain Donaldson visited the British Flying Training Schools in a Curtiss P-40 fighter. After his talks, Donaldson also included a low level aerobatic display, which delighted the school staffs and British students. A picture exists of Donaldson's P-40 coming across the No. 4 BFTS tarmac at full throttle with the propeller only scant feet above the ground. The student who took the picture, Wyn Fieldson, is described as the only one on the ramp who did not join the other cadets, who "fell flat on their faces."[50]

After almost a year and a half in the United States, Group Captain Carnegie, the man most responsible for launching the British Flying Training Schools, received a well-deserved promotion to Air Commodore and returned to the Air Ministry in Britain to become the Director of Training. Wing Commander Hogan, previously assigned to the South Eastern Air Corps Training Center, took over as the Director of Flying Training (U.S.A.). Wing Commander K. J. Rampling, the chief flying instructor at No. 5 BFTS in Clewiston, assumed Hogan's position at Maxwell Field in Alabama. Squadron Leader (soon promoted to Wing Commander) T. O. Prickett, a former bomber pilot in the Middle East and Malta, arrived in Clewiston to command No. 5 BFTS.

Following the departure of Air Marshal Harris in 1942, Air Vice Marshal Douglas Evill and then Air Vice Marshal William Welsh commanded the Royal Air Force Delegation in Washington. The final RAFDEL commanding officer, Air Marshal Douglas Colyer, CB, DFC, arrived in Washington in early 1945 as Air Officer Commanding the Royal Air Force in the United States of America. Colyer directed the vast organization, which had grown from one RAF officer at a borrowed desk in the War Department through the final victorious six months of the war, then presided over the dissolution of the Royal Air Force Delegation.

CHAPTER 9

OPERATIONS

Graduates of the British Flying Training Schools, now Royal Air Force pilots, undertook a journey back to Britain that in many ways mirrored the original journey to the schools. Shortly after graduation, the new pilots assembled at the train station, said goodbye to local townspeople and traveled back to Moncton, New Brunswick. From the Canadian Personnel Centre the new pilots traveled to Halifax and boarded ships to Britain. There they undertook additional training before being posted to an operational unit or other duties. This later training and service assignments varied depending on the stage of the war.

One of the grim realities of wartime service for RAF pilots is that graduates of early courses suffered heavy losses after posting to operational squadrons due to the strength of the Axis forces, the intensity of the fighting during the early war years, and the limited manpower of the RAF. As the various training programs turned out a surplus of aircrew and the status of the war grew more favorable for the Allies, many graduates of later courses encountered delays reaching operational squadrons, while graduates of the last courses saw little or no action.

It would be impossible to recount the operational careers of each graduate of the BFTS program. Here is a small representation of the diverse experiences these young men encountered after they left the British Flying Training Schools.

Keith Durbidge graduated with Course 3 at No. 6 BFTS, returned to Canada and then undertook an uncomfortable voyage back across the Atlantic. "We disembarked at Liverpool and boarded a train for the Reception Centre at Bournemouth. The only food provided on the train was ship's biscuits, four inches square, one inch deep, hard as concrete and full of weevils. We realized we were back in a war theatre."[1]

Douglas Sivyer, a graduate of Course 3 at No. 1 BFTS, traced the operational records of the graduates of his early course. Of the thirty-eight who completed the course, only fourteen survived the war. Eight graduates of Course 3 attended an Operational Training Unit (OTU) on Spitfires. One of these, Eddie McCann, flew with 131 and 165 Squadrons at Tangmere and then 232 Squadron in the Mediterranean where he escorted American medium bombers. Of the others, Johnny Gallon and Frank Seeley were killed while operating with 11 Group in England; Vernon Brooker, Blondie Reeves, and George Richardson were killed in North Africa; Bob Wood was killed on Malta, and Peter King was killed on Sicily. Of the original eight who trained on Spitfires, only McCann survived the war. Many of the official descriptions of the last flights of those killed in action contain nothing more than the poignant epitaph "failed to return."

Geoffrey Hirons graduated with the first course at No. 5 BFTS. After he returned to England, Hirons trained at a fighter OTU then traveled to Cairo, Egypt, for service in North Africa. Hirons joined 94 Squadron flying Hurricanes for a complete operational tour. In June 1943 Hirons converted to Curtiss P-40 Kittyhawks and joined 112 Squadron. Hirons flew another operational tour in Italy where he received the Distinguished Flying Cross and a commission. Hirons' squadron converted to P-51

Mustangs and by the end of the war he had 1,012 flying hours and had attained the rank of flight lieutenant.

Anthony Payne graduated with the first course at No. 3 BFTS. After returning to England Payne converted to twin-engine aircraft on Avro Ansons, then undertook several courses to master R/T procedures, IFF, and flying the Lorenz beam, all conducted against the background of "the very real problem of navigation in the constant industrial haze of factory-strewn England," which was as Payne recalled, "about as far removed from Miami as is possible to imagine."

Payne then attended a Wellington twin-engine bomber Operational Training Unit at Moreton-in-Marsh. Payne's previous experience in only single-engine aircraft apparently presented no problems, because he soloed the Wellington in under two hours and then advanced from co-pilot to pilot half way through the course as new crews formed. At the conclusion of the course, the crew left Britain in a new Wellington Mark 1c and flew to Gibraltar. After a few days' break, officials selected Payne's crew to make the first non-stop flight to Libya, cutting out the hazardous refueling stop at Malta. The twelve-hour and thirty-five-minute flight over the Mediterranean Sea occurred mostly at night. "We hit our landfall on the button, all credit to Jack Strain the navigator, later to be awarded Poland's highest decoration."

Payne and his crew joined 37 Squadron flying from a desert airfield, "miles and miles of damn-all, surrounded by miles and miles of damn-all." Engine trouble on their first raid on Benghazi resulted in a forced landing fifty miles behind enemy lines and a four-day hike with vital assistance from local Bedouins. "This qualified us for membership in the exclusive Late Arrivals Club."[2]

During leave in Tel Aviv, Payne contracted polio and spent the next two years in a Johannesburg hospital. He returned to flying in the spring of 1944 and became an instructor on AT-6 Harvards, "a very happy reunion." Toward the end of the war Payne instructed on gliders and finished the war as a warrant officer.

Michael Giddings graduated as the top student in the first course at No. 1 BFTS. In July 1942 Giddings flew a Spitfire from the carrier HMS *Eagle* with thirty others to bolster the defense of the island of Malta. As the group winged its way over the Mediterranean, an air traffic controller in perfect English ordered the flight to turn to a northerly heading. As the group commander considered this puzzling order, another, almost profane, voice ordered the group to continue on the original heading, thus averting a German ruse to lure the Spitfires to Sicily. Over the next four months Giddings participated in fierce combat over Malta, often flying three or four sorties a day. He returned to England after a takeoff accident in which his Spitfire collided with a construction truck that had pulled onto the runway. Back in Britain, Giddings flew Spitfire IXs during the airborne operations at Arnhem. His squadron reequipped with Mustangs and participated in long-range bomber escorts. On one of these escort missions, Giddings engaged and damaged a Messerschmitt 262, the new German jet fighter. He ended the war in Europe commanding 129 Squadron.

The RAF officers and students in the United States, as well as their American hosts, were thrilled to learn of the first 1000-bomber raid on Germany. American newspapers headlined front page stories of the attack on Cologne carried out on the night of 30/31 May 1942. Air Marshal Arthur Harris, the former head of RAFDEL in Washington and the new commander of Bomber Command, staged the attack by assembling every bomber in his command including second line aircraft, as well as aircraft from training units. Later critics have minimized the attack as little more than a publicity stunt, but at the time this attack caused considerably more damage than previous bombing raids, raised the morale on British and American home fronts, and caused considerable consternation within the German civilian population and the German high command (although it would be some time before attacks of this magnitude could be repeated with regularity).

It is doubtful that any graduates of the British Flying Training Schools participated in the first 1000-bomber attack on Germany. Graduates of the first BFTS courses would have still been engaged in conversion training at Operational Training Units and would not have yet joined operational units. But since Training Command aircraft were used in the raid (usually flown by instructors) some BFTS graduates may have participated in the attack.

The first course at No. 5 BFTS graduated without fanfare except for a dinner in Miami. The school facilities were still not complete, the graduates received no wings because the RAF had failed to supply any, and no decision had been made on commissioning, so the entire class graduated as sergeants. The graduates included nineteen-year-old Gerald Frank Russell Cooke, who always went by Russell. The class returned to Canada along a different route, which included a stop in New York City and Cooke recorded the experience, "I count myself extremely lucky having seen New York as I did and will never forget it. Pennsylvania Station, Fifth Avenue, Broadway & Times Square, Radio City, Empire State Building and all the rest. Some of the buildings actually hid their tops in the clouds on that day."[3] Sometime after the class returned to Canada, about one-third of the Clewiston graduates, including Cooke, received commissions as pilot officers.

Cooke always wanted to fly bombers. After returning to England he attended a twin-engine conversion course on Airspeed Oxfords in Grantham, Lincolnshire. "It seems quite a nice ship. In the plane the dual controls are side by side and you sit right up in front of the engines. It is also quite a change to walk through a door instead of climbing over the side to get in."[4]

After twin-engine training, Cooke traveled to Topcliffe near Thirsk, Yorkshire, for Blind Approach Training. "This training consists of radio navigation and work with the radio beam. It enables one to find the direction to an airfield, approach it in the correct direction and lose altitude at the correct time so as to land on the right spot even though the ground is obscure owing to fog or bad weather."[5]

Cooke then went to Bassingbourne, near Royston, Cambridgeshire, and joined a bomber Operational Training Unit flying Wellingtons. Cooke soloed a Wellington at night after only two hours of dual instruction. "This is rather unusual and only goes to praise the Yanky training. I am going up again tonight to knock off most of the four circuits required before cross-countries. You can imagine how I like this night flying. After finishing in the early hours of the morning I can go to bed leaving a note on the door 'not to be disturbed until mid day'. After lunch I can stroll up to the flights and talk things over with the boys."[6]

While training in England, Cooke celebrated his twentieth birthday. Now part of a Wellington crew, Cooke described a typical three-and-a-quarter-hour training flight in a letter home. The flight flew over the midlands at 2000 feet, climbing to 4000 feet to cross the Welsh hills. "Nearing the coast we couldn't see much of the ground as the clouds became fairly thick. Two minutes before we were due to arrive the clouds broke up and Aberystwyth lay right in front of us. I never knew Aberystwyth was so beautiful. After we left the hills again the clouds thickened and we climbed up and rode along the top of what looked like a huge wash tub of soap suds. We couldn't see the ground at all so we turned south again when we reached our estimated time of arrival over Hemslow. We came lower and found ourselves dead on track and finally landed at Steeple."[7]

In July 1942 Cooke and his Wellington crew joined 156 Squadron flying from Alconbury, a satellite field for Wyton. The officer's quarters in the prewar Royal Air Force stations were usually quite nice, even luxurious, with a decided club atmosphere. Airbases built quickly after the start of the war, such as Alconbury, could be anything but luxurious. "The officer's mess is in an old house, Upton House and I am living in one of the huts placed around the garden. The food seems very good. It's a pretty ghastly place for getting anywhere. There is only one bus into

Huntingdon each night. As is expected our mess is on the other side of the field to the town which is therefore eight miles away. The accommodation is not so hot either. Four to a room with no water laid on."[8]

Several days after twenty-year-old Pilot Officer Russell Cooke wrote that letter to his parents, his bomber went down in the dark skies over Germany. None of the crew survived. The crew was buried next to each other in Oldenburg, Germany.[9]

William Reid, a graduate of No. 2 BFTS, received the Victoria Cross for extreme heroism on a bombing mission to the German city of Dusseldorf in which German night fighters heavily damaged his Lancaster bomber and killed three of the crew. Although badly wounded himself, Reid managed to fly the crippled bomber back to England. After recovering from his wounds, Reid returned to Bomber Command and joined 617 Squadron. He took part in attacks on V-1 flying bomb sites until 31 July 1944 when a bomb dropped from another bomber hit Reid's Lancaster and he was forced to bail out. Reid spent the rest of the war as a POW and survived to return home.

Arthur Aaron, a graduate of Course 6 at No. 1 BFTS, received the Victoria Cross for a night bombing mission over Italy. The initial report indicated that an attack by German night fighters severely damaged the Stirling bomber and seriously wounded Aaron. Later reports suggest that fire from the rear gunner of another British bomber may have hit Aaron's aircraft. Although weak and in intense pain from his wounds, Aaron refused shots of morphine and helped fly the Stirling for five hours back to North Africa aided by the flight engineer (the two communicated by written messages since Aaron's jaw had been shattered). Aaron and the flight engineer succeeded in landing the crippled bomber at Bone after several attempts. Aaron died nine hours later.

Robert Richardson graduated with Course 3 at No. 5 BFTS and after OTU joined 18 Squadron flying Blenheims in North Africa. The squadron had just shifted to night operations after incurring heavy losses carrying out attacks by day. One night over Tunisia flying in the moonlight at 1,000 feet the wireless operator saw a faint reflection from a line of trucks draw up in cover along the side the road. Richardson came around and dropped a string of forty-pound anti-personnel bombs and 250-pound general purpose bombs. The gunner raked the area with his twin Brownings. Richardson brought the Blenheim around for several more runs and then attacked a heavy machine gun emplacement with his wing gun. In the darkness Richardson almost hit the roof of a house in the process. "I pulled the stick back, desperately trying to avoid the house and sure death. We whizzed so close to the roof that the roof tiles were ripped loose. Peter, who had a grand but terrifying view from the Blenheim's nose, came back to the cockpit. 'Don't you ever do that again,' he screamed, 'or I'll kick you up your arse.' I could well understand his feelings. Had I been in that nose cone, I can't imagine what I would have done."[10]

Charles George Waller graduated with the first course at No. 2 BFTS. Waller was dismayed when he was assigned as a twin-engine instructor upon his return to Britain in spite of the fact that coming from a BFTS he had only flown single-engine aircraft. Posted to an advanced flying school, "One of my first jobs was to take a pupil up and teach him formation flying in a twin-engine aircraft. The pupil was in his last week of training and had far more flying hours on twin-engine aircraft than I had."

Waller joined Coastal Command in January 1944. "I was on anti-shipping patrols off the coasts of France and Holland. This lasted until the end of the war in Europe when I converted to Liberators. These had been modified to carry troops and I was then on troop carrying from England out to India."[11] Waller left the RAF in 1946 with 2,014 flying hours.

Robin Sinclair, the son of the wartime Secretary of State for Air, graduated with Course 6 at No. 2 BFTS. After graduation Sinclair remained in the United States as a Basic flight instructor assigned to Gunter Field, Alabama. After eight months at Gunter, Sinclair transferred to the Western Flying Training Command and did an instructor's course on twin-engine aircraft at Sacramento, California. For a time, he served as an advanced twin-engine instructor in the desert at Yuma, Arizona,

before returning to Canada for assignment as second pilot ferrying a
Lockheed Hudson from Montreal to the U.K. Subsequently, Sinclair flew
De Havilland Mosquito aircraft on operations in Southeast Asia.

Nick Berryman chaffed under the strict army discipline of the Arnold
Scheme and washed out of flight training. Back in Canada, a panel of
officers allowed Berryman to continue training at a BFTS. He graduated
with Course 7 at No. 1 BFTS. After training at an OTU on Hurricanes,
Berryman flew low-level search missions in Boulton Paul Defiants and
Spitfires looking for aircrew downed at sea. Berryman also flew air-sea
rescue missions in a Supermarine Walrus.

Trevor Parfitt, the young man from a remote mining village, arrived
in the United States at No. 3 BFTS and struggled. His first instructor
provided little encouragement and informed Parfitt that he would never
make a pilot. The negative instructor sent Parfitt on his first solo with the
comment, "go ahead and kill yourself." Parfitt persevered, graduated, and
then joined Transport Command after his return to England. Parfitt flew
throughout the war, first in support of fighter squadron operations by
transporting ground crew and supplies to various aerodromes and then
flying passengers and cargo from Britain to India through the Middle
East and later into Europe. Parfitt also engaged in parachute dropping
and glider towing flying Dakotas (military version of the Douglas DC-3).
He was demobilized in 1946.

During the Blitz, Stanley James Endacott's home in Plymouth had been
damaged by bombs. He joined the RAF in July 1941 and graduated with
Course 4 at No. 5 BFTS. After arriving back in England, Endacott trained
at a fighter OTU then joined 164 Squadron flying Hurricanes armed with
40mm rockets. Following a number of missions from England, Endacott
transferred to Southeast Asia. From India he flew Hurricanes armed with
bombs in close support of the Fourteenth Army from Imphal-Kohima to
Mandalay and Prome. During his last months in the RAF, Endacott flew
Austers as a warrant officer in a communications squadron in Malaysia.

Jack Taylor graduated with Course 4 at No. 3 BFTS. After further training, Taylor flew both Spitfires and Hurricanes on operations. Toward the end of the war, Taylor was flying a Hawker Typhoon when he was shot down over Germany. Taylor managed to land the damaged Typhoon, but was murdered by German civilians.

Rodney Scrase graduated with Course 3 at No. 5 BFTS in March 1942. After returning to England, Scrase joined 72 Squadron just before the unit moved to support Operation Torch, the Allied invasion of northwest Africa. This was at a time of intense aerial combat with the German Luftwaffe, but a combat pilot's life consisted of more than aerial combat. The squadron's Spitfire Vs were replaced by Spitfire IXs. The new model offered improved performance, but did not have the Mark V's tropical air filters. The new aircraft suffered numerous mechanical problems from blowing dust on the primitive North African airfields; that is unless it rained, which turned the fields into quagmires of mud.

Returning to base one afternoon, the squadron flew into a tropical storm. Before the aircraft could reach the airfield, the storm broke over the field and the runway became flooded and visibility rapidly diminished. The squadron Operations Record Book recorded, "Two of our aircraft landed at Tingley while Sgt Hussey made a very good 'wheels down' landing at another airstrip under bad condition there. P/O Corbin's aircraft tipped on its nose on the runway due to the appalling conditions. The airscrew suffered most damage. All the remaining pilots managed to land successfully except Sgt Passmore who misjudged his landing speed and in trying to correct the aircraft, stalled and spun in. He was thrown about 25 yards from the aircraft and was killed. The aircraft was a complete wreck."[12]

Besides the weather extremes, 72 Squadron lived in appalling conditions in tents at makeshift airfields, which changed frequently. Millions of biting flies inhabited these temporary airfields. Airmen lived under mosquito netting and meals were prepared behind netting, which received a liberal coating of DDT before each meal. Meals became a race as the flies covered food and utensils. Temperatures often reached 120 degrees.

Following the capture of Sicily and the Allied landings in Italy, the squadron moved to Tusciano, but conditions remained primitive. Sleep was impossible due to the noise of the artillery and anti-aircraft fire. The mosquitoes inhabiting the area proved to be the large, fierce variety, resistant to all repellents. Living under these conditions sapped the strength of the crews, both air and ground, and within a few weeks many were suffering from malaria. Examining the aircraft each morning also became a chore to assess any damage caused during the night. "Shell fire damage was an obvious risk but several aircraft were damaged by great white oxen that roamed the field at night and scratched their hides on the wings, which damaged the all-important pitot head extensions, the externally mounted tubes that measured air speed."[13]

In December 1944 Scrase returned to England and joined 1 Squadron flying Spitfires on escort missions and fighter sweeps.

Martin John Burgess graduated slightly later than Course 5 at No. 4 BFTS because he had to stay and retake the navigation section of the Wings Exam. Burgess first joined 239 Squadron flying the North American Mustang I, then 225 Squadron in North Africa where he flew Hurricanes modified to carry bombs, commonly called Hurribombers, out of Algeria. The squadron converted to Spitfire Vs and concentrated on reconnaissance flights for the remainder of the campaign in Tunisia. After combat in Italy, Burgess was assigned to Palestine as an instructor on Harvards, Hurricanes, and Spitfires. After his tour instructing, Burgess returned to Italy and 225 Squadron, now equipped with the Spitfire IX. After the war ended Burgess returned to the U.K., but while waiting for demobilization he became ill with tuberculosis contracted overseas. Burgess spent two years in a hospital before his discharge from the RAF.

After graduation from No. 2 BFTS, John Robert Baldwin joined 609 Squadron flying the new Hawker Typhoon. At first the aircraft experienced considerable problems caused by an unreliable engine and an alarming propensity to shed the tail assembly in flight. Despite these problems, Baldwin shot down three German Bf-109s on an early mission and received the Distinguished Flying Cross. On another mission he was shot down in flames over the English Channel, but survived unharmed. His victory total continued to climb and in November 1943 he became commanding officer of 198 Squadron. Baldwin continued to fly the Typhoon, now armed with deadly rockets, on ground attack missions. Toward the end of the war he was promoted to group captain and assumed command of 123 Wing. Group Captain Baldwin is the top scoring Typhoon ace of World War II with fifteen victories and one shared.

Cecil Bridges joined the RAF in 1935 and trained as a fitter (mechanic) at the technical school at Halton. He applied for flight training and arrived at No. 4 BFTS with Course 8. After graduating as the top cadet of his course and receiving a commission, Bridges remained in the United States for further training and an assignment with the Army Air Forces as an instructor on twin-engine aircraft. Bridges returned to Britain after his tour of instructing. In August 1944, Bridges joined 627 Mosquito (Path Finder) Squadron based at Woodhall Spa, Lincolnshire. "Until the end of the war in Europe, operated by day and night against targets in Germany and occupied territories, mainly executing low level (800 feet) visual marking of target aiming points with illuminating flares, but also including very low level mine laying of inland waterways and precision low level bombing of selected targets (e.g. Gestapo Headquarters in Oslo). Final number of flying hours about 1200, final rank Acting Squadron Leader."[14]

After graduating with the second course at No. 3 BFTS, Felix Block returned to Britain and received further training on Wellington bombers. Block joined 179 Squadron in Coastal Command and flew some 1,500 hours by the time he was demobilized from the RAF as a warrant officer.

Joseph E. Ekbery graduated with the second course at No. 2 BFTS. Ekbery heard the news of the Japanese attack on Pearl Harbor while traveling back to Canada. In England Ekbery trained at a fighter OTU and then joined No. 222 (Natal) Squadron at North Weald flying Spitfires on fighter sweeps over northern France and later transferred to 232 Squadron. "We shipped out to North Africa on corvettes in the depths of winter, and became operational from Bone, Algeria, 5 January 1943 on Spitfire VBs. I was shot down over the Mediterranean on 25th February and ditched a hundred yards off shore. I remember thinking the Me-109 firing at me had missed, but bang! —a hole in the wing and no prop! I thought I could land back at the aerodrome, but a Spit without a fan glides like a brick. I didn't inflate my dinghy, so I didn't qualify for the 'Goldfish Club'."

Ekbery got his first confirmed victory on 26 April 1943, but like most successful fighter pilots felt sure of other victories that could not be confirmed. The month before he had been involved in a head-on dual with an Fw-190, which shattered his windscreen "right through to the last layer and the Fw-190 spun into a low cloud." Not long after the fight with the Fw-190, Ekbery encountered a Ju-87 dive bomber, "and emptied all my 303 ammunition in his general direction. We had de Wilde ammo, and I could see strikes all over it, but it flew gracefully on. I formated on it—the gunner was obviously dead, and the pilot seemed to have a fixation and kept straight and level. I waved and flew home. This taught me a strong lesson to hold my fire and make sure of my range. All my subsequent successes were achieved with single short bursts."

Ekbery finished his first tour and after a short stint in training flights in North Africa, he joined Neville Duke's 145 Squadron equipped with Spitfire VIIIs. Ekbery received the Distinguished Flying Cross, then as fighter opposition waned the squadron shifted to ground attacks after the invasion of southern France. "We made quite a few trips strafing the fleeing Germans on the roads and in trains (the steam from the boilers, when they go up, is quite amazing!)."

Ekbery ended his second tour and returned home after two years and five months on operations. "My final confirmed score was 6 enemy aircraft destroyed, 2 probably destroyed and 1 damaged. I had completed

370 hours on operations out of a total of 750 hours flying." Ekbery served in several training commands until demobilized in March 1946. "I was one of the lucky pilots flying right up to the last day."[15]

Collyn Warwick Warren was born in 1922 in Cologne, Germany. He graduated from No. 1 BFTS in 1943 and then returned to England and joined No. 12 OTU at Edgehill. The official report of Warren's last training flight is brutally terse. "Taken off at 1502 hours from Edgehill for an initial dual training sortie in Wellington III (BK455) at 1518 hours eyewitnesses saw the bomber stall at one hundred feet and upon hitting the ground, it rolled onto its back and began to burn fiercely."[16]

Dennis John Mason graduated with Course 4 at No. 2 BFTS and returned to Britain and received a commission and a posting to a flight instructors course. Mason taught in several schools, became a flight commander, and remained a flight instructor until his demobilization in April 1946. "During my flying career, I crashed twice, had one mid-air collision, was awarded the Air Force Cross, and ended my career with more than 1500 flying hours and the rank of Flight Lieutenant."[17]

Ken Bickers graduated from No. 1 BFTS, then joined Bomber Command after transition training. While on operations Bickers received the Distinguished Flying Cross. An excerpt from Bickers' second DFC reads, "103 Squadron RAF (DFC) Airborne 1839 24.03.1944 from Elsham Wolds for an operation against Berlin in Lancaster ME665 PM-C. Homebound, came down 2 km E of Luckenwalde and exploded with great force three crew members were found and are buried at Berlin, four others were not found. Sq. Ldr. Bickers was on the third sortie of his second tour, and at 21, he was one of the youngest flight commanders to be killed on Bomber Command operations."[18]

Even before going on operations, Christopher Harrison followed an unusual path through flight training. Before joining the RAF, Harrison had been employed by Rolls Royce working on the Merlin engine. Harrison volunteered for the RAF and arrived in the United States to begin flight training in the Arnold Scheme. After completing primary training, Harrison received orders for detached duty with Packard Motor Car Company in Detroit, Michigan. Packard had received a license to manufacture the Rolls Royce Merlin engine.

Harrison worked for nine months at Packard as a trouble shooter and then resumed flight training with Course 13 at No. 3 BFTS. After graduation and his return to England, Harrison trained on Beaufighter Mk IIs ("the worst plane I ever flew") and Mk VIs, ("one of the best!"). In February 1944, Harrison was posted to Little Snoring, Norfolk, for conversion to the de Havilland Mosquito. Afterward, he joined 515 Squadron flying the Mosquito, Mk VI "Cat's Eye" designed for low-level intruder night operations against German night fighter airfields. "Our job was to locate and patrol one or sometimes two night fighter bases and on the odd occasion the flare path was lit, to attack whatever moved. We also attacked 'targets of opportunity' en route."[19] Harrison flew forty-three missions over the continent.

Douglas Wilkinson trained with Course 11 at No. 4 BFTS in Arizona where he enjoyed the heat, the food, the local hospitality, and long walks in the desert. After his return to England, Wilkinson converted to twin-engine Airspeed Oxfords and then trained at a heavy conversion unit to qualify on the Handley Page Halifax, a four-engine heavy bomber. After completing training, Wilkinson and his crew joined 158 Squadron in Bomber Command. Wilkinson's bomber was shot down on his first mission over Germany and he spent the next sixteen months as a prisoner of war.

Alastair Michie graduated as the top cadet on Course 3 at No. 5 BFTS. Michie converted to twin-engine aircraft and flew Blenheims, Bisleys, Havocs, and Bostons. Michie joined 605 Squadron and flew Mosquito fighter bombers on intruder missions on two combat tours of about eighty total missions. "Our tasks were quite varied—to patrol German night-flying bases; to harass, bomb, and destroy targets of opportunity; and to search the seas for mine-layers, all at low-level and mostly at night. I flew twice to Berlin at 20,000 feet, mixing with the bomber stream and attempting to intercept German night fighters."

Michie was stationed in East Kent when the first V-1 flying bombs were directed toward London. "We would patrol off the French coast at about seven thousand feet where we tried to intercept them, successfully at times. They were fast, of course, and flew at about five hundred feet so that a high-speed dive was required to catch them."[20]

Richard Alan Day of Course 11 at No. 4 BFTS returned to England and flew Hurricanes at a fighter OTU before a posting to North Africa. In Egypt, Day joined 253 Squadron flying several marks of Spitfire fighters. In July 1944 the squadron moved to support Tito's partisans in Yugoslavia. On one flight, Day was wounded and then two months later he was shot down, survived, and evaded capture long enough to join a partisan force. Day returned to his squadron a month later. He received the Distinguished Flying Cross in 1945 and left the RAF in 1946.

J. R. Sutton graduated with Course 4 at No. 3 BFTS, returned to Britain and received a commission. After twin-engine conversion training on Airspeed Oxfords, Sutton attended No. 21 Operational Training Unit at Moreton-in-March on Wellington aircraft. Sutton and his crew flew a Wellington from Lyneham to Gibraltar in October 1942, then to Mersah Matruh, which had just been re-captured from the Germans, and then on to Cairo. "On arriving in Cairo from Mersah Matruh, we found that no further aircrew, or indeed aircraft, were required there. After carrying out some local ferry duties, we were ordered to take a Wellington aircraft through to India."[21]

Due to a surplus of pilots in India because Wellingtons were being converted from a six-man crew with a pilot and co-pilot to five-man crews with only one pilot, Sutton left his crew and joined 215 Bomber Squadron at Rawalpindi. In more than a year 215 Squadron performed many tasks including training Ghurka and Indian paratroops and flying combat operations out of Jessore, Bengal, by day and by night over Burma. During this time Sutton was "Mentioned in Dispatches" and awarded the Distinguished Flying Cross. Sutton later served as an instructor on Wellingtons in Palestine, as a test pilot in Iraq, and as a staff officer at RAF Headquarters Persia (Iran). After V-J day Sutton returned home for demobilization.

Harry Lister trained with Course 5 at No. 3 BFTS. On arrival back in Britain, Lister received a two-week leave and then a posting to No. 12 (P) A.F.U. at RAF Grantham where he converted to twin-engine Airspeed Oxfords. "Towards the end of the course, we were asked to make a choice of aircraft and branch of service in an attempt to put square pegs into square holes. However, it did not always work out and my choice of Strike Aircraft—Coastal Beaufighters, turned out as a posting to No. 45 Staff Navigator Navigation Course at Central Navigation School, RAF Granage."

Lister served as a staff navigation training officer and during this time managed to get attached to operational bomber squadrons for short periods to observe their procedures and navigation techniques. "I managed an attachment to 158 Squadron flying Halifax aircraft and went along for the ride as a supernumerary on two night bombing operations to Hamburg and Essen in July 1943. The Hamburg operation was the first on which the 'Window' anti-radar device was used, so I spent some time pushing bundles of paper strips down the flare chute."

Following the end of the war in Europe, Lister was posted to Transport Command in October 1945. "I trained in Dakota aircraft for Army Support, Supply Dropping, Paratrooping, glider towing, etc, finally being posted to 78 Squadron RAF Almaza, Egypt where I did straight transport work, passengers and cargo, along the North African Coast, Italy, Greece, and down to the Persian Gulf, Trucal Oman, etc. from where I was demobbed in April 1946."[22]

Keith Base graduated with Course 5 at No. 3 BFTS and returned to Britain and conversion training on twin-engine Airspeed Oxfords. He then attended a Wellington bomber OTU. Base subsequently served as an instructor, then went on to fly operations with both Coastal Command

and Fighter Command. Promoted to squadron leader, Base became a test pilot, but was severely injured in an accident. Base underwent reconstructive surgery at the famous McIndow Clinic in East Grinstead, Sussex, then embarked on an extensive rehabilitation program.

James Deans had been a motorcycle dispatch rider with the Royal Corps of Signals attached to the British Expeditionary Force sent to France in 1940. His unit had been one of the last evacuated from Cherbourg. Deans transferred to the RAF, graduated with Course 5 at No. 6 BFTS and received a commission. Deans joined 169 Squadron in Bomber Command where he received the Distinguished Flying Cross following a raid on Mannheim on the night of 5/6 September 1943 when his aircraft was repeatedly attacked by enemy fighters, one of which was shot down. Deans flew the badly damaged bomber back to base and made a successful emergency landing. Deans died one month later when his Sterling bomber crashed into the North Sea during a test flight. The cause of the crash was never determined.

Roddy Robertson graduated as the top cadet of Course 6 at No. 3 BFTS, received a commission, and then remained in the United States as an instructor. After attending the USAAF instructors course at Kelly Field, San Antonio, he instructed at Eagle Pass, Texas, until near the end of 1943.

Ernest Charles Wilson graduated with Course 13 at No. 4 BFTS. After his return to England, Wilson attended a twin-engine conversion course and then a Wellington Operational Training Unit. Wilson and his new crew joined 104 Squadron in Italy. The squadron had just moved to a new airfield and lived in primitive conditions. "Our living quarters were in tents and they had seen far better times. The one we found suitable was not too worn, but was dank, not entirely bare of any grass inside, but had a sort of trench running through the middle." Wilson discovered the reason for the trench, and the necessity to deepen it, later that night during a driving rain storm.

Wilson and his crew flew a mixed assortment of operations from August to December 1944: "we went to Austria, Hungary, Northern Italy,

Jugoslavia, and Greece, mostly at night. December operations were to harass retreating Germans in Greece and were carried out in daylight."

One particular supply-dropping flight did not go well. German flak opened up on the solitary Wellington after the supply drop. "From there being no flak at all, there was flak everywhere, and it was bloody dangerous stuff. Jack Garnsey in the rear turret was a soft spoken man and he advised me to take evasive action in a voice as evenly pitched as that of a Sunday School teacher."

When it was almost out of range, the German gunners hit the Wellington. "I was near deafened as well as sprayed with minute particles of glass. The Wireless Operator called out that he thought the starboard engine was on fire, which it was! He also said that the Rear Gunner had appeared from his turret badly injured with blood streaming or frothing from his mouth."

The fire was put out, the engine shut down and the propeller feathered, the abandon aircraft procedure considered, and the crew advised as to the situation. "The aircraft had been severely damaged; there were no flaps, very little brake pressure, no hydraulics, and was gradually losing height. Most Wellingtons on one engine will maintain height at about 6,000 feet; our big snag was that the land over which we flying was about 8,500 feet above mean sea level." One of the crew spotted what looked like a small landing field with something on the end. Wilson was not sure, but by now he was out of options. Down to 400 feet, the co-pilot frantically pumped the landing gear down by hand. The third green light, indicating the landing gear was down and locked, came on just in time for the co-pilot to take his safety position just behind the bulkhead door. "Somehow, with God's help, the aircraft was leveled out with no flaps, just at the right place on the landing strip at 120 miles per hour. I knew I had a little brake power, and I've never seen the end of a landing strip come up so fast. I saw what that thing at the end was; it was a road making machine, so I could not afford to collide with that. Fortunately, a lead off road come in sight and with an almighty heave and the use of the entire brake supply, I swerved onto it and came to rest in a cloud of dust!"

The crew had landed on an airfield under construction by American army engineers. Jack Garnsey, the wounded tail gunner, was immediately taken to a hospital in Florence where he was operated on within an hour of being hit. Garnsey made a complete recovery, but never flew again. "The Wellington was a write-off, I was sorry to see it land up in such a mess; it was my favorite and I had always flown it whenever it was available."[23]

L. J. Taylor graduated with Course 17 at No. 5 BFTS. After a rough voyage home on the RMS *Andes*, Taylor reported to the aircrew reception center at Harrogate for assignment. A month later Taylor boarded a ship for Alexandria, Egypt, where he undertook operational training on Hurricanes and Spitfires. After training, Taylor joined 111 Squadron at Rimini, Italy, on the Adriatic Sea. The squadron performed low-level strafing and later dive-bombing with a 500-pound bomb slung under the fuselage. "This is highly hazardous work and we were an easy target in the dive. Sure enough, the Germans got me with their deadly 88 mm flak, and I had to ditch in the River Po delta. I was pulled out of the water by two Salvation Army girls who had witnessed the action. I suffered some minor injuries—a few bits of shrapnel in the leg. A small piece worked its way out of my foot four years later."[24]

John Younie graduated with the second course at No. 5 BFTS and flew fighter reconnaissance and ground attack missions in North Africa and the Balkans. Flying Mustangs on numerous dangerous low level attacks over Yugoslavia, Younie received a bar to his earlier DFC for "consistently displaying a high standard of keenness and courage."

William A. Cory graduated with Course 9 at No. 3 BFTS. Back in England Cory trained on multi-engine aircraft and then joined 427 Squadron, 6 Group (Canadian)in Bomber Command, where he served from September 1943 to July 1944. "I completed 34 operations on Halifaxes and was awarded the D.F.C. and was promoted to Acting Flight Lieutenant in December 1943. After completing my tour at 427 Squadron at Leeming, Yorkshire, I was posted back to an OTU and finished my RAF career as an instructor on Wellingtons."[25]

Thomas William Reece trained with Course 10 at No. 3 BFTS. After his return to England, Reece received twin-engine conversion training on Airspeed Oxfords and then attended an OTU on Wellingtons. Reece received additional heavy bomber training on Short Stirlings and Avro Lancasters. In November 1944, Reece and his crew joined 90 Squadron at Tuddenham, Suffolk. By VE Day in May 1945, Reece had flown thirty-four operational missions by both day and night. In the summer of 1945 Reece was posted to 158 Squadron, Transport Command. For more than a year, he flew converted Stirling III bombers from the U.K. to Tripoli, Lydda, Basra, Karachi, and return, transporting troops to and from these distant points.

For his service with 90 Squadron, Reese received the Distinguished Flying Cross. "During the war, medals such as the DFC were awarded by the King at Buckingham Palace. However, there was always a back-log and my DFC had not been awarded before the end of the war. Mine was sent through the post with a polite letter. The phrase 'For King and country' lost much of its flavour for me."[26]

John Hanbury Smith-Carrington trained with Course 4 at No. 3 BFTS. After traveling back to Halifax, his group boarded the troopship HMT *Banfora*. "It was most unpleasant leaving Halifax, as a number of French Canadian soldiers mutinied and tried to leave ship. The situation was saved by a very brave Canadian Roman Catholic padre who persuaded them to keep the peace. Nevertheless, throughout the voyage we could not venture on deck alone."[27]

After his arrival in Britain, Smith-Carrington attended a conversion course on twin-engine aircraft. He joined 98 Squadron flying North American B-25 Mitchell medium bombers, "the first RAF Squadron to be equipped with them." Based at RAF Foulsham, Norfolk, RAF Honeley, Warwickshire, and RAF Dunsfold, Surrey, 98 Squadron flew low- and medium-level operational sorties over Europe. On completion of an operational tour in January 1944 Smith-Carrington spent three months instructing on Mitchells at No. 13 OTU, RAF Bicester.

In late April 1944, Smith-Carrington embarked from Gourock, Scotland, bound once again for Halifax, Nova Scotia. From May to December 1944, he served as an instructor at No. 7 OTU, Debert, Nova Scotia on Mosquito aircraft. In January 1945 he returned to the U.K. on a second operational tour where he again flew B-25 Mitchells on support missions. When the war ended, he became a flight commander on 98 Squadron and flew Mosquitoes at a number of RAF stations in occupied Europe. In June 1945, Smith-Carrington received a permanent commission in the RAF.

Alan Watson graduated with Course 11 from No. 6 BFTS and received a commission. Back in England Watson flew as a supernumerary attached to 78 Squadron, equipped with Halifax IIIs, on several missions to the Ruhr valley to gain operational experience. After his missions with 78 Squadron, Watson became a flight instructor. On 5 December 1944, while Watson was instructing Pilot Officer Wilson in aerobatics in a de Havilland Tiger Moth, the wing struts failed, which allowed the top wing to fold back, trapping Wilson in the rear seat. A Perthshire farmer in the village of Stanley reported seeing pieces falling from the aircraft. The farmer had the impression that Watson was trying to shift the wing from the rear cockpit just before he bailed out. Watson jumped too low and died on impact. His parachute was later tested and found to be working properly.[28]

Leonard J. Timperley graduated with Course 13 at No. 6 BFTS. Back in England, Timperley joined a new Wellington bomber crew at No. 12 Operational Training Unit at Chipping Warden, Oxfordshire. On a navigation training flight the Wellington encountered heavy thunderstorms with icing and severe turbulence. The Wellington broke up in the air and only the navigator survived. He somehow managed to parachute out of the disintegrating aircraft and land safely in spite of the extreme turbulence.[29]

Operational service in the RAF often had no uniform pattern. After Archie Venables graduated with Course 11 at No. 3 BFTS and returned to England, he flew for some time as a glider tow pilot with a glider training unit. "I was very disappointed at not being posted straight to an O.T.U., but consoled myself with the thought that I would have a few more flying hours under my belt before joining a squadron. I had no idea I would be towing gliders from 25th May 1943 to 20th February 1945." By February 1945 he had flown 550 hours towing Hotspur gliders with Miles Master II and Lysander aircraft, some of the time at night. With Venables' extensive experience towing gliders (and seven hours flying gliders) his next assignment is somewhat surprising. Venables attended an OTU to train on single engine fighters. After completing training on Spitfire Vs he went on to fly Typhoons with 55 Squadron and then flew Mustangs with 126 Squadron. After the end of the war, Venables and 126 Squadron participated in the massive flyover of London on 15 September 1945 led by Group Captain Douglas Bader. "I was in the centre of 600 fighter aircraft—tight formation, very low over the centre of London, down the Mall and over Buckingham Palace. This fly past was featured at the end of the film *Reach for the Sky*."[30]

Venables continued to fly Mustangs until March 1946 when he joined 19 Squadron at RAF Molesworth, Huntingdonshire, flying Spitfire XVIs. After service in Germany, 19 Squadron came home to its old peacetime base at RAF Wittering in Stamford, Lincolnshire. Venables flew home alone on 29 June 1946 on a very nostalgic journey. "As a small boy, my father used to drive us to the edge of Wittering Airfield in the 1920s to watch the old biplanes flying. I did not know until later, I was watching the pilots of 19 Squadron. Close by is Burghley House, an Elizabethan mansion which Hermann Goering had chosen as his residence when they conquered Britain. On my last flight, I was really coming home. I did a wide circuit to include Burghley House, it is a magnificent sight from the air. Someone came out to wave me a welcome home."[31]

Another No. 3 BFTS graduate, Kenneth Henry Butler of Course 12, returned to England and received twin-engine conversion training on Airspeed Oxfords. He then flew Armstrong Whitworth Whitleys at an Operational Retrieval and Training Unit at Thruxton where he towed and recovered gliders. Butler joined 296 Squadron flying Halifaxes on operations that included re-supply flights to resistance movements and glider tows to Arnhem in September 1944 and the Rhine River crossing in February 1945. Butler continued in RAF Transport Command until 1947.

Sydney Urch graduated with Course 11 at No. 6 BFTS and returned to England where he found "the RAF had enough fighter pilots and needed bomber pilots." Urch underwent conversion training to twin-engine aircraft and then shipped out to India. There things took a different direction. Urch attended a conversion course on Hurricanes at Mauripur airport, Karachi, and then waited for an operational posting. "While waiting around, asked to ferry a Harvard to Jodhpur. When I delivered it, the O.C. asked me, would I deliver another Harvard to Ceylon, a three day trip. When I got back it was a Tiger Moth to the forward area in Burma, and that's how I became a ferry pilot, all by accident."[32]

While considerable numbers of British Arnold Scheme graduates were retained as instructors at U.S. Army flight schools, fewer graduates of the British Flying Training Schools served as instructors in the United States. One of these, Philip E. Mitchell of Course 9 at No. 2 BFTS, recalled, "A few days before graduation, each cadet was interviewed by the RAF Commandant W/C Greaves. I was told that I had been selected to stay in the USA for training as an instructor in the U.S. Army Air Force. This did not please me, but when I appealed against the decision, I was told to do as ordered. Not until some time much later did I realise how lucky I was."[33]

Mitchell returned to Canada where he received a commission, then traveled to Kelly Field, San Antonio, Texas, to attend an army instructors course. "The course was concentrated lasting exactly a month. We were given impressive certificates by the USAAF pronouncing us qualified instructors."

Assigned to the Waco Army Air Field, Mitchell found, "There were about three hundred and fifty aircraft, BT-13A basic trainers, and over two hundred instructors, of whom twenty were RAF. The work was intense; each instructor had five pupils for a period of eight weeks."[34]

After his tour in the United States as an instructor, Mitchell returned to Britain. Hoping to fly Mosquitos, Mitchell attended a conversion course, but it became apparent that all graduates were being sent on heavy bombers, which Mitchell did not want. Mitchell and fellow student Les Titcumb went to the medical officer. "After perusal of AMOs and measurement of leg length and reach, the M.O. pronounced us both as being too small to fly heavies!"[35]

Mitchell's relief was short-lived and he received a posting to 38 Group flying heavy bombers towing gliders, dropping supplies and paratroops. "I protested to Wing Commander flying, but was told that nothing could be done about the transfer. Later, when I flew Stirlings, I could never take off with my safety harness fastened. My arms were not long enough to open the throttles with the harness fastened!"[36]

Mitchell continued to fly four-engine aircraft until the end of the war. "I was posted to 1588 Heavy Freight Flight at Santa Cruz, Bombay, India. One of the first units of Transport Command. I picked up a virtually new aircraft, a Short Stirling Mark V at Melton Mowbray and took off for India via Malta, Libya, Palestine and Iraq. During the time in India, we carried freight all over the sub-continent and in March 1946, I embarked on the S.S. *City of Paris* at Bombay for repatriation and release."[37]

After returning to Britain, many of the BFTS graduates served as RAF flight instructors. In one of the more unusual cases, Kenneth Dean graduated with Course 12 at No. 1 BFTS in March 1943. Officials in Terrell evaluated Dean's flying training and recommended him for single-engine fighters. The recommendation specifically noted that Dean was psychologically unsuited as an instructor. Also, coming from a BFTS, Dean had never flown a multi-engine aircraft. On returning to England Dean received an assignment as an instructor on multi-engine aircraft!

Dismayed and disappointed at first, Dean eventually became an instructor training future multi-engine flight instructors.

In another unusual case, Ian Glover graduated with Course 9 at No. 4 BFTS, received a commission and was selected to remain in the United States as an instructor. After he arrived at Maxwell Field in Alabama, army doctors discovered that Glover was color blind and disqualified him as an instructor. Glover traveled back to England, where he was selected for training as an instructor. By the end of the war, Glover had logged more than 1,200 hours as a flight instructor.

Brian Partridge graduated with Course 9 at No. 5 BFTS and returned to England and operational training on Hurricanes, getting married along the way. In June 1944 Partridge joined 611 Squadron flying Spitfires covering the Normandy invasion beaches. As the Allied armies moved inland, Partridge's squadron provided fighter cover for Lancaster bombers and by March 1945 the squadron was operating out of an airfield outside of Brussels. The squadron then converted to Mustang IVs, which had an endurance of four or five hours. "Now we could stretch our legs. Amongst others we covered ramrods [missions with one thousand bombers] to Hamburg, Nuremberg and Munich. The most exciting was on April 16th when we covered 617 Squadron bombing a cruiser at Swinemunde and then swept south to the Berlin area, (on the way waggling our wings at some Russian Stormoviks), where we had a dogfight with 10 Fw 190's near Finow airfield and shot down six of them." This mission lasted five hours and fifty-five minutes and was the squadron's longest trip, yet the fuel tanks still held thirty minutes of fuel when they landed at Hunsdon, north of London. "The Mustang was a flying bowser!"

The most frustrating mission occurred on 31 March escorting an attack on Hamburg, "when we watched helplessly as twenty plus Me 262's dived down from above and shot down eleven Lancasters. We reached 450 knots in pursuit, but, they left us standing. Thank God they didn't have sufficient numbers or fuel to regain control of their airspace. After VJ day, I stayed in the RAF until early retirement in 1961."[38]

After graduating as the top cadet on Course 4 at No. 5 BFTS, Robert G. F. Lee became a night fighter pilot. In August 1944 German ground fire hit Lee's fighter and he made a high speed wheels up forced landing. Immediately after the stricken fighter touched down it flipped over, trapping Lee in the cockpit. The area around the crashed fighter became a no-man's land of contention between German and American ground forces. As the battle ranged back and forth, the area came under intense artillery fire and the wrecked plane, with Lee still trapped inside, received many shrapnel hits. After the battle, Lee was finally discovered by famed war correspondent Ernie Pyle and an American war graves registration officer. A severely injured Lee had been trapped in the wrecked plane without food or water for eight days. It took American soldiers with tools more than an hour to extricate Lee from the plane. Lee became a symbol of personal endurance and survival under the most horrific circumstances when Pyle published a story about his ordeal. Lee spent many months in the hospital recovering from a shattered leg and numerous other injuries. In April 1945 Lee's father wrote to Embry-Riddle, where Lee had received his flight training. "I am pleased to say that Robert has recovered from all his wounds apart from the injury to his left leg, and this will, I am afraid, still take some time before it is well and of use to him."[39]

After graduation, Angus Eades, of Course 9 at No. 1 BFTS, remained in the United States and became an instructor at the Waco Army Air Field in Texas. Eades and his student were both killed when their basic trainer crashed while practicing forced landings. Philip Mitchell, another RAF instructor at the base, accompanied Eades' body to the Fort Sam Houston National Cemetery in San Antonio, Texas, where Eades was buried with full military honors.

Malcolm Thomas Sydney Davis graduated with Course 4 at No. 2 BFTS and then had a varied operational career. After his return to Britain, Davis received a posting to a flying instructor's course at Dalcross, Scotland, and then an assignment as an instructor on twin-engine Oxfords. After a crash, Davis became a glider pilot instructor. After training pilots of the

First Glider Pilot Regiment, Davis received a posting to the Middle East. Following varied familiarization flying experiences, Davis was assigned to an OTU at Chandeur from which he was posted to 500 Squadron, flying daylight interdiction operations on Baltimore twin-engine bombers. Davis was shot down flying a Baltimore, but survived. At the end of the war, Davis, then a flight lieutenant, had logged 1,800 flight hours.[40]

John A. B. Keeling completed flight training with Course 4 at No. 3 BFTS in February 1942. Commissioned pilot officer, Keeling returned to Britain and received twin-engine conversion training on Airspeed Oxford aircraft. Keeling then attended No. 51 OTU flying Blenheims, Douglas A-20 Havocs, and Boston IIIs. Keeling served first with 605 Squadron at RAF Ford, Hampshire, then later joined 23 Squadron on Malta flying de Havilland Mosquitos. In the course of thirty-five operational missions he received the Distinguished Flying Cross and a promotion to flight lieutenant. On completion of his operational tour, Keeling returned to Canada as an instructor at a Mosquito OTU. When the war ended, Keeling returned to the UK and spent his last months in RAF service ferrying Mosquitos, Beaufighters, and Bostons to Cairo.

Some graduates of early courses experienced delays in reaching an operational squadron. Ronald Charles Lamb trained with Course 2 at No. 3 BFTS. After graduation and his return to Britain, Lamb was posted to a Spitfire OTU. A forced landing after an engine failure gave Lamb a seven-day leave, but he dropped back on the course. When he graduated there were no operational postings for Lamb and seven others. Lamb and the others were sent to a gunnery school in Scotland to fly training flights. "To our dismay, we discovered that there was an 'Ops Ladder' on display in the Flight Office and only one pilot was being posted each month. However, a new Air Gunnery School was being opened at Andreas on the Isle of Man. The 8 of us volunteered en masse, reasoning that as we would be first in, we would be at the top of the new 'Ops Ladder'. This proved to be correct and I was the first one away on 8th November 1943."

With a surplus of pilots and fewer losses than expected, Lamb was again sent to a Spitfire OTU and then to a Tactical Exercise Unit in anticipation of the invasion of Europe. Lamb and a friend volunteered for overseas duty and within days boarded the *Arundel Castle* bound for Algiers. "Once again, however, we were stuck in a camp. Then we read in the forces newspaper, *The Union Jack* about the Balkan Air Force and Spitfires supporting the Partisans fighting in Jugoslavia. We immediately went to see the Commanding Officer and asked if he could get us posted there." A few days later, in July 1944, Lamb and his friend joined 332 Squadron at Cannae on the Adriatic coast of Italy flying the Spitfire VB with clipped wings. "We used to fly across the Adriatic to the Island of Vis, which was occupied by the partisans, there we would bomb-up and then fly to Jugoslavia to bomb and strafe German transport, etc."

On one trip Lamb attacked a train and was hit by flak in the coolant tank. He managed to fly some distance away over the Pindus Mountains before bailing out. "I spent some time with the E.L.A.S. partisans and eventually got flown back to Italy."

Lamb subsequently joined 93 Squadron at Ravenna in northern Italy and flew with them during the final push over the River Po. The squadron was in Udine on V-E Day and then moved to Klazenfurt in Austria. "I was with 250 Squadron flying Mustangs from August until I went back to England for demobilisation in December 1945. I did not have a great operational career flying 42 missions, total number of flying hours was 860. Highest rank held was Warrant Officer."[41]

William Allen joined Course 10 at No. 3 BFTS after training with the first and only primary course at No. 7 BFTS. After his return to England, Allen attended an Advanced Flying Unit at Peterbourough flying twin-engine aircraft. While at the AFU, Allen was sent on a commando course at Whitley Bay. He was seriously injured during training and taken off flying. After his recovery, Allen went into the British Army and spent the remainder of his military service as an artillery radar instructor.

Being eliminated from flight training was a devastating blow to young men who had dreamed of becoming Royal Air Force pilots. Those washed out of a British Flying Training School left with heavy hearts to return to Canada and an uncertain future. But being washed out of flight training did not necessarily mean the end of a flying career.

When William Davis washed out of No. 5 BFTS he had particular reason for resentment. Davis felt that his elimination had more to do with an incident at the school (unrelated to flight training) and the unfair reaction of the RAF commanding officer, rather than any flying deficiency.[42] Regardless of the reason for the elimination, Davis returned to Canada and remustered as an observer ("navigator" in American usage). After graduation from the observer course and promotion to sergeant, Davis reported to 103 Squadron. Due to their proficiency, officials selected Davis' crew to join a Pathfinder squadron, which were specially chosen elite units tasked with marking specific targets with flares or incendiaries for the bomber streams that followed. "We took on jobs that presented much more than ordinary challenges. Blind illuminators involved a technique for dropping large long-burning magnesium flares, using radar when the target was obscured. Planes carrying visual bomb aimers would fly behind us at a lower altitude and drop their markers on targets identified by the brilliant magnesium flares."[43]

By the end of the war Davis had been commissioned as an RAF officer, received numerous medals and commendations, and had been decorated by the king. After the war Davis received a coveted position on the staff of Air Vice-Marshal J. D. Breakey at Air Headquarters, Malaya, in Kuala Lumpur, which gave him a unique tour of the Far East. Davis returned home to England in 1947 and was demobilized. Many years later Davis commented on his service: "Even today I get a feeling of fright hearing the names Frankfurt, Wilhelmshaven, Dusseldorf, Essen, Karlsruhe, Cologne, Zeitz, Stettin, Leipzig, Chemnitz, Nuremberg, Hamburg, Hanover, and Kiel. I completed forty-three operations, plus a food-dropping trip to a field just outside The Hague. That trip was very rewarding because we knew that Dutch families were near starvation."[44]

Norman Nichol Brown arrived in Oklahoma with Course 11 at No. 3 BFTS, but was eliminated from flight training and returned to Canada. Brown remustered as a bomb aimer, completed his training in Canada and returned to England aboard the *Queen Elizabeth*. After his return, Brown joined a Wellington bomber crew with 102 Squadron at RAF Bruntingthorpe, Leicestershire. On operations, Brown received a commission, rose to the rank of flight lieutenant, and was awarded the Distinguished Flying Cross.

A few graduates of the British Flying Training Schools experienced problems after their return to Britain that are difficult to understand. John Jeffrey graduated with Course 6 from No. 2 BFTS and returned to Liverpool. Jeffrey attended a conversion course on Oxfords, but was considered unsuitable for operational type aircraft and lost his wings and sergeant stripes. Jeffrey then attended and passed an Airfield Control course and regained his rank. "Conditions in England were vastly different from flying over great stretches of desert, and I didn't consider that many of us got time to re-adjust, hence the high toll in lives of many of my friends who were killed in a few weeks of coming home."[45]

United States Army Air Forces cadets trained with seven courses at British Flying Schools. These American cadets were destined for either ferry or transport command after graduation.

Kenneth Anderson graduated with Course 13 at No. 4 BFTS. Anderson received additional training in Michigan and Colorado before being assigned to C-47 training with Continental Air Lines at Stapleton Field in Denver. During training, Anderson and his crew carried military cargo from Sacramento, California, to Wright-Patterson Field in Ohio. Subsequently, he was posted to India and flew Curtiss C-46s over the Hump to China. For this duty, Anderson received the Distinguished Flying Cross and an Air Medal.

Another American aviation cadet, Blaine H. Schultz, graduated with Course 12 at No. 5 BFTS and then traveled to Brownsville, Texas, where the army contracted with Braniff Airways to provide transition training on multi-engine aircraft. "I completed training with Braniff and was sent to St. Joseph, Missouri, for instrument training. I was then assigned to the 3rd Ferry Group. Most of my ferry flights were taking P-39s from Niagara Falls to Great Falls, Montana [these aircraft were destined for the Soviet Union via Alaska]."[46]

After ferrying aircraft throughout the United States, Schultz flew transports, as well as fighters across Europe. "After the surrender of Germany I was sent to Oran, Algeria, on the Mediterranean to fly C-47s and C-46s, both cargo aircraft, across North Africa to Italy and then to Cairo. There aircraft would then be picked up and flown to the China, Burma, or India Theaters for the war against Japan. I moved around a great deal: Oran, Casablanca, Tunis, Cairo, and Marrakech until the Japanese gave up and we were gradually sent home. I made the trip by Liberty ship."[47]

Another Army Air Forces cadet, Ralph A. Bass, graduated with Course 15 at No. 3 BFTS. After additional training, Bass joined Ferry Command where he delivered Martin B-26 medium bombers to the European Theater of Operations. In Casablanca, on the last leg of a delivery flight, Bass experienced trouble starting an engine on the B-26. Due to the delay, a B-17 waiting to take off behind Bass took off in their place. While flying across the Bay of Biscay, this B-17 was attacked by several Ju-88s operating from airfields in southwest France. The B-17 suffered severe damage and had two crew members killed before escaping out to sea. When Bass and his crew finally reached Cornwall, the heavily damaged B-17 was sitting on the ramp. "If we had made our scheduled departure time at Casablanca, quite possibly we would not have reached England in as much as we would not have had the fuel for the evasive action taken by the B-17."[48]

Paul G. Charbonnet, Jr., a USAAF aviation cadet, graduated with Course 15 at No. 3 BFTS, and then joined Air Transport Command. After a stint at Wilmington, Delaware, as a check pilot for Womens Airforce Service Pilots assigned to ferry duties, Charbonnet traveled to Homestead, Florida, for four-engine transport training. After conversion training, Charbonnet flew the South Atlantic ferry run from Miami to Trinidad to Georgetown, British Guiana, to Natal, Brazil, to Ascension Island, to Accra, Gold Coast (now Ghana), then to Dakar and finally Casablanca, and return. By the end of the war Charbonnet had made eighty-one ocean crossings.

The British RAF and American AAF graduates of the British Flying Training Schools were not the only personnel to go on operations. During the war many of the civilian instructors left the schools and joined the fledgling Air Transport Command and flew cargo and supply missions around the world. These missions took the former instructors over both the Pacific and Atlantic oceans and for many included flights over the treacherous Himalayan Mountains between India and China, known as the Hump.

While many graduates of early courses from the British Flying Training Schools saw considerable active service and graduates of middle courses often encountered lengthy delays before going on operations, graduates of later courses often found few if any openings in operational squadrons and languished in holding centers or were assigned to other duties. Many later graduates were retrained as glider pilots, remustered as flight engineers, or assigned non-flying duties. Many of these graduates never went on operations.

R. A. Eadie, who trained with a relatively early course at No. 6 BFTS, commented on the waiting. "It is perhaps worth noting that almost two years elapsed between joining the R.A.F. and joining an operational squadron. Of this time at least three months were spent either traveling or in transit camps; the same amount of time that was spent on Basic and Advanced training combined."[49]

The ship carrying Andrew L. Bayley of Course 17 at No. 1 BFTS back to England docked at Liverpool and Bayley and the other aircrew boarded a train to Harrogate, North Yorkshire. "I had several postings primarily aimed at keeping me busy. Finally, I was posted to St. Athan's in South Wales to take a Lancaster Flight Engineer's course. In future new pilots were to act as Second Pilot/Flight Engineers and complete 15 operational trips in this capacity before having a crew of their own. After St. Athan's, I was posted to 1660 Heavy Conversion Unit at Swinderby, Lincolnshire, and there duly teamed up with a crew."[50]

Eric Tomlinson graduated with Course 14 at No. 4 BFTS in July 1943 as a sergeant. Tomlinson returned to England and arrived at the pilot pool in Harrogate, Yorkshire, where he waited four months before an assignment to a "Pre-A.F.U. Course." He then drew assignment to airfield control with 10 Squadron at Melbourne, Yorkshire. Tomlinson was then posted to No. 6 AFU, Little Rissington where he converted to twin-engine Airspeed Oxfords. He completed the course and reported to No. 12 OTU at RAF Chipping Warden where he converted to Wellington bombers and picked up a crew, sixteen months after he graduated from flight training in the United States. Tomlinson and his crew waited three months before a posting to No. 1669 Heavy Bomber Conversion Unit, where the crew received a flight engineer (a sergeant pilot re-mustered as a flight engineer) and converted to Lancaster bombers. After the conversion to Lancasters, Tomlinson and his crew went on operations with 149 Squadron. The war in Europe ended one month after the crew's first operational mission, and twenty-two months after Tomlinson graduated from No. 4 BFTS.

Occasionally the needs of the service could suddenly interrupt the tiresome waiting. Michael Hirst also graduated with Course 14 at No. 4 BFTS, returned to England and spent the next year in various conversion courses on Dakota transports. As the routine continued, Hirst unexpectedly received orders to India. "The journey was so urgent that I left the south coast of England with my crew September 16th and arrived

September 19th in India by Sunderland Flying Boat! We were then in the
thick of it from the Imphal front in north Burma right down to Rangoon."
Hirst joined 31 Squadron RAF Southeast Asia Command under Lord
Louis Mountbatten. The area included crews from Canada, Australia,
and New Zealand, as well as Americans flying C-46 Commandoes. Hirst
flew some 700 operational hours, duty which often included two or three
missions a day, supply dropping or landing supplies. "There was nothing
to do on base—jungle all around us. I was invalided home in June 1945
and remained in Transport Command at RAF Lyneham, Wiltshire, on Air
Traffic Control duties. I had been promoted to Flight Sergeant in 1944,
Warrant Officer in 1945, commissioned in 1946 and eventually became
a Squadron Leader in 1951 until I left the Volunteer Reserve in 1965."[51]

Although official records are sketchy, many graduates from Courses 16
through 20 were retrained in England to fly gliders. Many of these pilots
were killed in operations such as Arnhem and the crossing of the Rhine.

Ian McEwan graduated with Course 19 at No. 3 BFTS. "Back in England,
we docked at Greenock, Scotland and traveled by train direct to Harrogate,
Yorkshire, a city bursting at the seams with aircrew, coming and going.
It seemed obvious to me that the war would have to last fifty years to
make use of all the fliers assembled there."[52]

McEwan and a great many newly graduated pilots were sent to various
fields to fly Tiger Moths to maintain proficiency. Flying the Tiger Moth
was fun, but unrewarding. "The Army needed glider pilots. 'Who wants
to volunteer?' The silence was deafening. All sorts of inducements
were made, but our group hung to the faint hope that eventually our
talents would be recognised and we would ultimately end up on a fighter
squadron. Of course, it wasn't to be and in November 1944 we ended
up as No. 1 Course, 23 H.G.C.U., Seighford, training to fly Horsa and
Hadrian gliders. Gliders? What a laugh! Flying boxcars with only one
flying direction—down!"

After graduation, four new glider squadrons were formed and McEwan
joined 670 Squadron. The squadrons were flown on C-47s through France

to Malta, and then on through Iraq to Karachi, India. The squadrons traveled by train to a base at Fatehjang, Punjab, about eight miles north of Rawalpindi. "Our training started in earnest in U.S. Hadrian Gliders and, although we never knew it at the time, we were being readied for a landing in Malaya. The Japanese were being pushed out of Burma, and I believe the idea was to outflank them." This operation never developed and became a moot point with the surrender of Japan. "The training during this period was interesting, a jungle self-preservation course given by Burmese tribesmen at Mahabaleshwar near Poona, use of automatic weapons, hand to hand combat, etc. Perhaps I should have joined the Army."[53]

Norman Crisp, a former bank clerk, graduated with Course 20 at No. 3 BFTS, then returned to England. "We were interviewed and assembled in the ballroom of the former hotel where we were billeted, and addressed by a Wing Commander. He began by saying, 'None of you will ever fly again.' (Long pause while we all took in this disagreeable news). 'Unless you volunteer for secondment to the Glider Pilot Regiment'." At this time the RAF had a surplus of pilots and the army gilder pilots had suffered severe losses on several operations. Crisp volunteered, "those who did not volunteer got posted to glider training anyway." During training, Crisp flew small obsolete Hotspur gliders, American Waco gliders ("don't know why"), and the massive British Horsa glider. After the actual flight training phase, "we were sent on other courses designed to provide some idea of soldiering. Army pilots of course were soldiers first and glider pilot second. Once on the deck, they became fighting men. We RAF pilots were definitely not soldiers."[54]

After the frantic early war years, John E. Lodge graduated with Course 17 at No. 5 BFTS, at a time when the RAF had a surplus of pilots. "I was one of those redundant RAF pilots selected for the glider program. We carried with us a certain casual, lighthearted attitude about dress and general conduct when not flying, and this didn't draw wild applause from our new associates. In a word, they were distressed. However, we were all business when engaged in operations. The glider people knew this, but could barely tolerate the fact that we didn't carry that same image on the ground."[55]

Some of the later graduates of the British Flying Training Schools expressed a certain disappointment in their RAF service.

Walter Albert Acott trained with Course 21 at No. 3 BFTS and is an example of being too young at the beginning of the war. "At the age of about 16 I joined the Air Training Corps which was a cadet scheme. I enlisted for the RAF, at the age of 17. The minium age for aircrew call up was 18 ¼ years, so I was placed on deferred service for a year." Acott graduated with Course 21 at No. 3 BFTS in November 1944. "I was placed top in terms of flying ability and recommended for single engine fighters or ground attack. The events that followed bore no relationship to that situation."

Acott returned to the Air Crew Receiving Centre at Harrogate, Yorkshire, in January 1945. Acott declined to become a glider pilot, because like so many others he still dreamed of becoming a fighter pilot. After a posting to an Elementary Flying Training School, flying primary trainers as a holding arrangement, Acott was assigned to a Flight Engineer's course. Following the course he joined a Heavy Conversion Unit in Lincolnshire, flying Lancaster bombers as a flight engineer. "I was there when the War finished, and I then assumed ground duties until demobilised in 1947. All in all, it was a disappointment to my ambitions, but it was an experience that I would not have missed, basically it was a case of being too young at the time of war, but one must console oneself in the thought of what might have happened had I been a year or two older."[56]

Another later BFTS graduate spent a lot of time waiting and finally retrained as a glider pilot just before the war ended. He left the RAF in 1946 with only 270 hours of flying time. "Was it all worthwhile? I could give you the usual patriotic platitudes but, in retrospect, I contributed very little to the 'war effort' and the three years spent in the Air Force were a terrible waste of time, time that could have been better spent."[57]

After the war most of the former students from the British Flying Training Schools left the Royal Air Force and returned to civilian life. Some stayed in the service and continued to experience varied assignments around the world.

CHAPTER 10

THE FINAL YEAR

British and American citizens followed the course of the war on their radios and in newspapers and national magazines, which regularly published situation maps depicting the positions of the Allied forces on the various war fronts. By late 1944 Allied armies that had landed in Normandy six months earlier were now advancing across northern France toward Germany. Allied forces that had landed in southern France were rapidly moving northward, while other Allied armies battled up the mountainous spine of Italy. Numerous massive Soviet armies steadily drove German troops back all along the broad eastern front. The situation maps graphically depicted a relentless tightening of the noose around Nazi Germany, which would lead to ultimate Allied victory.

The only exception to this unremitting advance came with a German counteroffensive through the Ardennes Forest toward the Belgian port of Antwerp, which was eerily reminiscent of the first German advance into France in the spring of 1940. Caught off guard by Hitler's last gamble, American forces were temporarily thrown back by a combination of surprise along a front weakly defended by second-line troops, poor and complacent intelligence, and vicious winter weather that grounded Allied air support. By the beginning of 1945, however, the German advance had literally run out of gas and had been forced back with heavy losses. The Luftwaffe was also running out of fuel, as well as aircraft and trained pilots as Allied air forces roamed over Germany in massive formations by day and by night striking targets at will.

Even with the increasingly favorable war news, flight training in the four remaining British Flying Training Schools (No. 1 in Texas, No. 3 in Oklahoma, No. 4 in Arizona, and No. 5 in Florida) continued unabated under the greatly expanded Royal Air Force Delegation in Washington and the Army Air Forces Flying Training Command. Although army flight cadets no longer trained in the British schools, the army detachment at each school actually increased, since responsibility for the schools belonged to the army under lend-lease. Now with a surplus of personnel, the RAF contingent at each school numbered fifteen officers and enlisted men. This staffing level contrasted sharply with the nine officers consti-tuting the total personnel assigned to the original six British Flying Training Schools just four years earlier (and several of these officers had not arrived or even been appointed when the schools opened). The civilian staff at each school had also increased.

John McKenzie-Hall, an RAF gunnery officer assigned to No. 1 BFTS, succinctly and accurately summed up the organization of the British Flying Training Schools. "I never fail to be amazed that such a hotch-potch of civilian and service personnel with all their different requirements and loyalties could work so well together in turning out a constant flow of very adequately trained aircrew."[1]

The Army Air Forces Flying Training Command continued to conduct periodic inspections of the schools. These inspections included not only essential items such as aircraft maintenance and parts inventories, but also covered mundane matters such as sanitary systems and vehicle tires. Even army chaplains from regional training commands routinely visited the schools to discuss "religious matters."

During a routine inspection of the No. 1 BFTS army supply unit in March 1945, the inspection team from the Central Flying Training

Command at Randolph Field in San Antonio, found serious procedural deficiencies. In response, the army supply officer told the inspection team that many of the army supply procedures were not applicable to a civilian flight school under Royal Air Force supervision. The supply officer further explained, "The British do not fully understand the ramifications of the AAF supply system and only insist on parts being available when needed; this was being accomplished." The inspection team's reply is not recorded, but can be surmised by the report's final remark. "Full compliance with all AAF regulations is now being effected."[2]

British students who trained in the United States had experienced overwhelming hospitality from local Americans. After four years and with the favorable war news and the inevitability of the war's conclusion, this hospitality did not diminish. Duncan Hancock of Course 27, the last course at No. 1 BFTS, later reflected, "RAF cadets had been training in Texas since 1941 and yet by 1945, practically every weekend some 300 of us disappeared into Dallas or Terrell, the great majority to be guests of families in the towns. We were entertained royally, sometimes in wealthy households, but frequently by families of quite limited means. Two families with whom I stayed on numerous occasions sent us food parcels for months after I had returned to the U.K. The affection I felt for America and for Americans has never diminished."[3]

Leslie M. Knibbs trained with Course 22 at No. 5 BFTS, which graduated at the end of March 1945, just six weeks before the end of the war in Europe. "It was not possible to take a walk in West Palm Beach because so many people would stop their cars and offer lifts. One of the large hotels in West Palm Beach offered us rooms over the Christmas holidays with food included and a gift for each cadet on Christmas morning—all at no charge."[4]

With final victory in Europe in sight, President Franklin Roosevelt died on 12 April 1945 in Warm Springs, Georgia, and the entire nation mourned. Servicemen in uniform openly wept at the death of the only president many of them had ever known. Government offices closed and memorial services were held in cities across the United States. The British Flying Training Schools suspended flight operations for the day so the British students, RAF officers and enlisted personnel, and the school staffs could participate in the local services. The national colors at the schools flew at half staff for thirty days.

A week before the president's death, Air Marshal Douglas Colyer, CB, DFC, arrived in Washington to assume command as Air Officer Commanding the Royal Air Force in the United States of America. One month later on 7 May, German General Alfred Jodl signed the instrument of unconditional surrender in General Eisenhower's European headquarters. The next day Prime Minister Churchill and Harry Truman, the newly sworn-in American president, jointly declared Victory in Europe or VE Day. The war in Europe had finally ended.

On 18 May 1945 Colyer issued an address to all RAF personnel in the United States commemorating VE Day. Colyer reminded everyone that the Royal Air Force had struck the first blows of the war and had also won one of the most decisive victories in history, which "saved our country when the prospect was bleakest." But he also reminded everyone that the job was not yet completed and that some Americans felt that Britain would now sit back since the war in Europe had ended. Coyler strenuously denied this and pointed out that considerable British territory still remained in Japanese hands and "we can not rest or relax until we have restored them to British Sovereignty.[5] All RAF personnel in the United States also received a copy of a victory message from Field Marshal Sir Bernard Montgomery praising the part played by the Royal Air Force in victory.

In spite of Coyler's stern comments about the continuation of the war, the Air Ministry began to promulgate guidelines for the release of certain servicemen. Releases would be based on age, length and type of service, marital status, and other factors. Releases were tentatively scheduled to begin in July 1945.

All overseas British service personnel age twenty-one or older on 15 March were allowed to vote by post in the 1945 general election. Each British school in the United States appointed an officer to oversee the election process. The election results were announced on 26 July while Allied leaders met in the Potsdam Conference. The results stunned the world. Clement Attlee, the Labour Party candidate for prime minister, scored a landslide victory over Winston Churchill. Although the rules allowed Churchill to remain in office for a certain period of time to settle affairs, he elected to leave immediately. Churchill issued a short farewell message to the nation which concluded, "I have therefore laid down the charge which was placed upon me in darker times. I regret that I have not been permitted to finish the work against Japan."[6]

In the Far East, British and American forces pushed the Japanese back in Burma and reopened the Burma Road while American forces cleared the last enemy resistance in the Philippines. Following the bloody fall of the island of Iwo Jima, Japanese troops prepared for a fanatical and suicidal defense of Okinawa, which lay only 340 miles from the Japanese home islands. As the direction of the war appeared headed to a final, readily discernible, conclusion, the savage fury of the unpredictable weather in the American southwest could still shock.

In the early afternoon of the last day of July, Falcon Field experienced a particularly violent thunderstorm with recorded winds of more than sixty miles-per-hour and heavy rains that flooded the field. Fortunately there were no injuries and the No. 4 BFTS school buildings and aircraft suffered only minor damage. Aircraft in the air had diverted to other fields to wait out the storm.

Falcon Field was not so fortunate the next day. Around 6:25 in the evening, a violent dust storm with winds gusting to forty-five miles-per-hour hit the field. School personnel noted that storms such as this were common in late summer, usually lasted about forty-five minutes, and "never necessitated further action to safeguard the aircraft."[7] After only ten minutes the dust storm developed into a severe thunderstorm with torrential rain and high winds with gusts to seventy-eight miles-per-hour. The Stearman primary trainers that faced into the wind actually began to fly, still secured to their tie downs. Instructors and maintenance personnel, as well as the British staff and students, rushed to secure the planes. These efforts proved to be futile, as well as dangerous, as the winds increased and the Stearmans began to break loose from their tie downs and career across the field toward the adjacent orange grove.

The next day primary flying at No. 4 BFTS had to be cancelled due to the total loss of thirty-seven Stearmans and one Harvard. The wreckage lay scattered, mangled, and overturned across the field and into the orange grove. In addition to the total losses, twenty-two aircraft including several Harvards suffered various damage. Fortunately no lives were lost, but three civilian workers suffered minor lacerations and another had to be admitted to the Mesa hospital with a possible neck fracture. The two-hour storm resulted in only minor damage to the school buildings, but the barracks were flooded and power, telephone, and water services were cut off until early the next morning.

Three days later, army pilots delivered forty-two Stearman PT-13s to Falcon Field from Minter Field in Bakersfield, California, to replace the PT-17s lost in the storm. Ten Harvards were also loaned to the school until the damaged advanced trainers could be repaired. Since the PT-13 aircraft came from an army primary school, these aircraft were not equipped for night flying or instrument flying and the RAF staff at Falcon Field reported, "it will not be possible to carry out the primary syllabus for 27 Course as laid down."[8]

Although Germany had surrendered, it appeared that the war in the Pacific would extend well into 1946. The RAF announced that the four remaining British Flying Training Schools would continue training until April 1946 and then close with the graduation of Course 28 (Course 27 at No. 5 BFTS), which was scheduled to arrive in late August 1945. But the devastation of two atomic bombs in early August and the subsequent Japanese surrender brought the war to a sudden conclusion.

Wildly enthusiastic crowds on both sides of the Atlantic thronged city streets in celebration. Personnel were granted forty-eight hours' leave to commemorate the end of World War II.

The schools received a victory message from "His Majesty the King to His Navies, Armies, and Air Forces, throughout the Empire." The eloquently simple message concluded, "By God's mercy the forces of evil have been overthrown. But many tasks remain to be accomplished if the full blessings of peace are to be restored to a suffering world. It is the duty of each one of us to ensure that our comrades have not died in vain and that your own hard won achievements are not lost to the cause of freedom in which you undertook them. On behalf of all my people, I thank you. God bless you all."[9]

Similar victory messages were received from the Air Council and a copy of another message from the Secretary of State for Air to the Air Ministry received wide distribution to the British students and RAF personnel in the United States.

The RAF cancelled the final course scheduled to arrive in late August and announced that the remaining four British schools would close in early September. Students in the two courses still remaining after the last graduation ceremony would continue training, but were given the option of completing flight training in Britain or returning to civilian life after the schools closed.

Air Marshal Colyer wished to attend the final graduation ceremonies of the four remaining British Flying Training Schools, but due to the distances involved, found this impractical. He did manage to attend three of the final ceremonies. Colyer traveled to Miami, Oklahoma, where he attended the Wings Parade for Course 25 at No. 3 BFTS on 23 August. He left the next day to attend the graduation of Course 25 at No. 1 BFTS in Terrell, Texas, and then traveled to Mesa, Arizona, the following day for the Wings Parade for Course 25 at No. 4 BFTS. Air Commodore E. D. H. Davies attended the Wings Parade for Course 24 at No. 5 BFTS in Clewiston, Florida.

Both Coyler and Davies addressed similar comments to the RAF staffs, school staffs, visitors, and the final British flight students in the United States. At No. 1 BFTS, Air Marshal Coyler stood under a hot azure Texas sky dotted with white puffy clouds as a warm breeze ruffled the Royal Air Force flag flying from a mobile flag staff, which had served so many graduation ceremonies and expressed "The fervent hope that friendship between the United States and England as it now exists would forever abide, making for the peace and prosperity of the world."[10]

The individual schools also issued parting thoughts to the British students. At No. 3 BFTS, M. J. Wagner of Spartan School of Aeronautics wrote to Course 25 in the final issue of the school magazine, *Open Post.* "It would please us to believe that you will remember us as a people whose feelings of hospitality toward you are as permanent as they are sincere. We invite you to return and emphasize that this invitation goes with you along with the technical knowledge you have gained here: may you be granted the good luck that will permit each to accomplish its separate end—lasting friendship and success."[11]

Wing Commander K. N. Sayers, the final chief flying instructor at No. 3 BFTS, had selected Patricia Smith of Miami as Miss Course 25, the last course representative. Miss Smith was also the fiancee of British student Douglas Gilbert and her picture is included in the final issue of the school magazine. The black and white photograph is full of strong as well as subtle nuances. Obviously depicting a beautiful young woman in the classic American small-town image, the photograph of Miss Smith also reveals thoughtful penetrating eyes and a captivating, almost mischievous, smile, which is both hopeful, and at the same time supremely confident of the future. This final issue of *Open Post* and the photograph of the beautiful Miss Smith perfectly capture the essence of the national mood at the end of the war.

Students of the last courses had a more relaxed trip back home since the war had ended. During a layover in Chicago after leaving No. 3 BFTS, Robert H. Tilney and several others became lost in the city and missed their train. "We were entertained royally—a Policeman on horseback led me from where I had gotten lost to a known place." When the group finally arrived at the departure camp in New York City, they found that there was no urgency in their return trip. "We were told to get lost for three weeks in New York. One of the doormen at Radio City Music Hall was from Cardiff, arranged tickets for me for the show. I also got tickets to the Metropolitan Opera for a performance by Grace Moore in Puccini's Madame Butterfly, it must have been about a month before she was killed in that aircraft accident in Scandinavia."[12]

The final fortnightly report from the RAF Delegation in Washington to the Air Ministry in London concluded, "With the cessation of the Japanese war this will be the last completed output from the B.F.T.S.s. In the four years and three months of their existence 6602 R.A.F. pilots have graduated and in addition 551 U.S.A.A.F. cadets were trained and received their wings." The report then summarized the contribution of the British Flying Training Schools:

> The unique constitution of these schools which, though civilian owned and operated were commanded and staffed by Royal Air Force personnel in a supervisory capacity, had in no wise handicapped them from fulfilling the highest expectations.

> The standards of economy of productive effort, efficiency, espirit de corps, and the quality and quantity of pilot output will stand favorable comparison with any similar organization in the British Commonwealth.

> Throughout the history of the schools there has not been one incident of any unsavory nature; on the contrary, the conduct and bearing of all ranks, on and off the stations, has been exemplary to a degree which has materially enhanced the prestige of both the Royal Air Force and the people it serves and represents.

> It is a pleasure to record that the schools and the Directing Staff in Washington have at all times received the utmost assistance from all commands, branches and ranks of the United States Army

Air Forces, and this co-operation has consistently been proffered in a spirit of cordiality and mutual respect equaled only by that existing between the schools and the civilian operators and staff.

Another chapter in the history of the Royal Air Force is closing, but it may be closed with satisfaction in the knowledge of duty well done. And this in the highest traditions of the Service.[13]

Even with the war over, the hazards of flight training did not end. As a final, although tragically premature, memorial service took place in Terrell on 3 September to commemorate those British students who had died in training at No. 1 BFTS, an AT-6 failed to return from a cross-country flight to San Marcos, Texas. Searchers located the wreckage of the Harvard the next day in Lake Travis near Austin and Thomas Beedie and Raymond Botcher joined their eighteen comrades in the Oakland Memorial Cemetery. These were the last casualties of the British Flying Training Schools. The first fatality had occurred five months before the United States entered the war and the last fatalities occurred after the war ended, just a week before the schools were scheduled to close and the RAF students return home.

Commanding officers from each school made the rounds of local officials, friends, and supporters to say goodbye. Wing Commander T. O. Pricket, the last chief flying instructor at No. 1 BFTS, wrote an open letter to local residents which concluded, "There are so many kindnesses we remember, our sojourn here has provided for so many pleasant memories that it is difficult for us to adequately express our feeling as we say goodbye."[14] The editor of the *Terrell Daily Tribune* replied in print. "To the RAF let us say your friendly courteous manner and your cooperation and interest in our civic and social life has made you many friends who regret having you leave our midst."[15] The *Dallas Morning News* editorialized on the closing of the school, "The little school whose runways cross-stitched the Kaufman County grasses and blackland was more than an emergency training base. It turned out to be a profitable bond between two great nations."[16]

Flight Lieutenant Palmer later commented on the lasting benefits of the American flight training program and the influence of the individual schools. "They have contributed much to Anglo-American understanding, interest and good will. And they have drawn closer the bonds of friendship, a friendship which will grow and endure long after the experiences on which it was founded have been forgotten."[17]

A RAFDEL report also acknowledged the contribution of the various training schemes in the United States. "R.A.F. training in the United States brought to that country many young men who otherwise would never have seen it. The proverbial hospitality of the Americans was extended to them with great generosity; and they, in turn, left with many Americans, the happiest impression of their Service and their country. The effects of this pleasant by-product of R.A.F. training will undoubtedly emerge in the future in the form of greater understanding between the two nations."[18]

An earlier farewell message from a departing course published in the No. 5 BFTS newsletter *Roger Out* also perfectly summed up the mood at the end of the war.

> Well, we come to the end, to take our leave of the
> Field, Clewiston, and Florida. We look forward,
> 'Yanks' and 'Limeys' alike, to seeing our friends
> and relatives again, maybe shooting a line or two;
> But we're going to miss folks that we have loved,
> worked, and played with here these last few months.
> So lets make do with the memories for a little
> while at least . . . .

> On the line "off" and going home,
> Out.

On 10 and 11 September the last Royal Air Force students (around 690), along with the RAF service personnel in the four remaining British Flying Training Schools boarded special trains destined for Fort Hamilton, New York, and from there back to the United Kingdom. The Army Air

Forces detachments remained at the schools to inventory the government property and prepare for disposal under the auspices of the Reconstruction Finance Corporation. By the end of the month most of the army personnel had also departed after locking the now-vacant school buildings.

For more than four years the British Flying Training Schools had reverberated with constant activity. The voices of young students, along with those of instructors, both in the air and on the ground, as well as administrative, dispatch, maintenance, and support staffs had been accompanied by the throaty roar of aircraft engines in the background. Now the schools fell strangely silent. Only the wind sighed forlornly through the vacant cavernous hangers, around the empty buildings, and across flight lines of deserted concrete. Faded wind socks, attached to poles standing like steadfast sentinels, still faithfully indicated wind directions to aircraft now gone and which would never return.

Autumn descended on a world at peace for the first time in six years and in the American northeast the green leaves of summer turned to various hues of golden browns, reds, and yellows. British officers departed from Washington as the Royal Air Force Delegation slowly dwindled. Desks and file cabinets were emptied, files and supplies were cataloged and boxed for shipment home, phones fell silent, and the long office corridors no longer echoed with hurried footsteps. In the last letter from the training section of the Royal Air Force Delegation in Washington to the Air Ministry in London, Wing Commander T. O. Prickett concluded, "I am the only person now remaining over here in training and expect to return at the end of this month."[19]

The great American flight training endeavor, which had grown from such humble beginnings into a triumphant undertaking involving so much planning, effort, expenditure, labor, and sacrifice, had been completed.

CHAPTER 11

AFTER THE WAR

When No. 3 BFTS closed at the end of the war, Spartan School of Aeronautics put together a small looseleaf booklet. This informal publication contained responses from each employee in the school's various departments to a short questionnaire. Flight instructors listed personal information such as permanent addresses, a summary of experience, ratings held, and total flight hours. Designed as a means for these now former employees to stay in touch, one question stands out. Among the flight instructors, all of whom had anywhere between 2,500 and 6,000 hours of flying time, in the space for "Future Plans" some had jobs, a few were returning to previous jobs, but the most prevalent answer was "Indefinite."

Following the end of the war, the former students of the British Flying Training Schools and the RAF officers and enlisted men who had served there, along with the schools' civilian employees, dispersed literally around the world. Most of the British students returned to various civilian occupations, married, and raised families; some remained in the Royal Air Force, while some returned to Canada or the United States to live. Many of the former students and staff who remained in the RAF rose to high rank during the cold war. The schools' former civilian employees usually entered various commercial or aviation fields.

It would be impossible to document the later careers and accomplishments of everyone associated with the British Flying Training Schools. Here are a few brief accounts representing the diversity of the individual experiences after the war.

BRITISH STUDENTS

Felix Block graduated with the second course at No. 3 BFTS then flew Wellington bombers before joining 179 Squadron in Coastal Command. Block left the RAF as a warrant officer and in 1948 he served as an Israeli Air Force staff officer during Israel's War of Independence.

Dennis John Mason of Course 4 at No. 2 BFTS had trained as an engineer before the war. After the war he went into engineering sales, became the chairman of a medium-sized company, and retired in 1979.

J. R. Sutton graduated with Course 4 at No. 3 BFTS. After the war he joined the Ministry of Civil Aviation and the Civil Aviation Authority with the National Air Traffic Service where he remained until retirement in 1981.

Malcolm Thomas Sydney Davis graduated with Course 4 at No. 2 BFTS. After the war he returned to Cambridge University and trained as a solicitor. Davis became a principal in a successful legal firm.

Hugh Tudor graduated with Course 5 at No. 5 BFTS and afterward participated in operations over France, Holland, and Germany. By the end of the war he had been promoted to squadron leader and decided to stay in the RAF. In 1949 Tudor served as second-in-command of a small RAF detachment assigned to the Norwegian-British-Swedish Antarctic Expedition, the first Antarctic expedition with an international team of scientists. The group traveled to the Antarctic aboard the *Norsel*, a 600-ton Norwegian vessel powered by a German U-boat diesel engine. Also on board were two Auster light aircraft, which were landed, assembled, and used by the RAF team for locating a suitable site for the expedition's base camp and also reconnaissance of the ice flow. In 1955 Tudor received the Air Force Cross for his command of a jet fighter squadron and an experimental aircraft squadron.

Douglas Wilkinson, a graduate of No. 4 BFTS, spent sixteen months in a German prisoner of war camp after being shot down on his first operational mission. After the war Wilkinson left the RAF as a warrant officer. He completed an aeronautical engineering degree at Loughborough University and then joined the scientific Civil Service. Wilkinson ended his career at the Royal Aeronautical Establishment at Farnborough as a specialist on helicopters.

Jeffery Richard Jones graduated with Course 4 at No. 3 BFTS. After returning to England, Jones served on operations with Air Transport Auxiliary and then trained as an instructor. A midair collision late in the war left him with a 60 percent service disability. In 1946 Jones returned to Keble College at Oxford to read philosophy, then after a period as a schoolteacher completed the Bar Finals. Jones went to Nigeria and became Chief Justice of Kano State and a CBE. In 1980 after a brief retirement, Jones accepted the post as Chief Justice of the island group of Kiribati in the central Pacific Ocean (formerly Tarawa in the Gilberts). Kiribati had received full independence from Great Britain the previous year.

Noel Robert Clark trained with the second course at No. 6 BFTS. His course graduated with no ceremony and he did not even receive his flying badge until he returned to Canada. Decades later Clark commented on his training. "I can honestly say that my six months in the U.S. in 1941–1942 were the best time of my life (but we better not tell my wife that!). The American civilian instructors fired me with tremendous enthusiasm for flying. They were absolutely wonderful and I don't think I could have gotten better training anywhere."[1] Clark must have been correct because he joined British Airways in 1946 and retired thirty years later with 19,600 hours of flight time.

After demobilization following the war, Robin Sinclair of Course 6 at No. 2 BFTS returned to Caithness, Scotland. He assumed the title of Viscount Thurso of Ulbster on the death of his father, Archibald Henry Macdonald Sinclair, wartime Secretary of State for Air. Sinclair took an active part in the House of Lords and was later instrumental in the founding of the highly successful Caithness Glass Company.

Frank Edward Winch of Course 11 at No. 3 BFTS served as a staff pilot flying Miles Masters and Marinets at No. 12 Air Gunnery School. Late in the war he converted to the Spitfire XXI and joined 91 Squadron just as the war ended. Winch remained with 91 Squadron until September 1946 and ended his service as a warrant officer. He stayed in the Royal Auxiliary Air Force until 1951 flying Vampire and Meteor jet aircraft and rose to the rank of flying officer. Winch then transferred to the RAFVR(T) and flew Chipmunks for several years, completing his service in the reserve forces in 1983 with the rank of flight lieutenant. Aside from his RAF service, Winch served for many years as a civil air traffic control officer.

Raymond Baxter graduated with Course 5 at No. 3 BFTS. After flying operationally as a Spitfire pilot, he left the RAF in 1946 and entered into a career with the British Broadcasting Corporation. Baxter aired as an outside broadcaster covering "mechanical sports," which included flying, motorcycling, and motor racing. He is best known as the host of *Tomorrow's World*, a highly successful program in which he previewed new scientific and technical products. During the show's long run Baxter introduced a diverse range of new products such as the pocket calculator, bar code readers, the first video games such as Pong, the first passenger hovercraft across the English Channel, and the supersonic Concord airliner. The show aired until 1977. Afterwards Baxter continued to produce commercials for British Leyland and promotional videos and films for various businesses.

Christopher Harrison, the young man who had his flight training interrupted by detached duty with Packard Motor Company, returned to Rolls Royce after the war. Harrison became assistant to the director of project review on Giffon and Eagle engines, then moved to technical services where he was in charge of all gas turbine ancillary and auxiliary units.

Harrison moved to Australia in 1954 to be chief test engineer at the Rolls Royce jet overhaul base in Sydney. Harrison remained in Australia when the Rolls Royce facility closed in 1960. After jobs with Bendix and the Atomic Energy Commission, Harrison joined Goodyear in 1965 and became product support manager (Aviation) covering the South Pacific and Asia. He also served as a flight instructor at the Royal Aero Club on New South Wales until he relinquished his commercial license around 1978.

After Laurie Nutton graduated with Course 13 at No. 4 BFTS, he returned to the UK and became an instructor. After the war Nutton left the RAF and flew charter flights for two years then joined British European Airways and retired in 1977. Not content with retirement, Nutton became a captain with Gulf Air and flew until 1982.

F. W. Barlow graduated with the course after Laurie Nutton at No. 4 BFTS and then followed a similar career. After the war Barlow stayed in the RAF long enough to fly the Meteor jet fighter then joined British European Airways in 1949. After retirement in 1980 Barlow joined Gibraltar Airways and continued to fly until his final retirement in 1982.

Alfred W. Syrett graduated with Course 13 at No. 3 BFTS. In the postwar period Syrett studied insurance, then became a fellow of the Chartered Insurance Institute and worked in aviation insurance with Lloyd's brokers for nearly ten years. After Syrett and his family emigrated to North America, he spent seventeen years with Air Canada in corporate insurance before retirement. Having spent much of his life since 1945 in the aviation insurance business, Syrett commented, "Thirty-seven years which all started when I got that first look at the U.S.A., it has been the springboard of a career."[2]

Sir John Gingell of Course 23 at No. 1 BFTS stayed in the postwar RAF and commanded 27 Squadron flying Vulcan strategic jet bombers armed with Blue Steel missiles. Gingell held several high level staff and operational positions, which included deputy director of the Defence Operations Staff at the Ministry of Defence and Air Officer Commanding 23 Group. He retired in 1984 after serving as deputy commander in chief Allied Forces Central Europe with the rank of air chief marshal. After retirement, Sir John Gingell served as Black Rod in the House of Lords (officially Gentleman Usher of the Black Rod in the Houses of Parliament) until 1992.

Roy Ullyett had been a well-known British sports cartoonist before he joined the RAF and trained at No. 3 BFTS. After the war, the six-foot three-inch Ullyett, with his signature handlebar moustache, resumed his career, which eventually spanned almost seventy years and 25,000 cartoons. Drawing under the pseudonym "Berryman" his cartoons appeared in publications such as the *Sunday Pictorial, Daily Mirror,* and *Daily Express.* By selling his cartoons, Ullyett raised more than £1 million for various charities and received the Order of the British Empire for his charity work.

Michael Giddings graduated with the first course at No. 1 BFTS as a sergeant. During the war he flew in the defense of Malta, earned a commission, and received both the AFC and DFC. At the end of the war Giddings commanded 129 Squadron and decided to stay in the RAF. He rose steadily through several staff and operational commands including a stint as a test pilot and C.O. of 57 Squadron flying the Handley Page Victor strategic jet bomber. After serving on the operational staff of Bomber Command, Giddings became deputy chief of Defence Staff. He was also involved in international talks leading to the Panavia Tornado attack aircraft. Giddings retired from the RAF in 1976 with the rank of air marshal.

Following his retirement, Giddings became an independent panel inspector with the Department of Environment from 1979 to 1991. During this time he presided over many, sometimes controversial, inquiries concerning British motorway expansion. On 1 January 1975, in the New Year Honours, he was appointed a Knight Commander of the Military Division of The Most Honourable Order of the Bath.[3]

Frank Miller graduated with the first course at No. 1 BFTS. A former art student, Miller continued his studies after the war and later became a successful architect in Australia.

Gordon Davies graduated with Course 10 at No. 4 BFTS then flew on operations with Bomber Command and with Air Sea Rescue. Davies stayed in the RAF after the war and received a permanent commission in 1948. He received the OBE from Queen Elizabeth for his involvement in redeployment, premature family reparations, UN affairs, and civilian administration in Cyprus from 1962 to 1965. Davies retired in 1974 with the rank of group captain. After leaving the RAF Davies became a regional manager in the hotel and catering industry primarily involved in staff training.

Norman Crisp graduated with Course 20 at No. 3 BFTS in August 1944. At this stage of the war the RAF had a surplus of pilots and Crisp volunteered to fly gliders. The war ended before his glider squadron could see action. Crisp served as an air traffic officer before demobilization in 1947. He then undertook several management and sales jobs. "In 1954, I began to write short stories evenings and weekends, selling them to many magazines including, in the U.S.A., *Saturday Evening Post* and *McCall's*. In 1959, I took the plunge and became a full time professional writer."[4] Crisp wrote several novels, including *Yesterday's Gone* about an RAF Lancaster bomber crew during the war (the fictional pilot trained in Oklahoma), and several stage plays, but he is best known for his prolific TV and screen writing. Crisp was a founding member of the Writer's Guild.

In 1988 Reg Gilbert of Course 14 at No. 6 BFTS established a trust that helps young people traveling in foreign lands to get a better understanding of the country's culture and people. For the duration of their stay the youth live with a local family and help in schools, hospitals, or assist with other community projects. Gilbert received the Order of the British Empire from Queen Elizabeth for his contributions to humanity.[5]

John Hanbury Smith-Carrington graduated with Course 4 at No. 3 BFTS. At the end of the war Smith-Carrington received a regular commission and remained in the RAF until 1972. He attended several service schools and served in various staff and instructional capacities in Southern Rhodesia, South Africa, and the UK. He received the Air Force Cross and the Queen's Commendation and served as Air Attache in Poland and Denmark, then as H. M. Inspector of Service Attaches (Army, Navy, and Air), worldwide from 1968 to 1971. After retirement from the RAF Smith-Carrington returned to his native Leicestershire and became active in local affairs.

Harry "Jimmy" Gill trained with the first and only primary course at No. 7 BFTS. After the school closed, Gill transferred to No. 6 BFTS and graduated. He remained in the United States as a basic flight instructor at Majors Field in Greenville, Texas, then returned to Britain in 1943. Gill flew the heavily armed Hurricane IIc with 279 Squadron escorting aircraft attacking German convoys off Norway and Holland, as well as air-sea rescue missions. After the war, Gill stayed in the RAF flying the Mosquito FB VI. High tone deafness ended his flying in 1949, but Gill enjoyed a successful career in the RAF Equipment Branch (later the Supply Branch). He joined Headquarters Middle East in 1966 and played a vital role in the evacuation of British forces and their families from Aden the following year. For his role in Aden, Gill received the Order of the British Empire. He retired in 1979 as director general, Engineering and Supply Policy, with the rank of air vice marshal. Following retirement Gill remained active in RAF affairs and after his death in 2008, *The Telegraph* eulogized, "Despite his senior rank, he displayed a complete lack of self-importance and was much loved and admired by all ranks."[6] Gill's favorite aircraft was the de Havilland Mosquito. The de Havilland Museum in London Colney has restored his personal aircraft, Mosquito TA 122, for static display.

Group Captain W. S. O. Randle, CBE, AFC, DFM, FRAeS, FBIM, graduated as a sergeant from No. 3 BFTS. Randle flew twenty-one missions on Wellington bombers with 150 Squadron and then flew Mosquitoes with 692 Squadron. Randle remained in the RAF after the war. He served in Malaysia and Borneo, became a flying instructor, and then flew helicopters in Korea as an exchange officer with the US Air Force. Randle attended the RAF staff college and received promotion to group captain in 1963. He retired from the RAF in 1972.

After taking early retirement from the RAF in 1961, Brian Partridge, a graduate of Course 9 at No. 5 BFTS, moved his family to Lagos, Nigeria, where he became chief pilot of a small charter company flying Piper Apaches and Aztecs. Partridge became a Piper dealer for a territory running from Dakar to Leopoldville and then added a Bell helicopter dealership. Civil war drove Partridge and his family back to the UK where he became sales director for Britten-Norman on the Isle of Wight. He sold Islanders in Africa, the Far East and in the Australasian Pacific area. Partridge flew until 1974 when cataracts forced him to give up his license after flying thirty-two years without an accident. Partridge later commented; "I have to thank the BFTS instruction for the quality of their training."[7]

David Green, a graduate of the first course at No. 3 BFTS, was demobilized in 1946. He joined British European Airways, but returned to the RAF in 1948. Green flew with 17 Squadron equipped with Spitfires and 28 Squadron in Hong Kong flying Spitfires and then Vampire and Meteor jets. After a stint as an instructor at the Oxford University Air Squadron, Green became flight safety officer in Fighter Command and a squadron commander at the Advanced Flying Training school on Vampire jets. After a posting as staff officer (air) at the Royal Military Academy Sandhurst, Green returned to the Far East as Squadron Commander 34 Squadron in Singapore flying Beverley transports. Back in the United Kingdom Green attended the College of Air Warfare before an assignment with Air Plans (Far East), in the Ministry of Defence and Senior

Tutor, College of Air Warfare. Promoted to group captain, Green served as Air Attache to Pakistan before returning to Britain and a final posting as Station Commander, RAF Swinderby. Green retired in October 1977.

Alastair Michie graduated as the top cadet of Course 3 at No. 5 BFTS and served during the war as a night fighter pilot. Michie, who had been born in France and educated in France and Scotland, then studied architecture at Edinburgh University. After graduation he attained world-wide recognition as an artist and sculptor. His work is featured in museums, universities, and major corporations, as well as private collections.[8]

Peter Shore, who trained at No. 3 BFTS, joined the British Labour Party in 1948. Following a number of staff and committee posts, Shore was elected Member of Parliament from Stepney in 1964. He remained in Parliament for the next thirty-three years and served as Parliamentary Private Secretary under Prime Minister Harold Wilson and three years later became a cabinet member as Secretary of State for Economic Affairs. Shore is well known for his opposition to British membership in the European Economic Community. After leaving Parliament in 1997, Shore took a life peerage as Baron Shore of Stepney.

Ray England, the top cadet of Course 9 at No. 1 BFTS, later served as an instructor at Waco Army Airfield in Texas. England became the chairman and chief executive officer of Jaguar Motors in 1972.

After Thomas William Reece graduated with Course 10 at No. 3 BFTS, he flew Sterling and Lancaster bombers and received the Distinguished Flying Cross. After the war, Reece trained as a primary school teacher and subsequently retired as Head Teacher of a Primary School in the Wirral. Forty years after the war, Reece offered this comment: "I am very proud to have served as a wartime pilot and have a very high regard for the friends who took part in the war, in all the Services. Generally speaking, there seems to be little regard for these people in this country."[9]

Ian Bryson Taylor of Course 14 at No. 4 BFTS returned to England and became a flight instructor. After the war, he returned to Aberdeen University and completed his engineering studies. After graduation, Taylor joined Richard Costain Engineering Contractors and from 1957 to 1961 worked for the firm in Barbados building the Barbados Deep Water harbor.

Clifford Ashley graduated with Course 12 at No. 4 BFTS then returned to England and spent twelve months as an instructor. Ashley volunteered for transfer to the Fleet Air Arm, but the war ended before he completed training. He stayed in the RAF until 1947 and then entered civilian aviation. Ashley retired from British Caledonian Airways in 1982 with more than 20,000 hours of flight time on fifty different types of aircraft.

Another No. 4 BFTS graduate, Thomas Southern of Course 12, graduated, returned to England and was seconded to British Overseas Airways Corporation where he flew flying boats from the UK to Africa, the Middle East, and India. After the war, Southern left the RAF and continued with BOAC (now British Airways). Southern retired as a senior captain with more than 20,000 hours of flight time.

William A. Cory of Course 9 at No. 3 BFTS flew thirty-four missions on Halifaxes with Bomber Command and received the Distinguished Flying Cross. Cory finished the war as an Operational Training Unit instructor where he was promoted to squadron leader. After leaving the RAF, Cory joined BOAC and retired as a senior captain in 1970.

After graduating with Course 10 at No. 1 BFTS, Thomas Round served as an instructor assigned to the U.S. Army Air Forces. After the war, Round became an internationally acclaimed operatic tenor. A fan of Gilbert and Sullivan, Round formed his own ensemble, Gilbert and Sullivan for All. He retired after performing for more than fifty years.

John Bruce of Course 14 at No. 4 BFTS returned to England and flew with No. 4 AFU Training Command in Scotland, piloting Avro Ansons for the advanced training of navigators, bomb aimers, and wireless operators. After the war, Bruce returned to Aberdeen University and took a Bachelor of Science degree in forestry. He then emigrated to Canada where he worked for the British Columbia Forest Services for thirty-five years before retirement.

Charles Kenneth Cooke graduated as the top cadet of Course 15 at No. 3 BFTS. After he returned to England, Cooke attended a staff navigation course and then had a varied wartime service, which included a brief tour on operations with Bomber Command, station navigation officer at RAF Outson, and a stint as commandant of a British prisoner of war camp. Cooke remained in the Royal Air Force after the war and held a variety of flying posts. He served as a flight commander with 60 Squadron in Malaya flying Spitfires and later Vampire jets and then served as commanding officer at RAF Wyton, where Victors, Canberras, and Comets were based. Group Captain Cooke retired from the RAF in 1975 with a total of thirty-three years' service, having flown sixty-two marks of aircraft. After retirement he became sales director for Chemring P.L.C. in Plymouth, England.

Frank Johnson graduated with Course 15 at No. 4 BFTS. After flying transports on operations in India, Johnson left the RAF after the war and returned to Oxford University. Due to his son's illness, Johnson moved his family to the milder climate of Australia. There he went into commercial banking and then became a stock broker and eventually a principal in his firm. After the death of his wife (whose health had been broken while a prisoner of the Japanese during the war) Johnson became an investment manager.

British actor Robert Hardy, noted for his portrayals of Winston Churchill and starring role in the Public Broadcasting System television series *All Creatures Great and Small*, trained with Course 27 at No. 1 BFTS, one of the last two courses that did not graduate in the United States.

Anthony Payne, a graduate of the first course at No. 3 BFTS, had been sidetracked by a bout of polio in the Middle East. After the war Payne went into banking, but in 1948 returned to instructing at the local RAF

Reserve Flying School. A Tiger Moth crash put him back in hospital for six months with a broken back. Payne returned to flying Chipmunks until the school closed in 1954 as part of government austerity measures. Payne then went into Fleet Street for a career with the *Sunday Times* in the circulation department. "I left flying with great reluctance; however, my Commercial licence was very restricted by reason of my medical history."[10]

William Reid, a graduate of No. 2 BFTS, received the Victoria Cross, Britain's highest decoration for valor, during a bombing mission in which he was wounded and his bomber heavily damaged. On a later mission after his recovery, Reid became a prisoner of war after his Lancaster bomber went down. Reid survived the war and returned home to Scotland where he attended Glasgow University, became an agricultural advisor, married, and raised a family. A quiet, unassuming man, Reid's family and friends apparently knew little of his wartime exploits. After his death in 2001, Reid's family placed his Victoria Cross up for auction. It sold for a record £384,000.

After being eliminated from flight training, Norman Nichol Brown of Course 11 at No. 3 BFTS remustered as a bomb aimer and flew on operations with a Wellington bomber squadron. Brown received a commission, rose to the rank of flight lieutenant, and received the Distinguished Flying Cross. After the war, Brown took a degree in Administration at Manchester University. Brown held positions with International Business Machines and the Wool Textile Employer Council, as well as senior lecturer in management in the Department of Industrial Administration at Bradford University, head of the Department of Management Studies at Sunderland Polytechnic, and vice principal of the College of Technology in Southall, Middlesex. In 1968 Brown became principal of West Bromwich College of Commerce and Technology.

Alan Bramson, the top cadet of Course 16 at No. 1 BFTS, became an instructor upon his return to England. After the war, Bramson continued in the aviation field. He wrote twenty-two aviation books and articles, including a well-received series of flight training manuals. At the age of seventy-eight Bramson continued to consult regularly on commercial aviation matters and was still certified to fly the most modern four-engine jet transports.

Many of the RAF students who trained in the United States returned to civilian life after the war, but stayed in the Volunteer Reserve. William Sydney Ellis, a Reserve pilot recalled to active duty for two years during the Korean War, flew the new Gloster Meteor jet fighter with 504 City of Nottingham Royal Auxiliary Air Force Squadron.

Group Captain John R. Baldwin, DSO and Bar, DFC and Bar, AFC, a graduate of No. 2 BFTS, and the top scoring Typhoon pilot of World War II with fifteen victories and one shared, continued in the Royal Air Force after the war. He commanded 249 Squadron in the Middle East and then, as part of the officer exchange program, flew North American F-86 Sabre jets with the United States Air Force in Korea. Group Captain Baldwin disappeared on a weather reconnaissance mission in March 1952 and is still officially listed as Missing in Action and presumed dead.

Several graduates of No. 1 BFTS returned to Texas after the war. After flying the new Avro Lincoln on weather reconnaissance missions, Eric Gill left the RAF and moved to Texas where he received a degree in petroleum engineering from Southern Methodist University. Jim Forteith flew against communist insurgents in Burma and Malaysia, then returned to Texas and married a young lady he met at a dance given for the British students during the war. Arthur Ridge flew in the Berlin Airlift, retired from the RAF, and then moved to Texas. Henry Madgwick returned to Terrell after the war and entered the insurance business. Madgwick was elected mayor of Terrell in 1998 and again in 2000, and was instrumental in the formation of the No. 1 BFTS Association (North America) and later in the creation of the No. 1 BFTS Museum.

AMERICAN STUDENTS

Colonel Gail Halvorsen, an Army Air Forces aviation cadet who trained with Course 18 at No. 3 BFTS, became internationally famous as the "Candy Bomber" during the Berlin Airlift. Berlin children would congregate off the end of the runway to watch the large transports on final approach to the beleaguered city. One day on impulse, Halvorsen tossed chewing gum to the children below as his plane passed overhead. This simple act of kindness blossomed as more and more children gathered and waited, recognizing Halvorsen's plane because he would dip the wings as he approached. Now with official approval, Halvorsen's generosity became a mini-relief effort as his buddies joined in collecting candy, rations, and other items, which were dropped by tiny parachutes made from handkerchiefs. Needy Berlin children returned the small parachutes for refills. International news organizations picked up the story and Halvorsen became an enduring symbol of American generosity and decency.

William Watkins grew up in an agricultural and ranching family in California. After learning to fly in the Civilian Pilot Training Program, Watkins joined the Army Air Forces and trained first at No. 6 BFTS and then, when that school closed, with No. 3 BFTS. After graduation, Watkins joined Ferry Command and flew both single-engine and multi-engine aircraft throughout the United States including ferrying aircraft destined for the Soviet Union to Alaska. After the war, Watkins remained in the Air Force Reserve and attended the University of California where he received a degree in Veterinary Medicine. He subsequently served with the State of California in various animal disease control and animal health programs. Watkins retired from the California Air National Guard as a colonel with thirty years of service.

Another Army Air Forces cadet, Ralph A. Bass, trained with Course 15 at No. 3 BFTS, then flew with Ferry Command delivering aircraft to the European Theater and with Transport Command flying Curtiss C-46s over the treacherous Hump from India into China. Bass completed his regular service in March 1946 and entered the reserves. In 1951 he returned to active duty during the Korean conflict and after the war remained in the USAF. During a varied career Bass advanced to Command Pilot. He left flying status in 1963 after serving in Panama, Korea, Hawaii, and several United States mainland bases. Before retirement as an Air Force colonel in 1972, Bass served in USAF Tactical Air Command, in USAF Headquarters, and completed a one year tour of duty with the 7th Air Force in Vietnam.

British Officers

Flight Lieutenant Palmer, the first administrative officer at No. 1 BFTS, served in the Judge Advocate General's office in Cairo, Egypt. He later became the head of the RAF legal department and retired as an air commodore.

Martyn Green, the first administrative officer at No. 2 BFTS, had been a well-known musical comedian before joining the Royal Air Force. After the war Green returned to the D'Oyly Carte Opera Company. In 1951 he left the company and moved to New York City and continued his career on Broadway, as well as television, recordings, and films. After a tragic accident in which he lost his left leg, Green returned to acting and producing with a prosthetic limb. His film roles included *A Lovely Way to Die* in 1968 and *The Iceman Cometh* in 1973. Green continued to perform until his death in 1975.

Wing Commander John Fergus McKenna, AFC served at No. 4 BFTS where he was noted, not only as the commanding officer, but for his distinctive car, a bright yellow 1938 Cadillac LaSalle coupe. McKenna originally earned his wings with the Royal Australian Air Force during the 1930s and was seconded to the RAF. After being placed on reserve status he attended medical school in Scotland. Recalled to duty at the beginning of the war, McKenna fought in the Battle of Britain and received the Air Force Cross. After the war, McKenna returned to Arizona and set up a medical practice in Phoenix. He died following an accident in 1970 and his ashes were scattered over Falcon Field.[11]

Before the Royal Air Force Delegation in Washington, early planning for British training in the United States came through the British Embassy. Air Commodore George Pirie, DFC, the air attache, had joined the Royal Flying Corps in 1916. Pirie remained in Washington until August 1941 when he briefly took command of RAF Northern Ireland and then HQ Middle East Command. After several substantive commands, Pirie was promoted to air chief marshal and returned to Washington in 1950 as head of the RAF Staff British Joint Services Mission. He retired in 1951.

Squadron Leader Stuart Mills, DFC, the combat veteran seconded to the British Embassy in late 1940, played a crucial role in the formation of the British Flying Training Schools and then commanded both No. 2 BFTS and No. 4 BFTS. Mills remained in the United States until 1945 and retired from the RAF in 1956 with the rank of group captain.

Group Captain Carnegie, the officer hurriedly assigned to the United States to supervise the new British flight training programs, returned to England toward the end of 1942. For the remainder of the war he served as director of Flying Training at the Air Ministry. Beginning in 1951 Carnegie served for three years as chief of staff of the Royal New Zealand Air Force. After retiring as an air vice marshal, Carnegie managed Burghley House, a massive country house begun in 1555 surrounded by a 9,000-acre estate centered on the beautiful market town of Stamford in Lincolnshire. The house contained an extensive collection of rare art and antiques dating from the time of Queen Elizabeth I.[12]

Wing Commander Hogan took over command of the training section of Royal Air Force Delegation in Washington from Group Captain Carnegie and continued until 1944. Hogan had been the top graduate at Cranwell in 1930, a pioneer in long distance record flights during the inter-war years, as well as a Battle of Britain squadron commander and fighter ace. After his tour in the United States, Hogan returned home and assumed duties as the assistant commandant at the Empire Central Flying School and the following year commanded No. 19 FTS at Cranwell. After the war, he was successively Station Commander at RAF Wattisham, Sector Commander Northern Sector, Air Officer Commanding 81 Group, then 83 Group as part of 2nd Allied Tactical Air Force Germany, and finally Senior Air Staff Officer Flying Training Command. Hogan retired from the RAF as an air vice marshal.

Wing Commander Charles A. Ball, the first commanding officer of No. 6 BFTS, arrived in Ponca City in May 1942 and was joined five months later by his wife, Irene, and two young daughters. Ball had joined the RAF in 1929 and from 1932 to 1934 helped form the Egyptian Air Force. Ball served in Bomber Command and as an RAF instructor before coming to America. Ball and his family emigrated to the United States after the war and settled in Portland, Maine.

Wing Commander David H. Lee, the first chief flying instructor at No. 3 BFTS, joined the RAF in 1930 and served in the rugged north west frontier of India. At the beginning of the war he served with 61 Squadron flying Hampden bombers. After leaving Oklahoma, Lee returned to the Air Ministry and in 1945 traveled to the Far East to take command of 904 (Fighter) Wing. At the end of the war, Lee's wing undertook the vital task of assisting in the rescue and repatriation of POWs and Allied internees in the Dutch East Indies which often involved his P-47 Thunderbolt squadrons in hostile action against insurgents and others in the unsettled region. After returning home, Lee served at the RAF Staff College and as commander of RAF Scampton, home to a wing of Canberra bombers. Three years later Lee moved to Aden as Air Officer Commanding Air Forces at the HQ British Forces Arabian Peninsula. In 1962 he returned to Britain as commandant RAF Staff College and then received a promotion to air marshal. Before his retirement from the RAF, Lee served for three years as U.K. military representative on the NATO Military Committee. Lee had been appointed OBE in 1943; CBE in 1953; KBE in 1965; and GBE in 1969. After his retirement, Lee published three books on RAF postwar history and served as vice president of the RAF Benevolent Fund in 1988.

Squadron Leader A. C. Kermode, the first chief ground instructor at No. 3 BFTS and for many months the only RAF officer in Miami, joined the Royal Naval Air Service in 1916. Before he came to Miami, Kermode had written several books on subjects such as the theory of flight which were widely used in the RAF.[13] Kermode retired from the Royal Air Force in 1960 as an air vice marshal and Director of Educational Services.

In the April 1960 issue of *Flight* magazine, an article titled "Airlines of the World, the British Carriers" listed Wing Commander H. A. Roxburgh as a director of Derby Airways, a British regional airline. Roxburgh had been commanding officer of No. 3 BFTS. Coincidentally, Derby Airways had grown from a British civilian flight school formed in 1938 to train pilots for the Royal Air Force. Derby Airways became British Midland International.

AMERICAN CIVILIAN STAFF

Lillian Taylor became a Link trainer operator at No. 6 BFTS. After the war, Taylor continued as a Link operator with Braniff Airways until she and her husband moved back to Ponca City. Taylor stayed in touch with many of the British students and she and her husband made numerous trips to England meeting with former students, organizing reunions, and promoting the memory of the British school in Oklahoma. Taylor became the unofficial spokesperson for No. 6 BFTS and the recognized authority for information related to the school. In 1986 former British student John Flannery wrote to the mayor of Ponca City to express his appreciation for the many kindnesses he received in Ponca City during the war. Flannery also had an unusual request. During training, he had bailed out of his heavily damaged Stearman after a midair collision that killed the two occupants of the other aircraft. Flannery wanted to thank the Darr Aeronautics employee who had packed the parachute that saved his life that day more than forty years earlier. Lillian Taylor supplied the name and current address of the former parachute rigger.

Many of the former civilian instructors continued to fly. Garnett Howell, a former advanced instructor at No. 1 BFTS, joined the new United Nations and flew in Mexico and Europe. The UN then sent Howell to Africa as an instructor. Several of his students went on to become senior captains with African national airlines.

C. Thomas Hill flew as a flight instructor at No. 6 BFTS. After the war, Hill continued in aviation and became a commercial airline pilot like many of the other instructors and graduates of the BFTS program. But then Hill decided to pursue another career and left aviation to attend medical school. Hill became a doctor and after his retirement returned to Ponca City to live.

Leon Schroeder, a primary and later an advanced instructor at No. 3 BFTS, also became a doctor after the war. Schroeder was instrumental in establishing an exhibit in the Air and Space Museum in Oklahoma City to commemorate the British students who trained in Oklahoma.

Former No. 1 BFTS primary instructor "Red" Vincell died in a crash while crop dusting in Arkansas.

Former Riddle Field instructor Jim Cousins joined Eastern Airlines and retired thirty-three years later. Another Riddle Field instructor, Tommy Teate, who never attended college, managed to earn a U.S. Army commission and retired as an Air Force lieutenant colonel. At the time of his retirement he had been a commercial airline pilot, a test pilot, veteran of three wars (WW II, Korea, and Vietnam), and a flight instructor for the British Royal Air Force, United States Air Force, and the Brazilian Air Force.[11]

J. E. Castleman, the last civilian chief flight instructor at No. 1 BFTS, continued instructing after the war. In 1967 Castleman and his student were both killed when a rogue cross wind flipped their trainer over during a landing approach.

Bill Hillman, a former advanced instructor at No. 3 BFTS, joined Eastern Airlines and retired in 1979 with 23,000 hours of flight time.

Another Spartan advanced instructor, Harold Morgenstern, who had been judged too old to join the U.S. Army or Navy at the beginning of the war, returned to New England after the school closed. Morgenstern joined Lockheed Overseas Corporation flying a converted B-17 bomber with a twenty-seven-foot lifeboat attached underneath on air-sea rescue missions out of Iceland. When the contract ended, Morgenstern became an executive pilot for an electronics research and development company. Company policy forced Morgenstern to retire at age fifty and he then secured a job flying for the State of Maine. "This was a surprise, as I knew no politicians." Again forced to retire at age sixty due to state policy, Morgenstern then flew freight and U.S. Mail until he finally retired for good after more than forty-one years and 16,000 flight hours, and with never an accident.

Some of the postwar careers took unexpected turns. After the war, Lloyd Nolen, a former advanced instructor at No. 1 BFTS, continued to fly as a crop duster in the Texas Rio Grande valley. In 1951 Nolen and four friends purchased a surplus P-51 Mustang fighter to fly for fun. Several years later the group acquired two surplus Grumman F8F Bearcats. The group, jokingly referred to as the Confederate Air Force (each member was a "colonel"), was shocked to learn that the government had systematically destroyed most of the tens of thousands of military aircraft built during the war. The Confederate Air Force set out to find, restore, and preserve in flying condition as many types of World War II aircraft as possible.

At the beginning of the second decade of the twenty-first century the renamed Commemorative Air Force with headquarters in Midland, Texas, is the largest flying museum in the world. The Commemorative Air Force collection contains military aircraft from Allied as well as Axis nations and includes the only flying Boeing B-29 Superfortress in the world. The B-29 was the largest and most sophisticated bomber built during World War II.

Louise Sacchi became a navigation instructor at No. 1 BFTS after she realized that finding a job as a woman pilot in the early 1940s was virtually impossible. Sacchi returned to Pennsylvania after the war and became a flight instructor. In 1962 she began a sixteen-year career ferrying new private aircraft overseas (the first woman international ferry pilot). By the time she retired in 1978, Sacchi had ferried around 340 aircraft, mostly Beechcrafts, over both the Atlantic and Pacific oceans, held several speed records, and had written two books about her life and experiences. Sacchi was the first woman awarded the prestigious Godfrey I. Cabot Award for distinguished service to aviation. She passed away in 1997 at the age of eighty-three.

George Mayer served as an advanced flight instructor at No. 3 BFTS until he left Spartan and joined the infant Air Transport Command where he flew 104 missions in China, Burma, and India and received the Distinguished Flying Cross. Mayer returned to Miami after the war and founded two manufacturing businesses and a real estate firm. In 1974 he was named Oklahoma Small Businessman of the Year. Mayer also served on several local boards and committees, and as a Federal Aviation Administration safety advisor.

Elsee "Dee" Dutton had been one of the first female control tower operators in the United States when she went to work for Darr School of Aeronautics in Ponca City. There she became friends with many of the British students. Dutton moved to Washington and joined a small government intelligence service that later became the Office of Strategic Service (OSS, the predecessor of the CIA). After training her on ciphers and codes, the OSS sent Dutton to London where she renewed several old friendships from Oklahoma, including Jack Barrington, a Lancaster bomber pilot who was preparing to ship out to the Middle East following an operational tour in Europe. They were married in 1947 and returned to Ponca City the next year. Barrington entered the insurance business and the couple became active in community affairs while raising two children.[15]

Besides Barrington, former No. 6 BFTS students Harold Cogman and Albert Sims also returned to Ponca City and married local women. Cogman had flown Hurricanes, Spitfires, and Mustangs in North Africa and Italy. After serving as an instructor, Sims flew Wellington and Lancaster bombers on operations. Both Cogman and Sims went to work for Continental Oil Company. Cogman retired after thirty-four years with the company.

The British government recognized the civilian school operators and directors for their wartime service. The citation given to Tony Ming of Spartan's No. 3 BFTS is representative: "I am commanded by the Air Council to inform you that they have learned with much pleasure that His Majesty the King has been graciously pleased to approve your appointment as an Honorary Member of the Order of the British Empire in recognition of your services to the Royal Air Force. The Council wishes me to convey to you their warm congratulations on this mark of His Majesty's Favor and to thank you for all you have done."[16]

Ming continued with Spartan after the war. He became the manager of Spartan's Tulsa Aero Repair Department and then transferred to the company's New Jersey repair facility. Ming also continued to fly charter flights. On a 1961 charter flight in heavy fog, Ming's aircraft flew into the ground near Charleston, South Carolina, taking his life.

Harding Lawrence, the former head of the No. 1 BFTS Link trainer department and later assistant director of the school, joined Major Long in the new Pioneer Airlines. After Continental Airlines absorbed Pioneer, Lawrence spent ten years with Continental then became the president and CEO of Braniff International Airways. Always controversial, Lawrence's flamboyant management style raised Braniff from a regional carrier to international prominence, but many blame him for Braniff's ultimate downfall.

THE OPERATORS

Major Long sold his interest in the Dallas Aviation School after the war, but continued in the aviation field. Long and General Robert Smith formed a new feeder airline, Essair, which became Pioneer Airlines in 1946. Pioneer Airlines operated in Texas and New Mexico until it merged with Continental Airlines in 1955. At the time of his death in 1976, Long served on the board of directors of Gates Learjet Corporation. His career had literally spanned the breadth of aviation history from the ninety-horsepower, fabric-covered JN-4D Jenny of World War I to the age of the corporate business jet.

Spartan Aeronautics never returned to the manufacture of aircraft even though the company had designed a new high-performance personal aircraft and flown the prototype. Owner J. Paul Getty felt that the much heralded postwar private aviation boom would prove risky and disappointing. Instead, Spartan developed a line of high-quality travel trailers using aircraft construction techniques. Spartan at one time offered nineteen different trailer models, but stiff competition from low-cost manufacturers forced an end to production in 1959.

Spartan successfully engaged in the aircraft overhaul, conversion, and service business until 1970. Spartan's last job, appropriately, was the complete restoration of a Spartan Executive to "like new" condition for the South Carolina owner, then the plant closed.

For a time another venture, Spartan Airlines, operated as a feeder airline, while the Spartan School of Aeronautics continued to prosper in the field of aviation training. J. Paul Getty managed the company until he sold his interest in 1968. Captain Maxwell Balfour remained executive vice president of Spartan Aeronautics until he retired in 1961. He passed away in 1977.

After leaving Embry-Riddle in 1944, John Paul Riddle formed Riddle Airlines. The airline flew freight and passengers between New York, Miami, and South America. Riddle also founded the Inter-American

Institute in Florida to train businessmen for future South American markets and a flight school in Brazil that operated under contract to the Brazilian government.

Riddle never realized his vision of a bright future for aviation training in South America. Even though Riddle's South American school enjoyed considerable initial success and at one time reached an enrollment of 3,000 students, his venture foundered on the shifting sands of Latin politics. Riddle Airlines continued although it struggled to survive in spite of contracts with the US military. A series of heart attacks forced Riddle to sell his various interests and he passed away in 1989. Riddle is buried in Arcadia, Florida, in the same plot with the twenty-three Royal Air Force students who died during training in World War II. John Paul Riddle would not be known as the most successful businessman, but he was always a tireless and passionate advocate for aviation.

After John Paul Riddle left the company, Embry-Riddle continued under the leadership of John McKay and his wife Isabel. The years following the war were lean and the company barely survived. After several years of declining health, John McKay died in 1951 and the task of operating the company fell to his wife. After suffering a stroke in 1961 she sold the school in 1963, but remained on the board of directors until her death in 1972. Jack R. Hunt, a former Navy blimp pilot, awarded the Harmon Trophy in 1956, became president of the school in 1964 and served until his death in 1984. During that time Embry-Riddle moved from Miami to Daytona Beach, Florida, and enjoyed considerable success.

At the beginning of the second decade of the twenty-first century, both Spartan College of Aeronautics and Technology in Oklahoma and Embry-Riddle Aeronautical University in Florida are among the premier aviation training schools in the world.

A final, albeit unfortunate, footnote to the story of No. 7 BFTS and Avenger Field did not involve the British. In early 1943, months after the British students and RAF staff had departed from Sweetwater, the United States government indicted Joe Plosser, Charles Prince, general contractor

Victor Nelson, auditor Robert Young, and several subcontractors for fraud involving the initial construction of the school. The indictment alleged that the defendants had conspired to bill the government for materials and services that were never delivered. The investigation originated when No. 7 BFTS experienced an unusually high number of construction defects, which were time consuming and costly to correct. The trial held in Federal District Court in Abilene, Texas, included charges, countercharges, and a litany of evidence which pitted the numerous defendants against one another. The trial also featured an abundance of old-fashioned fiery legal rhetoric such as the federal prosecutor's description of Joe Plosser and Charles Prince as "arch criminals." The high point of the trial came when attorney Dan Moody, a popular former Texas governor (and still the youngest governor ever elected) representing Plosser and Prince, delivered an impassioned closing argument lasting almost an hour. In the end, the jury took little time to exonerate Plosser, Prince, and the subcontractors, but found that the general contractor and the auditor had falsified payment invoices. In spite of the not guilty verdict, the Defense Plant Corporation had already cancelled the Plosser and Prince contract and transferred operation of the Sweetwater school to Aviation Enterprises of Houston.

The newly formed (1947) independent United States Air Force turned its back on the former civilian flight schools. Some sources have suggested that high-ranking Air Force officers still resented General Hap Arnold's 1939 decision to involve civilian schools in the army flight training effort. Some Air Force officers openly stated that by the time the Army Air Forces trained, supported, and supervised the civilian flight school operators, the army could have performed the entire pilot training program more efficiently and at lower cost than the civilian schools. This is an oversimplification which ignores the magnitude and the overwhelming complexity of the wartime flight training program, as well as the ultimate success of the venture.

Lieutenant General Yount expressed a far different opinion when he wrote to Captain Balfour in 1944: "It seems only yesterday that the command placed its entire future in the hands of a few patriotic men such as yourself. Without this small nucleus of civil contractors this command could not possibly have expanded from four or five hundred a year to the astounding rate of 110,000 pilots per year."[17]

Apparently the Air Force prejudice against the civilian schools applied only to pilot training because Spartan Aeronautics, Embry-Riddle, and Major Moseley's Cal Aero Tech received postwar Air Force contracts to train aircraft mechanics.

With pressure from the rapid expansion resulting from the Korean War, the Air Force again (but reluctantly) turned to civilian schools for flight training in the early 1950s. One of the limited number of contracts went to Harold Darr, the previous operator of No. 6 BFTS. Locals in Ponca City maintain that Darr wanted to reopen the school due to his fondness for the former school site, but commercial leases on portions of the facilities and the deteriorated condition of some of the remaining buildings made a return to Ponca City impractical. Instead, Darr built a new contract school at Marana Air Base northwest of Tucson, Arizona. The new school, with a staff of 800 employees, utilized 30 primary trainers and 156 AT-6s, a far cry from the days of No. 6 BFTS.

As with several of the former school operators, Darr also entered the postwar airline business. In 1947 Darr rescued the financially struggling Monarch Airlines. Three years later, Darr became the first president of Frontier Airlines, which originated from the merger of Monarch, Arizona Airlines, and Challenger Airlines. Frontier Airlines, with headquarters in Denver, Colorado, operated a route system that spanned forty cities along the Rocky Mountains from Montana to the Mexican border. Frontier grew to become one of the most profitable regional airlines in the United States. Harold Darr retired as president of Frontier Airlines in 1953.

In 1954 Harold Darr founded Darr Equipment Company to rent, service, and maintain heavy construction equipment. Even though Darr passed away the following year at the age of sixty-one, Darr Equipment Company is still (2015) a leading regional heavy equipment service company. In 2000 Darr Equipment Company employees dedicated one of the main flagpoles at the entrance to the new Dallas-Fort Worth National Cemetery to the company's founder, Harold S. Darr.

Major Moseley had purchased the historic Grand Central Air Terminal (substituting the word "airport" for "terminal") and continued his aviation school to train aircraft mechanics, technicians, and engineers at Cal-Aero Technical Institute. Moseley also operated a successful aircraft servicing and overhaul operation. For several years Cal-Aero Tech did well, due to the postwar GI Bill and the Korean War-era Air Force mechanics contracts. As the war diminished, the Air Force canceled its contract in 1952 and the city of Glendale closed a portion of the airport runway, severely limiting the types of aircraft able to use the field. Enrollment drastically declined and Major Moseley's school closed in 1954. The historic airfield that had been inaugurated with such fanfare in 1929 became an industrial park.[18]

In 1952 Major Moseley, along with partner Charles E. Bartley, the inventor of rubber-based solid fuel rocket propellants, formed the Grand Central Rocket Company. In 1958 the company provided the Altair third stage of the Explorer I rocket, as well as one of two Altair designs for Project Vanguard, which launched early American satellites into orbit. The founding partners sold the company in 1961 to Lockheed Aircraft Corporation.

With the end of the war, Southwest Airways also left the flight training business and began scheduled airline service in California. Still led by John Connelly and Leland Hayward, the regional airline, flying surplus Douglas DC-3s, which were both plentiful and inexpensive, adorned with a thunderbird emblem reminiscent of the Thunderbird Field logo, quickly expanded its route system. Noted as a no-frills airline, Southwest pioneered cost savings measures and reduced turn around times between landings and departures. A 1948 *Time* magazine article reported, "Connelly serves no food ('let them bring their own'), provides no chewing gum ('we never fly high enough to need it and besides it sticks to the floor') or magazines ('takes too long to unwrap them')." In 1958 the airline changed its name to Pacific Air Lines (with a more modern and stylized thunderbird emblem) and began to upgrade equipment. During the 1960s, the airline faced stiff competition and difficult economic times, exacerbated by a fatal crash in 1964. In 1968 Pacific joined in a three-way merger to form Air West.

Even with his leadership role in Southwest Airways, Leland Hayward continued in the entertainment field. In 1945 Hayward sold his talent agency and became a successful Broadway, motion picture, and televison producer. He produced the original stage production of *South Pacific* and *The Sound of Music*. In 1948 he produced the play *Mister Roberts* and then the film of the same title in 1955. His credits also include *The Spirit of St. Louis* (starring Jimmy Stewart, an original investor in Southwest Airways), *The Old Man and the Sea*, *Gypsy* and the film version of *The Sound of Music*. In 1960 Hayward married Pamela Churchill, former wife of Randolph Churchill, Winston Churchill's tumultuous son. Leland Hayward and John Connelly both passed away in 1971.

THE CEMETERIES

For years Mrs. Frantie Manbeck Hill cared for the RAF graves in Miami, Oklahoma. Mrs. Hill died in 1989 and is buried in the RAF section of the Miami, Grand Army of the Republic cemetery, alongside the graves she so lovingly tended. Her tombstone reads, *Mrs. F.M. Hill of Miami, buried alongside, voluntarily tended these fifteen British Airmen's graves and helped their loved ones from 1941 to 1982. These selfless human actions were unknown to most. She was awarded the King's medal for service in the cause of freedom by King George VI.*

In Terrell, a group from the Terrell War Relief Society, primarily Bertha Brewer, Neil Griffith, Mrs. James Marriet, Margaret Bass, and Mary Boyd took over care of the British graves. The RAF section of the Terrell Oakland Memorial Park cemetery contains a small stone monument dedicated by Lord Halifax in April 1942 with the poignant epitaph from a Rupert Brooke poem: *Some corner of a foreign field that is forever England.*

In the other cities where the British students who died during training are buried, local women, the War Relief Society and the American Legion, as well as other organizations or groups of volunteers, also tended to the British graves.

THE SCHOOL SITES

With the conclusion of the war, the Defense Plant Corporation either sold the former school facilities or conveyed ownership of the sites to local governments for whatever use they could make of them.

The original frame buildings that housed No. 1 BFTS disappeared in a sea of industrial expansion and a four-lane road now cuts through the original school site to provide access to industrial plants. The two-story operations building survived into the late 1960s as the airport management office, then was torn down. The two original hangars were incorporated into manufacturing facilities. The distinctive curved hangar roofs are still discernible, but few people today notice. The third hangar was also converted to commercial use, but then later burned to the ground. Curious metal rods imbedded in the wide concrete apron now used to store material and park heavy trailers can still be seen. These tie downs once secured scores of trainers that taught young British students to fly.

The government conveyed War Eagle Field, the home of No. 2 BFTS, to Los Angeles County. The wartime structures outside of Lancaster were used as a county jail and later modernized and replaced by an INS detention facility. The original hangars are still in use.

Most of Spartan's wartime training facilities in Tulsa, the temporary home of the first British students of No. 3 BFTS, were torn down in 1970 to make way for runway expansion. The demolished buildings included five barracks that had housed British students, American Refresher students including Lance Wade, the RAF's distinguished American fighter pilot, and the beautiful original stone cafeteria.

Spartan Aeronautics continued to use the school buildings in Miami in conjunction with Northeast Oklahoma Junior College (known as the North Campus) to give flight instruction under the GI bill. In time the program ended, the buildings, including the unique Pennant Terminal, fell into disuse, and several of the vacant buildings suffered minor fires. All have now been torn down. The only reminder of the British school is the aircraft hangars. Two of the hangars have been considerably modified into commercial facilities and the original small hangar still remains dedicated to aviation use.

Mesa is now the third largest city in Arizona with a population of more than 440,000. Falcon Field, once an outpost in the desert, is surrounded by broad avenues, upscale housing, retail development, commercial facilities, master planned communities, and a golf course. The airport is a bustling general aviation airport and home to the Arizona wing of the Commemorative Air Force. A large Boeing plant dedicated to support of the Apache helicopter program is located just north of the field. Two of the original hangars are still in use and little changed from the war years. To the west of the field the extensive orange groves are still there, but are now separated from the field by a four-lane road. The only portion of a school structure still remaining is the stone fireplace and chimney from the recreation hall, maintained as part of a small city park. A plaque on the fireplace commemorates No. 4 BFTS, the Royal Air Force, and the students and instructors who died during training at the school.

Cecil Bridges returned to Mesa forty years after graduating as the top cadet of Course 8.

> I drove out to Falcon Field and stood beside my rented American car and looked about me. Whole tracts of orange and grapefruit groves had vanished to be replaced by retirement homes, and the

fat catfish no longer lurked in the irrigation channels. The neat buildings and parade ground with the twin flagpoles—one for 'Old Glory' and one for the Union Jack—the swimming pool, all these had gone and a jumble of hangars and crates and untidy roads offended the eye.

There had once been a common sense of purpose and achievement—a sense of unity—in every building, every aircraft, every person on the field. Now there was only a myriad individual entities. I was reminded of the words of George Borrow when writing of the prize ring, "How for everything there is a time and a season and then how does the glory of a thing pass from it, even like the flower of the grass".[19]

In October 1941 Air Marshal A. G. R. Garrod toured the new British Flying Training Schools along with an entourage of high-ranking RAF and Army Air Forces officers. In Clewiston, Florida, Garrod commented on the criticism of the cost to build No. 5 BFTS and Riddle's vision of a postwar use for the school. Garrod felt the criticism unwarranted. "In ten, twenty, and even thirty years from now his wisdom would be proven."[20] Sadly that never occurred. After the war the former No. 5 BFTS school facilities fell into disuse and deteriorated. Itinerant crop dusters occasionally used the field and a new flight school lasted less than two years. Other uses included a mobile home park, a small factory to manufacture ladies' undergarments, and for a time the old buildings housed migrant workers employed in the nearby sugar cane fields. County officials encouraged proposals from developers interested in the site, but these ideas always proved mostly fanciful, with little financial backing.

In the 1980s the old school buildings, including the hangars, were bulldozed to the ground. Today one of the original runways has been lengthened and improved and new hangars erected. The airport, renamed Airglades Air Park, serves as the Hendry County airport, as well as the Clewiston municipal airport, supporting a few local aircraft owners, transient pilots, and skydivers. All that remains of John Paul Riddle's postwar vision is a number of faded photographs in the airport office, the distinctive diamond-shaped ring road (which now encompasses only bare ground), a number of old fire hydrants hinting at the once extensive utility system, and a small section of one original taxiway, which leads nowhere.

In 1991 the original school buildings at Darr School of Aeronautics in Ponca City, were "almost as we left them" according to J. C. Price when he returned for the fifty-year anniversary reunion (and he included a photo taken on final approach to the airport to prove it). The school buildings are now gone, except one. This original building still stood at the beginning of the second decade of the twenty-first century, vacant, neglected, and shabby, with windows and doors boarded, but still capable of further use with a little care, more than seventy years after it was built. Typical of the other school sites, the aircraft hangars have been converted to commercial use.

All of the school buildings from the short-lived No. 7 BFTS are gone. But the small original hangar, built in 1929 when the municipal field opened, is still there. The hangar houses a museum dedicated to the Womens Airforce Service Pilots (WASPs), who trained at Avenger Field after the army took over the British school.

REUNIONS AND ASSOCIATIONS

Not long after the end of the war, it became common for veterans of a particular British Flying Training School to get together for informal lunches or dinners, usually in London or other British cities. As these gatherings became larger, invitations were extended to former members of the school's RAF staff, former members of the Royal Air Force Delegation in Washington, and the previous school owners and staff.

When graduates of No. 3 BFTS planned a reunion in 1949, Group Captain Kermode wrote from his post in Singapore.

> 3 BFTS was the greatest experience of my life. The cadets and staff carried on everything that we tried to start in those early days.

> Those of us who served either as cadets or staff at 3 BFTS have 'got something' which not only the RAF, but perhaps even the Nation, could well do with in these days. We had our difficulties, struggles and arguments, but we learnt to work with the Americans and learnt to work with each other, we helped a large number of cadets to be better officers and NCO's and pilots, and I believe that the majority of that number feel an affection, perhaps even a debt to 3 BFTS that is shared by graduates of very few other Flying Training Schools.[21]

In time these informal gatherings evolved into formal organizations. Former students organized associations that represented each of the British wartime training schools in the United States, except No. 7 BFTS. Because of the number of ex-students living in the United States, each association had a comparable North American organization or liaison. These associations maintained close ties with former students, shared information, published newsletters, and organized reunions, both in Britain and in the United States.

Captain William McCash, AFM, of Course 20 in Mesa and others organized the No. 4 BFTS Association and put together probably the most complete list of former students and subsequent service of any of the British schools.[22] The program for the 1991 No. 4 BFTS fifty-year reunion held at Falcon Field contains the notation, "Guest of Honor— Jimmy Stewart—First Stockholder of Southwest Airways."

These associations flourished during the 1980s and 1990s, as members retired and children left home, but began to decline after the turn of the century due to poor health and diminishing numbers. Most of the associations had closed by the beginning of the following decade, but some activities continued. In 2011 several members of the No. 5 BFTS Association returned to Clewiston, Florida, for a visit.

CONCLUSION

There are still reminders of the BFTS presence in the United States. Oklahoma governor Frank Keating declared 23 September 1992 as "#3 British Flying Training School Day." Each cemetery plot where the British students are buried is under the supervision of the Commonwealth War Graves Commission with North American headquarters in Ottawa, Canada. These sites are well maintained and most local communities hold a commemorative ceremony each year, usually on Memorial Day or Veterans Day.

The No. 1 BFTS Association (North America) evolved into a separate entity, The No. 1 British Flying Training School Museum, Inc. This group maintains a museum at the Terrell airport, the former No. 1 BFTS school site. The museum displays artifacts, photographs, and a model of the school as it appeared during the war.

The Clewiston Museum has a display commemorating the British school and a collection of school records. Other local libraries, museums, and schools, such as Northeastern Oklahoma A&M College in Miami, Oklahoma, have displays or maintain records and materials related to British flight training.

In 1997 Beth Lawless, an elementary school teacher in Ratan, Oklahoma, asked her sixth grade reading class to select a topic for a research project. The class decided to research the story of a local plane crash. The class learned that the story involved the two AT-6s from No. 1 BFTS, which crashed in the nearby mountains on a training flight in 1943. The project expanded to two reading classes, which researched the crashes and then wrote a comprehensive final report.[23]

After the report, the schoolchildren decided to raise money for a memorial to the four British students who died in the Kiamichi mountains. The project became a community project. Ms. Lawless and the children asked the British Broadcasting Corporation to help locate any relatives of the crash victims. The story aired by the BBC generated considerable interest. People throughout Great Britain were deeply moved to learn that schoolchildren in a small Oklahoma town no one had ever heard of cared enough to erect a memorial to young British flyers who had died almost sixty years earlier. Following the publicity, British Airways offered to fly the relatives to Dallas for the dedication ceremony.

On February 20, 2000, exactly fifty-seven years to the day after the crashes, a large crowd estimated at more than 700 gathered just outside Moyers, Oklahoma, to dedicate the grey granite memorial, under clear blue skies. The beautiful day and warm temperature offered a stark contrast to the cold misty overcast day on February 20, 1943. At the ceremony, the Antlers, Oklahoma, high school band played, "God Save the Queen" and the "Star Spangled Banner," while a National Guard honor guard presented the colors. Buglers played both the British "Last Post" and the American "Taps." The Lord Mayor of the London Borough of Redbridge, complete in the official robes of office, and the New Zealand Military attache from Washington, D.C. attended. Seventeen relatives of the four students sat in several rows of metal chairs arranged under a canvas awning. John Wall from New Zealand and Gordon Wright from England, the students in the other At-6 that made a precautionary landing in a nearby valley, sat behind the relatives.

Wartime Aircraft Recovery Group is an organization of volunteers in England who recover and display artifacts from aircraft crashes. Around 1994 the group investigated the World War II crash of an Airspeed Oxford, which crashed and burned in poor weather shortly after takeoff from RAF Ternhill, killing the pilot. More than fifty years after the crash, the group recovered a small crumpled metal disk from the site. Carefully straightening the disk revealed the still pristine inscription.

POLARIS FLIGHT ACADEMY

THIS IS TO CERTIFY THAT

J. JENKS

HAS THIS DATE COMPLETED THE

PRESCRIBED COURSE OF FLIGHT

TRAINING AT THIS SCHOOL

WAR EAGLE FIELD

LANCASTER CALIFORNIA

The number of British pilots trained in the United States represents a relatively small portion of the Allied worldwide flight training programs during World War II. The true significance of the program is represented by the close ties of friendship which developed between the young British students and Americans of all walks of life, friendships which continued during the war and remained long after the end of the war.

On the international level, the British Flying Training Schools program was one of the greatest cooperative ventures ever undertaken between nations. Aircrew training, along with other cooperative ventures such as lend-lease, cemented the alliance between Great Britain and the United States that transcended national interest and continued after the war, throughout the cold war, and exists to this day.

Appendix

BFTS Fatalities

In accordance with British policy, Royal Air Force students who died while training at the British Flying Training Schools were buried in the United States. The care and upkeep of these graves are under the authority of the Commonwealth War Graves Commission, whose North American headquarters is located in Ottawa, Canada. Below is a list of British Flying Training School graves in the United States arranged by school.

No. 1 British Flying Training School

Terrell, Texas. Oakland Memorial Park

1. Richard D. Mollett, November 10, 1941

2. William L. Ibbs, January 18, 1942

3. George I. Hanson, January 21, 1942

4. Raymond A. Berry, February 7, 1942

5. Leonard G. Blower, February 7, 1942

6. Aubrey R. Atkins, February 14, 1942

7. James Craig, May 28, 1942

8. Geoffrey M. Harris, September 17, 1942

9. Allan S. Gadd, October 27, 1942

10. Thomas Travers, October 27, 1942

11. Alan R. Langston, February 1, 1943

12. Vincent H. Cockman, February 20, 1943

13. Frank R. W. Frostic, February 20, 1943

14. Michael J. Hosier, February 20, 1943

15. Maurice L. Jensen, February 20, 1943

16. Kenneth W. Coaster, September 17, 1943

17. M. W. A. Williamson, November 27, 1943

18. H. Gilbert Slocock, February 7, 1945

19. Thomas S. Beedie, September 3, 1945

20. Raymond B. Botcher, September 3, 1945

Nineteen of the No. 1 BFTS fatalities were due to aircraft accidents. The other fatality, Gilbert Slocock, died of natural causes shortly after his arrival in Terrell. In addition to the British casualties, three civilian instructors, T. O. Somerville, M. D. McDonald, and Cliffard A. Levan, along with one Army Air Forces aviation cadet, Howard W. Perry, died in aircraft accidents at Terrell. The bodies of the American casualties were returned to their home towns for burial.

No. 2 British Flying Training School

Lancaster, California. Lancaster Cemetery
1. Maier B. Himelstaub, February 13, 1942

No. 3 British Flying Training School

Tulsa, Oklahoma. Memorial Park
1. Ronald D. Harrison, July 11, 1941

Miami, Oklahoma. Grand Army of the Republic Cemetery
1. Fred Tufft, October 27, 1941

2. Peter McCallum, November 13, 1941

3. Alan Brown, August 31, 1942

4. Harold A. Burman, August 31, 1942

5. Herbert Horace Hacksley, August 31, 1942

6. Donald Arthur Harfield, August 31, 1942

7. Ralph K. Price, October 3, 1942

8. William C. Speirs, April 8, 1943

9. Walter E. Elliott, October 20, 1943

10. Kenneth Raisbeck, June 26, 1944

11. James Boyd, December 14, 1944

12. William G. M. Mann, March 21, 1945

13. Cecil J. Riddell, May 2, 1945

14. Frederick D. Beverley, May 30, 1945

15. Dennis M. Mitchell, August 10, 1945

In addition to the British casualties, three civilian instructors, D. Gale Hendrix, Clifford Pitts, and Leonard D. Weaver, and one Army Air Forces aviation cadet, C. E. Walter, died in aircraft accidents at No. 3 BFTS.

Frantie Manbeck Hill is also buried in the same plot as the Royal Air Force students. Mrs. Hill lovingly tended the RAF graves until her death in 1989. In recognition of her care and devotion, she received the King's Medal of Service from the British government.

No. 4 British Flying Training School

Mesa, Arizona. Mesa City Cemetery
1. Alexander T. Brooks, October 20, 1941

2. Paul C. J. Colling, October 21, 1941

3. Alec H. Sutton, December 28, 1941

4. Peter D. Campbell, January 7, 1942

5. William Burke, January 14, 1942

6. Frank Glew, April 1, 1942

7. Harold E. Hartley, April 15, 1942

8. Jack Payne, April 15, 1942

9. William J. Watters, December 24, 1942

10. Robert Lawther, January 18, 1943

11. Horace R. J. Partoon, March 5, 1943

12. George Davison, April 8, 1943

13. James G. Buchanan, April 14, 1943

14. Robert B. Horn, April 14, 1943

15. John L. Gomm, August 13, 1943

16. John G. Versturme-Bunbury, August 17, 1943

17. Walter W. Chamberlain, October 28, 1943

18. Reginald G. H. Clarke, October 28, 1943

19. Arthur R. Lewis, October 30, 1943

20. Anthony S. Lovett, December 17, 1943

21. John R. Durston, March 8, 1944

22. Albert Morris, May 23, 1944

23. Peter F. Mitson, November 27, 1944

In addition to the British casualties, four civilian instructors were killed at Mesa: Barney John Gordon, Bob Hammond, Willard W. Schendel, and Donald Walker. Another instructor, James Earl Netser and Army Air Forces aviation cadet, Lawrence A. Janson, both died of natural causes while at Falcon Field. After No. 4 BFTS closed, Course 26 returned to England to continue training and two students, Ronald Oubridge Ayres and Algernon Stewart Bailey were killed in flying accidents and are buried in Britain.

No. 5 British Flying Training School

Clewiston, Florida. Oak Ridge Cemetery (Arcadia, Florida)

1. Charles F. Russell, July 22, 1941

2. Alfred T. Lloyd, January 5, 1942

3. Roger B. Crosskey, January 20, 1942

4. William Meekin, June 30, 1942

5. Richard B. Thorp, July 16, 1942

6. Geoffrey R. King, December 3, 1942

7. Ronald A. Purrett, December 14, 1942

8. Derek R. Clandillon, January 19, 1943

9. John A. Clay, January 19, 1943

10. Forbes M. Robertson, April 24, 1943

11. Mervyn H. E. Thomas, April 28, 1943

12. Dennis H. Washer, April 28, 1943

13. Leonard G. Stone, August 24, 1943

14. Edward C. F. Vosper, August 24, 1943

15. George H. Wilson, September 15, 1943

16. Robert A. Wood, September 15, 1943

17. Anthony J. Oakley, January 14, 1944

18. Thomas J. Parry, January 14, 1944

19. Michael K. Hinds, July 13, 1944

20. Lionel M. Viggers, October 9, 1944

21. Horace Bowley-Booth, May 4, 1945

22. Thomas W. Calderhead, May 4, 1945

Louis Wells, an Arnold Scheme RAF student who died in an aircraft accident on December 9, 1941, is also buried in Arcadia along with the twenty-two BFTS students.

When John Paul Riddle M.B.E., aviation pioneer and founder of Embry-Riddle Company and Riddle-McKay Aero College, died in 1989, he elected to be buried in Arcadia alongside his British students.

No. 6 British Flying Training School

Ponca City, Oklahoma. Independent Order of Odd Fellows' Cemetery

1. Raymond Haslam, January 27, 1942

2. Joseph A. Neild, September 30, 1942

3. John F. Swain, November 3, 1942

4. Owen W. Phillips, July 5, 1943

5. Gerald O. G. Worrall, August 19, 1943

6. Harry A. Dinnage, January 7, 1944

7. Raymond D. W. Eyres, January 18, 1944

Also buried in the Royal Air Force section of the Ponca City Cemetery is Charles Bradlaugh Thompson, Esquire, M.B.E. "Born Lancaster England Sept. 26, 1892 Died, Aug. 3, 1984"

Thompson tended the British graves for many years and was knighted for his service to the school.

ENDNOTES

NOTES TO INTRODUCTION

1. Townsend, *Duel of Eagles*, 19.

2. Saward, *Bomber Harris*, 13.

3. When Peter Townsend, an RAF fighter squadron commander during the Battle of Britain, reported to his first squadron in 1934 he was told, "Only fools and owls fly by night." Townsend, *Duel of Eagles*, 168.

4. AIR 32-14, *The History of Flying Training, Navigation Training.*

5. Guinn, *Arnold Scheme*, 17–19.

6. Terraine, *A Time for Courage,* 86.

NOTES TO CHAPTER 1

1. A German attack on the RAF training base at Brize Norton in August 1940 destroyed forty-six aircraft and considerably disrupted the training schedule.

2. Hatch, *Aerodrome of Democracy*, 7.

3. Canada had officially created an Air Force two months before the end of World War I, but it was disbanded shortly after the end of hostilities.

4. Barris, *Behind the Glory*, 15. In fairness, there is evidence that Lord Riverdale approached the negotiations with a certain arrogance and considered the Canadians as little more than crude colonials.

5. Hatch, *Aerodrome of Democracy*, 33.

6. Others have suggested the name change was due to accounting reasons in order to keep the various training schemes separate.

7. Richards, *Royal Air Force 1939–1945, Vol I*, 74.

8. Caine, *Eagles of the RAF*, 40.

9. Ibid.

10. Hatch, *Aerodrome of Democracy*, 90.

11. Ibid., 93.

12. AIR 45/2, "History of R.A.F. Delegation, Annex B."

13. AIR 20/1387, "Notes of Meeting in U.S. of S.'s Office on Saturday, 7 th Sept, 1940."

14. AIR 45/2, Letter dated 15 February 1941 from Air Attache to Air Marshal A. G. R. Garrod, Air Ministry, "History of R.A.F. Delegation, Section IV, Appendix 4."

15. AIR 20/1387, Memo dated 30 March 1941 from A.M.T. titled "Empire Air Training Scheme Committee."

16. AIR 45/2, Letter dated 15 February 1941 from Air Attache to Air Marshal A. G. R. Garrod, Air Ministry, "History of the R.A.F. Delegation, Section IV, Appendix 4."

17. AIR 20/1387, Memo dated 30 March 1941 from A.M.T. titled "Empire Air Training Scheme Committee."

18. AIR 45/2, Letter dated 15 February 1941 from Air Attache to Air Marshal A. G. R. Garrod, Air Ministry, "History of the R.A.F. Delegation, Section IV, Appendix 4."

19. AIR 20/1387, Memo dated 30 March 1941 from A.M.T. titled "Empire Air Training Scheme Committee."

20. Ibid.

21. AIR 20/1387, unsigned and undated memo titled "Notes on Scheme for Training Pilots and Observers in the U.S.A."

22. AIR 20/1387, Memo dated 30 Mar '41 from A.M.T. titled "Empire Air Training Scheme Committee."

23. Edner is regarded as the first American casualty of the cold war after he was savagely murdered in 1949 during the Greek Civil War.

24. Michael D. Montgomery, *Aviation History*, November 2004.

Notes to Chapter 2

1. Guinn, "British Aircrew Training in the United States 1941–1945," *Air Power History* (Summer 1995): 9.

2. While the military did not use the light civilian planes for training, the Civilian Pilot Training Program taught many young men destined for military flight training the essentials of flight in these planes.

3. AIR 20/1387, "Notes of Meeting held in U.S. of S.'s Office on Saturday, 7th Sept. 1940."

4. AIR 20/1387, memorandum by A.M.T. dated 28 August 1940, "Development of Training Facilities in U.S.A."

5. Ibid.

6. AIR 20/1387, A.C.39(40) Memorandum by A.M.T. dated 10 September 1940, "Air Council: Training of Pilots in the United States of America."

7. Ibid.

8. AIR 20/1387, memorandum dated 11 September 1940 titled "Training of Pilots on a Civilian Basis and as a Commercial project at Civil Schools in the United States of America."

9. Churchill, *Their Finest Hour*, 553.

10. Ibid., 566.

11. Ibid., 569.

12. Nicknamed "Hap" early in his career because he was always happy, Arnold graduated from West Point in 1908 and later joined the aviation branch of the Signal Corps where he learned to fly from the Wright brothers in 1911. Coffee, *Hap: The Story of the U.S. Air Force*, 40–45.

13. One of Arnold's staff officers, Lt. Col. Ira Eaker, summed up the staff's opposition to using civilian training schools when he argued that the new policy would be "just plain murder." Coffey, *Hap: The Story of the U.S. Air Force*, 196.

14. There were nine schools in the original plan, which has led some sources to refer incorrectly to nine contractors. Oliver Parks operated two schools.

15. Three of the operators, Long, Moseley, and Darr, later received contracts to provide basic flight training.

16. Arnold, *Global Mission*, 181.

17. Aircraft allocation ratios would continue to be a source of negotiation and endless revision throughout the war.

18. AIR 45/2, letter dated 13 April 1941 from A. G. R. Garrod Air Member for Training to S. Of S. (Secretary of State for Air) located as Annex C to "History of R.A.F. Delegation."

19. Ibid.

20. Arnold, *Global Mission*, 215–38.

21. AIR 20/1388.

22. Towers graduated from the Naval Academy in 1906 and became naval aviator No. 3 after being taught to fly by the legendary Glen Curtiss.

23. The U.S. Coast Guard trained fifty British Fleet Air Arm pilots to fly helicopters later in the war.

24. Hammerton, ed., *ABC of the RAF*, 75.

25. AIR 20/1388.

26. AIR 20/1388, letter dated 24 April 1941 to Commodore G. C. Pirie from Air Commodore The Hon. R. A. Cochrane, C.B.E., A.F.C., Director of Training, Air Ministry.

27. Garrod, AMT, reports to Air Council about US, Sept. 7, 1940.

28. Coffey, *Hap: the Story of the U.S. Air Force,* 40–45.

29. AIR 20/1387, letter dated 13 March 1941 from George Pirie to Air Marshal A. G. R. Garrod, Director of Equipment, Air Ministry, London. Also AIR 45/2, letter dated 2 April 1941 from George Pirie to Air Marshal Garrod, "History of R.A.F. Delegation Section IV, Appendix 6." Also, AIR 32/14 *History of Flying Training,* 468–75.

30. AIR 20/1388, letter dated 12 June 1941 from Group Captain D. V. Carnegie to Air Attache, British Embassy, Washington, D.C.

31. AIR 20/1387, memorandum titled "Ab Initio Flying Training in the U.S.A. Conclusions of a meeting held in Whitehall on 7 March 1941."

32. AIR 20/1388, letter dated 26 April 1941 from B. A. Cochrane to Commodore G. C. Pirie, M.C., D.F.C. Air Attache, British Embassy, Washington.

33. Ibid.

34. Ibid.

35. AIR 45/2, letter dated 13 March 1941 from Pirie to Air Marshal A. G. R. Garrod, "History of R.A.F. Delegation Section IV, Appendix 5."

36. AIR 45/2, letter dated 2 April 1941 from Air Commodore Pirie to Air Marshal A. G. R. Garrod, O.B.E., M.C., D.F.C.

37. Letter dated 31 March 1941, from Air Commodore G. C. Pirie to Major F. H. Alexander, Office of the Chief of the Army Air Corps. "History of the Dallas Aviation School, Love Field, Dallas, Texas, 1 July 1939–15 March 1941."

38. Wiener, *Two Hundred Thousand Flyers*, 43–44.

39. AIR 45/2, letter dated 2 April 1941 from Pirie to Air Marshal A. G. R. Garrod, Air Ministry, London, "History of the R.A.F. Delegation."

40. Ibid.

41. Ibid.

NOTES TO CHAPTER 3

1. Carnegie had been a Royal Naval Air Service flying boat pilot during World War I flying dangerous North Sea patrols. During the inter-war years, Carnegie served in numerous staff and operational positions, commanded a seaplane training unit, and attended the RAF Staff College.

2. AIR 20/1388, letter dated 24 April 1941 to Commodore G. C. Pirie M.C., D.F.C. Air Attache, British Embassy, Washington from R. A. Cochrane.

3. AIR 20/1388, letter dated 4 May 1941 from Carnegie to Air Commodore The Hon. R. A. Cochrane, C.B.E., A.F.C., D. of T. Air Ministry.

4. Ibid.

5. AIR 45/2, Section IV, Appendix 9.

6. AIR 20/1388, letter dated 4 May 1941 from Carnegie to Air Commodore The Hon. R. A. Cochrane, C.B.E., A.F.C., D. of T., Air Ministry. Carnegie's reference is to Brig. Gen. Davenport Johnson, later promoted to Major General and command of the 11th Air Force in Alaska.

7. Ibid.

8. Ibid.

9. Churchill, *The Grand Alliance*, 764.

10. Hogan participated in a 1938 record-setting long distance flight in which three Wellesley bombers flew non-stop in formation from Egypt

to Australia. During the Battle of Britain Hogan scored five victories and received the Distinguished Flying Cross.

11. AIR 20/1388, letter dated 12 June 1941 from Carnegie to "Air Attache, British Embassy, Washington, D.C."

12. AIR 20/1388, undated memo titled "U.K. Training in U.S.A. Present Allocation of R.A.F. Personnel."

13. AIR 20/1388, letter dated 12 June 1941 from Carnegie to "Air Attache, British Embassy, Washington, D.C."

14. *Terrell Daily Tribune*, May 30, 1941.

15. Quoted in a collection of undated essays arranged by the Terrell Heritage Society titled *Terrell Centennial 1873–1973*. The quote has been attributed to either Bertha Brewer or her sister Virginia.

16. Letter dated 26 May 1941, from Balfour to Colonel T. D. Harris located in Ponca City library and reproduced in Peek, *The Spartan Story*, 107.

17. The B-19 did not go into production. The only XB-19 (with a gross weight of 162,000 pounds and powered by four Wright R-3350 engines) served throughout the war as a long-range transport. Retired after the war, the giant aircraft was scrapped in 1949.

18. AIR 20/1388, letter dated 12 June 1941 from Carnegie to "Air Attache, British Embassy, Washington, D.C."

19. Letter dated 10 June 1941, from Carnegie to Captain James Price, Training and Operations Division, U.S. Army Air Corps, War Department, Washington, D.C.

20. Hayer, "Falcon Field Beginnings," 175.

21. *Miami News-Record*, 17 October 1982.

22. AIR 20/1388, letter dated 12 June 1941 from Carnegie to "Air Attache, British Embassy, Washington, D.C."

23. *Mesa Journal-Tribune*, 27 June 1941.

24. AIR 20/1388, letter dated 12 June 1941 from Carnegie to "Air Attache, British Embassy, Washington, D.C."

25. Ibid.

26. Guinn, *The Arnold Scheme*, 188–189.

27. AIR 20/1388, training memo written by Carnegie dated 23 July 1941.

28. AIR 20/1388.

29. James, *Teacher Wore a Parachute*, 158.

30. AIR 20/1388, untitled memo dated 23 July 1941.

NOTES TO CHAPTER 4

1. Guinn, student questionnaire.

2. Ibid.

3. Ibid.

4. Ibid.

5. Ibid.

6. Ibid.

7. Ibid.

8. Ibid.

9. Ibid.

10. Ibid.

11. Ibid.

12. Ibid.

13. Ibid.

14. The V1 flying bomb Stugnell referred to as a "doodle bug" had just enough fuel to reach its target. As soon as the engine quit those on the ground knew the bomb was coming down.

15. Guinn, student questionnaire.

16. Ibid.

17. Ibid.

18. Ibid.

19. Ibid.

20. Ibid.

21. Ibid.

22. Ibid.

23. Ibid.

24. Ibid.

25. Ibid.

26. Watson diary supplied to Dr. Gilbert S. Guinn by W. E. J. Bishop, March 1987.

27. Guinn, student questionnaire.

28. Ibid.

29. Ibid.

30. Ibid.

31. Ibid.

32. Ibid.

33. Ibid.

34. Falcon Field Association newsletter February 2002.

35. Guinn, student questionnaire.

36. Ibid.

37. Ibid.

38. Ibid.

39. Ibid.

40. Ibid.

41. Ibid.

42. Ibid.

43. Denson, *The Royal Air Force in Oklahoma*, 91.

44. Ibid.

45. Guinn, student questionnaire.

46. Ibid.

47. Ibid.

48. Ibid.

49. Ibid.

50. Ibid.

51. Ibid.

52. Ibid.

53. John A. Cook wartime letter, copy to Dr. Gilbert S. Guinn.

54. Guinn, *The Arnold Scheme*, 199.

55. Guinn, student questionnaire.

56. Comments to Dr. Gilbert S. Guinn.

57. Guinn, *The Arnold Scheme*, 200.

58. Lee Randall wartime diary, provided to Dr. Gilbert S. Guinn.

59. Guinn, student questionnaire.

60. Frank Rainbird diary provided to Dr. Gilbert S. Guinn.

61. John Roberts Davies wartime letters provided to Dr. Gilbert S. Guinn.

62. Guinn, student questionnaire.

63. Ibid.

64. Ibid.

65. Ibid.

66. "Notes for the Guidance of Airmen Trainees Selected for Pilot and Observer Training at Certain Training Centers Overseas." Located in No. 1 BFTS ORB.

67. John Roberts Davies wartime letters provided to Dr. Gilbert S. Guinn.

68. No. 3 BFTS Association newsletter, July 1995.

69. John Roberts Davies wartime letters provided to Dr. Gilbert S. Guinn.

NOTES TO CHAPTER 5

1. *The Daily Times Herald*, June 3, 1941, and *Dallas Morning News*, 3 June 1941.

2. AIR 29/625, report from W/C Hilton to G/C Carnegie dated 7 June 1941.

3. No.1 BFTS ORB, 2 June 1941

4. AIR 29/625, report from W/C Hilton to G/C Carnegie dated 7 June 1941.

5. *Terrell Daily Tribune*, 18 April 1941.

6. No. 1 BFTS ORB, 14 June 1941.

7. Toward the end of the war the barracks would also be air conditioned.

8. Bert Allam, letter to Tom Killebrew, 30 November 1999.

9. Guinn, student questionnaire.

10. AIR 29/625.

11. Guinn, student questionnaire.

12. Ibid.

13. Ibid.

14. War Department, Air Corps Materiel Division, Memorandum 24-41A, dated 6 June 1941. Copy located in No.1 BFTS ORB, June 1941.

15. Guinn, student questionnaire.

16. Flight Lieutenant Martyn Green (actually William Martyn-Green, but he always went by Martyn Green) had been wounded while serving in the infantry in World War I. After the war Green became a renowned comedian in Gilbert & Sullivan comic operas performed by the D'Oyly Carte Opera Company and other troupes during the interwar years.

17. Guinn, student questionnaire.

18. AIR 29/625, report from W/C Hilton to G/C Carnegie dated 7 June 1941.

19. *Tulsa Daily Tribune*, 16 June 1941.

20. Ibid.

21. AIR 29/625, report dated 24 June 1941.

22. Guinn, student questionnaire.

23. *The Tulsa Tribune*, 12 July 1941.

24. Ibid., 20 August 1941.

25. As a young pilot serving in the rugged North West Frontier, Lee once delivered vital bubonic plague serum to Gilgit, a mountain outpost in the Karakoram mountains astride the old Silk Road from Chinese Turkestan to India.

26. Guinn, student questionnaire.

27. Ibid.

28. *Mesa Journal-Tribune*, 1 August 1941.

29. Dawson, *RAF in Arizona*, 17.

30. AIR 29/627.

31. Dawson, *RAF in Arizona*, 43.

32. Ibid., 44.

33. AIR 29/627.

34. Ibid.

35. *Mesa Journal-Tribune*, 3 October 1941. The month after Metcalf arrived in Mesa, his mother passed away in England.

36. AIR 29/627, No. 4 BFTS ORB, Course 1 Final Report.

37. Dawson, *RAF in Arizona*, 46.

38. AIR 29/627.

39. Russell Cooke wartime letters, Clewiston Museum.

40. Ibid.

41. *The Clewiston News*, 11 July 1941.

42. Craft, *Embry-Riddle at War*, 81.

43. Largent, *RAF Wings Over Florida*, 64.

44. Russell Cooke wartime letters, Clewiston Museum.

45. Ibid.

46. Ibid.

47. *The Ponca City News*, 10 August 1941.

48. No. 6 BFTS ORB, 26 August 1941.

49. *The Ponca City News*, 19 August 1941.

50. *Tails Up!* Volume One.

51. AIR 20/1388, 20 October 1941, 75–77.

52. Southwest Air Fast Express (sometimes referred to as SAFEway Lines) later became part of American Airlines. Monde, *Wings Over Sweetwater*, 10.

53. *Sweetwater Reporter*, 7 September 1941.

54. Monde, *Wings Over Sweetwater*, 19–20.

55. *Sweetwater Reporter*, 7 September 1941.

56. Monde, *Wings Over Sweetwater*, 20–21.

57. *Nolan County News*, 9 April 1942.

58. Mr. G. E. Dotsun also submitted the name Avenger Field, but he was disqualified because his brother-in-law was one of the contest judges.

59. *Sweetwater Reporter*, 28 June 1942.

60. *Nolan County News*, 11 June 1942.

61. There has been some confusion about the date the first British students arrived in Sweetwater. The 20 June date was confirmed by Mrs.

Diana Gill, widow of British student Jimmy Gill, from Gill's wartime logbook, in a 22 January 2011 letter to Tom Killebrew.

62. Mary Curry personal interview with Tom Killebrew, Sweetwater, Texas, 11 October 2007.

63. *Nolan County News*, July 9, 1942.

NOTES TO CHAPTER 6

1. Guinn, student questionnaire.

2. Ibid.

3. *Open Post, the Last of Many.*

4. Ibid.

5. Hammerton, *ABC of the RAF*, 78.

6. A half roll on top of a loop is essentially an Immelmann, but the British preferred not to use the name of the World War I German ace.

7. Guinn, student questionnaire.

8. Ibid.

9. John Roberts Davies diary provided to Dr. Gilbert S. Guinn.

10. *Terrell Tales No. 4*, published in the No. 1 BFTS Association newsletter.

11. Ibid.

12. Arthur Ridge, interview by Tom Killebrew, Dallas, Texas, 29 January 2000.

13. Douglas Rorman Byrne letter of 22 January 1987 to Dr. Gilbert S. Guinn.

14. James, *Teacher Wore a Parachute*, 160.

15. Larsen, *RAF Wings Over Florida*, 135.

16. The Dalton, or E6B computer, is still in widespread use.

17. *A System of Elementary Flying Training*, 27.

18. Guinn, student questionnaire.

19. Ibid.

20. Ibid.

21. John Roberts Davies wartime letters provided to Dr. Gilbert S. Guinn.

22. Dawson, *The RAF in Arizona*, 77.

23. James, *Teacher Wore a Parachute*, 63.

24. Ibid.

25. *Open Post, the Last of Many.*

26. Largent, *RAF Wings Over Florida*, 66.

27. Russell Cooke wartime letters, Clewiston Museum.

28. "A System of Elementary Flying Training," Air Ministry, London, April 1941.

29. Bert Allam letter to Tom Killebrew, 12 January 2000.

30. Guinn, student questionnaire.

31. Ibid.

32. Harold Morgenstern letter dated 3 October 1983 to Dr. Gilbert S. Guinn.

33. Guinn, student questionnaire.

34. Ibid.

35. Ibid.

36. Don Stebbings, "Terrell Tales No. 36," published in the No. 1 BFTS Association newsletter.

37. Guinn, student questionnaire.

38. Largent, *RAF Wings Over Florida*, 107.

39. Ibid., 185.

40. Letter dated 18 December 1942 from Wing Commander E. W. Moxham to Group Captain Hogan located No. 1 BFTS ORB, appendix A, 434.

41. AIR 29/627, No. 4 BFTS ORB Course 1 Final Report.

42. *Jane's, Fighting Aircraft*, 251.

43. *Open Post, the Last of Many.*

44. A. J. Allam, unpublished manuscript titled "Into the Wild Blue Yonder," 1979 in the possession of the author. Jack Bolter and his entire bomber crew disappeared on a mission over Germany in March 1945, just two months before the end of the war in Europe.

45. William W. Watkins wartime diary, provided to Dr. Gilbert S. Guinn.

46. John Roberts Davies wartime letters provided to Dr. Gilbert S. Guinn.

47. Himelstaub's parents were Polish Jews incarcerated in a German concentration camp. There is evidence that Himelstaub's mother survived the camps and relocated to Tel Aviv after the war.

48. Dawson, *The RAF in Arizona*, 133.

49. Jane Howell phone interview with Tom Killebrew 18 December 2000.

50. Email from Kenneth Dean to Tom Killebrew 23 August 2011.

51. *Terrell Daily Tribune*, 22, 23, and 24 February 1943.

52. John Price wartime diary provided to Dr. Gilbert Guinn.

53. Jim Millward letter dated 28 April 2004 to Tom Killebrew.

54. AIR 20/1387, extract from Bulletin from RAFDEL Washington to Air Ministry for fortnight ending 6 March 1943.

55. No. 3 BFTS ORB, 24 April 1943.

56. Ibid., 8 April 1943.

57. Guinn, student questionnaire.

58. Alan Lummis letter (no date) to Dr. Gilbert Guinn.

59. Largent, *RAF Wings Over Florida*, 152.

60. Don Ashby, "Terrell Tales No. 37," published in the No. 1 BFTS Association newsletter.

61. Guinn, student questionnaire.

62. Ibid.

63. Ibid.

NOTES TO CHAPTER 7

1. "Notes for the Guidance of Airmen Trainees Selected for Pilot and Observer Training at Certain Training Centers Overseas." Located in the No. 1 BFTS ORB.

2. John Roberts Davies wartime letters provided to Dr. Gilbert S. Guinn.

3. Largent, *RAF Wings Over Florida*, 114.

4. Ibid., 106.

5. AIR 20/1387.

6. No. 1 BFTS ORB, 9 June 1941.

7. *Terrell Daily Tribune*, 15 August 1941.

8. *Dallas Morning News*, 7 June 1941.

9. *Terrell Centennial 1873–1973*, 82.

10. *Dallas Morning News*, 10 December 1941.

11. Guinn, student questionnaire.

12. Ibid.

13. Denson, *The Royal Air Force in Oklahoma*, 52.

14. *The Scurry Times*, 2 July 1942.

15. Ibid.

16. Largent, *RAF Wings Over Florida*, 96.

17. Guinn, student questionnaire.

18. Ibid.

19. Ibid.

20. Ibid.

21. More than seventy years later Phyllis still has the watch, a treasured possession. Long after the war Phyllis and her husband Bruce Spoon continued to stay in touch with the families of the three British students.

22. Alan Norton Watson diary, copy supplied to Dr. Gilbert S. Guinn by W. E. J. Bishop.

23. *Terrell Daily Tribune*, December 30, 1941.

24. Guinn, student questionnaire.

25. Ibid. Four decades later, Keeling admitted to Dr. Gilbert S. Guinn that he was embarrassed by some of his youthful remarks.

26. Guinn, student questionnaire.

27. Alan Norton Watson diary, copy supplied to Dr. Gilbert S. Guinn by W. E. J. Bishop.

28. Guinn, student questionnaire.

29. Frank Rainbird wartime diary provided to Dr. Gilbert S. Guinn.

30. When local newspapers published the story of Rainbird's meeting with the governor, the Associated Press picked up the story and it ran in other major U.S. cities.

31. Largent, *RAF Wings Over Florida*, 99.

32. Ibid.

33. Guinn, student questionnaire.

34. Dawson, *RAF in Arizona*, 48.

35. Guinn, student questionnaire.

36. Ibid.

37. Largent, *RAF Wings Over Florida*, 115–116.

38. Guinn, student questionnaire.

39. Largent, *RAF Wings Over Florida*, 210.

40. Russell Cooke wartime letters, Clewiston Museum.

41. William W. Watkins wartime diary provided to Dr. Gilbert S. Guinn.

42. *Open Post*, June 1944.

43. Craft, *Embry-Riddle at War*, 67.

44. Russell Cooke wartime letters, Clewiston Museum.

45. Letter dated 25 August 1942 in Appendix, No. 1 BFTS ORB, 375.

46. Largent, *RAF Wings Over Florida*, 112.

47. Guinn, student questionnaire.

48. Countess Appoyi, Queen Consort to King Zogi of Albania.

49. Largent, *RAF Wings Over Florida*, 103–104.

50. Guinn, student questionnaire.

51. Harry Hewitt, "Terrell Tales" published in the No. 1 BFTS Association newsletter.

52. Largent, *RAF Wings Over Florida*, 80.

53. Jim Millward, "Terrell Tales" published in the No. 1 BFTS Association news letter.

54. Guinn, student questionnaire.

55. Denson, *The Royal Air Force in Oklahoma*, 64.

56. John A. B. Keeling wartime letters provided to Dr. Gilbert S. Guinn.

57. Guinn, student questionnaire.

58. *Terrell Daily Tribune*, October 31, 1942.

59. Ibid., November 25, 1944.

60. Largent, *RAF Wings Over Florida*, 223.

61. Dawson, *RAF in Arizona*, 215, 217. Flt. Lt. Lord, the pilot of the Dakota, received the Victoria Cross posthumously.

62. *Terrell Daily Tribune*, 29 July 1943.

63. *Mesa Journal-Tribune*, 20 June 1941.

64. Ibid., 13 March 1942.

65. *Terrell Daily Tribune*, 19 December 1942.

66. Ibid., 30 May 1945.

67. Guinn, student questionnaire.

68. Ibid.

69. *Dallas Morning News*, 9 September 1945.

70. Ibid.

71. Ibid.

72. Ibid.

NOTES TO CHAPTER 8

1. AIR 20/1388, memorandum, no title, to A.M.T. 23 July 1941.

2. AIR 29/625, Appendix I, letter dated 4 October 1941.

3. AIR 20/1388, memorandum, no title, to A.M.T. 23 July 1941.

4. No. 1 BFTS ORB, Introduction, 2.

5. No. 6 BFTS ORB, 31 December 1942.

6. No. 3 BFTS ORB, 1 May 1942.

7. AIR 29/625, Appendix C.

8. No. 1 BFTS ORB, Attachment, 421.

9. AIR 29/626, 90.

10. Ibid.

11. Ibid.

12. Tredrey, *Pilot's Summer*, 91.

13. Ibid, 145.

14. AIR 20/1388, memorandum dated 17 October 1941.

15. AIR 20/1388, memorandum dated 20 October 1941.

16. Pauline (Bond) Baxter, interview by Tom Killebrew, Kaufman, Texas, 17 August 2000.

17. *Spartan News*, issue #7, September 1942.

18. Ibid.

19. Craft, *Embry-Riddle at War*, 216–217.

20. AIR 29/626, 94.

21. No. 1 BFTS ORB, Attachment, 421.

22. Guinn, student questionnaire.

23. Twin-engine bombers such as the Wellington would also be modi-fied to eliminate the copilot.

24. AIR 20/1388, extract from Bulletin for fortnight ending 8 September 1941.

25. The memo is signed "K.P.Mc." and is almost certainly from Colonel (later brigadier General) Kenneth P. McNaughton on the staff of Major General (later Lieutenant General) Barton K. Yount, commander of United States Army Air Forces Flying Training Command. Located in Maxwell, microfilm roll A2281.

26. AIR 29/627, fortnightly report dated 12 June 1943.

27. Letter dated 29 December 1943, located in Maxwell, microfilm roll A2281.

28. Guinn, student questionnaire.

29. Ibid.

30. Largent, *RAF Wings Over Florida*, 161.

31. Ibid., 164.

32. Records Group 234, Defense Plant Corporation, National Archives, Suitland, Maryland.

33. AIR 20/1387, Bulletin, fortnight ending 12 December 1942.

34. Ibid., fortnight ending 31 October 1942.

35. No. 6 BFTS ORB, 8 November 1942.

36. AIR 29/625, letter from Dr. Johnson dated 2 March 1942 to Squadron Leader Beveridge, 286.

37. AIR 20/1387, Bulletin, fortnight ending 28 November 1942.

38. No. 3 BFTS ORB, 8 July 1943.

39. AIR 29/625.

40. Dawson, *RAF in Arizona*, 55.

41. Ibid., 83.

42. AIR 20/1387

43. Lenzner, *The Great Getty*, 110.

44. Ibid.

45. Copy of John Price diary provided to Dr. Gilbert S. Guinn.

46. AIR 20/1387, bulletin for fortnight ending 12 June 1943.

47. No. 1 BFTS ORB, 20 and 22 February 1943.

48. No. 3 BFTS ORB, 14 February 1943.

49. MacLachlan returned to operations and his Mustang was shot down by ground fire on 31 July 1943. After being taken prisoner, MacLachlan died in captivity. He was 24.

50. Dawson, *RAF in Arizona*, 35–36.

NOTES TO CHAPTER 9

1. Keith Durbidge letter dated 10 January 1987, to Dr. Gilbert S. Guinn.

2. Guinn, student questionnaire.

3. Cooke wartime letters, Clewiston Museum.

4. Ibid.

5. Ibid.

6. Ibid.

7. Ibid.

8. Ibid.

9. The Commonwealth War Graves Commission re-interred the crew to the new (1951) Becklingen War Cemetery in northern Germany.

10. Largent, *RAF Wings Over Florida*, 121–122.

11. Guinn, student questionnaire.

12. Mansfield, *Spitfire Saga*, 53.

13. Ibid., 136.

14. Guinn, student questionnaire.

15. Ibid.

16. Royal Air Force (Volunteer Reserve) Officers 1939–1945. www.unithistories.com

17. Guinn, student questionnaire.

18. Royal Air Force (Volunteer Reserve) Officers 1939–1945. www.unithistories.com

19. Guinn, student questionnaire.

20. Largent, *RAF Wings Over Florida*, 97.

21. Guinn, student questionnaire.

22. Ibid.

23. Ibid.

24. Largent, *RAF Wings Over Florida*, 109.

25. Guinn, student questionnaire.

26. Ibid.

27. Ibid.

28. Note added to Alan Watson diary provided to Dr. Gilbert S. Guinn by W. E. J. Bishop.

29. Denson, *The Royal Air Force in Oklahoma*, 95.

30. Guinn, student questionnaire.

31. Ibid.

32. Ibid.

33. Ibid.

34. Ibid.

35. Titcumb received an appointment to a Mosquito conversion course and died in an accident one week later.

36. Guinn, student questionnaire.

37. Ibid.

38. Brian Partridge letter, Clewiston Museum.

39. Largent, *RAF Wings Over Florida*, 92–95.

40. Guinn, student questionnaire.

41. Ibid.

42. Another British student remembered the RAF commanding officer: "He is the sort of Englishman who makes the rest of the world loathe all Englishmen."

43. Largent, *RAF Wings Over Florida*, 88.

44. Ibid., 91.

45. Guinn, student questionnaire.

46. Largent, *RAF Wings Over Florida*, 153.

47. Ibid., 159–160.

48. Guinn, student questionnaire.

49. Letter dated 30 January 1983 from R. A. Eadie to Dr. Gilbert S. Guinn.

50. Guinn, student questionnaire.

51. Ibid.

52. Ibid.

53. Ibid.

54. Ibid.

55. Largent, *RAF Wings Over Florida*, 117.

56. Guinn, student questionnaire.

57. Ibid.

NOTES TO CHAPTER 10

1. Guinn, student questionnaire.

2. "History of the 2564th AAFBU, 1 July 45–30 Sep 45." Maxwell, microfilm roll A2281.

3. Guinn, student questionnaire.

4. Ibid.

5. AIR 29/627, Weekly Routine Orders, No. 5 BFTS, 18 May 1945, 573.

6. Churchill, *Triumph and Tragedy*, 675.

7. AIR 29/627.

8. AIR 27/629.

9. Distributed to each school the surviving example is from AIR 29/627, Weekly Routine Orders, No. 5 BFTS, 644.

10. *Terrell Daily Tribune*, 24 August 1945.

11. *Open Post*, Volume IV, August 1945.

12. Guinn, student questionnaire.

13. AIR 20/1387.

14. *Terrell Daily Tribune*, 7 September 1945.

15. Ibid., 10 September 1945.

16. *Dallas Morning News*, 23 August 1945.

17. Flt. Lt. M. W. Palmer, "British Flying Training Schools in America," *Transatlantic* (April 1945): 27.

18. AIR 45/2, "History of R.A.F. Delegation."

19. AIR 20/1387, Letter dated 8 November 1945 from W/C T. O. Prickett to Mr. J. P. Winckworth of the Air Ministry.

NOTES TO CHAPTER 11

1. Noel Robert Clark letter dated January 13, 1987 to Dr. Gilbert S. Guinn.

2. Guinn, student questionnaire.

3. *London Gazette*, 1 December 1976, 2–3.

4. Guinn, student questionnaire.

5. Denson, *The Royal Air Force in Oklahoma*, 103.

6. *The Telegraph*, 19 March 2008.

7. Letter from Brian Partridge, Clewiston Museum.

8. Largent, *RAF Wings Over Florida*, 96.

9. Guinn, student questionnaire.

10. Ibid.

11. Dawson, *The RAF in Arizona*, 151.

12. Burghley House retains its original sixteenth-century appearance and has been featured in many movies including *The Da Vinci Code*, *Pride and Prejudice*, and *Elizabeth: The Golden Age*.

13. One of Kermode's books, *The Mechanics of Flight*, first published in 1932, is still (2015) in print in updated form.

14. Largent, *RAF Wings Over Florida*, 193.

15. Denson, *The Royal Air Force in Oklahoma*, 79.

16. Peek, *The Spartan Story*, 110.

17. Wiener, *Two Hundred Thousand Flyers*, x.

18. Walt Disney Studios, a tenant in the industrial park, purchased the original, badly deteriorated, art deco airport terminal building. In 2013 Disney proposed a plan to completely renovate the historic structure.

19. Guinn, student questionnaire.

20. *The Clewiston News*, October 24, 1941

21. Newsletter, "No.3 British Flying Training School Annual Reunion" June, 1949.

22. Reprinted in Dawson, *The RAF in Arizona*.

23. "AT-6s Crash Near Moyers During WW II." Sixth grade reading project Ratan, Oklahoma, elementary school 1997–98, copy in the Terrell Public Library.

BIBLIOGRAPHY

I. PRIMARY SOURCES

A. United Kingdom.

Each British Flying Training School kept a unit diary known as the Operations Record Book. Copies are located in the National Archives, London (formerly the Public Record Office), on micro film rolls AIR 29/625 and AIR 29/626. Certain entries have letters, reports, appendix, or other attachments.

Additional information concerning the British Flying Training Schools is found on microfilm rolls AIR 20/1387 and AIR 20/1388, National Archives, London. These files contain copies of correspondence from RAF officers in Washington, D.C. to officials at the Air Ministry, London, concerning training in the United States.

Many of these official records are incomplete.

B. United States.

U.S. Air Force Historical Research Agency archives located at Maxwell Air Force Base, Alabama. These records are contained on microfilm roll A2281. These reports, not always complete, are for each of the army units assigned to the individual British Flying Training Schools and are arranged by date and are usually either bi-weekly or quarterly. Toward the end of the war the army assigned various historical personnel to write histories of the various British schools and the army units.

These histories should be used with caution and contain obvious errors.

II. SECONDARY SOURCES

Arnold, H. H. *Global Mission.* New York: Harper and Brothers, 1949.

Barris, Ted. *Behind the Glory.* Toronto: Macmillan Canada, 1992.

Berryman, Nick. *In the Nick of Time.* West Sussex, England, Woodfield Publishing, 2001.

Bishop, Patrick. *Fighter Boys: The Battle of Britain, 1940.* New York: Viking Penguin, 2003.

Bowyer, Chaz. *History of the RAF.* London: Bison Books, 1990.

Brendon, Piers. *The Dark Valley: A Panorama of the 1930s.* New York: Alfred A. Knopf, 2000.

Caine, Philip D. *Eagles of the RAF; The World War II Eagle Squadrons.* Washington, DC: National Defense University Press, 1991.

Chandler, Graham. "The Bombing of Waziristan." *Air & Space Smithsonian,* June/July 2011.

Churchill, Winston S. *The Second World War: Their Finest Hour.* Boston: Houghton Mifflin Company, 1949.

———. *The Second World War: The Grand Alliance.* Boston: Houghton Mifflin Company, 1950.

———. *The Second World War: Triumph and Tragedy.* Boston: Houghton Mifflin Company, 1953.

Clarke, I. F. *Voices Prophesying War 1763–1984.* Oxford: Oxford University Press, 1966.

Coffey, Thomas M. *Hap: The Story of the U.S. Air Force and the Man Who Built It, General Henry H. "Hap" Arnold.* New York: The Viking Press, 1982.

Cooper, Alfred Duff. *Old Men Forget.* New York: Dutton, 1954.

Craft, Stephen G. *Embry-Riddle at War: Aviation Training during World War II.* Gainesville: University Press of Florida, 2009.

Craven, Wesley Frank, and James Lea Cate, eds. *The Army Airforces in World War II, Vol. I: Plans and Early Operations January 1939 to August 1942.* Chicago: University of Chicago Press, 1948.

Dawson, Jim. *The RAF in Arizona, Falcon Field, 1941–1945*. Newnan, GA: Stenger-Scott Publishing, 2002.

Denson, Paula Carmack. *The Royal Air Force in Oklahoma; Loves, Lives, and Courage of the British Air Crews Trained in Oklahoma During World War II*. Oklahoma City: Oklahoma Heritage Association, 2006.

de Quesada, A. M. *Images of America, The Royal Air Force over Florida*. Charleston, SC: Arcadia Publishing, 1998.

Dunmore, Spencer. *Wings for Victory; the Remarkable Story of the British Commonwealth Air Training Plan in Canada*. Toronto: McClelland & Stewart, 1994.

Eaton, Elbert Lee. *Weather Guide for Air Pilots*. New York: The Ronald Press Company, 1939.

Golley, John. *Aircrew Unlimited: the Commonwealth Air Training Plan during World War II*. London: Patrick Stephens, 1993.

Green, David, ed. *Open Post, the Last of Many. A Souvenir Edition of the Official Journal of No. 3 British Flying Training School, Miami, Oklahoma, United States of America, a One-Time Branch of Spartan School of Aeronautics, Tulsa,Oklahoma*.

Guinn, Gilbert S. *The Arnold Scheme; British Pilots, the American South and the Allies' Daring Plan*. Charleston, SC: The History Press, 2007.

———, and G. H. Bennett. *British Naval Aviation in World War II, The US Navy and Anglo-American Relations*. London: Tauris Academic Studies, 2007.

Hammerton, Sir John, ed. *ABC of the RAF: Handbook for all Branches of the Air Force*. London: The Amalgamated Press Limited, 1942.

Hart, B. H. Liddell. *History of the Second World War*. New York: G. P. Putnam's Sons, 1970.

Hatch, F. J. *The Aerodrome of Democracy; Canada and the British Commonwealth Air Training Plan, 1939–1945*. Ottawa, Canada: Directorate of History, Department of National Defense, 1983.

Hayer, Charles. "Falcon Field Beginnings." *AAHS Journal*. American Aviation Historical Society, Fall 1985.

Jane's Fighting Aircraft of World War II. London: Jane's Publishing Company, 1946; Reprint, Singapore: Random House, 1994.

James, Joe. *Teacher Wore a Parachute.* New York: A. S. Barnes and Company, 1966.

Killebrew, Tom. *The Royal Air Force in Texas: Training British Pilots in Terrell during World War II.* Denton: University of North Texas Press, 2003.

Largent, Will. *RAF Wings over Florida: Memories of World War II British Air Cadets.* West Lafayette, IN: Purdue University Press, 2000.

Lenzner, Robert. *The Great Getty.* New York: Crown Publishers, Inc., 1985.

Lukacs, John. *Five Days in London May 1940.* New Haven: Yale University Press, 1999.

MacMillan, Margaret. *Paris 1919: Six Months That Changed the World.* New York: Random House, 2003.

Manchester, William. *The Last Lion: Winston Spencer Churchill, Visions of Glory 1874–1932.* Boston: Little, Brown and Company, 1983.

———. *The Last Lion: Winston Spencer Churchill, Alone 1932–1940.* Boston: Little, Brown and Company, 1988.

Mansfield, Angus. *Spitfire Saga, Rodney Scrase DFC.* Stroud, Gloucestershire, UK: Spelmount Publishers, 2010.

Monde, Major Bennet B. *Wings Over Sweetwater, the History of Avenger Field, Texas.* n.p. 1995.

Morgan, Hugh. *By the Seat of Your Pants, A Consideration of the Basic Training of RAF Pilots in Southern Rhodesia, Canada and the USA during World War II.* Cowden Kent, UK: Newton Publishers, 1990.

Peek, Chet. *The Spartan Story.* Norman, OK: Three Peaks Publishing, 1994.

Philpott, Ian M. *The Royal Air Force: An Encyclopedia of the Inter-War Years, Volume I, The Trenchard Years 1918 to 1929.* Barnsley, South Yorkshire, UK: Pen and Sword Books, 2005.

———. *The Royal Air Force: An Encyclopedia of the Inter-War Years, Volume II, Re-Armament 1930–1939*. Barnsley, South Yorkshire, UK: Pen and Sword Books, 2008.

Price, Alfred. *Spitfire: A Complete Fighting History*. New York: Dorset Press, 1992.

Reynolds, Clark G. *Admiral John H. Towers: The Struggle for Naval Air Supremacy*. Annapolis, MD: Naval Institute Press, 1991.

Richards, Denis. *Royal Air Force 1935–1945, Vol. I: The Fight at Odds*. London: Her Majesty's Stationery Office, 1953.

Round, Thomas. *A Wand' ring Mistrel, I: The Autobiography of Thomas Round*. Lancaster, UK: Carnegie Publishing, 2002.

Simmons, Virgil. *Air Piloting: Manual of Flight Instruction*. New York: The Ronald Press Company, 1941.

Terraine, John. *A Time for Courage: The Royal Air Force in the European War, 1939–1945*. New York: Macmillan, 1985.

Thomas, Lowell. *History as You Heard It*. Garden City, NY: Doubleday and Company, 1957.

Townsend, Peter. *Duel of Eagles*. New York: Simon and Schuster, 1971.

Tredrey, Frank D. *Pilot's Summer, An R.A.F. Diary*. Oxford, England: Kemp Hall Press, 1939.

Wellum, Geoffrey. *First Light, the Story of the Boy who Became a Man in the War-Torn Skies above Britain*. London: John Wiley & Sons, Inc., 2003.

Wiener, Willard. *Two Hundred Thousand Flyers, the Story of the Civilian-AAF Pilot Training Program*. Washington: The Infantry Journal, 1945.

III. Official Publications

A System of Elementary Flying Training. Air Ministry, April 1941.

Instrument-Flying Instruction on the Standard Panel. A.M.

Pamphlet 123, September 1941.

Principles of Flying Instruction. Air Ministry, June 1939.

Index